Computer Chips and Paper Clips

Technology and Women's Employment

VOLUME II

Case Studies and Policy Perspectives

Heidi I. Hartmann, Editor

Panel on Technology and Women's Employment
Committee on Women's Employment and Related Social Issues
Commission on Behavioral and Social Sciences and Education
National Research Council

D1440902

NATIONAL ACADEMY PRESS
Washington, D.C. 1987

National Academy Press • 2101 Constitution Avenue, NW • Washington, DC 20418

This project has been supported by funding from the Women's Bureau of the U.S. Department of Labor, the National Commission for Employment Policy, the Economic Development Administration of the U.S. Department of Commerce, and by the National Research Council (NRC) Fund. The NRC Fund is a pool of private, discretionary, nonfederal funds that is used to support a program of Academy-initiated studies of national issues in which science and technology figure significantly. The NRC Fund consists of contributions from a consortium of private foundations including the Carnegie Corporation of New York, the Charles E. Culpeper Foundation, the William and Flora Hewlett Foundation, the John D. and Catherine T. MacArthur Foundation, the Andrew W. Mellon Foundation, the Rockefeller Foundation, and the Alfred P. Sloan Foundation; the Academy Industry Program, which seeks annual contributions from companies that are concerned with the health of U.S. science and technology and with public policy issues with technology content; and the National Academy of Sciences and the National Academy of Engineering endowments.

Library of Congress Cataloging-in-Publication Data
(Revised for vol. 2)

National Research Council (U.S.). Committee on Women's Employment and Related Social Issues. Panel on Technology and Women's Employment. Computer chips and paper clips.

Bibliography: v. 1, p. 183–199.
Includes index.
Contents: v. 1. [without special title] — v. 2. Case studies and policy perspectives / Heidi I. Hartmann, editor.
    1. Women white collar workers—Effects of technological innovations on. 2. Office practice—Automation. 3. Microelectronics—Social aspects. 4. Women—Employment. 5. Women—Employment—Goverment policy—United States. I. Hartmann, Heidi I. II. Kraut, Robert E. III. Tilly, Louise.
HD6331.18.M39N38   1986   331.4 ' 8165137 '0973   86-18113
ISBN 0-309-03688-7 (v. 1)
ISBN 0-309-03727-1 (v. 2)

Panel on Technology and Women's Employment

Committee on Women's Employment and Related Social Issues

Contents

Contents, Volume I

Preface

Striking advances in microelectronic and telecommunications technology have transformed many worlds of work. These changes have revolutionized information storage, processing, and retrieval, with immediate and long-range consequences for clerical work. Since women—nearly 15 million of them—are the overwhelming majority of clerical workers, they are and will be disproportionately affected by this type of technological change. Jobs may be created or eliminated, but they are also transformed. So far, knowledge about these large processes of change has been scattered and incomplete. Thus, there is great need for more systematic evaluation and understanding of technological change and its specific effects on the conditions of and opportunities for women's employment.

In light of this need, the Committee on Women's Employment and Related Social Issues established its Panel on Technology and Women's Employment in March 1984. The tasks of the panel included gathering existing data, identifying areas in which research is most needed and commissioning scholars to undertake this research, and preparing a conference and a two-volume report to present the panel's findings and recommendations. This work was supported by the Women's Bureau of the U.S. Department of Labor, the National Commission for Employment Policy, the

Economic Development Administration of the U.S. Department of Commerce, and the National Research Council Fund.

A number of questions faced the panel: To what extent do current changes differ from earlier ones? Is the new microelectronic and telecommunications technology creating or eliminating jobs? In what ways is it affecting the quality of employment for those whose job organization and content are being transformed? Are there differential effects that depend on the skill, occupation, industry, or demographic characteristics, such as minority status or age of workers? If jobs disappear or change drastically, what kind of support—training, retraining, or relocation—might be needed for displaced workers? What institutional arrangements might be necessary or desirable for planning and implementing change or devising support programs?

The panel's answers to these questions are presented in Volume I (a listing of its contents precedes this preface). This second volume gathers many of the papers commissioned by the panel during the course of its work. Each illuminates, from the author's own perspective, one or more aspects of those questions examined by the panel. Often these perspectives differ, indicating the contradictory interpretations of fact that characterize the research on technology and employment, particularly because the phenomena being studied are still unfolding and the data are very much less than adequate to the task. Each paper has been revised by its author(s) to take into account the comments of panel members and others who participated in a workshop held in February 1985 to discuss early versions of the papers.

Professor Eli Ginzberg's overview provides a context for the volume. He presents his view of the changes that have taken place in the participation of women in the labor market, noting that some of the economic sectors that in the past provided the bulk of job growth for women workers may no longer do so, at least partly due to new office technologies. He stresses, however, that technological change is a critical factor in fostering economic growth and creating new types of jobs. His policy prescriptions include continued research and development to enhance technological change and economic growth, full employment, improved education and retraining, continued enforcement of equal employment opportunity laws and regulations, and increased provision of child care.

The four case studies in Part II describe the impact of information technology in the insurance industry, among bookkeepers (between 1910 and 1950), among secretaries, and in computer-related occupations. The first three case studies trace how the opportunities of women workers tend to change along with alterations in the organization of work and the implementation of innovations. Barbara Baran, Sharon Strom, and Mary Murphree all argue that women's opportunities have become more limited as the division of labor has become increasingly structured. Baran notes the current contradiction within the insurance industry that as jobs become more skilled in many ways as a result of computerization they also offer less mobility; she also anticipates declines in the number of jobs likely to be available to clerical workers, particularly the least-skilled workers. Strom's history of changes in women's role in bookkeeping, an important clerical occupation, gives equal weight to changes in the organization of work and to the various innovations in calculating machines available to bookkeepers over the years. Up to 1950, bookkeepers grew in number and became preponderantly female; their work was increasingly tied to machines and their opportunities increasingly circumscribed. Murphree's contemporary case study shows how the effects of office technologies on secretaries vary according to the way these technologies are used. A critical variable, Murphree finds, is the number of bosses the secretary serves; accordingly, with new equipment, her work may become more or less challenging. In nearly all cases, however, Murphree finds that the patrimonial nature of office work, in particular its strong reliance on differences in gendered roles, remains little changed.

Strober and Arnold examine the newly emerging occupations related to computers: computer scientists and systems analysts, computer programmers, and computer operators. Using data available from the Census Bureau, they find that even in these new occupations gender-based earnings differentials exist. One explanation suggested is that women and men in these occupations tend to work in different industries, with women less likely than men to work in the "high-tech" industries.

The pessimistic impression left by these case studies of the impact of computers (and their forerunners) is somewhat mitigated by the sweeping historical analysis provided by Claudia Goldin. The first of three authors in Part III who connects technological change with trends in women's employment, Goldin reviews the history of women's employment and productivity growth since the 1800s. She reports that across industries women have tended to increase their representation where productivity growth has been greatest and also notes that the entrance of women into manufacturing in the 1800s, where technological and organizational change was especially pronounced, tended to raise women's wages. Together these facts indicate that technological and organizational change generally enhance women's opportunities. In the more recent period, however, Goldin sees the increase in women's education as the single most important factor in changing women's labor force status.

Allan Hunt and Timothy Hunt, in their review of trends in clerical employment from 1940 to the early 1980s, attempt to identify specific impacts of office automation. Like Ginzberg, they note that it is easier to attach technological explanations to areas of decreasing employment than to anticipate the new jobs technology may create. Their findings suggest that although employment growth in clerical jobs has slowed (probably permanently), technological change cannot in most instances be identified as the reason. For example, despite the increased capital investment in the financial sector, no trend toward increased productivity (and possible job displacement) was discerned.

Eileen Appelbaum points to other important trends in the recent period: the significant increase in temporary work, shifts in part-time work, and the modest increase in home-based work. All these shifts, she argues, are facilitated by computerization, but also reflect changes in the organization of work. In Appelbaum's view, these new forms of work are likely to become increasingly important as employers continue to face the need to minimize costs. Although new work may provide some important options for women workers, Appelbaum believes that on the whole these trends have more negative consequences than positive ones.

The four papers in Part IV provide policy perspectives on important subjects. Alan Westin reviews recent experiences of a sample of major employers with office automation and offers his suggestions for how best to implement new office system technologies. He reports that increasing attention is being given in workplaces to enhancing the quality of employment and notes that the most important factor in determining how well an employer uses new technology is the overall quality of its human resources policy. Bryna Fraser describes available options for attaining education and training related to new technologies and recommends important improvements in the delivery of education and training. Like many of the authors in the collection, she notes the importance of continuing education over a lifetime. Thierry Noyelle, on the basis of his analysis of changes in the service sector, argues that education will become even more important in the future in ensuring employment opportunity. Like Appelbaum, Baran, and others, Noyelle believes the structure of employment opportunities within firms is undergoing fundamental change. Internal labor markets, with clear job ladders providing upward mobility, are disappearing. Instead, increased hiring of skilled workers is occurring, and workers must have greater skills to obtain entry-level jobs; on-the-job training is a less sure route to upward mobility for the less skilled. Felicity Henwood and Sally Wyatt, two researchers from the United Kingdom, provide an overview of employment policies related to technological change in Western Europe. They note that workers are more involved in decisions involving the implementation of technological change in many European countries than they are in the United States. Henwood and Wyatt also review European education and training policies and policies related to easing unemployment, some of which may be due to technological change. Throughout, they stress that women, because of their specific locations in paid and unpaid employment, tend to have perspectives and needs different from those of men. They note in particular that women have often been more sensitive to issues concerning quality of work.

The panel offers these papers, with their divergent viewpoints, not only because they were helpful to it in its own deliberations, but also in the belief that they will stimulate further discussion and research. The issues raised in these papers about the current transformations in employment concern both men and women workers, although the particular examples are taken primarily from areas of predominant employment for women.

LOUISE A. TILLY, *Chair*
HEIDI I. HARTMANN, *Study Director*
Panel on Technology and
Women's Employment

Acknowledgments

These papers were commissioned by the panel to inform its work. The authors have earned our appreciation for the insight and timeliness of their research. Many of them present here the fruits of original data-collection efforts, vastly more involved than could be described in the space allotted to them here. Others have spent considerable effort to create consistent data series from published and unpublished sources. All have brought their considerable analytical skills to bear on questions of importance to the panel. Thanks also to the panel members for identifying topics for the papers, thinking carefully about the questions that needed to be addressed, and reviewing the work of the authors at many stages.

Even after the major effort of summarizing research results in a written product has been completed, producing a published volume of collected papers is a formidable task. Lucile DiGirolamo, staff associate to the panel, ably organized much of the process, from the contracting and fiscal management involved in commissioning papers to keeping track of the numerous drafts and assisting in checking references and tables. She ably elicited cooperation from the authors in matters both of format and substance. Gillian Marcelle, a student intern with the panel, who served as editorial assistant for this volume, made important intellectual contributions to the overall shape of the volume. She also edited several of the papers, making organizational and substantive improvements. In this era of incomplete automation, many of these papers were produced on word-processing systems incompatible with that used by the National Academy Press. Much of the translation and cleanup involved were done by William Vaughan, staff assistant to the panel, and Estelle Miller, electronic composition specialist, National Academy Press, in addition to Lucile and Gillian. Estelle Miller used laser composition software to produce camera-ready copy. Nancy Winchester, project editor, National Academy Press, supervised the production of the manuscript. To all we express our appreciation for a great deal of hard work, often performed under tight time pressures. Throughout this process, too, the authors were unusually responsive.

We also thank Alice S. Ilchman, chair of the Committee on Women's Employment and Related Social Issues, for the many ways in which she facilitated the panel's work. Eugenia Grohman, associate director for reports for the Commission on Behavioral and Social Sciences and Education, provided useful advice and coordinated production with the Press. David A. Goslin, executive director of the commission, has our appreciation for his continued support of the work of the committee and its panels.

Several organizations made this report possible through their financial support. We thank both the organizations and the individuals who provided liaison. At the Women's Bureau of the U.S. Department of Labor, we thank Collis Phillips, Mary Murphree, and Roberta McKay. In addition, we would like to recognize Lenora Cole-Alexander, former director of the Women's Bureau, for her interest in and strong support of the project. Carol Romero and her staff at the National Commission for Employment Policy provided the impetus and the funds for a major review of clerical employment trends, which was carried out by Allan Hunt and Timothy Hunt and reported briefly here. Beverly Milkman and Richard Walton, at the Economic Development Administration of the U.S. Department of Commerce, aided the panel with a grant to allow it to complete the project in a timely manner. Crucial early funding was provided by the National Research Council Fund.

LOUISE A. TILLY
HEIDI I. HARTMANN

Part I

Overview

Technology, Women, and Work: Policy Perspectives

ELI GINZBERG

THE CHANGING ROLE OF AMERICAN WOMEN

In the mid-1950s, the National Manpower Council decided by only a single vote that "womanpower" was a subject worth exploring (National Manpower Council, 1957). And in the early 1960s, when Barnard College required that its students attend a series of lectures on jobs and careers, my lecture elicited only bored faces and clicking knitting needles. Most of the students were not interested in the advice that I offered: to study calculus and to gain mastery over the quantitative approaches in one of the natural or social sciences, which, I assured them, would provide them not only access to a job, but to a job with prospects. Early in the era of the feminine mystique, their minds and emotions were focused in other directions (Ginzberg and Yohalem, 1966; Ginzberg et al., 1966).

These recollections are presented to contrast with the situation today, when many college-educated women are studying a broader range of subjects and are making an increasing commitment to the labor force. The growing importance of women in the U.S. labor market, where they now account for 43 percent of all workers, a

3

percentage that continues to grow, is a recent phenomenon. But during this short time—since around 1950—there have been many striking changes in the relation of women to work. Witness the following:

- Over half of all women aged 16 to 64 work, and the proportion is almost two-thirds for those who are at the end of their childbearing period.
- Although it is true that more women than men work less than full-time, year-round, most women who work, like most men, are regular workers who hold full-time jobs.
- Gender remains a critical determinant of the types of jobs and careers available to women, but it is not nearly as strong a discriminatory influence as it was in the past. In law, medical, and graduate business schools, women students account for at least one-third of the graduates, up from less than one-tenth as recently as the mid-1960s.
- For the first time in the nation's history, women outnumber men among students enrolled in colleges and universities.
- In the third of a century since 1950, women have accounted for three out of every five new additions to the labor force.
- The explosive growth of the service sector, which today accounts for more than 70 percent of total employment and total output, was both a cause and an effect of the availability of women workers (Stanback et al., 1981).
- Although the antidiscrimination laws and regulations of the 1960s and early 1970s and the changed attitudes and behavior of employers opened up many hitherto restricted fields of work to women (beyond the professions noted above), women continue to be heavily concentrated in a narrow set of occupations. Some 20 fields account for two out of every three women workers.
- Over the last half century the occupational group that has experienced the most rapid rate of growth has been clerical workers, which is a reminder of the need to consider not only the broad potential impacts of technology but to narrow the focus to specific technologies that are likely to have a strong impact on women workers.
- For the first time in the nation's history, white men no longer constitute the majority of the work force. Women, together with black, Hispanic, and other minority males, today account for more than half of the work force.

These observations suggest that our analysis pursue a middle road. We must continue to be sensitive to the patterns that underlie the place of women in the world of work, but we must also consider that women account for close to half of the entire work force and their future jobs and careers will therefore be affected by the broad labor market developments that will affect all workers.

OBSERVATIONS ON CHANGING TECHNOLOGY

Technological changes are a way of life for industrial societies, but most innovations involve changes in processes or products that are relatively circumscribed. Even when a significant technological improvement occurs, such as the discovery and manufacture of nylon or the development of the electric typewriter, the impact on the labor market is likely to be absorbed without serious job losses, because among other reasons the lower price or improved quality tends to increase demand. The number of jobs placed at risk by even significant new technology is relatively small and is likely to be stretched out over a period of years. Most textile mills made the transition from natural to artificial fibers without having to lay off large numbers of workers; the same was true of some of the companies that had earlier manufactured standard typewriters and had made the transition to electric, electronic, or computerized typewriters.

There have been major technological breakthroughs, however, such as the development of the railroad, the telephone, electric power, the automobile, and the airplane, in which the impacts on work and workers were more pervasive, although it should be noted that these impacts were fully diffused only after long periods, often decades or generations. Whereas we will soon celebrate the hundredth anniversary of the first automobile, some outlying families still are not connected to an electric grid, and in some areas a home telephone is still not affordable by every family.

The development of the microprocessor and the linking of personal computers into communications networks are major technological breakthroughs that have the promise of affecting the U.S. economy and way of life on the order of magnitude of the railroad and the automobile. We must allow for the possibility that the computer will prove even more revolutionary, since it has the potential of altering not only the movement of people and goods but the nature of work itself (Ginzberg et al., 1986).

It must be emphasized, however, that no matter how dramatic
the new technology may become, it has been in existence for a third
of a century and it would be difficult to point to its having had
large-scale adverse effects on significant groups of workers, male
or female, during that period. The most serious charges that can
be levied against it are that there have been "silent firings" (that
is, workers not hired) and other negatives such as some deskilling
of jobs, downscaling of opportunities, and health hazards. But to
date the new technology has been positively correlated with the
continued growth of the service sector and in particular with the
expansion of women's employment.

Of all the effects of economic forces on the labor market—
overall growth, cyclical change, structural shifts, and technological
change—the last will surely be the least important a decade from
now. The Bureau of Labor Statistics estimates that in the 1980s
only about 15 percent of the changes that occur in job structure will be ascribable to technology; 85 percent will be due to
the cyclical and structural movements of the economy (Kutscher,
1985).

In sum, the following conclusions are evident: (1) women's
share of total employment has been mounting rapidly and is likely
to increase further, until women account for half of all workers;
(2) this growth has been closely associated with the differentially
rapid growth of the service sector; (3) while women are no longer
as closely confined to a few major occupational fields, they remain heavily concentrated; (4) the microprocessor and computer-
communications linkages are likely to affect disproportionately the
clerical arena in which women workers are heavily concentrated;
and (5) even if the new technology were to have a strong impact
on existing patterns of work, the consequences would be manifest
only over relatively long periods of time.

POLICY PERSPECTIVES

FRAMING THE ISSUES

As noted above, the single most important short-term determinant of the labor market experience of women (in fact, all)
workers will be the growth rate of the U.S. economy and the timing and severity of the next recession. We are now in the fourth
year of recovery from two back-to-back recessions, which started

in 1979 and ended in 1982. If past is prologue, there is only 1 chance in about 100 that, if President Reagan remains in office throughout the whole of his second administration, the nation will escape a new recession. At this time (August 1986), the outlook for the year still appears to most forecasters to be positive. The expansionary capacity of the economy does not appear as yet to have met its potential. But it would be an error to overlook the major economic problems that continue to exist: (1) the $900 billion debt of the less developed countries (LDCs); (2) the annual $170 billion deficit of the United States in its foreign trade; (3) the continuing high value of the dollar against many currencies; (4) the federal budgetary deficits that loom ahead as far as one can see; and (5) the still high real rate of interest. In my view, if the leading industrial countries fail to attack these five problems conjointly and effectively, the prospect of a severe recession with large-scale labor market consequences is not only possible but probable.

There is steadily accumulating evidence that the United States and other advanced economies are confronting a sea change in the internationalization of their economies as evidenced by the following:

- the spectacular spurt in imports to the United States from the LDCs (with adverse effects in this country on many nondurable manufacturing sectors with large numbers of women workers, such as apparel manufacturing);
- the relocation overseas of major labor-intensive jobs in durable manufacturing such as electronic components (again with a heavy impact on women workers);
- the extraordinary transfer of capital funds to the United States, mostly from Europe and Japan, part of which are for investment in plant and equipment and part of which are held in money market instruments;
- the never-ending trade negotiations that are aimed, in the short run, at protecting U.S. jobs (as in automobiles and steel) and, in the longer run, at reducing tariff and nontariff barriers in international trade (the United States has been taking the leadership to expand the General Agreement on Trade and Tariffs [GATT] to include services, a high employment area for women workers [Noyelle and Dutka, 1987]).

As long as the U.S. economy remains expansionary, the odds favor the maintenance, or even the reduction, of barriers affecting international trade in goods and services. But, in my view, we are dangerously close to a reversal of our long-term efforts to reduce trade barriers. If the next recession is severe or prolonged, it is probable that we will not be able to avoid new barriers. Since the United States is the dominant market for the exports of both developed and developing countries, we must exercise restraint to avoid erecting new protective trade barriers. The decade of the 1930s provides one salient example of beggar-your-neighbor policy. The lessons learned have helped to set and keep the developed world on the path to freer international trade, but there is a growing risk that these lessons have begun to fade.

The most important question with regard to the future impact of technology on women's employment is whether the sanguine results of the last 20 years can be projected to the remaining years of this century and beyond. The optimist might contend that there is no reason to expect more "disturbance" in the years ahead than we have experienced over the past two decades, which saw the computer revolution resulting in few, if any, dysfunctional effects. The pessimist, of course, sees the future differently. In his or her view, the linkage of the computer to communications networks, which is only now hitting its stride, will have a range of adverse consequences for women's employment: first, by eliminating a number of white-collar positions, and second, by making possible the further relocation of many back-office positions from central cities to the suburbs, to distant communities, and also to overseas locations, particularly to English-literate populations. The pessimist goes further and points to the downskilling of jobs and the degrading of careers that often accompany accelerated computerization.

As an iconoclast, I am unpersuaded by either the optimistic or the pessimistic forecast. There are three key elements in my view of the future.

First, the computer revolution has reached a point where it is likely to have a greater "displacement" effect on women's employment over the next 15 years than it has had in the past. A simple projection of the past fails to take into account the fact that computer technology is now on a steeper curve; employers and employees are more willing and able to adapt to it since more than 70 percent of all jobs are in the service sector. Moreover, since U.S.

management is striving to become and remain cost-competitive in the world marketplace, it must reduce its white-collar payrolls; wider reliance on the computer offers reasonable prospects for success in this effort.

Second, productivity can increase in the service sector. Over the last half century, employment in agriculture has decreased from 20 percent of the total labor force to under 3 percent; in manufacturing, employment has declined from close to two-fifths to under one-fifth. For many years neither the tools (computer) and communications resources nor the organizational structure and managerial know-how were available to run large organizations without many layers of staff. Further, we learned only recently how to tie large numbers of small units, owned or franchised, into a single organization, but today we are the world's leader in these structures—from hotels and fast food establishments to banks. This experience has proved that earlier economists were wrong when they said that services were immune to economies of scale and postulated that they suffered from the "cost disease," with continued dependence on additional labor resulting inevitably in higher costs (Baumol, 1967).

Third, the new products and services that may be developed are as yet unknown. The expectation that the computer will first slow, and eventually reverse, the absolute and relative gains made by clerical workers in the past several decades is only one aspect of the future. What remains uncertain is whether and how quickly the computer-communications link-up is likely to generate the creation of new products and services that will lead to the employment of large numbers of new workers, both women and men. One has to engage in a historical experiment and identify the types of employment opened up by the widespread introduction of the automobile from the tens of thousands of people who obtained new jobs in our national parks to millions of construction workers who built homes in the suburbs. As the time period is extended and the technology becomes more pervasive, it is more difficult and less relevant to assess the impact of a new innovation on total employment. Too many other factors intervene to influence the outcome.

TABLE 1 Large Occupations (more than 1 million workers) in Which Women
Accounted for at Least Half of All Workers, 1982

Occupation	All Workers (millions)	Percent Women
Registered nurses, dieticians, therapists	1.7	92
Teachers, except college	3.3	71
Sales workers, retail	2.4	70
Bookkeepers	2.0	92
Cashiers	1.7	87
Office machine operators	1.1	75
Secretaries	3.8	99
Typists	1.0	97
Assemblers	1.1	54
Food service workers	4.8	66
Health service workers (excluding nurses)	2.0	90
Personal service workers	1.9	77
Private household	1.0	97

NOTE: Civilians, 16 years old and over.

SOURCE: Bureau of the Census (1983:Table 696).

ARE WOMEN WORKERS AT RISK?

The question of whether women workers are at risk is critical
for the reasons noted earlier, namely, that such a high proportion of women workers are concentrated within a relatively limited
number of occupational groupings and they account for a differentially larger number of all workers in selected industries. Tables 1
and 2 provide the critical data.

Two important points can be derived from Table 1. First,
the 13 occupational groups shown in the table account for more
than half of all women workers. Second, the six occupational fields
dominated by women (90 percent or more of all workers) account
for one out of every four women workers. What the table does not
show is that the occupational distribution of men workers is much
less concentrated.

Since our primary concern is to assess the probable impact
of technology on women's employment in the remaining years of
this century, it may be helpful to consider what happened in
the years 1972–1982 to the female-dominated occupational areas,

particularly those areas in which technology in general and computer technology specifically have made significant advances. The total number of sales workers remained stable during the years 1972–1982, as did the proportion of women workers. There was a significant increase in the number of bookkeepers, from 1.6 million to 2.0 million, and the share of women in the field increased from slightly under 90 percent to slightly over this proportion. The number of cashiers increased at a far higher rate than the number of bookkeepers, from 1.0 million to 1.7 million, but there was no increase in the proportion of women, which remained at 87 percent. Office machine workers expanded from under 700,000 to 1.1 million, and the proportion of women increased from 71 to 75 percent. There was a modest increase in the number of factory assemblers, from 1.022 million to 1.087 million, and the share of women increased from 47 to 54 percent.

Several points are worth noting. In a number of fields in which women workers predominated, total employment (men *and* women) increased significantly. For the most part, the proportion of women workers as a percentage of all workers did not change appreciably. Most important, none of the data suggest that the computer and related technology displaced large numbers of workers in fields where women were heavily concentrated.

We can supplement our understanding of what transpired in the recent past by looking at employment in industries where women account for half or more of all employees. Table 2 illustrates that, with the single exception of private household employment, which sustained a decline of one-half million, the industries characterized by a predominance of women workers expanded in the years following 1970.

The optimistic implications of this recent experience with respect to total employment trends and their impact on women workers, however, must not be uncritically projected into the future. It is important to review the projections to 1995 of the Bureau of Labor Statistics [BLS]. Table 3 presents the 8 female-dominated occupational categories of the 13 categories for which the BLS foresees the largest job growth: secretaries, nurses' aides, salespersons, cashiers, professional nurses, office clerks, waitresses, and kindergarten and elementary school teachers. Each of the above categories will add, according to the BLS, between 230,000 and 560,000 new jobs by 1995. Together they account for 20 percent of all anticipated job growth. Most of these occupations are

TABLE 2   1970 and 1982 Employment in Industries in Which Women Accounted
for at Least Half of All Workers in 1982

Industry	All Workers (millions)		Percent Women	
	1970	1982	1970	1982
Retail trade	12.3	16.6	46	52
Finance, insurance, and real estate				
Banking and finance	1.7	2.8	58	64
Insurance and real estate	2.2	3.5	45	52
Personal services				
Private households	1.8	1.3	89	85
Hotels and lodging chains	1.0	1.3	68	66
Professional and related services				
Hospitals	2.8	4.3	77	76
Health services	1.6	3.5	71	76
Teachers, all levels	6.1	7.6	62	66

NOTE: Civilians, 16 years old and over.

SOURCE: Bureau of the Census (1983:Table 698).

TABLE 3   Female-Dominated Occupations with Largest Projected Job Growth,
1984-1995

Occupation	Change in Total Employment (thousands)	Percent of Total Job Growth
Cashiers	556	3.6
Nurses, registered	452	2.8
Waiters and waitresses	424	2.7
Nurses' aides and orderlies	348	2.2
Salespersons, retail	343	2.2
Teachers, kindergarten and elementary	281	1.9
Secretaries	268	1.7
General office clerks	231	1.4

SOURCE: Silvestri and Lukasiewicz (1985:Table 3).

not the most rapidly growing ones, but even a slow-growing large
occupation adds more to women's employment.

The BLS forecasts have held up reasonably well, at least in
total if not in all subsectors. But our concern here is with selected areas where the new technology is likely to have its greatest

ELI GINZBERG

women workers are substantial. We will look more closely at
two industries, banking and hospitals, each of which reveals serious difficulties in assessing the future impacts of technological
and other forces on women's employment. The computer and
computer-communications linkages, including satellites, have had
a head start in banking and finance, and the new technology has
also been making headway, although more slowly, in the administrative and financial, and more recently, in the clinical areas of
hospitals. Moreover, each industry has a large number of workers:
in 1982 banking and finance employed about 2.8 million workers,
of which women accounted for two-thirds, and hospitals employed
4.3 million individuals, with women accounting for three-quarters
of the labor force (see Table 2).

Banking and Finance

One reason that it is difficult to sort out clearly what has
been happening in banking and finance is the multiplicity of forces
affecting the employment profile. In addition to computers taking
over most of the number crunching from clerks, the number of
locations where such work is carried out has grown. The new
technology is also leading to changes in hiring standards. Most city
banks prefer high school and junior college graduates because they
have come to recognize that the dynamism of the new technology
will require the continuing retraining of staff. The high rate of
turnover of new employees, particularly women clerical workers,
has enabled most banks to accommodate the changes to date
without layoffs. But they have reduced new hires (Dutka, 1983).

The foregoing is only part of the story. In the last decade, while
these changes were occurring in back-office work, many large city
banks were opening new branches, which required more personnel,
and most recently, with deregulation, they moved aggressively to
introduce a wide range of new financial services, adding many new
workers to fill expanding front-office jobs.

To complicate matters further, the narrowed spread between
the rates at which the banks have been able to borrow and to
lend, particularly in the early 1980s, caused an adverse effect
on their profitability and liquidity. In short, the changes from
the side of technology were dwarfed by cyclical and structural
alterations, which have buffeted and continue to buffet commercial

banking. But we must be careful not to minimize the technological factors, since major structural transformations are under way that will permanently transform conventional banks into providers of financial services of which the full reach remains to be revealed.

A cautionary assessment of the technological impacts on women's employment in banking and financial services would have to include the following:

• A substantial reduction has already taken place in lower-skilled clerical positions in insurance and banking as well as in the other sectors of finance, insurance, and real estate (FIRE).

• It is likely that in addition to back-office clerical positions that have already been relocated out of urban centers, additional jobs will migrate to outlying areas and even overseas locations. This trend will have a particularly adverse effect on the employment prospects of urban minority women.

• The raising of hiring requirements will close out most opportunities for young women who do not possess at least a high school diploma and preferably a junior college degree.

• The likelihood that many middle management positions will become redundant could have adverse effects on many women who have been able to gain a toehold on the executive ladder.

• In contrast to the foregoing, which are "downbeat" forecasts, allowance must be made for the extent to which the new technology will continue to stimulate and possibly accelerate the growth and development of new financial services for which there will be a substantial and sustained demand.

Once this last potentiality is taken into account, there is a reasonable prospect that the long-term employment effects of the new computer-communications technology on women's employment in FIRE will be positive, not negative (Noyelle, 1987).

Hospitals and Health Care

Let us now look at what has been happening to women's employment in hospitals and the likely changes in the future. First, hospital employment increased in the 12 years after 1970 by no less than 50 percent, from 2.8 million to 4.3 million, and in both years women accounted for about three of every four members of the work force. A little noted phenomenon in this period of expansion in employment has been the trend of most acute care institutions to raise the qualifications of their nursing staff and technicians by hiring and retaining those with more education and training, a preference reflecting the increasing intensity of care and the greater reliance on sophisticated technology. Many hospitals have shifted their employment patterns in the direction of more registered nurses and have reduced the numbers of practical nurses and nurses' aides.

The introduction of the diagnosis-related group (DRG) system for the reimbursement of Medicare patients has acted as a major spur to hospitals to move aggressively to modernize their administrative and financial record keeping via computerization. Their survival hinges on how quickly they are able first to understand their admissions and then control treatment regimens and length of stay, since under DRGs they are paid a fixed price per admission.

As noted earlier, the Bureau of Labor Statistics and most other forecasters assume that health care in general, and hospitals in particular, will continue to be a major growth industry between now and 1995. But that assumption must be inspected anew. Hospital admissions have leveled off; length of stay is dropping; the financing of hospital care is being tightened by third-party payers (government and insurance); and the DRG system is encouraging all providers to tighten their cost controls, including their use of personnel. In 1984 and again in 1985, total hospital employment, instead of expanding, experienced a small decline.

With for-profit enterprises playing a larger role in the provision of health care, the future structure of the federal government's financing of Medicare still evolving, the numbers of older persons requiring more care continuing to increase, medical knowledge and techniques continuing to advance, and the shift from inpatient to ambulatory settings accelerating, it would be a serious error to use the past as guide to the future, especially if the focus is centered on hospitals, not on the totality of health care services.

There is no question that the computer and other new technologies have already left their marks on the hospital indirectly. The strong trend toward for-profit and nonprofit chains; the shift from inpatient to ambulatory care settings; radical changes in surgical procedures, particularly cardiac, ophthalmic, and urologic surgery and many other changes have occurred during the period of increased computerization, from the introduction of the computer into medical education to its use in nurses' procedures.

The combined influence and impact of these technological and related changes (economic, organizational, managerial) on the positive employment of women hospital workers are not clearly discernible, but the following may be considered a middle-of-the-road assessment.

• The dominant view as of mid-1986 is that hospital employment has peaked and that a decline of up to 20 percent in hospital employment over the next decade and a half is possible, some would say, even probable. Clearly, such a decline would have a differentially adverse effect on women workers because they account for about 70 percent of all hospital employees and also are more heavily concentrated in the lower-skilled occupational categories that are most vulnerable to the inroads of the new technologies.

• On the basis of selected field investigations in New York City and in Boston, my associates and I have become aware of the increasing trend of late for hospitals to cut back on hiring less-educated and less-skilled persons. This means that minority women who improved their employment prospects in the 1960s and 1970s by obtaining jobs in hospitals are definitely at risk. Some are being let go; many more who would have been hired in an earlier period are not even being interviewed.

• It is true that at the upper end of the occupational distribution, women physicians and nurses with a master's or doctorate degree are well positioned both with respect to employment and advancement. On the other hand, the much bruited shortage of nurses that commanded attention only 5 years ago has evaporated with little likelihood that a shortage will reappear. Part of this striking shift within such a short time period reflects the pressure of the new resistant climate on hospital administrators and their ability through computerization to exercise much closer control over their personnel costs, particularly their nursing personnel costs.

For a more balanced overview, it should be noted that the above relates solely to hospital employment, not to total employment in the health care sector. The latter is likely to expand as physicians treat more people in their offices and as more patients, including patients who are quite ill, can now be cared for in their homes. Women workers, in particular registered nurses, practical nurses, technicians, and nurses' aides will unquestionably find that jobs are expanding in these out-of-hospital settings. On the whole, total health care employment is expected to continue to increase. A small percentage of women workers, those with higher-level skills, will continue to advance; many more with limited skills will have to work at less attractive jobs with little upward mobility (Ginzberg, 1985).

POLICY RECOMMENDATIONS

Currently, more than half of all adult women are in the labor force and many more would probably work if suitable jobs were available. Six major factors have accelerated the growing importance of women workers in the U.S. economy during the post-World War II decades:

• The need of the economy for more labor and the availability of women willing and eager to fill such jobs.

• The differentially rapid expansion of the service sector whose employers were often seeking part-time workers while many women preferred or were willing to take such jobs.

• Many of the new service jobs in clerical work and sales required individuals with a general education and little in the way of specific skills. Women met these basic requirements.

• In the long period of rapid expansion and high profits many corporate employers built up large staffs. Declining profits and the increased use of the computer have in recent years encouraged employers to operate with fewer white-collar workers.

• The increasing participation of women in work has been paralleled by a greater percentage of women investing in higher education so as to be able to improve their career prospects.

• Despite these major changes in the relation of women to the world of work, the earlier concentration of women workers in a relatively few occupational and industrial groupings has continued (although the concentration has been reduced). A high proportion of all women workers continues to be employed in the service sector at the lower end of the wage scale.

In light of these six principal changes in the shape of women's employment, policy makers should focus on the following:

Full Employment Women, like men, need employment opportunities if they are to find jobs and enjoy career prospects. The U.S. economy has been slack since 1979 as we have attempted to control inflation. We have redefined full employment in terms of 7 or 8 percent not 3 to 4 percent unemployment. Moreover, the federal government, the only agency capable of affecting macro-economic policy, has permitted the employment issue to drop off its agenda, although the Humphrey-Hawkins Act obligates both the Congress and the administration to address a host of job issues. The first and most important contribution of policy makers should be to strive to bring and keep the economy as close to full employment as possible. At a minimum they should avoid ill-advised actions such as new trade restrictions, radical reforms in the tax structure, and excessively large defense programs, which could reduce the capacity of the U.S. economy to move toward a high and sustainable level of employment.

Continued R&D   There is every reason for the government and the corporate sector to maintain and increase their efforts to strengthen their R&D structures. These hold the best promise for the continuing growth and profitability of the U.S. economy in an increasingly competitive world economy. Although new technology has the potential for placing people's skills, jobs, and careers at risk, the penetration of new technology usually proceeds at a rate that permits adjustments to be made through retraining, attrition, and early retirement rather than through job displacement. While a rapidly penetrating new technology can on occasion result in job losses, most workers who are displaced lose out because of the inability of their employers to remain competitive, as has been the case in steel, autos, apparel, and many branches of electronics.

Strengthened Education and Retraining   Policymakers should recognize that the best approach to the prevention of increasing instability in the world of work is a strengthened educational system that will enable workers to be properly educated, trained, and retrained. The economy needs expanded government and corporate funding for retraining programs. The large numbers and high proportion of young minority women, particularly in large urban centers, who fail to graduate from high school, need special attention and help. As we noted, the new technology is leading large employers to raise their hiring standards. Hence young women, including teenage mothers who do not have high school diplomas, may be permanently restricted to the peripheral labor force. We need more and better second-chance programs such as the

Job Corps. The Job Training Partnership Act is not adequately responsive to the needs of the hard-to-employ.

A National Jobs and Education Program   The advances in computer-communications technology will, as we have seen, considerably reduce the demand for clerical workers and result in the relocation of many clerical jobs from large high-cost urban centers to outlying and even foreign locations. These developments will make it even more difficult for the urban high school drop-out to fashion a permanent attachment to the labor force, particularly in jobs that offer prospects of advancement. It may be desirable, even necessary, for our society to reappraise the need for a national jobs program (with an educational component) that will assist poorly educated young people to acquire work experience and at the same time overcome their educational deficiencies. A national jobs program could also serve as an important bridge for older women, particularly those who have been on and off welfare for some period (Hollister, 1984).

Continued EEO Enforcement   There is no question that the crowding phenomenon referred to above has been a major factor in keeping women's wages considerably below men's and in limiting the opportunities of many to advance into better-paying jobs and careers. Antidiscrimination legislation and administrative procedures have made some contribution to reducing wage discrimination, but the major positive force has been the expansion of the economy and the willingness and ability of more and more women to prepare for technical and professional careers. We should continue to use legal and administrative techniques to reduce discrimination in the labor market, even while we recognize that major gains to improve women's earnings and career opportunities depend primarily on the expansionary potential of the economy. Of equal if not greater importance is the response of the urban school systems. They currently fail to provide many low-income women with a proper educational foundation—without which their entrance into and advance in the world of work will be seriously circumscribed.

Child Care   No one who has reflected on women's employment can overlook the importance of strengthening the social service infrastructure, particularly the expansion of child care facilities. Most women who work must also care for their children and run their households. Greater equity and career opportunities for women require that society recognize that women workers carry excessive burdens and seek to lighten these burdens (Economic Policy Council of UNA-USA, 1985).

A CONCLUDING NOTE

The thrust of the foregoing policy recommendations has been to emphasize that the major preconditions for the continued expansion and improvement of employment opportunities for women hinge on the continuing strong growth of the economy and on strengthening the educational preparation of women for adulthood and for the world of work. A full employment policy and strengthened educational system are the two principal foundations for further progress. Supplementary support can come from strong antidiscrimination mechanisms and from expanded child care facilities.

However, it is unrealistic to expect our economy, or any developed economy, to perform continuously at a high level of employment. Similarly, even a well-functioning educational system will not be responsive to the needs of all young people. A significant minority is likely to reach working age inadequately prepared for the world of work. Large-scale shifts in markets and new technological breakthroughs introduce further disturbances that will result in job losses, skill downgrading, and reduced earnings, even while they also open up new opportunities for job growth, skill improvements, and higher earnings. A responsible and responsive democracy must act to assist those who are most vulnerable to the inadequacies of our schools and the labor market. It can do so by providing second-chance opportunities for the many who need to improve their basic competences if they are to be successful in obtaining a private-sector job; for interim public employment if they are not capable of competing successfully for such jobs; and for access to training and retraining in the event that they are victimized by market or technological change.

Our society confronts a paradox that it can no longer ignore. It cannot hold on to its conviction that all persons should work to support themselves and their dependents and at the same time ignore the reality that many lack the required competences for getting and holding jobs and that many others, competent others, cannot find jobs. If we reaffirm our commitment to the work ethic, we must see that everyone, men and women alike, who need or want to work have an opportunity to do so.

REFERENCES

Baumol, William J.
  1967   Macroeconomics of unbalanced growth: the anatomy of urban crisis. *American Economic Review* 57(3):415–426.
Bureau of the Census
  1983   *Statistical Abstract of the United States, 1984.* 106th edition. Washington, D.C.: U.S. Department of Commerce.
Dutka, Anna B.
  1983   A Review and Analysis of the Citibank Office Technology Pilot Project Program at Martin Luther King, Jr. High School. Report, Conservation of Human Resources, Columbia University, New York. January.
Economic Policy Council of UNA-USA
  1985   *Women and Family in the United States: A Policy Initiative.* Report of the Family Policy Panel. New York: United Nations Association of the United States of America.
Ginzberg, Eli
  1985   The restructuring of U.S. health care. *Inquiry* (Fall) 22(3):272–281.
Ginzberg, Eli, and Alice M. Yohalem
  1966   *Educated American Women: Self Portraits.* New York: Columbia University Press.
Ginzberg, Eli, Ivar E. Berg, Carol A. Brown, John L. Herma, Alice M. Yohalem, and Sherry Gorelick
  1966   *Life Styles of Educated Women.* New York: Columbia University Press.
Ginzberg, Eli, Thierry J. Noyelle, and Thomas M. Stanback, Jr.
  1986   *Technology and Employment: Concepts and Clarifications.* Boulder, Colo.: Westview Press.
Hollister, Robinson G., Jr., ed.
  1984   *The National Supported Work Demonstration.* Madison: University of Wisconsin Press.
Kutscher, Ronald
  1985   Factors Influencing the Changing Employment Structure of the United States. A paper given at the Second International Conference of Progetto Milano, Milan, Italy, January 25. Washington, D.C.: Bureau of Labor Statistics.
National Manpower Council
  1957   *Womanpower.* New York: Columbia University Press.
Noyelle, Thierry J.
  1987   *Beyond Industrial Dualism: Market and Job Segmentation in the New Economy.* Boulder, Colo.: Westview Press.

Noyelle, Thierry J., and Anna B. Dutka
　1987　*Business Services in World Markets: Lessons for Trade Negotiations.*
　　　　New York: Ballinger.
Silvestri, George T., and John M. Lukasiewicz
　1985　Occupational employment projections:　the 1984–95 outlook.
　　　　Monthly Labor Review 108(11):42–57.
Stanback, Thomas M., Jr., Peter J. Bearse, Thierry J. Noyelle, and Robert
A. Karasek
　1981　*Services/The New Economy.* Totowa, N.J.: Allanheld, Osmun & Co.

Part II

Case Studies of Women Workers and Information Technology

The Technological Transformation
of White-Collar Work:
A Case Study of the Insurance Industry

BARBARA BARAN

Although white-collar automation has received considerably less press than robots on the assembly-line, the introduction of computer-based technologies into the office has generated growing concern that industrialized working conditions and technological redundancy may be spreading to white-collar settings. Because of the pervasiveness of occupational sex segregation within the office work force, it is also feared that women will bear the brunt of the restructuring process. Feldberg and Glenn (1983), for example, argue that whereas women's jobs are disproportionately disappearing and their opportunities for upward mobility declining, men may actually benefit from the new technologies both because they will dominate the more highly skilled technical and professional jobs being created and because automation may centralize control in the hands of (male) senior managers and systems analysts.

The limited numbers of case studies that have been published on the impacts of office automation report conflicting findings.

With regard to changes in the occupational structure, some researchers have found that job loss is concentrated among low-skilled clericals (Faunce et al., 1962; Roessner et al., 1985; Shepherd, 1971), implying a general upgrading of labor. Other studies indicate, on the contrary, the elimination of skilled clerical activities, resulting in a polarization of the occupational structure (Feldberg and Glenn, 1977; Hoos, 1961; U.S. Bureau of Labor Statistics, 1965). Similarly, whereas some analysts have reported less task fragmentation as the technology becomes more sophisticated (Shepherd, 1971; Matteis, 1979; Sirbu, 1982; Adler, 1983; Appelbaum, 1984), others suggest that job content is narrowed and worker autonomy reduced (Murphree, 1982; Greenbaum, 1979; Cummings, 1977; Feldberg and Glenn, 1983, 1977). Finally, although in all cases women experienced the greatest job loss, in some reports it appeared that after automation women were relegated to lower-skilled activities (Feldberg and Glenn, 1977; Murphree, 1982), whereas in other accounts female clericals seemed to benefit from the new labor process (Matteis, 1979; Cummings, 1977).

The intent of my research on the insurance industry was to contribute to this nascent literature. The findings reported here are based on a two-year study of the impacts of automation on that industry. The first phase of this research was an in-depth case study of a major national property/casualty carrier, which included 26 interviews with employees in various parts of the company's operations (home office, branch office, data-processing center, commercial group, and personal lines centers) and different levels of the occupational hierarchy, as well as analysis of extensive quantitative personnel data which the company made available. The second phase involved lengthy interviews with executives, personnel managers, and systems analysts in 18 other companies, loosely stratified by size, product type, growth rate, distribution system, and so on; members of the industry's trade associations, agents' associations, and vendor companies were also interviewed. Third, a structured telephone survey was conducted of 37 companies—21 life firms and 16 property/casualty firms—again loosely stratified. All of the firms in both samples were among the top 100 companies in their industry segment. Together these 55 insurers account for approximately 55 percent of industry employment; they range from firms of over 50,000 employees to firms of less than 1,000. Finally, I have supplemented this field work with secondary source material from government agencies, trade publications, and documents and survey data kindly provided by the trade associations and consultants to the industry.

Two kinds of conclusions emerged from this effort. The first, of course, are numbers of concrete observations which will be presented in summary form in this paper. In addition to these sectorally specific findings, however, analysis of the insurance industry generated a set of more general hypotheses concerning the kinds of factors it is necessary to consider when attempting to assess the impacts of office automation technologies on a work force. Since the following discussion is not sufficiently comprehensive to cover all these issues, I want to discuss them briefly here before turning to the more detailed findings of the study.

First, as the case of the insurance industry made clear, it is virtually impossible to separate technological innovation from other factors affecting the competitive dynamics of an industry. The competitive environment is both a major determinant of the speed of diffusion of innovation and—quite apart from technological change—significantly affects the demand for labor.

Second, and closely related, is that the impacts of the new technologies on the labor force are not limited to their effects on the organization of the work process. In insurance, changes in product offerings and in the structure of both the industry itself and the firms within it promise to be equally important influences on the kind and amount of labor employed.

Third, it was clear from this study that "office automation" cannot be analyzed as a single phenomenon. Impacts vary on the basis of the specific kinds of technology being introduced (including, importantly, the generation of that technology) and the nature of the work process being automated (originating often in the unique characteristics of the product, market, and organizational structure of the industry). In terms of the first, I would underline the importance of periodizing the process of office automation; some of the disagreement in the literature can be attributed to differences in the generation of the technologies observed. In terms of the second, it is obvious that even in this one industry, the new labor processes will vary widely by product line. It is also important to point out that the insurance industry is very different from office-type settings in which word processing is the core application since systems development in the insurance industry has been driven by its data-processing needs. In fact, in some regards, more accurate parallels can be drawn between automation in the insurance industry and automation in manufacturing industries. In both cases, production work is increasingly performed by machines while administrative support activity remains relatively labor-intensive (although, in insurance, services activities are also becoming extremely automated).

Fourth, in assessing the impacts of automation on skill requirements and on the occupational structure of an industry, I would stress the importance of analyzing the changes occurring in the *entire* labor process. In failing to do so, analysts often miss the forest for the trees. When the organization of work is being fundamentally restructured, it is not so useful to talk about how specific jobs are changing; instead, we need to begin to assess how particular job functions or activities are being reconstituted and recombined to produce new kinds of job categories.

Although this observation may seem banal, most studies of the effects of office automation have focused almost exclusively on the clerical work force. As such, they miss one of the most important features of the current wave of applications, that is, the automation of professional functions and their transfer to less-skilled labor. As a result, these studies may be overly pessimistic both about the decline of clerical-type occupations and their likely skill levels; at the same time, they may be overly optimistic about the expansion of higher-level, challenging, well-paid work.

Fifth, we have to be careful not to assume any necessary identity between skill levels and other job attributes, such as pay, satisfaction, or occupational mobility. Indeed, many of the new jobs emerging in the insurance industry may require fairly high levels of skill and yet offer few rewards, material or otherwise.

Finally, this last point is true in part because different categories of workers will not only be differentially affected by the process of transformation, but the nature of the available labor force also shapes job design. In this case, the nature of the female labor market may be an important determinant of the emerging occupational structure.

Some, although not all, of these themes will be explored in greater depth in the remainder of this paper. To give context to the discussion of the ways in which new technologies are having an impact on the labor force, the first section begins by describing the significant changes that have occurred in the last decade in terms of the rate of diffusion and the kinds of computerized systems implemented in the insurance industry.

THE PACE OF DIFFUSION AND
THE NEW IMPLEMENTATIONS

Insurance companies, along with financial institutions and the government, were among the earliest users of electronic data-processing (EDP) computers. As early as 1959, the finance, insurance, and real estate sector boasted the greatest number of computer installations per million employees (Phister, 1979); by 1970, the insurance industry employed a higher ratio of computer specialists than any except the high-technology manufacturing industries (Bureau of Labor Statistics, 1981b).

Size of the organization was initially the primary factor influencing the implementation decision; companies attempted little, if any, formal cost-benefit justification. Applications were generally limited to structured accounting tasks, billing, and claims disbursements. With the exception of the move to direct billing—a transaction which had traditionally been handled at the agency level, the automation of these functions had little impact on the rest of the organization.

For the first two decades, the pace of diffusion was extremely civilized and the industry proceeded much as it had for the last hundred years. The barriers to rapid adoption of more sophisticated office systems were both technological and organizational.[1] Beginning in the early 1970s, however, systems development took two important new turns. First, the focus of automation shifted

---

[1] The technological barriers included (a) equipment incompatibility, both among the various vendors and even within the product offerings of a particular vendor, that prevented network extension and integrated system development; (b) substantial work station connection costs and communications costs; and (c) the difficulty of representing more complex white-collar activities in computer algorithms. The attempt to impose a standardized logic on many procedures often generated too many exceptions to be cost-effective and in some cases even diminished the efficiency of the organization. The organizational problems associated with the introduction of the new systems were perhaps even more substantial than these technical problems: these integrated systems required a fundamental reorganization of production, service, and distribution, since their effect was not limited to clerical labor in word-processing and data-processing departments; higher-level workers had their jobs redefined and in some cases even eliminated. Their resistance erected a powerful barrier to diffusion.

from administrative functions such as accounting to automation of the production process itself, meaning primarily the underwriting, rating, and physical production of the insurance policy and the handling of claims disbursements. Second, in the place of single-task, batch-oriented machines, multitask, multimachine systems began to be introduced, often operating on-line.

The process of systems integration was an evolutionary one. As the price/performance ratio of the hardware continued to improve and the software became more sophisticated, more and more functions in the operational areas were automated and systems became increasingly decentralized. Independent systems began to proliferate, often geared exclusively to a company's in-house data-/word-processing activities. Gradually, however, a counter-tendency developed as companies moved to link these systems together into what at first were fairly rudimentary networks. Initially, in some of the local settings, applications were developed that went beyond the automation of a discrete task toward the performance of a wider set of connected operations. Automated linkages were then slowly constructed among systems, so that information could be electronically transferred and shared.

On this basis, entry and processing functions were increasingly decentralized and distributed throughout the organization, but data bases were integrated and centralized. In the mid to late 1970s, what are often referred to as "office automation" (OA) applications also began to be linked to these DP-based systems. A multitude of new office machines were introduced. Optical character recognition devices were applied to premium billing and collection operations; computer output microfilm (COM)—which permits the transfer of data directly from computer to microfiche— was used extensively by all insurers, and in conjunction with computer-assisted retrieval technology, increasingly replaced paper files; finally, more and more companies began to experiment with electronic mail, teleconferencing, electronic fund transfer, interactive data access via television, and other "office of the future" technologies.

To an important extent, the introduction of these more sophisticated systems in the 1970s was driven by a new competitive environment. Unprecedented levels of inflation and correspondingly high interest rates and important demographic and socioeconomic changes[2] combined to shake up this once stodgy industry by increasing uncertainty in financial markets and, consequently, dramatically increasing competition in the financial services sector. Deregulation fueled these competitive flames. Giants in the industry found themselves struggling for survival; and companies with a long, proud history of paternalism were suddenly forced to lay off up to 1,500 employees virtually overnight. In many ways, in fact, the insurance industry was hit by a crisis not unlike the one faced by U.S. auto manufacturers; and in both cases, one important response on the part of companies was to turn to automation—both to increase the efficiency of their operations and to enhance their product offerings.

Whereas the early applications were basically limited to the automation of discrete tasks (e.g., typing, calculating), the new implementations called for rationalization of an entire procedure (e.g., new business issuance, claims processing), and ultimately the restructuring and integration of all the procedures involved in a particular division, product line, or group of product lines. As such, in the categories of Bright's (1958) original analysis, there has been a dramatic leap in the span, level, and penetration of the automated systems and, therefore, in the impacts on the labor force. The changes that have occurred in the underwriting and claims support systems best illustrate this evolution, although I will also touch briefly on three others: administrative/clerical, decision support, and agency systems.

---

[2] On the demand side, inflationary pressures initiated the demand for alternatives to ordinary insurance that would provide adequate protection at lower cost or higher rates of return on savings. Demographic shifts fueled these trends. Dual income households—and the more affluent dual career households—grew rapidly and consumer assets were increasingly concentrated here. The needs and tastes of this population differed significantly from the traditional insurance consumer—with more emphasis on investment over mere savings, less concern with thrift and more with spending, and a demand for a fuller range of sophisticated financial services. On the supply side, competitors outside the insurance industry responded to the new market conditions by offering reasonable substitutes for many traditional insurance products and services. In addition, commercial banks began to lobby for the lifting of regulatory restrictions which bars them from the sale of insurance. Finally, insurance companies themselves moved to diversify their product offerings and successfully lobbied authorities to deregulate rates.

Underwriting and Claims Support Systems

The underwriting function is a critical component of the insurance policy production process; it entails an analysis of the risk involved and acceptance or rejection of that risk. As such, the heart of this operation has always been performed by professional labor: insurance underwriters. However, today, in numbers of product lines, clerks—aided by decision parameters embedded in computer software—are responsible for the risks their companies accept; and in the most standardized lines, computers are even performing this risk calculation task themselves. The underwriting systems now being used to produce property/casualty personal lines products (such as auto and homeowners' insurance) are a good example of these new applications.

Traditionally, the production process for personal lines products involved roughly the following: an agent gathered the client's policy information and forwarded this to an underwriting department, located either in the home or branch office; the underwriters established a file on the client, evaluated the risk, and determined the risk parameters, then sent the policy to the rating section. A rater (a skilled clerical employee) calculated the premium charges based on guidelines contained in numerous manuals; sometimes that information had to be communicated back to the agent so that the client could make a decision whether or not to use this particular company. In most cases, the policy went back to the underwriter who reviewed it and then sent it to a typing pool where policy typists prepared the various forms and documents. Finally, the policy was mailed back to the agent who forwarded it to the customer.

In most large property/casualty carriers the first applications of computerized equipment to the underwriting process were implemented in the early 1970s and were aimed at speeding the underwriter's access to client files, shortening the time involved in rate making, and of course improving the efficiency of policy production. A typical system of this vintage might simply have involved a stand-alone computerized rating system—with most of the rating guidelines from the manuals built into the machine—and an automated policy issuance system, which performed the typing and assembly function.

In many personal lines departments today, this kind of configuration remains the current state of the art. Beginning in the late 1970s, however, some of the largest carriers moved to institute what they variously call "underwriting by exception," "pigeon-hole underwriting," or "computer-assisted underwriting." The aim is very simply to have the computer itself perform the risk assessment function on as large a fraction of policies as possible, on the basis of underwriting decision rules which are built into the machine.

In general, the production process associated with these kinds of systems looks something like the following: the agent sends the policy information to a personal lines department where a clerical worker screens it and enters all routine risks directly into the machines; these policies are then often relayed in batch form to the carrier's national (or regional) computer center; the computer evaluates the risk, rates the policy, and produces it. Policies which fail to fit within the pre-established guidelines are kicked out by the machine and returned to an underwriter, who often now calls up the information on a terminal and works with it on the screen. Although these systems are extremely new, a few companies already report that 50 percent to 90 percent of their personal lines policies are completely underwritten by the computer.

Most personal lines systems fall between the two just described in their level of sophistication, but, in almost all cases, clerks are assuming greater, and sometimes almost exclusive, responsibility for underwriting. For example, in one major property/casualty carrier, the introduction of computer-assisted underwriting two years ago shifted the bulk of the underwriting function from the underwriting department to the operations department, a clerical operation which had formerly been confined to assembling and producing the physical policies. Although auto policies still go to the underwriters for an initial screening process, most property policies are sent directly to skilled clerks in the operations department, who themselves order all necessary inspection reports and issue the policies.

In some rare instances, the underwriting function has even been integrated into the activity of a sales worker, entirely eliminating it as a separate department. In these cases, a highly skilled clerical position—customer representative—has been designed; this job includes answering inquiries from potential customers over the phone; accessing a terminal to produce on-the-spot rate quotes; negotiating the rates; and then if a sale is made, capturing additional information on-line. The computer underwrites and produces the policy that same night.

Similar kinds of work process configurations have emerged in the claims departments of large insurance companies. In the life insurance division of the industry, for example, group health claims systems—which were implemented early in the 1970s and are now probably the most sophisticated in the industry—have allowed skilled clerks to take over 75 percent or more of the claims function.

ADMINISTRATIVE/CLERICAL, DECISION SUPPORT, AND AGENCY SYSTEMS

In contrast to the underwriting and claims support systems, neither office automation applications nor decision support systems have, as yet, made a significant change in the organization of work, although in the case of the former, companies have reported fourfold productivity increases when word-processing equipment is substituted for traditional typewriters and 70 to 85 percent rises in output per operator when CRTs replace MagII equipment (Life Office Management Association, 1979). By the late 1970s, word processors were widely diffused throughout the industry. Companies concentrated on installing the text-processing systems first, since that is where large and immediate savings could be realized, and then gradually added more sophisticated technologies and applications—electronic mail, voice mail, image processing, electronic office support, and decision support. In most cases, word processing and data processing have been both organizationally and technically independent; companies have moved extremely slowly to merge the two through electronic communications capabilities.

Management information or decision support systems are thus truly in their infancy. Although the integrated systems described earlier have made a wealth of information available on a timely—often daily—basis, few insurance managers have on-line access to these data bases. In the last few years, however, user acceptance has improved significantly due largely to the proliferation of personal computers. One of the promises of these systems is that they can begin to bypass middle management and provide top executives with ongoing access to the performance of their various departments.

The story of the agency support systems is somewhat more complex. As in the case of the carriers, the greatest leaps in productivity have been attained in the production and servicing functions, but this is largely the result of extensive networking with the carriers and has therefore been highly dependent on the nature of the distribution system.[3] Over the last 5 to 6 years, insurers with captive or salaried agency forces have moved rapidly to integrate sales electronically into the company's overall operations, allowing them to substantially rationalize the flow of work. For example, the keying function can be moved to the field office, closer to the point of data generation; much of the servicing of the policies can be computerized and moved from the field to the home office; sales proposals and policies can often be printed on-site in the field offices, eliminating bulk ordering. The benefits of these integrated systems include improved speed and quality of quotations, policy production, billing and customer service; greater sophistication in marketing techniques; error reductions; and less duplication of clerical effort.

EFFECTS OF AUTOMATION ON THE SIZE AND COMPOSITION OF THE WORK FORCE

Taken together, the effects of these new systems on the insurance work force has already been dramatic and because integrated implementations did not begin in earnest until fairly recently, we can expect even more significant changes in the future. Work is being both eliminated and redesigned.

According to a recent study funded by the U.S. Department of Labor (Drennan, 1983), productivity in the insurance industry as a whole grew rapidly between 1969 and 1979, at an average annual rate of 2.7 percent (in contrast to a 1.1 average annual growth rate for all private industries); and these productivity gains accelerated

---

[3] The four major marketing systems in the insurance industry are independent agents and brokers, exclusive or "captive" agents, salaried employees (the "direct writers"), and direct mail. Both independent and exclusive agents are independent contractors, but the latter represent only one insurer. The great advantage of the direct writers and exclusive agency systems is the organizational integrity which has allowed them to make full use of integrated, computer-based systems.

so that by 1975–1979 the average annual percentage increase in productivity was 6.7 percent using a GNP deflator and 4.2 percent using an industry deflator.[4]

Also significant, registered productivity improvements varied within the industry. In the life insurance segment, where automation of policy production proceeded most rapidly, purchases of policies increased by 49.2 percent (between 1970 and 1980) while the labor force expanded by only 9.8 percent. In the property/casualty segment, on the other hand—where fewer lines of business were easily automated and, more important, insurers were expanding capacity to reap the benefits of high interest rates— employment kept pace with gains in output. From 1970 to 1978, average annual employment gains in property/casualty carriers were 3.2 percent, approximately one-fourth again higher than the industry-wide average and just slightly less than four times higher than the average gains of 0.85 percent annually in life carriers. By 1980, however, reckless expansion caught up with these companies. Between 1980 and 1982, sales plunged by 6.5 percent and employment growth slowed considerably. Since then there may even have been some labor-shedding. Every property/casualty company we visited, with one exception, had experienced serious layoffs in the last four years, ranging between 5 percent and 15 percent of their work force. In the coming years, labor savings are expected to accelerate in all segments of the industry.

With respect to future job loss, three fairly comprehensive employment forecasts for the insurance industry have been recently published (Drennan, 1983; Leontief and Duchin, 1986; Roessner et al., 1985); all three predict dramatic declines in industry employment—particularly clerical employment—between

---

[4] Relatively crude measures of real productivity figures are presented here, because of the difficulty in calculating inputs from real estate, stock brokerage houses, and so on (estimated roughly at 6 percent of total industry employment). Unpublished productivity figures for the insurance industry calculated by the U.S. Department of Commerce show the dramatic improvement over the previous decade but suggest somewhat slower average annual gains during this period (2.0 percent). However, the Department of Labor figures were based solely on insurance carriers, whereas the Department of Commerce estimates include agents and brokers. The average annual employment gain for agencies and brokers during these years was 4.5 percent, or almost double the industry-wide figure. This then explains the discrepancy and strengthens the hypothesis that the new technologies were indeed paying off in terms of labor savings at the insurance carriers.

1980 and the turn of the century. If, relative to output, requisite
clerical labor input in the industry declines by even 10 percent
between 1981 and 1991, approximately 100,000 fewer clerical jobs
would be created. If, by the end of the century, the clerical labor coefficient were to fall to 70 percent of its present level—the
smallest decline predicted by these forecasters—over 400,000 fewer
clerical jobs would be created; and between 1990 and 2000, approximately 100,000 clerks would actually lose their jobs through
layoffs or attrition (Baran, 1985:225–234). Clerical job loss may
well be even more serious. One of the studies is considerably more
pessimistic; in addition, none of these studies take into account
the effects of structural shifts likely to occur in the industry. For
example, because agencies were responsible for 61 percent of all
new clerical jobs in the last decade, a reorganization and consolidation of the distribution function—which most industry observers
expect—should have a major effect on clerical employment.

   Although layoffs in response to the overcapacity common in
the 1980s (and the anticipated job loss) could affect the entire
occupational structure, the impacts of technological change can
be more discriminate. Over the last two decades, there have been
visible shifts in the composition of employment and effects have
varied with waves of implementation.

   The first impacts of computerization were, as we have seen,
on the accounting functions of carriers; in addition, billing shifted
from agencies and sales offices to the insurers' data-processing
departments, and probably coincidentally, reporting requirements
to state regulatory agencies increased (Appelbaum, 1984). As a
result of these various forces, the most significant change in the
occupational structure of the industry during the 1960s was an
extraordinary influx of technical personnel (see Table 1). Whereas
in 1960 professional and technical workers had constituted 3.2
percent of all employment, by 1970 this share had grown to 5.8
percent (U.S. Bureau of Labor Statistics, 1969, 1981b).[5]

---

[5] There are substantial problems involved in developing a longitudinal
data series on employment in the insurance industry. There are three
principal data bases: the first, the U.S. Census of Population, remained
consistent between 1960 and 1970 and permits useful comparisons of occupational change over that decade, although even for this time period
the extent of disaggregation by occupation—particularly insurance-specific
occupations—is woefully inadequate. By 1980, census data were truncated
and occupational categories were significantly reorganized and redefined; this

Over the next decade, data-processing technology continued
to diffuse and text-processing equipment was introduced; competition had heated up markedly and firms were rushing to reduce unit
labor costs. By the end of this period, the impacts of technological
change on clerical labor are strikingly clear (see Table 1): clerical
employment as a percentage of total employment in the industry
fell from 50 percent to 45 percent; 73,000 clerical jobs were eliminated. This dramatic drop in employment share contrasts with
the experience of clerical labor in the economy as a whole and
in other similar industries such as banking, securities, business
services, and credit agencies. It occurred because the introduction
and subsequent diffusion of new technologies occurred earlier for
the insurance industry and was therefore more widespread by the
late 1970s (Drennan, 1983).

Virtually all clerical categories experienced relative decline,
but routine clerical occupations—such as keyboarding, filing, traditional office machine operators, and so on—were particularly

---

makes comparison with earlier years difficult and, in some cases, useless.

The second important source, the Bureau of Labor Statistics' Occupational Employment Matrix, provides data reported for 1970, 1978, and 1980
which are estimates based on other surveys. In 1980, the Matrix shifted
from basing itself primarily on census data to relying principally on data
from the BLS Occupational Employment Survey (OES). However, the OES
data fail to correspond even generally to the census data. To illustrate, the
table below compares the occupational structure of the insurance industry
as reported by the 1978 Matrix based upon the census and the 1980 Matrix
based upon the OES:

	Census (1978)	OES (1980)
Professional/technical	6.79%	15.4%
Managers/officials	12.08	13.8
Sales workers	34.54	14.6
Clerical workers	45.42	54.4

The third source of occupational data, the employer-based OES series,
which appears to be the most reliable, has limited usefulness since it is
available for the insurance industry only for the years 1978 and 1981. Despite
this limitation, this report has relied on it and the OES-based Matrix and
has used the census-based Matrix only when necessary for the earlier years.
Although wide discrepancies in the data exist, at least the *direction of change*
is the same in most cases. Finally, we have used the BLS *Employment and
Earnings* series in comparing aggregate employment changes, since these data
were the only longitudinal ones available disaggregated by major industry
division. See Hunt and Hunt (1985) for a fuller discussion of methodological
problems.

TABLE 1 Percentage Distribution of Insurance Employment by
Occupation, 1960, 1970, 1978

| Occupation | Percent of Total Employment | | | Percent Change from 1970 to 1978 |
	1960	1970	1978	
Managers/officers	13.3	11.8	12.1	21.4
Professional/				
technical workers	3.2	5.8	6.0	24.0
Clerical workers	47.4	50.0	45.4	8.0
Computer operators		0.7	1.3	119.0
Keypunch operators		.1.8	1.2	-21.9
Statistical clerks		2.8	2.5	6.4
Bookkeepers		3.6	2.8	-7.4
Adjusters/examiners		7.3	9.8	58.8
File clerks		2.5	1.7	-19.7
Mail handlers		0.7	0.5	-10.7
Secretaries		13.2	12.0	8.2
Typists		6.9	5.1	-11.7
Sales	33.6	30.0	34.5	37.2

NOTES: Percents for subcategories under the category "Clerical workers" do not total the percents for the category as a whole due to other clerical occupations not listed. Columns do not add to 100.0 due to other occupations not listed.

SOURCE: 1960 data, U.S. Bureau of Labor Statistics (1969); for all other years, U.S. Bureau of Labor Statistics (1981b:Vol. I).

seriously affected. In absolute terms, the number of bookkeeping machine operators fell by 60 percent, calculating machine operators and duplicating machine operators by 41 percent, tabulating machine operators by 76 percent, keypunch operators by 22 percent, file clerks by 20 percent, and typists by 12 percent (Bureau of Labor Statistics, 1981b).

Secretarial employment in the insurance industry continued to grow at about 1 percent a year—reflecting the relatively small impact of automation on traditional administrative support tasks, yet this growth rate was less than one-third that of secretarial labor in the economy as a whole and less than half the rate of employment growth in the insurance industry. Even in this occupational area, then, the introduction of word-processing equipment and rationalizing moves such as the pooling of secretaries took a toll on employment opportunities. Professional, managerial, and especially sales jobs, on the other hand, grew at a fairly rapid clip.

Although there are no current data available to reflect the recent implementations of integrated on-line systems, it is clear that, especially in the carriers, clerical jobs are continuing to disappear (see Table 2). Between 1978 and 1981, of the clerical occupational titles reported in the BLS Occupational Employment Survey of Insurance, approximately two-thirds grew more slowly than overall employment and close to one-half experienced absolute job loss.

TABLE 2 Percentage Change in Employment in Insurance
Carriers by Selected Occupation, from 1978 to 1981

Occupation	Percent Change in Employment
Total employment	5.6
Managers and officers	10.9
Professional and technical	9.5
Actuary	21.7
Systems analyst	42.5
Accountant/auditor	-51.1
Claims examiner, property/casualty	10.8
Underwriter	3.0
Computer programmer	36.2
Clerical	3.5
Computer operator	0.4
Bookkeeper, hand	-15.2
Claims adjuster	-7.7
Correspondence clerk	-1.5
File clerk	-15.9
General clerk	-5.9
Rater	-1.6
Secretary	6.6
Stenographer	-31.4
Typist	-2.9
Sales	6.6

SOURCE: Unpublished data from the U.S. Bureau of Labor
Statistics (1978, 1981a).

However, clerical categories such as "claims examiner, life, acci-
dent and health," "insurance clerk," and "policy change clerk"
continued to experience steady growth, probably reflecting the
growing responsibility of clerks for the claims and underwriting
processes.

Significantly, from 1978 onward the impacts of automation on
professional work have become evident in aggregate data. Between
1978 and 1981, underwriters lost employment share and the number of accountants and auditors plunged dramatically. Although
the professional and technical category still grew faster than total
employment, most of this expansion was directly attributable to
the continued addition of computer professionals (systems analysts
and programmers); excluding these two categories, professional occupations grew at about half the rate of total employment. Growth
in the number of sales personnel also began to slow down (to about

half the rate of the previous period)—probably reflecting declining profitability and the attempts on the part of insurers to improve the efficiency of their distribution systems; but managerial ranks continued to swell.

Three conclusions can be drawn from these data: First, at least in relative terms, insurance is employing fewer people; and in increasing numbers of occupational categories, the relative decline in employment share has escalated into absolute job loss. Second, the weight of the occupational structure has shifted upward, tilting toward the higher-skilled categories of labor—managerial, professional, and sales. Third, however, even within the clerical category, routine occupations are being eliminated most rapidly. In contradiction, then, to observers who feared that widespread deskilling would accompany automation of this industry, the new technologies seem to be raising aggregate skill levels—both across occupations and within occupations. When the declining and growing clerical occupations in the life insurance segment of the industry are ranked on the basis of current wage levels (as a proxy for complexity of the job), this upward shift in clerical skills is confirmed. Almost without exception, all occupations at the bottom of the pay scale are shrinking more rapidly than those at the top. Similarly, when the average skill level of declining and growing occupations in both the 1970–1978 and 1978–1981 periods are computed on the basis of the U.S. Department of Labor's (1977) *Dictionary of Occupational Titles* job evaluation scheme, growing occupations in both time periods ranked higher in the areas of mathematical skills, language requirements, and specific vocational training (Baran, 1985:115–118).

Although these aggregate data are suggestive, they fail to capture the logic of the new implementations and therefore are not very useful either in predicting the future or in describing the kinds of new jobs actually emerging. For that kind of detail, it is necessary to go to the level of the shop floor.

CHANGES IN THE NATURE OF WORK: THE VIEW FROM THE SHOP FLOOR

Conceptually, what is perhaps most notable about the emerging organization of work in the insurance industry is that it represents an electronic transcendence of the assembly-line, or more

precisely of the detailed division of labor which has come to dominate all modern industry, both blue and white collar. Despite the
fact that the office automation literature, particularly the critical
literature (see, for example, Braverman, 1974; Cummings, 1977;
DeKadt, 1979; Driscoll, 1979, 1980; Feldberg and Glenn, 1977,
1983; Greenbaum, 1979; Hoos, 1961; Nussbaum and Gregory,
1980), has been dominated by the fear that industrialized labor
processes would accompany the rising capital intensity of white-
collar production, ironically it was the *pre*-automated rather than
the newer highly automated labor processes in the insurance industry that most closely resembled an industrial assembly-line.
Traditionally, in huge open offices, white-collar insurance workers
sat grouped by function—underwriters, raters, typists, file clerks,
and so on; the paper flowed manually from one station to another
as each worker completed his or her portion of the production
task. In line with established principles of industrial engineering
and scientific management over the last two decades, this work
was increasingly fragmented into its component parts and simpler
functions were turned over to less-skilled labor. Just the check
issuance procedure in a preautomated claims office illustrates the
extraordinary degree to which work was divided:

> If a check had to be issued, first it was typed by a typist;
> then another clerical verified the amount; a third person audited
> the claim to insure that the doctor charged appropriately for the
> service provided; a fourth person actually "burst" the check (took
> apart the carbons); and a fifth then put the check through the
> signing machine. Including supervisorial oversight, between six and
> seven people were involved in this one procedure alone (personal
> interview).

Task fragmentation was not limited to processing functions. In
many property/casualty companies, for example, underwriting
was also rationalized; at the bottom end, routine underwriting
tasks were turned over to a newly created clerical position, "underwriting technical assistant," and, at the top end, the number
of specialty underwriters increased.

The early applications of data-processing and text-processing
equipment tended to follow and intensify the Taylorist logic underlying this form of work organization, producing ever more
highly "industrialized" work settings. In the case of data processing, the early mainframes were large, noisy, and often required
special rooms. Because of these technical requirements and the

tendency to automate in conformity with the rationalized bureaucratic structure, separate data-processing departments were established in all insurance companies. These eventually generated their
own hierarchy of systems analysts, programmers, computer operators, data-entry operators, and so on. With the improvements
in telecommunications in the last decade, the entry function was
often separated sharply from the rest of the operation and frequently spatially isolated in suburbs or small towns where land
and labor were cheaper. These were the "electronic sweatshops."
Work within the centers was machine-linked, machine-paced, and
often machine-monitored as well; correspondingly, turnover was
extremely high. Many of the early applications of word processing had a similar character in that key entry was often separated
from other clerical activities and centralized in a word-processing
center.

Beginning in the late 1970s, however, as companies began to
introduce integrated systems, they also embarked on a serious redesign of the labor process, which promises to reverse many of
these earlier trends. Whereas the organizing logic of the last several decades produced an amazing proliferation of "detail" workers, today the white-collar assembly-lines are being internalized
within the machines themselves; an electronic reintegration of the
work process is manifesting itself in at least three important new
trends.

First, multifunction jobs are replacing the extremely narrowed
occupational categories of the past. On the basis of the new integrated systems, insurers have been able to consolidate all policy
holder data into central master records stored in the company's
main computer installation. In the past, these records were du-
plicated in up to a dozen functional units; now users in remote
sites can access and alter relevant policies and the changes can be
integrated into the master record. One individual can therefore
handle multiple service transactions and functional units can be
consolidated since the individual master record for each policy is
a complete data base.

Second, "mental" and "manual" labor are (slowly) being reintegrated as entry functions are slipped unobtrusively into the activity of higher-level workers, such as underwriters and claims
adjustors. The apocryphal example is the insurance salesman,
equipped with a portable terminal, who enters all necessary policy data directly from the customer's home; through a regular

telephone link, that information is received by the company's mainframe which then underwrites, rates, and produces the policy. Although the current state of the art is perhaps a decade away from this futurist scenario (and many procedures simply do not lend themselves to such extensive automation), companies are beginning to install systems that require professionals to perform some, if not all, of the requisite data entry.

Finally, apart from this kind of electronic integration of tasks, in several procedures and product lines, single-activity units are being eliminated in favor of multiactivity teams. Whereas formerly typists, raters, and underwriters were divided into separate units, each with its own supervisor, now a small team consisting of one or two of each kind of worker will service some subset (often geographical) of the company's customers.

Although these overall trends are visible throughout the entire industry, a variety of actual job configurations are emerging both within companies and across companies largely reflecting differences among product lines. In the case of high-volume, standardized lines, two principal types of work organization seem to be developing. The first of these is found in purest form in the highly automated personal-lines underwriting departments of many large property/casualty carriers. Here both rating and risk assessment have been largely assumed by the computer; as a result, functions formerly divided among entry clerks, raters, underwriting assistants—as well as additional low-level underwriting tasks—have been consolidated and turned over to a highly skilled clerical worker.

Although closely circumscribed in their decision making, these clerks are a long way from the typing pool. Judgment is required, and often they are required to interact directly with the agents, a level of responsibility formerly reserved for professional underwriters. Most important, these workers (limited by the decision parameters built into the machines) are almost solely responsible for the soundness and accuracy of the millions of routine risks their companies write.

Underwriters have also had their jobs redefined as clerks have taken over their lower-level functions. First, they have become "exceptions" handlers, responsible only for the policies that fail to fit into the "pigeon-holes" of the computerized system; thus, their work has become more complex. Second, there has been a

reorientation of the job function away from churning out policies and toward planning and marketing.

A similar job configuration has emerged in the claims operation of many group life and health insurers. On the basis of highly integrated computer systems, clerks have taken over most of the work of professional claims examiners; the small number of remaining examiners handle only the problem cases.

The emergence of this kind of work organization, where routine clerical work is eliminated, professional jobs are reduced in number while being enlarged in depth and scope of responsibility, and skilled clerks become the bulk of the work force, seems to depend on several factors. First, the operation is high volume, making automation cost-effective; second, the product is standardized, making it relatively easy to translate the decision parameters into algorithmic form; third, these operations still involve semiskilled functions that cannot be automated, often because interpersonal interaction is required.

Alternatively, where products are standardized and volume is high but semiskilled functions *can* be assumed almost entirely by the computer system, the work force is highly bifurcated between a large number of routine data-entry clerks and a very small number of skilled professionals. At the clerical level, there is little real decision making and no interaction with agents or clients.

Finally, in product lines that are too low in volume, unique, or complex to lend themselves to this level of standardization, automation is less extensive and more confined to discrete tasks. Clerical work is routinized and narrow; professional work is computer-assisted to the extent technically feasible, but professionals are not being replaced either by clerks or by machines. In these situations, there are serious constraints on the automation of professional functions, either because low volume makes such sophisticated systems unjustifiably costly or because the work itself is too complex or unstructured. In the longer run, it is possible that some professional functions will be turned over to less-skilled labor as the software improves; but it is also likely that clerical labor will be bypassed entirely as data entry is increasingly folded into the activity of higher-level originators.

The nature of the product may be the primary determinant of which of these job configurations emerges. The second seems to be considerably more prevalent in life insurance companies (about

75 percent of our sample, as opposed to 50 percent for property/casualty firms); and even within property/casualty personal lines, the production of homeowners policies often afforded clericals greater discretion and wider responsibility than auto policy production. The crucial parameter in both cases seemed to be the difficulty of interpreting the necessary supporting reports (e.g., medical records, auto history, property evaluation). However, there were important differences in apparently identical product situations to emphasize the importance of a managerial decision level in the design of the labor process.

Although each of these job configurations has different ramifications for the employed work force, there are certain important similarities among all three that distinguish them from the earlier labor processes, beginning with their impacts on skill requirements. First, even in the case of routine entry operators, clericals have an increasingly important responsibility for the quality of the data. In the context of integrated data bases, errors are more significant, more costly, and more difficult to detect and correct, because data entered anywhere throughout the system is immediately recorded in all relevant files. There are multiple reasons for the new organizational and occupational designs just described, but in all cases an important motivation was the reduction of error; in each instance greater accountability was assigned to first-line workers. Single-source entry and team systems, for example, both encourage and demand that an individual or small group—often aided by feedback from the machines—assume responsibility for the accuracy of their work. The move to decentralize and despecialize entry was encouraged to an important degree because centralized work settings generated intolerably high error rates. To the extent then that responsibility is an essential component of skill, skill requirements have been rising.

Similarly, there is evidence that even routine data-entry positions involve greater levels of mental concentration than traditional text entry, to the extent that the work requires the operator to know and use a multiplicity of codes (Adler, 1983). In the old-fashioned insurance typing pools it was possible, after sufficient experience on the job, to semi-automatically pull out the appropriate forms from the appropriate stack and fill in the requisite information virtually without thinking, much like driving a car down a familiar route; the work was boring and demanded little in the way of mental effort.

As Adler notes when reviewing recent research, this kind of comfortable familiarity is never achieved when the language of the work is algorithmic. In addition, with increased computerization the span of functions for which any individual worker is responsible has widened; each transaction involves the entry of a wide variety of codes and discrete pieces of information, each step of which must be performed quickly, accurately, and in the correct sequence. The new systems then demand a kind of continual mental alertness which might also appropriately be understood as a new kind of skill. Finally, the fact that the systems are continually changing—both in response to technological improvements and in the interest of product innovation—means that the work force must be unusually flexible and adaptable and sufficiently polyvalent to easily learn new routines, new codes, and new procedures.

On the other hand, as Adler noted in the case of routine clerical activity in banking, what may be most notable about many of the new jobs is precisely the extent to which they demand much of the worker with little reward (Adler, 1983): "If the abstraction of means increases training requirements and mental effort, the abstraction of ends leads to a very different result—work is often experienced as boring." There are also other roots to this perceived disaffection. Although objectively work has been reintegrated through the expansive reach of the computerized system, for any individual worker, task variety may have diminished. For many insurance clerks, the previous work process involved a multiplicity of activities, which in combination relieved the boredom of the day. Now all these functions are of the same quality, that is, they center around the machine and the manipulation of its abstract symbols. Worse, the sustained concentration that is required introduces a new element of stress. Finally, the sociability of a job declines dramatically in the transition to a computerized work setting.

Evaluating the new skilled clerical categories is even more difficult. On the one hand, there is no doubt that they are an improvement over most clerical jobs along a series of dimensions: task variety has widened rather than narrowed, the span of decision making is broader, the responsibility for production is greater, and general training and educational requirements have risen. However, pay scales remain low and in some cases work is closely monitored and even paced by the system, heightening occupational stress. A recent survey by the 9 to 5, National Association of Working Women (1984) found that respondents whose work is subject to computerized monitoring are much more likely to rate their jobs as "very stressful" than other office automation users. Similarly, those working under production quotas report significantly higher levels of stress than other office workers.[6] Equally important, although skill levels may be rising, opportunities for occupational mobility may be diminishing. As lower-level professional categories are eliminated, there is, in the words of one manager, increasingly a "quantum leap" between the computer-linked clerical positions and the next step up the occupational ladder. In this sense, career paths may be *structurally* truncated.

Even for the professional and managerial labor forces the reorganization of work is only a mixed blessing. Although their work is likely to become more challenging, many jobs may be eliminated.[7]

WOMEN AND MINORITY WORKERS

Because of the prevalence of occupational stratification by gender and race, this reshaping of work and of the occupational structure has particularly affected female and minority workers.

---

[6] The survey presented a picture of two prototypical skilled, computer-linked clerical occupations: customer service representative and claims examiner in which white claims examiners were more likely than any of the other clerical categories reported to find their work always "interesting and challenging" (50 percent of claims examiners as compared to 30 percent of white legal secretaries, the second-ranked occupation). They were almost twice as likely as other clerks to work under production quotas and 44 percent described their jobs as "always very stressful" (as compared to 29 percent of general clerks in automated settings). Customer service representatives were even more likely to have set production quotas (72 percent) and to experience their jobs as very stressful (60 percent).

[7] In the case of sales workers, competitive pressures have probably been a more important source of change than automation—although the two are clearly integrally connected. The primary impacts of the new technologies on the agency employees have been: first, a decline in their role as service providers and an increased emphasis on their sales function; second, a much closer connection on all levels with the rest of the organization. Skill requirements have clearly risen in some product lines—particularly financial services planning—as evidenced by new training and licensing requirements. However, in more standardized product lines, both the role and necessary competencies of the sales worker are being eroded; the direct marketing clerk described earlier is a good example of this kind of change.

TABLE 3 Number of New Jobs Created in the Insurance Industry by Gender, 1960-1982

| Year | Number of New Jobs (thousands) | | | Percentage of New Jobs Held by Women |
	Total	Women	Men	
Insurance carriers				
1960-1970	198.0	109.1	88.9	55.1
1970-1978	143.9	144.7	-0.8	101.0
1978-1982	63.2	58.6	4.6	92.7
Agents/brokers				
1960-1970	70.7	46.6	24.1	65.9
1970-1978	115.2	86.6	28.6	75.2
1978-1982	71.0	55.3	15.7	77.9
Total				
1970-1982	393.3	345.2	48.1	87.7

SOURCE: U.S. Bureau of Labor Statistics (1983).

Therefore, it is impossible to evaluate the effects of the new technologies on the work force without considering these more selective impacts.

EFFECTS OF AUTOMATION
ON THE FEMALE WORK FORCE

Despite the fact that female-dominated jobs are disappearing in great numbers, empirically the proportion of women in the insurance industry has grown dramatically in the last decade. By 1982, women comprised 61 percent of the industry's entire work force, up from 54 percent in 1970 (Bureau of Labor Statistics, 1983).

Between 1970 and 1978 women claimed approximately 231,000 of the 259,000 new jobs created; and over the next 4 years women gained 113,900 jobs, whereas men gained only 20,300 (see Table 3). In total during this period, female employment rose by 49 percent compared to a meager 8 percent rise in male employment.

Since during this same decade clerical workers declined as a percentage of the work force, the increase in female employment cannot be explained by the disproportionate growth of traditionally female-typed jobs. On the contrary, what seems to be occurring is a major movement of women into traditional male occupations—professional, managerial, technical, and even clerical.

Between 1970 and 1979, the proportion of female managers and officers grew from 11 percent to 24 percent of the insurance work force; professionals grew from 17 percent to 38 percent; and technicians, from 38 percent to 65 percent. The percentage of women insurance examiners and investigators (formerly male clerical occupations) grew from 9 percent in 1962 to 26 percent in 1971 and to 58 percent in 1981 (Appelbaum, 1984).

Overall in the insurance industry, the ratio of women to men in professional and technical occupations rose by 19 and 27 percentage points in 1971 and 1981, respectively, as opposed to a 4.3 percentage point gain for women throughout the economy in professional and technical occupations combined. Although the disaggregated comparative statistics are not extremely reliable, women in the insurance industry seem to have increased their share of professional employment more rapidly than in any other major sector of the economy (see computations in Baran, 1985:144).

There are a number of plausible explanations for this rapid transition from male to female labor. The first is simply affirmative action victories. Because of EEOC oversight and successful affirmative action suits waged against numbers of insurers, companies throughout the industry have developed more egalitarian hiring and promotion policies.[8] At the same time, however, there is evidence that women are being hired in preference to men for the new computer-linked jobs, whether those are presently designated professional, technical, or clerical. For example, the professional staffs in the new highly automated personal-lines centers of one company are so overwhelmingly female that an administrator of one joked that they are under pressure to develop affirmative action goals for men. She explained that the reason the company chose to hire women was that they are more flexible than men in adjusting to the computer-mediated labor process.

In another company, the introduction of computer-assisted underwriting has shifted the bulk of policy processing from a

---

[8] For example, in response to affirmative action litigation, between 1977 and 1983, one company we studied increased its percentage of female managers from 4 percent to 33 percent; professionals, from 27 percent to 46 percent; and technicians from 29 percent to 67 percent.

department that is over 60 percent male to one which is entirely female. In still another, the change to a computerized claims process was accompanied by an increase in the percentage of female employees from approximately 25 percent of the claims force to over 60 percent.

In line with this hypothesis also, the percentage of female professional and technical workers in the industry varies widely by product line. In the more highly automated life and medical/health segments, women's share of employment in these occupational categories is considerably higher.[9]

The differences in the proportions of female labor are not solely attributable to automation; other characteristics of the job militate for or against the employment of women. For example, in all firms women hold a greater percentage of professional and managerial positions in the personal lines of business where external contacts are individual rather than corporate; similarly, women have been preferred for office rather than field operations (such as claims adjustment or sales). Nevertheless, the jobs which have been more accessible to women also lend themselves more easily to automation. Thus, although the congruence between female presence in an activity and its level of mechanization to some extent reflects an older discriminatory structure of employment, the growing dominance of women in these occupations and product divisions threatens to strengthen and perpetuate the inequality.

In a small number of companies, there seems to be some concern over this prospect. A personnel manager in one major property/casualty carrier said that she worries that numbers of occupational categories are segregating females and may be devalued as a result. Despite the rapid movement of women out of the clerical ghettos in this company, 79 percent remained in positions that were 80 percent or more female and 71 percent were in occupations that were 90 to 100 percent female. Approximately 20 percent of *nonclerical* jobs were overwhelmingly occupied by women.

---

[9] In 1979, 40 percent of all professionals in life carriers and 43 percent of professionals in medical/health carriers were women, as opposed to 35 percent in property/casualty companies. Similarly, 68 percent of all life insurance technicians were female and 81 percent of all medical/health technicians, whereas women held only 50 percent of all technical jobs in the property/casualty segment.

Not surprisingly, then, although women are moving up in the occupational hierarchy, female wage rates in the industry remain extremely low. In our case study company, for example, female professionals earn only 16 percent more than male clericals (whereas male professionals earn 50 percent more); and the majority of white female managers (57 percent) earn on the average $4 *less* per week than white male clericals. Overall in the insurance industry, real average hourly earnings for nonsupervisory personnel fell by 4 percent between 1968 and 1978, in contrast to a slight rise in real wages during this same period across all industries. Disaggregating by industry segment, the drop in wages corresponds directly to the increase in the proportion of female labor (Bureau of Labor Statistics, 1983).

Automation and feminization are thus proceeding as twin and highly interrelated processes—and we should expect this trend to continue. Automation of professional functions is creating precisely the kinds of jobs women have traditionally held in offices: the work is fairly routine, semi-skilled, and responsible, but offers low monetary reward and little opportunity for occupational mobility. As Oppenheimer (1968) has argued, employment of men instead of women in such occupations would mean a rise in the price of labor, a decline in its quality, or both.

In today's environment, however, insurance companies are having an increasingly difficult time finding low-cost, high-quality female labor. As a result, such labor may be becoming a significant locational determinant. Nelson's (1982) study of the locational determinants of automated office activities (including insurance) concluded that, holding land costs constant, companies have chosen to site such operations in areas with a disproportionately high percentage of suburban married women. Compared with women in the central cities, suburban wives are often less career-oriented and may therefore be more willing to accept jobs with limited occupational mobility; because they are much more likely to be supplementing rather than solely providing the household income, they may be more content with modest pay scales.[10]

---

[10] An executive of the Fantus Co., a subsidiary of Dun and Bradstreet, which specializes in corporate location, made an argument similar to Nelson's regarding insurance company relocations in particular (*Best's Review*, 1979); see also Kroll (1984).

Ross's (1985) study of insurance company relocations and our own case work and survey tended to corroborate this hypothesis. Of the 75 percent of our sample who indicated that major spatial changes had occurred in their company within the last 5 years, 71 percent had moved a greater percentage of their operations to suburban locations. Overwhelmingly, they cited labor quality, labor costs, or both as the primary locational criteria.

EFFECTS OF AUTOMATION ON MINORITY WORKERS

Although the relocations and, more generally, the changes occurring in the labor process may favor some categories of female labor, they threaten to have a negative effect on other categories. The situation of minority workers is particularly problematical.

In general over the last 15 years, paralleling the progress of women, the position of minority labor in the insurance industry has improved significantly. Whereas in 1970, the percentage of blacks in insurance was seriously below the economy-wide average in all occupational categories, by 1980 the EEOC reports indicated higher than average minority employment in many occupational categories—including higher percentages of black employment. Disaggregating these gains by industry segment, it is clear that minority workers also fared best in highly automated sectors.[11]

Given the occupational structure of the industry, the majority of these minority employees are women. Approximately one-fifth of the female work force is composed of minorities as opposed to one-tenth of the male work force. Overwhelmingly these women are concentrated in clerical positions (74 percent). Minority men also hold a disproportionate share of clerical jobs; 32 percent of all minority men in the industry are clericals compared to 7 percent of all white men.

---

[11] In the medical/health segment, in 1980, minority workers held 24 percent of all jobs; although their greatest share of employment was in clerical work (almost 30 percent), minority workers held unusually high percentages of jobs in all occupational categories. Minority employment was lowest in property/casualty firms (14.1 percent) and insurance agencies (12.4 percent), although even here in both cases minority workers held a disproportionate share of clerical jobs (U.S. Equal Employment Opportunity Commission, 1980).

The explanation for the influx of minority workers is identical in most respects to the argument I made with regard to women: affirmative action gains and the automation of the labor process. At the same time, there was an important difference in the dynamic of entry that may be extremely important in the longer run.

Long excluded from office-type employment, at least in the private sector, minority women—especially black women—began entering the clerical work force in significant numbers for the first time in the late 1960s. To some extent these women sought—and were granted—new job opportunities as a result of the Civil Rights movement and its demands for greater equality in the job market; to some extent, they were pushed to enter the clerical labor force as opportunities for employment as domestic service workers declined. Nevertheless, they entered the office after the division of labor in administrative support activity had become excessively detailed—and they entered at the bottom, in what are often referred to as "back-office" jobs.

This is still where minority clericals are overwhelmingly concentrated—in the data-processing centers, typing pools, and filing departments. As of 1980, almost 90 percent of all secretaries and 84 percent of all receptionists were white, whereas minority workers represented 25 percent of all typists; 27 percent of all file clerks, office machine operators (other than computer operators), and messengers; and 28 percent of all mail clerks.[12]

Undoubtedly, then, the high proportion of minority clericals in the insurance industry is a direct indication that much of its office activity is production-oriented, rather than more traditional administrative support. In addition, the kinds of industrialized work settings created by the first waves of mechanization in the industry favored minority employment.

Today the concern is that these jobs are disappearing, through mechanization, relocation, and perhaps also the new labor process configurations. First, as Table 4 suggests, of the eleven clerical occupations with the greatest minority representation, all but two are declining; in contrast, virtually all of the growing occupations are dominated by whites. Second, the movement of automated insurance activities out of the central cities to suburbs and white

---

[12] These data are for the economy as a whole (U.S. Equal Employment Opportunity Commission, 1980).

TABLE 4 Occupations in the Insurance Industry, by Race

Occupation	Percent White	Percent Black
All occupations	82.0	10.0
Professional/technical/sales		
Underwriter	88.95	6.27
Computer systems analyst	89.05	4.64
Operations and systems research	88.73	6.02
Actuary	94.16	1.79
Statistician	84.86	7.88
Computer programmer	86.75	5.58
Insurance sales occupations	90.81	5.16
Clerical: above average black[a]		
General office supervisor	83.12	10.17
Computer operator	80.13	11.64
Peripheral equipment operator[b]	79.44	12.67
Typist[b,c]	75.30	15.78
Correspondence clerk[c]	81.08	13.43
Order clerk	81.08	11.69
File clerk[b,c]	73.13	17.52
Billing, posting, calculating machine operator[b]	77.67	12.50
Duplicating machine operator[b,c]	73.25	17.48
Office machine operator, not elsewhere classified[b,c]	73.17	17.12
Telephone operator[b]	79.05	14.38
Mail clerk[b]	72.28	18.72
Messenger[b,c]	73.03	17.59
Clerical: below average black[a]		
Computer equipment supervisor	86.78	7.30
Financial record-processing supervisor	90.16	4.67
Secretary	89.00	5.73

TABLE 4 (continued)

Occupation	Percent White	Percent Black
Stenographer[b,c]	84.74	9.10
Receptionist[b]	84.24	8.15
Bookkeeper/accountant/audit clerk	90.01	4.33
Payroll/timekeeping clerk	85.53	8.15
Billing clerk	85.34	7.95
Cost and rate clerks		
(including raters)[c]	85.29	7.88

NOTE: Employment share percentages are for the entire economy, not the insurance industry, for 1980.

[a]Clerical occupations are grouped according to whether the proportion of blacks is higher or lower than the proportion of blacks for "All occupations" (10.0 percent).
[b]Absolute decline 1970-1978 in insurance industry employment (Occupational Employment Matrix, Bureau of Labor Statistics, 1981b).
[c]Absolute decline 1978-1981 in insurance industry employment (Occupational Employment Survey, Bureau of Labor Statistics, 1978, 1981a).

SOURCE: U.S. Equal Employment Opportunity Commission (1980).

towns also threatens minority employment. Again using the example of our case study company in the absence of reliable aggregate data, the three new, highly automated "personal-lines" centers described earlier were located in towns where minorities represented 3.1 percent, 3.3 percent, and 14.3 percent of the population (whereas their representation in the population as a whole is closer to 20 percent). This company's centralized data-processing center (soon to be closed) and home office also relocated from a central city with a minority population of over 40 percent to suburban locations which are 90 percent white. Third, and somewhat more speculatively, the move to team-type work configurations, which involve close working relations among high-level and lower-level employees, may well favor the hiring of "socially compatible" white women (Nelson, 1982; Storper, 1981). The historically low level of minority representation in secretarial and receptionist jobs lends circumstantial evidence to this hypothesis. As the bulk-processing centers are closed and key entry functions are moved to decentralized settings, minority clericals are in real danger of being displaced. And the centers *are* closing. A vice president in one company we interviewed predicted that within 2 years their six processing centers located across the country, which now employ approximately 1,500 to 1,800 women, will have been closed. Although word processing is still somewhat centralized in many companies, over 70 percent of our sample in the survey responded that the trend in their company is toward decentralization of this function.

Finally, and perhaps most important, are the prior disadvantages minorities face in the educational arena. If it is true, as I believe, that the lesser-skilled jobs in the industry will continue to disappear, workers without adequate mathematics and literacy skills will be disadvantaged. To the extent that these occupations increasingly involve interpersonal communication, workers for whom English is their second language may also be passed over.

CONCLUSION

To conclude, it seems appropriate to return briefly to the primary concerns raised in the office automation literature and to summarize the perspectives presented here on the most contentious questions: Will automation deskill white-collar work? Will office automation result in widespread technological redundancy? Will women workers bear the burden of the restructuring process?

In terms of the deskilling debate, I have argued that three kinds of processes seem to be *raising* skill requirements in the insurance industry. First, the rapid automation and elimination of much low-skilled work—as computers assume responsibility for the most-structured functions—is making the occupational structure increasingly top heavy. Conservatively, we can expect that during this coming decade roughly two-thirds of all new jobs in the industry will be nonclerical; over the next decade, net job gain should all occur in nonclerical job categories (Baran, 1985:234–238). Second, the transfer of higher functions to less-skilled labor—as decision parameters are embedded within computer software—is creating new categories of skilled clerks, biasing the clerical hierarchy upward as well. For just this reason, in fact, there is some evidence that *clerical* skills are higher in mass-produced product lines where clerks are able to assume greater responsibility for the entire production process than in specialty lines where they remain adjuncts to professional labor. Finally, especially within the context of integrated data bases, computer-mediated work seems to demand *new* skills of the clerical work force. In all these ways, therefore, what we are witnessing is a rolling process of deskilling and reskilling which, in aggregate, should increase the industry's demand for skilled labor. At the same time, however, as I suggested at length earlier, opportunities for occupational mobility may decline, the quality of work life may deteriorate, and salary scales may remain low.

Turning to the question of job redundancy, an important corollary to this argument about skills, I have argued that clerical job loss may indeed reach serious proportions over the next two decades.

In the last 10 years women have moved rapidly into professional, technical, and managerial occupations. However, since approximately 70 percent of the almost 1 million female employees in the insurance industry are clericals, the predicted drop in clerical jobs would have important implications for employment opportunities for women. Assuming that women gain even 50 percent of all new nonclerical jobs and continue to constitute 94 percent of all clerical employment gained or lost, under conditions of moderate declines in clerical employment women will gain slightly less than half of all new jobs created in the industry over the next two decades; in contrast, between 1970 and 1980, women gained closer to 88 percent of all new jobs. If the decline in clerical employment is more substantial—as two of the studies cited predict (Leontief and Duchin, 1986; Roessner et al., 1985)—female employment in the industry would actually fall by 10 percent or more, unless, of course, women claim a much larger share of nonclerical employment (Baran, 1985:238–239).

While women are moving up the occupational hierarchy in significant numbers, at the same time women at the bottom may be losing their jobs. In this sense, the effects of automation on the female work force will vary importantly by class and race. For minority clericals and less-educated white women, especially in the central cities, the threat of redundancy is serious. For skilled clerks, particularly in suburbs and small towns, there will probably be jobs but not opportunities, unless new kinds of training programs are developed. For college-educated women, there may be new opportunities but there is also the danger, discussed earlier, that numbers of professional, technical, and lower managerial positions may resegregate females and be implicitly or explicitly reclassified downward as a result.

The truth is that in a real sense the future is both uncertain and open-ended. Ultimately the question of whether the new technologies are used to create more good jobs than bad ones will depend on decisions made by the leadership of the firm; these decisions will be nonetheless shaped in significant ways by public policy. There is, for example, historical evidence that skill availabilities and shortages impact directly on job design (Levitan et al., 1981). Public programs that absorb the costs of training— including both general education and the kind of ongoing retraining that a period of rapid technological change requires—make "working smarter" strategies both more attractive to companies and, in fact, possible.

Policy will also play an important role in determining which workers bear the burden of the transition. Without a greater public emphasis on education and training, for example, it is likely that many of the workers presently employed in great numbers in the insurance industry will not only be expelled, but may also find themselves unable to secure comparable work. Similarly, aggressive affirmative action policies might act as a countertendency to the gender bias of job loss.

One of the greatest dangers of studies such as this, which attempt to analyze the impacts of technological change on the work force, is their underlying assumption of technological determinism. In fact, the findings of these studies are ambiguous and indeterminate not only because the processes we are analyzing are in a state of flux but, more important, because collectively we have considerable control over the eventual outcome of these processes. Nevertheless, with these caveats firmly in mind, I think that it is safe to predict that we need to begin to prepare our work force— particularly our female work force—for a labor market in which there will be many fewer routine clerical jobs.

REFERENCES

Adler, Paul
    1983   Rethinking the Skill Requirements of the New Technologies. Work-
            ing Paper. Boston: Harvard Business School.
Appelbaum, Eileen
    1984   The Impact of Technology on Skill Requirements and Occupational
            Structure in the Insurance Industry, 1960–1990. Unpublished pa-
            per. Temple University, Philadelphia.
Baran, Barbara
    1985   Technological Innovation and Deregulation: The Transformation
            of the Labor Process in the Insurance Industry. Final Report for
            the U.S. Congress Office of Technology Assessment under Contract
            No. 433-3610.0. University of California, Berkeley.
Best's Review
    1979   Insurance office locations in the 1980s. *Best's Review* (August):62–
            63.
Braverman, Harry
    1974   *Labor and Monopoly Capital.* New York: Monthly Review Press.
Bright, James R.
    1958   Does automation raise skill requirements? *Harvard Business Review*
            (July–August):85–98.
Bureau of Labor Statistics, U.S. Department of Labor
    1965   *Impact of Office Automation on the Insurance Industry.* Bulletin 1468.
    1969   *Tomorrow's Manpower Needs. Vol. II. National Trends and Outlook:
            Industry Employment and Occupational Structure.* Bulletin 1606.
    1978   Occupational Employment Survey: Insurance. Unpublished data.
    1981a   Occupational Employment Survey: Insurance. Unpublished data.
    1981b   *The National Industry-Occupation Employment Matrix, 1970, 1978, and
            Projected 1990.* Bulletin 2086, Vols. I and II.
    1983   *Employment and Earnings* 30(January).
Cummings, Laird
    1977   The Rationalization and Automation of Clerical Work. Unpub-
            lished Master's thesis. Brooklyn College, New York.
DeKadt, Maarten
    1979   Insurance: a clerical work factory. Pp. 242-256 in Andrew Zim-
            balist, ed., *Case Studies in the Labor Process.* New York: Monthly
            Review Press.
Drennan, Matthew P.
    1983   *Implications of Computer and Communications Technology for Less Skilled
            Service Employment Opportunities.* Final Report to the U.S. Depart-
            ment of Labor under Grant No. USDL 21-36-80-31. New York:
            Columbia University.
Driscoll, James W.
    1980   Office Automation: The Dynamics of a Technological Boondoggle.
            Presented at the International Office Automation Symposium,
            Stanford University.
    1979   People and the automated office. *Datamation* (November):106–112.
Faunce, William, Einar Hardin, and Eugene H. Jacobson
    1962   Automation and the employee. *Annals of the American Academy of
            Political and Social Science* (340):60–68.

Feldberg, Roslyn, and Evelyn Nakano Glenn
1983   Technology and work degradation: effects of automation on women clerical workers. Chap. 4 in J. Rothschild, ed., *Machina Ex Dea: Feminist Perspectives on Technology.* Elmsford, N.Y.: Pergamon.
1977   Degraded and deskilled: the proletarianization of clerical work. *Social Problems* 25:52–64.
Greenbaum, Joan M.
1979   *In the Name of Efficiency.* Philadelphia: Temple University Press.
Hoos, Ida
1961   *Automation in the Office.* Washington, D.C.: Public Affairs Press.
Hunt, H. Allan, and Timothy L. Hunt
1985   An assessment of data sources to study the employment effects of technological change. Pp. 1–116 in *Technology and Employment Effects.* Interim Report of the Panel on Technology and Women's Employment, Committee on Women's Employment and Related Social Issues, National Research Council. Washington, D.C.: National Academy Press.
Kroll, Cynthia
1984   Employment Growth and Office Space Along the 680 Corridor: Booming Supply and Potential Demand in a Suburban Area. Working Paper 84-75, Center for Real Estate and Urban Economics. Berkeley: University of California.
Leontief, Wassily, and Faye Duchin
1986   *The Future Impact of Automation on Workers.* New York: Oxford University Press.
Levitan, Sar, Garth L. Mangum, and Ray Marshall
1981   *Human Resources and Labor Markets: Employment and Training in the American Economy.* New York: Harper and Row.
Life Office Management Association
1979   *Word Processing Survey.* Atlanta, Ga.: Life Office Management Association.
Matteis, Richard J.
1979   The new back office focuses on customer service. *Harvard Business Review* 57(March–April):146-159.
Murphree, Mary
1982   Impact of Office Automation on Secretaries and Word Processing Operators. Presented at the International Conference on Office Work and New Technology, Boston.
Nelson, Kristin
1982   Labor Supply Characteristics and Trends in the Location of Routine Offices in the San Francisco Bay Area. Paper presented at the 78th annual meeting of the Association of American Geographers, San Antonio, Tex.
9 to 5, National Association of Working Women
1984   *The 9-to-5 National Survey on Women and Stress.* Cleveland, Ohio: National Association of Working Women.
Nussbaum, Karen, and Judith Gregory
1980   *Race Against Time: Automation of the Office.* Cleveland, Ohio: Working Women's Education Fund.
Oppenheimer, Valerie
1968   The sex labeling of jobs. *Industrial Relations* 7(3):219-234.

Phister, Montgomery, Jr.
  1979   *Data Processing Technology and Economics.* Santa Monica, Calif.:
         Santa Monica Publishing Company.
Roessner, J. David, Robert M. Mason, Alan L. Porter, Frederick A. Rossini,
A. Perry Schwartz, and Keith R. Nelms.
  1985   *The Impact of Office Automation on Clerical Employment, 1985-2000:
         Forecasting Techniques and Plausible Futures in Banking and Insurance.*
         Westport, Conn.: Quorum Books.
Ross, Jean
  1985   Technology and the Relocation of Employment in the Insurance
         Industry. Unpublished master's thesis. Department of City and
         Regional Planning, University of California, Berkeley.
Shepherd, J.
  1971   *Automation and Alienation: A Study of Office and Factory Workers.*
         Cambridge, Mass.: MIT Press.
Sirbu, Marvin A.
  1982   Understanding the Social and Economic Impacts of Office Au-
         tomation. Unpublished paper. Cambridge, Mass.: Massachusetts
         Institute of Technology.
Storper, Michael
  1981   Toward a structural theory of industrial location. In J. Rees, G.
         Hewing, and H.A. Stafford, eds., *Industrial Location and Regional
         Systems.* New York: J.F. Bergen Publishers, Inc.
U.S. Department of Labor
  1977   *Dictionary of Occupational Titles,* 4th edition.
  1981   *Selected Characteristics of Occupations Defined in the Dictionary of Oc-
         cupational Titles.*
U.S. Equal Employment Opportunity Commission
  1980   *Minorities and Women in Private Industry.*
Zuboff, Shoshanah
  1982   Problems of symbolic toil. *Dissent* 29(Winter):51–61.

"Machines Instead of Clerks": Technology and the Feminization of Bookkeeping, 1910–1950

SHARON HARTMAN STROM

The nineteenth-century office was a world inhabited by men. Chief clerk, bookkeeper, copyists, and messenger boys supervised the office, kept financial records, produced documents, and transmitted information. In the 1870s and 1880s women were recruited to use the telephone and the typewriter as the production of documents and transmission of information were mechanized. But, to most observers it seemed that financial matters and record keeping were still where they belonged: in the secure grip of the male bookkeeper. The bookkeeper, C. Wright Mills said (1951:191), "was at the very center of the office world. He recorded all transactions in the day book, the journal, the cashbook or the ledger; all the current orders and memoranda were speared on his iron spike; on his desk and in the squat iron safe . . . were all the papers . . . which the office and its staff served."

But the traditional bookkeeper was soon to lose his importance and more often would be a woman and not a man. Women were only 5.7 percent of the bookkeepers, cashiers, and accountants in 1880, but were 38.5 percent of them by 1910. Along with the rising number of women classified as stenographers, typists, and machine operators (many of whom were doing some sort of bookkeeping), these women, newly classified as bookkeepers, caused the number of females working in offices to triple between 1910 and 1920. By

1930 the Census showed that more than half of all the bookkeepers were women. In 1940, the Women's Bureau of the U.S. Department of Labor (1942:2) found that women were 42 percent of the hand bookkeepers and 82 percent of the bookkeeping machine operators in Philadelphia, a major center of office employment.

Why did women become bookkeepers and why was the feminization of bookkeeping linked to the mechanization of office work? This paper will argue that management initially sought women workers to use bookkeeping machines because they could pay them less and because they thought women would offer less resistance to the deskilling of bookkeeping than salaried male workers familiar with the traditional craft of posting books by hand. Yet the extent to which bookkeeping could be deskilled and mechanized remained problematic. Workers continued to apply hidden skills of judgment and to integrate a number of tasks, particularly to jobs in the middle levels of bookkeeping, even though these jobs required the use of machines. Work done by machine operators had to be supervised, checked, and prepared for use by head bookkeepers and accountants. Some of the machine work was statistical or inappropriate for "factory"-like regimens. Most of this kind of work had never been performed by traditional bookkeepers. The increasing numbers of women holding these jobs before World War II were thus neither "unskilled" nor "deskilled," yet their duties remained largely unarticulated in official job titles and descriptions.

Workers responded to these changing conditions in the office in a number of somewhat contradictory ways. Some male office workers sought to protect their jobs from feminization. Postal and railroad clerks, who had powerful craft unions at the turn of the century, were largely able to do this. Men might try to move into the new profession of accounting, more clearly off limits to most women. Some women tried to improve their status in the office hierarchy by moving up to more interesting and better-paying positions. Some women and men joined together and began to unionize to resist the worst aspects of mechanization, speed-up, and deskilling. And some women began to agitate for new job titles and higher salaries because they recognized the "hidden skills" they were using and because they perceived that male clerks received more pay than women for the same work.

Before taking up these issues, however, it must be explained why the changes in bookkeeping and accounting after 1910 had such wide-reaching consequences for American office workers. Both the size of business and government and the number of bookkeeping and paperwork functions they performed increased. The cost of producing these functions became a matter of concern as overhead costs rose and margins of profits declined in the 1920s and as depression hit in the 1930s. New kinds of corporations and agencies based on extensive financial record keeping appeared, such as department stores, public utilities, life insurance companies, savings and loan companies, the Internal Revenue Service, and the Social Security Administration. The technology of the fine machine tool and die industry made possible significant breakthroughs in the mass production of office machines. At the same time a vast supply of women workers suitable for office work were available to employers when sufficiently educated male workers were in short supply. The typewriter and telephone had already established a link between the mechanization and feminization of the office. Finally, there was an explosion in the volume of financial record keeping after 1910 due to the widespread introduction of cost accounting. Corporate and government managers, under internal pressure to produce more information in comprehensible form, and under external pressure to make themselves publicly accountable, turned to new methods of accounting and office management, which necessitated, from their point of view, both the mechanization and feminization of traditional bookkeeping.

SCIENTIFIC MANAGEMENT, THE COST ACCOUNTING REVOLUTION, AND THE ACCOUNTANT

Braverman (1974) and Davies (1982) have both noted that by the turn of the century principles of "scientific management," first developed for use in industry by F.W. Taylor, were being applied to office work. These principles included scientific observation of work (time and motion studies) to develop more efficient work patterns, the subdivision of tasks, standardized forms and office furniture, rewards for employees based on measured output (bonus plans), a pace of work which encouraged workers to work as fast as possible without loss of efficiency, and close supervision of workers to prevent slow-downs, sabotage, and error. What is not as widely known is that the scientific managers also urged reconstruction of not only how the office worked but the kind of work it produced. Bookkeeping, accounting, and statistical analysis were intrinsic to the new systems because they allowed corporate managers to gain real control of their enormous organizations. The office, once scientific management and cost accounting had been introduced, was far more than a "paper-pushing" sideline to real production and in fact became the nerve center that kept everything functioning smoothly (Galloway, 1921:ix):

> When it is seen that the activities of production and distribution are made possible only through the operations covered by the term "office work," then we approach the truer appraisal of the office as a necessary economic factor. The office managers and employees cease to be passive agents. . . . They at once rise to the dignity of active forces which furnish constructive ideas, and co-ordinate the activities of the business into smoothly working units of enormous size and power.

The chief goal of the new management thinkers was to coordinate factory and office by first defining and then integrating such functions as purchasing, production, inventory control, pricing, and personnel management through a series of administrative units which did not exist before 1900. At the heart of these changes lay a new concept of bookkeeping which pinpointed the actual cost of components of production and distribution: labor, overhead, materials, energy, shipping, and the like. Nelson (1975) argues that "cost accounting" thus demanded the breaking down into smaller operations of jobs once performed by the bookkeeper and the foreman and a consequent reduction of their control over the workplace.

At the same time federal and state government investigations of railroads, life insurance firms, and public utilities were revealing that the largest economic institutions in America had the shoddiest accounting procedures imaginable. A progressive reformer like Louis Brandeis argued for standard cost accounting partly because he admired efficiency but also because agencies like the Interstate Commerce Commission or the New York State Public Service Commission needed better records to review rates charged to consumers (Brock, 1981). The term "scientific management" was coined after a meeting between Taylor and Brandeis during the Eastern Railroad Rates cases in 1910 (Merkle, 1980:59).

During World War I government contracts spurred the growth of both cost accounting in private industry and government accounting procedures, which were rapidly becoming more and more

sophisticated. A wave of municipal reform after 1910 modernized many town and city accounting systems. Widespread growth
of department stores and retail chains necessitated mechanized
billing procedures and inventory control. The corporate income
tax and the Federal Reserve System forced banks and corporations
to audit their books more thoroughly and responsibly.

Chandler (1962) argues that cost accounting was instituted
also in response to a series of crises which faced the larger corporations after 1900, including overexpansion, excess inventory,
growing labor unrest, and a sharp drop in demand in 1921. New
"strategies and structures" for meeting these crises led to the creation of the multidivision form of corporate organization. At the
heart of the multidivisional corporation lay a new level of executive management, "company headquarters." Here the financial
managers sought and manipulated the pieces of information which
allowed them to account for costs, manage inventory, analyze sales,
gauge profits and losses, raise capital through sale of stock or commercial loans, and, above all, plan for and predict the future. In
contrast to the old offices, which had often been located in or near
plants and whose executives roamed between factory and office
with ease, the new headquarters were geographically and psycho-
logically separated from plants, and were often housed in towering
buildings in the center of town.

At the center of the new style of financial management was
a relatively new professional: the accountant. By 1910 some
state universities, commercial business schools, and prestigious
educational institutions like the Wharton School or the Harvard
Graduate School of Business Administration offered accounting
degrees. The schools advertised that accountants were needed
everywhere (*System*, November, 1918:767):

> Accountancy firms need them. Business concerns need them.
> The Federal Government needs them. Financial knots must be
> uncovered and untangled. Waste must be cut down and output
> speeded up. Operating plans must be worked out and operating
> staffs organized and directed. Related branches of industry must
> be coordinated and made to function together. These and similar
> problems which confront the Government and Organized Business
> are squarely up to the accountants—the business technicians—of
> the country.

The emergence of cost accounting after 1910 did give the accountant new prestige. Unlike the bookkeeper, who kept track of
all financial transactions, or the auditor, who checked the books

over for mistakes or fraud, the accountant was now as important to a large company's well-being as a vice-president or treasurer. Accountants purposely tried to emphasize the distinction between themselves and bookkeepers. Accountants were to plan or manage, not to actually "do the books" (Bennett, 1926). One management expert (McAdams, 1927, no. 26:2, in Office Management Series, 1967) described cost accountants as "business doctors" who could put a firm in the pink again by providing "budgets, methods, standards, and measurement." The accounting division of Standard Oil of New Jersey employed 51 people in 1912, but had doubled in size by the mid-1920s, even though auditors and comptrollers had been moved to a separate department (Gibb and Knowlton, 1956). Nonetheless, an ongoing problem with affiliate divisions, which were served by 20 traveling auditors from the home office, "made comparative cost studies virtually impossible. . . ." Standard Oil hired Price Waterhouse to prepare a comprehensive accounting manual for in-house use, which was completed in 1934. This new grip on the company's finances allowed Standard Oil to radically change its operating methods. A smaller and more professionally trained executive committee was installed at the new Rockefeller Center along with 900 office employees to oversee the larger picture, to divorce itself from the petty interests of individual affiliates, and to "consider all questions from the standpoint of the general interest of the company" (Larson, Knowlton, and Popple, 1971:26–27).

Accounting seemed to be a man's world. By 1982 nearly two-thirds of those studying business in high school were women, but 84 percent of those majoring in business training courses in colleges and universities were men (Morse, 1932:24). Some women were trained as accountants before World War II but they were sometimes excluded from taking CPA exams, and certainly women were never seen as potential business executives.

The Census of 1930, however, reported more than 17,000 women auditors and accountants. Education for accounting remained more accessible to the general population than for the other professions. This was partly true because bookkeepers lobbied so effectively to keep an exam, not educational degrees, as the chief requirement for certification. Anyone who could gain permission to take and then pass a CPA exam could be certified, and would-be accountants could go to night school or take correspondence courses from schools like Pace and Pace of New

York. While an advertisement (*System*, August, 1918:259) by the Walton School in 1918 was clearly aimed at men, "Be a Walton-Trained Man," Pace in the same year (*System*, November, 1918:767) claimed that "demand for trained accountants, both men and women, is increasing daily, hourly."

During the Great Depression the interests of enlightened business planners and progressive reformers came together in a body of federal legislation which continued to transform accounting procedures. The securities act of 1933 and 1934 required all firms selling stock to be independently audited and to publicly disclose their financial statements. The Federal Power Act of 1935 mandated new systems of accounting for public utilities. FHA legislation spurred the growth of monthly installment home mortgages, and the Federal Banking Act of 1935 brought far more banks into the Federal Reserve System and its accounting methods for credit control. The new social security, unemployment insurance, and income tax legislation required all but the smallest employers to adopt new methods of financial record keeping for employees.

The amount of financial paperwork that changes in accounting, management, and regulation created was staggering, and without fundamental changes in the organization of the clerical labor force, its composition, and the machines it used, the changes would not have been possible.

OFFICE MACHINES AND THEIR HISTORY

Most of the technology required for the mechanization of bookkeeping had been developed by the late nineteenth century in small machine tool and die shops near factories, in large manufacturing cities by engineers, and by businessmen inventors seeking more efficient office methods. William Patterson, a former railroad owner, built the first cash registers (adding machines on drawers) for use in his Dayton coal yard business in 1882, and later founded the National Cash Register Co. Joseph Burroughs, a former bank clerk from St. Louis, named his adding machine the American Arithometer, and sold a grand total of 1,435 machines between 1895 and his untimely death in 1898. After renaming the firm Burroughs, his successor sold nearly 8,000 machines in 1905 and was producing 100,000 calculating machines by 1930 (Coleman, 1949; Morgan, 1953). Frank Baldwin's machines were adopted by the accounting department of the Pennsylvania Railroad and a leading life insurance company. A young college graduate and employee of the Western Electric Company, Jay Monroe, helped Baldwin develop a higher-speed machine and by the mid-1920s the Monroe Calculating Co. had 165 branch offices in the United States (Morse, 1932:83–85).

Listing adding machines required two motions: punching the keys and turning a crank. Any additional functions made them bulkier, heavier, and more difficult to use. While electrical adding and calculating machines became more common during the 1930s, the fancier machines were still very large, expensive, and most likely to be used by accountants or statisticians. Consumers wanted more lightweight and affordable machines. Heavy competition developed between companies to produce the most reliable lightweight adding machine in the teens and early 1920s. In 1899 there were 18 establishments making cash registers, calculators, and tabulating machines valued at less than $6 million in total, but by 1919 65 firms made more than $83 million worth of products (Bureau of the Census, U.S. Department of Commerce, 1933:1120).

The comptometer, developed by Felt and Tarrant in Chicago, was often more popular than the calculator because it was key-driven, lightweight, and inexpensive; and once a special system was learned, it could be used to do subtraction, multiplication, and division. Its chief drawback was that it was non-listing; that is, there was no printed tape which showed each item entered, only a window in which a running total appeared. Since the bulk of financial record keeping required simple addition, the comptometer was suitable to a wide variety of purposes. Some of the first machines were ordered by the U.S. Treasury Department and the Equitable Gas Light and Fuel Company (Darby, 1968). The Comptometer Corporation developed training schools for operators, and in 1930 placed an estimated 27,500 operators in offices in the United States and Canada (Morse, 1932:78).

Bookkeeping and billing machines, used to enter transactions and to make up bills, invoices, and purchase orders, were simple combinations of typewriters and adding machines. Remington made an "adding and subtracting" typewriter in the teens, but both typewriter and calculating machine firms made all kinds of bookkeeping and billing machines after World War I. The productivity of both bookkeeping and duplicating machines was greatly enhanced if used in conjunction with the addressograph, which permitted the mechanical reproduction of alphabetized names and addresses on mailings and statements.

Tabulating and keypunch machines became well known to the general public because of their role in compiling the Census of 1890. The principle was to mechanically keypunch individual pieces of data onto a small card and then use a mechanical sorter to compile the cards into different categories. Although any number of patents for such machines had been filed in the 1880s, Herman Hollerith, an engineering graduate of Columbia University, was the first to receive assurances from the Bureau of the Census that his machines would be used once produced. A variety of agencies and corporations began to use the machines, including the Surgeon General's office, the Baltimore Department of Health, and the New York Central Railroad.

Most of the renown went to the compilation of vital statistics, but the cost-accounting possibilities of the new machines were also significant. The New York Central could, after the installation of its Hollerith system (Austrian, 1982:125), "tell on a nearly current basis how many hundreds of tons of freight were moving East or West, which of hundreds of stations along its lines were profitable; where freight cars should be sent or returned; which freight agents were being paid. It would give the railroad a much firmer command of its far-flung business." By 1900 Hollerith was at work on a standardized cost-accounting machine to be used in conjunction with time tickets filled out on the factory floor. In 1910 a renamed Russian immigrant, John Powers, was hired by the Bureau of the Census to supervise production of the Bureau's own census machines. He developed a new keypunch machine which more closely resembled a typewriter keyboard and a method for printing tabulated information onto rolls of paper. Hollerith's machines eventually served as the basis of IBM's empire, and Powers' machine was picked up by Remington Rand.

By the 1930s office machines were more likely to be electrified. They required less operator strength and were far more automatic and productive. The International Labour Office reported in 1937 (p. 495) that "an employee addressing envelopes by hand could not do more than 500 in a day's work; a hand-worked addressing machine can print 1,000 addresses in an hour, and the number rises to 1,500 for machines worked by the foot, and 2,000 for those actuated by electric motors, or even 10,000 in the case of special work for which the machine has been prepared." Considerable progress had been made in combining office machines in fairly compact electrified systems to perform more complicated functions. At the 1934 office equipment manufacturers' show in New York, IBM offered a new check proofing machine for banks (*Business Week*, October 20, 1934:14):

> The operator runs an adding mechanism with her right hand. Her left controls 24 sorting keys for alphabetical division, clearing house bans, and other classifications. After recording the amount of each check, she presses one of the 24 keys and drops the check in a slot. The checks come out sorted in 24 bundles. A master tape gives a complete listing with code designation opposite the amount.

Remington Rand offered a "central records control" system to department stores, which combined the dial telephone, punch card, and tabulating and adding machines. In 1935 National Cash Register sold a machine that "would perform all the bookkeeping required under the new Federal Home Loan Act," and in 1936 Burroughs and Monroe offered special payroll machines to accommodate new social security legislation (*Business Week*, October 24, 1936:16).

By the 1920s, a handful of large diversified office machine companies had been created by merger or acquisition and dominated the industry until the 1950s: Adressograph-Multigraph, Burroughs, National Cash Register, International Business Machines, Remington Rand, and Underwood Elliott Fisher. While all firms showed a drastic decline in sales in 1931, by 1935 the industry had regained its highs of the 1920s and saw record profits in 1937 and 1938. The year 1941 was a banner one, and office machine firms received handsome war contracts because of their fine machine-tooling capacities. Many of them made war materials such as bomb sights and rifles as well as office machines. The war spurred demand for more diversified and sophisticated machines as the size and complexity of institutions and their functions grew; most new developments in technology were commissioned and financed by the federal government. The government literally devoured most office machines for its agencies and war-related industries during the war (*Fortune*, August, 1944:127–132, and December, 1944:150–154, 194–196).

Soma (1976) argues that all the technology needed to create the digital computer was available by WWI, but that no one in government saw the need to provide massive funding for its research and development until WWII. While his assumption that government capitalization of computer research was inevitable is somewhat perplexing, it points out how important government patronage of the office machine industry was and continues to be. We might add that the growing size and complexity of both business and government in the 1940s made it inevitable that computers would be used if produced. The development of office machine technology responded to demand for machines more than inventions influenced demand. As Mills (1951:193) argued, machines were mass manufactured because they complemented the changing social reorganization of the office: "Thus machines did not impel the development, but rather the development demanded machines, many of which were actually developed especially for tasks already socially created."

MECHANIZATION, FEMINIZATION, AND SCIENTIFIC MANAGEMENT

Substantial numbers of women began to work in bookkeeping departments in the decade before WWI. Some had studied in business schools, were hired with the title of bookkeeper, and held jobs comparable to those of men. But most were specifically hired to use office machines. Women and their machines sometimes replaced men. Edward Page (1906:7683), a dry goods jobber, instituted the use of carbon forms, loose-leaf ledger sheets, a vertical file, a typewriter, and some computing machines in his office at the turn of the century. Six male clerks were replaced by one billing clerk and a "girl who sits at a desk with a comptometer and an arithometer. She adds the yards on the comptometer and then extends the bills on the arithometer, and does the work of six men with great ease."

In a scientific management text from 1914, one expert (Banning) titled his chapter "Machines instead of Clerks" and gave a number of examples of how women machine operators might replace male hand clerks. In the payroll department of one manufacturer, it had taken six clerks two days to compute the payroll. Two women using calculating machines could do the same work in the same time with fewer errors. Felt and Tarrant reported that a Kansas City steel firm had eliminated the jobs of three men in the estimating department by installing a woman machine operator

(Jadden, 1914:85). One promoter of business machine products (Beach, 1905:8) reminded his readers that "girls" were perfectly capable of using the new machines and could be "employed at a comparatively small compensation."

We do not know how many male clerks lost their jobs as women machine operators replaced them, but given the labor shortages of the teens and the explosion of clerical work tasks, it is more likely that men were simply moved to other positions. Many women machine operators were being hired to fill new jobs created by the introduction of machines to accomplish new tasks. Murolo (1982) found that the first woman to be hired by Aetna Life Insurance Co. was a telephone operator in 1908, but she was joined by 35 temporary female employees who came to work Hollerith machines in 1911 for a study of mortality statistics. Three stayed on as permanent employees but were asked to use the back elevators so they would not be seen by the company president, who did not approve of women working in the insurance business. Although the number of women working at Aetna had grown to 150 by 1916, they remained in sex-segregated typing, filing, and machine-operating departments until WWI.

The boom in business, finance, and trade during WWI, combined with a general labor shortage, meant that many of those who remained resistant to women clerks had to give in to the modernizers. One study found that the large increase in female clerks in Ohio between 1910 and 1920 was almost entirely due to hiring during the war (Rotella, 1977:210). F.W. Rowland (1933, no. 61:3, in Office Management Series, 1967) of the Lincoln Insurance Co. recalled that during WWI office managers " . . . were called upon to organize . . . a rapidly increasing volume of business with male members of our staff leaving for the service in ever increasing numbers. We advanced junior clerks to positions of responsibility and trained large groups of girls to perform duties formerly considered as strictly male jobs." At Aetna women now worked in departments with men, and by 1922 44 percent of the home office was female (Murolo, 1982). The Women's Bureau (Erickson, 1934:16) found that the use of female bookkeeping machine operators in banks became general practice during the war, and by its end women were "entrenched as bookkeeping machine operators on customer accounts and other applications of listing and balancing."

Office machine companies urged businesses to buy their machines and avoid wartime labor supply problems by training women to use them. They claimed their products were so easily operated that even those with no previous bookkeeping training might be put to work. "Uncle Sam took my experienced clerks. In their place I have willing workers but INEXPERIENCED. So I must have simple office machines . . . inexperienced operators soon become lightening fast on the 10-KEY DALTON." The same machine promised to "substitute woman-power for manpower; . . . with little practice a girl . . . does the figure work of three or more experienced men." Burroughs announced that "anyone who can read can post ledgers with a Burroughs Automatic Bookkeeping machine," and by 1925 the pretty "Monroe girl" was routinely used to advertise the company's adding machine in a way which suggested women were firmly entrenched at calculating machines: "The Monroe girl turns out more figure-work in a day's time, smoothly and pleasantly. Monroe simplicity and lightening speed keep her work moving rapidly, without mental or physical effort. Any girl in your office can be a Monroe girl if you provide a Monroe Adding Calculator" (*System*, July and November, 1981:endpieces; January, 1925:79; September, 1925:316).

Banking, insurance, manufacturing firms, public utilities, and consumer services all experienced expansion in the 1920s, but they also faced declining margins of profit. Mergers and acquisitions increased the size of economic institutions and while grumbling over the cost of clerical costs continued, it became obvious to executives and office managers alike that the more complicated the business, the larger the clerical staff it required. "Overhead," the bane of those who sought higher profits, grew dramatically during the 1920s as office staffs and departments mushroomed (Melman, 1951). One way to keep costs down was to hire women; they cost substantially less, particularly if given job titles which didn't connect them to bookkeeping. One employer tersely informed the Women's Bureau (Erickson, 1934:34) that he had hired women to replace male ledger clerks because the same volume of business could be produced at "a lower unit cost. Women [were] paid less than men so cost [was] reduced." Another way to cut costs was to apply scientific management principles. So likely were mechanization, feminization, and scientific management to be applied to office work together in the 1920s that we think of them as being inherently linked, or even causing one another. We should keep in mind, however, that these are three separate processes.

Scientific management experts repeatedly argued there was no reason why the office could not be a factory. Streamlined and rationalized, the office assembly line might be as efficient as its manufacturing counterpart. There were important areas of resistance to scientific management in the office; executives, supervisors, male clerks, and private secretaries resented measurement and rationalization of their jobs (Davies, 1982). But young women who had never worked before could be placed at machines, stopwatched, and encouraged to work even faster through bonus plans and as a condition of continued employment.

Bookkeeping, billing machine, and comptometer operations were perfectly suitable to the drive system, including time and motion studies, bonus plans, and assembly-line production. Managers had pretty much achieved the fine art of this labor process by the 1920s and had put it to use extensively in department stores, utilities offices, insurance firms, and large banks. The Milwaukee Electric Railway and Light Company reported in 1930 that it had doubled its billing production by measuring tasks and using wage incentives. "Each bill necessitates about 35 key and motor bar strokes which means that in addition to striking 116 keys per minute, the operator must insert and remove the bill, insert and remove proof sheets, turn meter records, obtain and return stacks of bills as well as take personal time. The best operator averages 4.5 bills per minute, about one bill every 13 seconds, 8 hours a day, 5.5 days a week." Six machine billers could produce 230,000 bills a month, or an average 200 bills an hour each (Seybold, OMS #54, 1930).

Other applications of scientific management included centralizing departments and creating stenography, typing, and computing pools. In 1927 the Roxana Petroleum Co. moved all its transcribing, filing, figure work, and recording personnel to one floor, from which they served 15 departments. Roxana began with the computing machine operators, and then moved on to the transcribers, wherein lay the "greatest resistance." By measuring work, using time charts, deducting errors from bonus payments, and providing intense supervision, the clerical staff produced nearly twice as much work with half as many people and saved the company $32,000 in salaries (Jones, 1928).

While it is dangerous to conclude overwhelmingly that the first women office workers who used these machines enjoyed doing so, impressionistic evidence indicates that at least some did. G.M., who went to work at the Rhode Island manufacturing firm Brown and Sharpe in 1913, used a comptometer in the cost-accounting section. "The section I was in had to check requisitions, and then add them and get a total. Then you had to post them and check your total. And stamp your initials. If you made more than one mistake, you were called down. But I liked it—to be able to do your day's work and feel that you had done it *good*." Since she was paid on a bonus plan she tried to work up to as much speed as possible. She recalled that it was important to keep your hand on the lower part of the machine to save time, "so we seldom used a 9, or an 8, we'd just press 4 twice." She was so valuable an employee she worked for 2 years after her marriage in 1916 and was later sent by the comptometer people to several other firms to teach the use of the machine for inventory and payroll systems (Rhode Island Working Women, 1981).

At Roxana Petroleum, managers claimed that the 50 percent of the women workers who survived centralization came to enjoy the new methods of work. By working together instead of for individual bosses, the workers enjoyed a "spirit of teamwork and competition." The new system allowed "girls" with particularly strong skills to shine because speed and accuracy were the basis of rewards instead of "personality factors." Finally, they were doing the work they had actually been hired to do, "where formerly they were doing considerable office and errand boy work for members of the staff" (Jones, 1928).

The depression offered many office managers incentives to further mechanize and rationalize their offices. Certainly feminization also continued, but the desperate need of men for employment may have mitigated this trend somewhat. Managers did admit that the high rates of unemployment between 1931 and 1933 had allowed them to permanently eliminate older male salaried workers and replace them with younger ones, many of whom were female. *Business Week* reported in 1936 (May 16:18–20) that the highest number of jobs available were for bookkeeper-stenographers and business machine operators, and that for every 13 women seeking work there were nearly 30 men.

While many marginal firms either went out of business or were forced to rely on improperly trained bookkeepers and antiquated machinery, larger and more stable ones probably modernized their bookkeeping systems for the first time. The Pierce School of Business Administration found that 14 of 59 financial companies they surveyed in 1931 had begun to take additional steps to cut office costs, including time and motion studies and the "use of new office equipment, such as dictaphones and bookkeeping and billing machines" (*Monthly Labor Review*, October, 1931:1058). A similar survey of 300 companies employing 35,000 office employees in 1936 showed "a pronounced increase in the use of plans for measurement of production and wage incentives during the depression" (Stivers, 1936, no.76:6 in Office Management Series, 1967). Complaints about both mechanization and speed-up were a common theme in office worker union literature of the period (Pell, 1937; Strom, 1985).

WOMEN OFFICE WORKERS: HOW MANY IN WHAT JOBS?

It is difficult to learn very much about the sexual division of labor in financial record keeping from the published census figures. The census figures show a steady increase in the proportions of women bookkeepers and business machine operators after 1910. But they also seem to show that women did not enter financial record keeping as rapidly as they did typing and stenography. Careful analysis of the subjective criteria used to identify and classify the clerical occupations in the census, the data themselves, and other information regarding job classification leads us to two somewhat different but not contradictory conclusions; women were underreported in financial record keeping jobs, and men continued to work in bookkeeping long after they left other clerical occupations. The entry of women into bookkeeping, in contrast to some other kinds of jobs, did not initially seem to lead to total feminization.

In all likelihood more women were performing accounting, auditing, and bookkeeping functions than indicated by the census records. First, as Conk (1978:78) notes, "census statisticians could not analyze, except in a very general way, the changes going on inside the factories, offices, shops and corporations where people were occupied." Occupations held by women, immigrants, and minorities in general received very little scrutiny and were far more likely to be listed as large aggregates than were occupations held by white native-born men. In the years when the clerical occupations were changing more rapidly than occupations in other sectors, most of the attention of the census takers went to differentiating the trades, manufacturing jobs, and the professions.

Second, the methods actually used by the Census Bureau may have distorted the data, especially for women and blacks. Edwards, director of the Census Bureau from 1910 to 1940, routinely instructed census clerks to reclassify individuals who did not fit into preconceived categories and to "make use of supplemental information on the census form" to change the respondent's original designation of her or his occupation. Conk (1978:144) concludes that

> there are serious questions about the extent to which Edwards and the census classifiers relocated women, blacks, and young workers from one occupation to another because such occupations were 'very unusual' for these groups. . . . If there were, for example, blacks and women in skilled trades or high status occupations, the census data would tend to obscure them.

Third, since published census figures did not differentiate accountants and auditors nor move them into the professional category until 1950, and since most of the professional white-collar workers were men, even the actual census data showed that women made up a larger percentage of bookkeepers than the earlier printed aggregate categories had implied (see the disaggregation of accountants and bookkeepers in Table 1).

Fourth, it also seems likely that many women who used bookkeeping and billing machines were listed as typists or secretaries since their machines incorporated typewriter mechanisms. But they were likely to be working in bookkeeping, purchasing, billing, sales, or accounts receivable departments, and were part of the bookkeeping process. While machine operators were placed in a separate category of clerical work in 1930, the relatively small total of them compared to workers in other categories suggests that only those strictly designated as "machine operators" by employers were so listed. It is also possible that some workers preferred to be thought of as clerks instead of machine operators and so reported themselves as clerks to the census takers. Nearly all bookkeepers, stenographers, and typists used machines but were not generally listed as machine operators.

Finally, there is the rapidly and suspiciously growing category of "clerical and kindred workers not elsewhere classified." As the

TABLE 1 Numbers of Employees for Selected Clerical and Office Work Professions, 1900-1950 (in thousands)

Occupation and Sex	1900	1910	1920	1930	1940	1950
Accountants/auditors	22.9	39.2	118.5	191.6	238.0	390.4
Male	21.5	35.7	105.1	174.6	218.3	332.6
Female	1.4	3.6	13.4	17.0	19.7	57.8
Bookkeepers/cashiers	232.0	446.8	615.5	738.2	721.1	993.5
Male	159.2	263.3	269.8	272.5	248.4	217.5
Female	72.7	183.6	345.7	465.7	472.8	776.0
Stenographers/typists	134.0	387.0	786.0	1,097.0	1,223.2	1,660.7
Male	38.0	86.0	80.0	66.0	81.3	92.4
Female	96.0	311.0	706.0	1,031.0	1,141.8	1,568.3
Office machine operators	n.a.	n.a.	n.a.	38.1	66.1	149.6
Male	n.a.	n.a.	n.a.	5.4	9.3	26.3
Female	n.a.	n.a.	n.a.	32.7	56.8	123.3
Clerical and kindred, not elsewhere classified[a]	234.7	654.3	1,323.3	1,680.5	2,026.1	3,177.5
Male	223.8	578.5	990.0	1,260.7	1,289.9	1,628.1
Female	10.9	75.8	332.4	419.9	736.1	1,549.4

[a]For 1900-1920 includes office machine operators, dispatchers, bank tellers, shipping and receiving clerks, and clerical and kindred workers. For 1930 includes all of the above except office machine operators. For 1940 and 1950 includes all of the above except office machine operators and shipping and receiving clerks.

SOURCE: Kaplan and Casey (1958).

data in Table 1 indicate, women began as about 4 percent of all these workers in 1900 but were nearly 50 percent of them by 1950, and by 1950 so many women clerical workers were in this catch-all category they nearly equaled stenographers and typists. What jobs they did in the office often remained unclear, although they must often have been using office machines other than typewriters. A survey of large offices in 1930–31 by the Women's Bureau led Erickson to conclude (1934:5):

> In today's offices with fifty or more clerical workers the book-keeping and letter writing activities frequently are overshadowed in the number employed by those engaged on the details of handling advertising, sales campaigns, market and credit analyses and collections, involved statistical and financial reports of costs, and a variety of other recording activities. The extent of these new office

activities and the policies and practices naturally vary markedly and are quite unstandardized, so it is only to be expected that job terminology for occupations is indefinite and not comparable from office to office. The duties of secretaries, typists, and machine operators vary considerably, and when an attempt is made to classify the work of most of the other office employees for analysis the variations seem to be legion.

The institution of personnel offices in many large businesses in the late teens and early 1920s made job classification and description an issue in the private sector as well as the public. Office management magazines began to print growing numbers of articles on the "science" of job classification in the 1920s. Most of these classifications placed clerical workers using machines throughout the spectrum of "unskilled" and "skilled" jobs. Inexperienced machine operators (usually bookkeeping, billing, and keypunch workers) fell at the bottom of the hierarchy, while steno machine operators, stenographers, comptometrists, and typists were in the middle. Bookkeepers, cost clerks, statisticians, and some secretaries and stenographers ranked near the top, just beneath managers and executives. A Women's Bureau survey of offices in major cities in 1930 (Erickson, 1934) showed that women were employed in all of these occupations and were as likely to be machine operators or general clerks as they were stenographers and typists (see Table 2).

Although the job titles used in business and listed in the *Dictionary of Occupational Titles*[1] (U.S. Department of Labor, 1939) were more accurate and more narrowly defined than those listed in the Census, these job classifications, like those of the Census Bureau, suffered from ambiguity and sex-stereotyping. Most office workers used machines, yet some were "operatives," some were "clerks," and some were "bookkeepers." Most of these workers were women. The tendency to assign women to certain job categories and not to others lent the manual and nonmanual dichotomy

---

[1] The *Dictionary of Occupational Titles*, developed by the United States Employment Service and first published in 1939, listed hundreds of clerical occupations, many of them requiring use of the business machines that had been developed since 1890. These occupation titles and definitions were based on observation of workers in their places of employment and augmented by information from 6,500 employers, trade associations, labor unions, and civil service commissions. Accountants and auditors were listed as "professionals and managers"; the Census did not move them to a separate category from bookkeepers until 1950.

TABLE 2 Percentage Distribution for Employment of Women in Offices in Seven Cities[a] in 1930

Occupation	All Types of Offices[b] (N = 42,844)	Advertising Agencies (N = 941)	Banks (N = 7,821)	Insurance Companies (N = 15,321)	Investment Houses (N = 2,870)	Mail-order Houses[c] (N = 4,951)	Public Utilities (N = 5,917)
General clerk	34.7	25.1	20.6	37.5	18.2	39.0	46.1
Secretary	4.4	17.1	6.5	3.1	9.7	1.6	2.4
Stenographer	14.4	17.5	18.0	14.1	22.4	7.2	13.5
Typist	15.2	17.0	15.2	20.4	16.6	10.2	7.3
Machine operator	12.3	4.7	23.0	8.6	11.1	11.8	12.5
File clerk	6.0	3.7	6.8	7.2	7.7	5.2	3.2
Supervisor	3.7	4.7	2.5	4.0	3.1	3.8	4.3
Telephone operator	2.1	3.2	3.6	1.2	3.2	0.4	3.8
Hand bookkeeper	2.3	4.7	0.6	1.9	6.5	2.0	3.1
Cashier, teller	1.0	1.0	2.0	0.5	0.2	0.2	2.3
Correspondence, messenger, and merchandising clerk[d]	3.2	0.4	0.9	0.8	0.3	18.3	1.3
Other[d]	0.6	1.0	0.5	0.8	1.0	0.2	0.2
Total[e]	99.9	100.1	100.2	100.1	100.0	99.9	100.0

[a]New York, Hartford, Philadelphia, Atlanta, Chicago, Des Moines, St. Louis.
[b]Publishing houses included in total but not listed as a column.
[c]Includes some chain stores.
[d]This small group comprises professional and semiprofessional women such as personnel directors, underwriters, and the like.
[e]Numbers do not add to 100.0 because of errors in rounding.

SOURCE: Erickson (1934).

a kind of sexual character, which also reflected the job classifiers' and census takers' disinterest in the actual qualifications of and skills performed by women workers. So many women had the skills and qualifications necessary for office work, and they were quite early on taken entirely for granted. Neither job titles nor pay scales adequately reflected them.

Leffingwell revealed much of this unintentionally when he argued in 1917(p. 125) that clerical jobs should be closed to working-class women because "to be a good stenographer . . . requires a much higher grade of education than many of them possess. The stenographer must be able not only to run a typewriter, but also to spell and use the English language better, as a rule, than her employer. . . ." Conveniently for employers, these attitudes coincided with an overwhelming tendency for women of all ages and classes to seek clerical work, partly because office work had status and prestige, because other jobs were not open to women because of discrimination, and because wages in office work remained relatively attractive compared to other kinds of employment for women, even though these wages were lower than those of men doing comparable work.

STRATIFICATION IN THE OFFICE

MARITAL STATUS, CLASS, AND RACE AND ETHNICITY

Before WWII clerical workers were overwhelmingly young, and younger than women in other occupations. Most firms had rules against hiring married women, and the Women's Bureau survey of 1930 (Erickson, 1934) found more married women reporting discrimination in office hiring than in any other line of work. During the 1920s larger numbers of women began to stay in clerical jobs after they were married. Coyle (1929) argued that some women had begun to hide their marriages from employers to keep their jobs. Some management experts suggested that there were no longer real barriers to married women working except custom and tradition (Leffingwell, 1934, no. 62, in Office Management Series, 1967), but there was considerable public pressure from legislators, the media, and the general public for both public and private employers not to hire married women during the depression. Nonetheless, the number of married women clerical workers increased, as did the number of married women workers in general. As late as 1941 three-fourths of all women office workers were single, but as the labor shortages of WWII began to be felt, most managers dropped strictures against married women with little reluctance (Niles, 1944, no. 96, in Office Management Series, 1967).

Jobs for women clericals between 1910 and 1930 were designed for white women with some high school education. Certainly in the early years the high school education requirement was also intended to exclude working-class women and immigrants from the office. But inexpensive business schools began to offer business training by the turn of the century, and working-class parents who were able to send daughters to these schools were able to place them in offices. While there were fewer foreign-born women in clerical jobs than in other nonagricultural occupations, there was a higher number of native-born white women with foreign-born parents. In 1910 these women were nearly 41 percent of all clerical workers; native-born women with native-born parents were 52 percent. About 7 percent were foreign-born (Rotella, 1977). Leffingwell complained in 1917 (p. 125) that the "profession" of stenography was already attracting the sort of women who devalued the office atmosphere.

> One trouble with the typewriting "profession" is that some of the mail order houses have so standardized the work that any girl who can read can learn to type off form letters and do addressing and fill in work. This tempts many girls to enter the field, and after a year or so . . . they consider themselves fit for higher position.

Despite Leffingwell's distaste for the policy, employers by the 1920s were consciously seeking working-class women to use office machines in departments which had been subjected to principles of scientific management. The Curtis Publishing Co., a pioneer in such techniques, reported that it had recruited ledger clerks to use Elliott Fisher bookkeeping machines (Morgan, 1925, no. 6:9–10, in Office Management Series, 1967): "We seek girls of seventeen years minimum age, at least two year's high school or its equivalent. . . . We prefer inexperienced girls and those who have some economic incentive to work as we have found they make the steadiest workers and we select from our recruits what we classify as the semi-dependent applicant, that is, the girl who is partially or wholly dependent on her earnings for her livelihood." Cheney Brothers, a New England silk mill which had been one of the first manufacturing firms to Taylorize, reported that it preferred to recruit women clerical workers from mill employees, and by 1923 had "promoted" 72 percent of its office staff from "minor mill positions." Only 14 percent of the office staff were foreign-born, but nearly 64 percent were American-born of foreign parentage, and 20 percent came from southern or eastern European ethnic groups (Lamb, 1926, no. 21, in Office Management Series, 1967).

More than half of Murolo's (1982) sample of women working at Aetna Life Insurance Co. between 1924 and 1930 were daughters of blue-collar men. Aetna's office management specialist, Marion A. Bills (1929, no. 44:17, in Office Management Series, 1967), said that it was easier to both hire and keep women office workers in towns with large numbers of manufacturing workers: "We studied the occupations of the fathers of all our people who were with us at a certain time, and also those who left us within five or six years. We found that if you rated these occupations from day laborers up to professional men, the chance of the person remaining with you increases as the social standing of the fathers' occupations decreased."

Of the tiny percentage of minority women working in clerical jobs (about 0.7 percent of the total by 1930) nearly all worked in businesses owned by Afro-Americans. Jones (1985:179) found that Montgomery Ward, a Chicago-based mail order house, was the largest employer of Afro-American clerical workers in the United States, with 1,050 of them on the payroll in 1920. But a 1930 survey of offices in Chicago and Atlanta found not a single incidence of white and black women working together in the same office. Black women clericals were generally older, more likely to be married, and received lower wages than other clerical workers (Erickson, 1934).

The growing incidence of high school education in the 1920s, along with vocational education in a business curriculum for most high school girls, created unlimited supplies of trained white workers for offices until WWII (Davies, 1982; Rotella, 1977). Weiss (1978:73–75) found that as early as 1915 more students were being educated in commercial courses in public high schools than in business colleges, and that by 1924, 66 percent of those enrolled in commercial courses in high schools were women. Discrimination against women in other kinds of education and training programs, the refusal of many middle-class parents to invest in college educations for daughters, and the desire of many working-class parents to get their daughters out of factories and into offices meant that most women had little alternative to office work. The economist Paul Douglas argued flatly in 1930 (p. 366) that the high schools "primarily served to recruit juveniles for clerical work." The importance of high school for nearly everyone cannot be underestimated, for it greatly expanded management's control in the industrialized countries over both industrial and clerical workers; even partial high school education conveyed a set of basic skills that made many workers interchangeable. As Lockwood (1958:37) says, "universal public education meant that every literate person became a potential clerk."

While the employment of clerical workers continued to increase steadily over the course of the twentieth century and to increase more rapidly than employment of industrial workers, the number of women and men seeking clerical employment increased at an even greater rate (International Labour Office, 1937). As early as 1928 there were three to five clericals seeking jobs for every one available in New York State, a greater disparity than in any other occupation (Coyle, 1929:187).

The crisis of women looking for clerical work, which was already serious before the depression began, became more acute by 1933 as many middle-class women and men, who were trained in the professions, sought clerical work because they were unable to find jobs as teachers, librarians, or editors. The competition became even more acute as more married women were looking for work. Many working-class women who could type or keep books were forced to work in manufacturing, restaurant work, or domestic service. Black women, who had always found that work in offices and most factories was hard to get because of racial discrimination, now faced competition from white women for even the lowest-paying jobs. The New York Employment Service reported in 1934 that one out of three women applying for work was a white-collar worker but only one out of eight got a white-collar job (Pell, 1937:8). In Philadelphia office workers were the fourth largest group of unemployed workers registered at the State Employment Office in 1933, and through 1936 were "one of the most numerous classes on the rolls" (Women's Bureau, U.S. Department of Labor, 1942:6).

WAGES AND CLERICAL WORK

One of the most important consequences of the rising literacy of the work force and the feminization of the office was a steady lowering of clerical wages compared to those in manufacturing. Male clerks particularly lost ground. Douglas (1930:363–366), after taking the rise in the cost of living into account, found that while all wage earners in manufacturing earned 29 percent higher wages in 1926 than they had in 1890, all salaried and clerical workers earned only 3 percent more. Certainly women clerks earned far less than male workers in industry and substantially less than the average male wage earner. Until WWII, however, they were likely to earn more than women in manufacturing jobs.

In his study of the male-female earnings differential in clerical work between 1880 and 1970, Niemi (1983) found that "male earnings levels consistently exceeded female earnings levels." As clerical occupations became more feminized the gap between men's and women's salaries within clerical work narrowed from a range of 25–45 percent in the early twentieth century to a 15 to 20 percent gap in the 1960s and 1970s. At the same time, clerical wages were falling relative to nonclerical wages.

From a working-class or middle-class woman's (or her family's) point of view, the salaries paid for office jobs must have looked good, even with the stagnating wages of the 1920s and 1930s, and may partly explain why so many women were still looking for office jobs before WWII. Since some high school was now compulsory for everyone, a daughter could receive free business training and move right into an office job, where she made higher wages than women in any other line of work except the professions. Moreover, if she could advance into the middle ranges of clerical work—stenographer, bookkeeper, statistical clerk, or supervisor, for example—she could earn more than most other working women and even as much as some men (see Table 3).

As clerical wages increased somewhat during the 1940s, these perceptions of women's clerical jobs continued, and with good reason. The Census of 1950 still showed that median yearly incomes for women clerical workers put them closer to managers, proprietors, and professionals of the same sex than any other occupation. And while female professionals, who needed to invest in expensive college educations to obtain jobs, made 65 percent as much as men in a similar category, on average women in clerical positions earned 71 percent as much as their male counterparts (Table 4).

TABLE 3 Average Annual Earnings of Clerical Employees Who
Worked 48 Weeks or More in 1939, by Occupation--Philadelphia

Occupation	Women	Men
Special office workers	$2,010	$2,704
Rate clerks	--	2,280
Secretaries	1,469	1,920
Bookkeepers, hand	1,446	2,016
Audit clerks	1,413	2,099
Cashiers, tellers	1,412	2,231
Bond, security, and draft clerks	1,404	1,716
Clerks, n.e.c.,[a] public utilities	1,360	1,948
Renewal clerks	--	1,926
Statistical clerks	1,332	1,989
Cost and production clerks	--	1,791
Payroll clerks, timekeepers	1,227	1,561
Clerks, n.e.c.,[a] finance and insurance	1,225	1,415
Stenographers	1,223	1,463
Accounting clerks	1,213	1,667
Clerks, n.e.c.[a], federal and state government	1,202	1,838
Claims examiners, adjusters	1,190	1,931
Billing machine operators	1,183	1,583
Actuarial clerks	1,181	1,209
Bookkeeping clerks	1,171	1,467
Billing, statement, and collection clerks	1,169	1,701
Bookkeeping machine operators	1,169	--
Tabulating machine operators	1,161	1,552
Calculating machine operators	1,151	1,508
Dictating machine transcribers	1,147	--
Order and shipping clerks	1,144	1,585
Keypunch operators	1,106	--
Telephone operators	1,095	--
Receptionists	1,061	--
Duplicating machine operators	1,060	1,290
Typists	1,056	1,384
File clerks	1,054	1,355
Credit clerks	925	1,612

[a]Not elsewhere classified.

SOURCE: Women's Bureau (1942).

TABLE 4 Median Yearly Income for Non-Farm Workers Working 50-52 Weeks/Year, 1949, by Occupation

Occupation	Men	Women	Ratio of Women's Income to Men's Income (percent)
Professional and technical	$4,030	$2,600	64.5
Managers, officers, and proprietors	4,327	2,536	58.6
Clerical and kindred	3,136	2,235	71.3
Sales	3,270	1,632	49.9
Craftsmen, foremen	3,378	2,265	67.1
Operatives	2,924	1,920	65.7
Laborers	2,366	1,900	80.3
Service workers	2,405	1,137	47.3

SOURCE: Kaplan and Casey (1958).

THE LIMITS OF RATIONALIZATION AND THE ISSUE OF UPWARD MOBILITY

Not all the new jobs for women in clerical work were for standardized use of business machines. A 1927 survey of the sex of workers managers preferred for certain jobs found that while men were strictly preferred for shipping clerks and timekeepers, and women for typists, stenographers, file clerks, and bookkeeping machine operators, either men or women would be hired as ledger, payroll, and statistical clerks or as bookkeepers (Rotella, 1977:25). Women were also hired to supervise machine departments or steno pools.

Accounting and bookkeeping functions were still growing rapidly. The number of workers with the job title of bookkeeper grew until 1930, and from 1930 to 1940 the number of bookkeepers declined only slightly while the number of machine operators and clerical workers not elsewhere classified increased. There were nearly 47,000 new jobs for accountants and auditors. New urgency was given to more sophisticated methods of cost accounting for the office because of the establishment of government regulation and the increasing need to justify prices and minimize taxes.

Scientific management planners initially wanted to create a sex-segregated labor force in which male professionals and head bookkeepers received salaries and female machine operators were paid on a piece-work basis. But the continuation, even growth, of large numbers of jobs in between these two groups, and the temptation to fill them with women, who were always paid less than men, created a more complicated labor force. G.L. Harris, active in the American Management Association and the author of a textbook on office work (1935:163), noted that "expert book-keepers are not so much in demand, but expert billing calculators are. There are more opportunities for young women in the departments than there are for men, and such young women can advance to responsible positions in the division." For many women the chance to work in bookkeeping departments represented not only slightly higher salaries but a chance to think of themselves as "advancing" in clerical work and even holding positions comparable to those of men. It is also important to keep in mind that while stenographers and typists used machines that were distinctly sex-stereotyped, both men and women used adding and calculating machines. And since so many educated middle-class men and women were unemployed and forced to take low-paying clerical jobs throughout the 1930s, women and men held some of the same jobs.

Once women worked in jobs also held by men, they were likely to gain some of the job privileges and self-esteem of men, if not comparable salaries. These privileges might include more self-pacing, self-direction, and a wider variety of tasks to perform. The comptroller of Fraton and Knight (Wilson, 1934, no. 63:18, in Office Management Series, 1967) argued that bonus plans were really only effective "when quantity is the predominanting factor" such as in transcribing, typing, ordering, and invoicing. For general accounting, sales, and cost estimating, however, "we find only the direct salary base is applicable." These employees "contribute materially to the financial success of the company . . ." and "it is evident that in this division quality of the work cannot be sacrificed to speed." Marion A. Bills of the Aetna Life Insurance Company (1929, no. 44:11, in Office Management Series, 1967) disagreed. We "find innumerable cases where people are still doing the simplest routine work . . . but whose salaries have grown by small increases so that they are paid two, three, and even four times what . . . they are worth. For example, we have the much misused term of 'bookkeeper.' In different companies we find bookkeepers who are simply posting clerks, a job which they could learn in a few weeks, and bookkeepers who need to be expert accountants."

Yet her success at implementing these ideas beyond the all-female departments at Aetna remained limited (Murolo, 1982).

Prior to 1928, women clerical workers at Roxana Petroleum were scattered throughout various functional departments. When the corporation announced plans for centralizing and rationalizing its typing, transcribing, and comptometer operations into one division, both male executives and female operatives were resistant to the change (Jones, 1928). The men were resistant because they would no longer control the operations performed by the women clericals, and the women clericals because "they seemed to think their work might be more humdrum and difficult. They felt in some cases that they might not be able to measure up to the standard and quality of work expected, that they might lose their freedom, that their chances for promotion would not be so good. . . ." These women workers, in other words, perceived that working alongside men improved their chances of securing better positions and working conditions.

Managers had intended women's office jobs to be held by "workers whose highest ambition will be realized when they are placed on your payroll as clerical workers—the kind that can be depended upon to perform faithfully routine tasks day in and day out without thought of promotion" (Nichols, 1934, no. 65:26, in Office Management Series, 1967). But many women did receive promotions to better jobs, held more responsibility than their job titles indicated, and became ambitious far beyond the expectations of managers. Everyone knew, however, that there was an unspoken law: advancement for women stopped short of the executive's door. Men, whether qualified or not, had to be the top managers and executives, and the shock of that reality must sometimes have disturbed women workers. One management specialist (Barnhardt, 1933, no. 61:18–19, in Office Management Series, 1967) worried about this problem in 1933:

> Some of my studies have revealed the extent to which firms employing women for doing certain kinds of clerical, especially secretarial work have used and promoted women so extensively that there is an absolute absence of men in the upper levels from which promotions to junior executives can be made. We checked the private secretaries and assistants to executives in one company, and found that in eighteen cases, fourteen assistants to executives were women who, if the executive went out of the organization, could not be promoted. Indeed at the time of our study some of these women were already falling down on the job because they

were sure they would not be promoted and could not see why
they should work very hard any longer. In this firm some of these
secretaries and assistants were college-trained women, high-grade
women.

Both women who worked in low-paying machine operator jobs
and women who had moved to more responsible positions remained problematic for employers. Employers complained as early
as the 1920s about higher rates of absenteeism and job turnover
for women than for men in office jobs. These rates reached epi-
demic proportions in the banking industry by the late 1940s (Mc-
Colloch, 1983). Other women expressed their dissatisfaction in
ways that sometimes perplexed employers. One industrial psy-
chologist (Giberson, 1939, no. 87:27, in Office Management Series,
1967) classified "wily females" with alcoholics, psychoneurotics,
paranoids, and other social misfits of the office. Their "devious
natures," she concluded, were partly attributable to the fact that
they are temporary workers frustrated by the "all-consuming matter of pay levels."

One question that arises here is when and how the issue of
job classification began to emerge in management-labor conflict in
the office. As noted above, managers in government and private
industry both had devised job-classification schemes to facilitate
hiring, job placement, salary setting, and the justification of a
multiply stratified labor system. But once jobs were classified
and given job descriptions employees could also argue that they
were not being paid wages commensurate with their duties or
that they should be moved to a higher job classification. There
is some evidence that women and minorities in the expanding
clerical labor force of the federal government of the 1930s and
1940s, with its highly refined civil service classification system,
were the first to use this as a tool to achieve upward mobility and
to attack sex discrimination. When the Bureau of Agricultural
Economics listed a new position "for men only," women workers
protested and the designation was changed to "male or female"
(*Federal Record*, Jan. 20, 1940:6). In 1941 ledger account clerks
in the Veterans Administration won what was claimed to be a
20-year battle to upgrade their position to a higher grade because
"they did work which required a broad knowledge of laws and legal
opinion governing the accounts handled by their division." Thirty-
one clerks, led by Mrs. Marvel Lockhart Ball, drafted their own
appeal to the Civil Service Commission. As their union newspaper

explained, "the greatest significance of this decision is that it raises questions concerning similar type advances for thousands of clerks in the Government service who are doing a calibre of work far above their rank" (*Federal Record*, November 7, 1941).

A flurry of such office workers' union activity between 1937 and 1950 began to address the issues of job classification, possibilities of promotion, working conditions and deskilling, and adequate compensation for men and women (Strom, 1983; McColloch, 1983; Strom, 1985). These unions were crushed by employers, government, and rival craft unions during the McCarthy period, and it was not until the emergence of the civil rights movement in the 1960s and the women's movement in the 1970s that the same issues emerged as political and trade union causes. By then the sexual composition of office work had changed dramatically. With the coming of WWII, men who had been willing to take office jobs during the 1930s had a growing variety of occupational choices, and competition for managers, accountants, and servicemen quickly decimated many male staffs of bookkeeping departments. In the long run the disappearance of men from the lower levels of clerical work proved to be a positive development for managers because it saved so much money. Management expressed concern over the shrinking pool of women clerical workers, but an immediate solution was simply to open office jobs to married and a small but steadily growing number of minority women. The hiring of minority and married women workers allowed office employers to continue their major objectives in the labor management of bookkeeping: to steadily cheapen wages through feminization, to mechanize and deskill traditional salaried jobs, and to raise the productivity of office staffs by reducing the number of privileged males.

As the number of married women—now likely to be in jobs for many years at a time—and the number of single middle-class college women—unable to enter the professions because of discrimination—increased, managers apparently imposed new forms of segmentation on the office in the 1950s. While male executives and top-level managers were still there to oversee things, older women may have more and more been asked to supervise young women and middle-class white women placed in more pleasant jobs. Minority women may have more frequently been assigned to machine operators jobs. There is every reason to believe that this pattern of segmentation still largely exists. What obstacles it presents to worker solidarity is something that warrants further investigation. But it should have come as no surprise that when more mass-based union movements appeared in the 1970s they emphasized higher wages, upgraded and fuller job classifications, adequate working conditions for machine operators, an end to sex discrimination, and the important connections between all of these.

REFERENCES

Austrian, G.D.
1982   *Herman Hollerith: Forgotten Giant of Information Processing.* New York: Columbia University Press.
Banning, K.
1914   Machines instead of clerks. *Library of Office Management,* 1. Chicago and New York: A.W. Shaw Co.
Beach, E.H.
1905   *Tools of Business: An Encyclopedia of Office Equipment and Labor Saving Devices.* Detroit: Bookkeeper Publishing Co., Ltd.
Bennett, G.
1926   *Accounting Systems: Principles and Problems of Installation.* Chicago and New York: A.W. Shaw Co.
Braverman, H.
1974   *Labor and Monopoly Capital: The Degradation of Work in the Twentieth Century.* New York: Monthly Review Press.
Brock, B.
1981   *The Development of Public Utility Accounting in New York.* East Lansing: Michigan State University.
Bureau of the Census, U.S. Department of Commerce
1933   Census of Manufactures, 1929, Volume II. Washington, D.C.: U.S. Department of Commerce.
Chandler, A.D.
1962   *Strategy and Structure: Chapters in the History of the Industrial Enterprise.* Cambridge, Mass.: MIT Press.
Coleman, J.S.
1949   *The Business Machine—with Mention of William Seward Burroughs, Josephy Boyer, and Others—Since 1880.* Princeton, N.J.: Newcomen Lecture, Princeton University Press.
Conk, M.A.
1978   *The United States Census and Labor Force Change, 1870-1940.* Ann Arbor, Mich.: UMI Research Press.
Coyle, G.L.
1929   Women in the clerical occupations. *Annals of the American Academy of Political and Social Science* 143(May):180–187.
Darby, E.
1968   *It All Adds Up: The Growth of the Victor Comptometer Corporation.* Victor Comptometer Corporation.

Davies, M.W.
1982 *Woman's Place Is at the Typewriter: Office Work and Office Workers, 1879–1930*. Philadelphia: Temple University Press.
Douglas, P.H.
1930 *Real Wages in the United States, 1890–1926*. Cambridge, Mass.: Harvard University Press.
Erickson, E.
1934 The employment of women in offices. *Women's Bureau Bulletin* 120. Washington, D.C.: U.S. Government Printing Office.
Fawcett, W.
1927 Uncle Sam rates the efficiency of his office workers. *Office Economist* 9(May):3–4, 13.
Galloway, L.
1921 *Office Management: Its Principles and Practice*. New York: Ronald Press Co.
Gibb, G.S., and E. Knowlton
1956 *The History of the Standard Oil Company of New Jersey: The Resurgent Years, 1911–1927*, Vol. 2. New York: Harper and Row.
Harris, G.L.
1935 *Business Offices: Opportunities and Methods of Operation*. New York: Harper and Bros.
International Labour Office
1937 The use of machinery and its influence on conditions of work for staff. *International Labour Review* 36(October):486–516.
Jadden, W.B.
1914 Keeping labor records by machinery. *Library of Office Management*. Vol. 4. Chicago, New York and London: A.W. Shaw Co.
Jones, J.
1985 *Labor of Love, Labor of Sorrow: Black Women, Work, and the Family from Slavery to the Present*. New York: Basic Books, Inc.
Jones, W.F.
1928 Centralization means economy. *Office Economist* (November):5–6, 13.
Kaplan, D.L., and M.C. Casey
1958 Occupational trends in the United States, 1900–1950. *Bureau of the Census Working Paper*, 5.
Larson, H., E. Knowlton, and C. Popple
1971 *The History of the Standard Oil Company of New Jersey: New Horizons, 1927–1950*, Vol. 3. New York: Harper and Row.
Leffingwell, W.H.
1917 *Scientific Office Management*. Chicago and New York: A.W. Shaw Co.
Lockwood, D.
1958 *The Blackcoated Worker: A Study in Class Consciousness*. London: George Allen and Unwin Ltd.
McColloch, M.
1983 *White Collar Workers in Transition: The Boom Years, 1940–1970*. Westport, Conn.: Greenwood Press.

Melman, S.
    1951   The rise of administrative overhead in the manufacturing indus-
            tries of the United States, 1899–1947. *Oxford Economic Papers*
            3(February):62–112.
Merkle, J.A.
    1980   *Management and Ideology: The Legacy of the International Scientific
            Management Movement.* Berkeley: University of California Press.
Mills, C.W.
    1951   *White Collar: The American Middle Classes.* New York: Oxford
            University Press.
Morgan, B.
    1953   *Total to Date: The Evolution of the Adding Machine. The Story of
            Burroughs.* London: Burroughs Adding Machine, Ltd.
Morse, P.
    1932   *Business Machines: Their Practical Applications and Educational Require-
            ments.* New York: Longmans, Green and Co.
Murolo, P.
    1982   White-Collar Women: The Feminization of the Aetna Life Insur-
            ance Co., 1910–1930. Unpublished paper. History Department,
            Yale University.
Nelson, D.
    1975   *Managers and Workers: Origins of the New Factory System in the United
            States, 1880–1920.* Madison: University of Wisconsin Press.
Niemi, A.
    1983   The male-female earnings differential: a historical overview of the
            clerical occupations from the 1880s to the 1970s. *Social Science
            History* 7(Winter):97–107.
Office Management Series
    1967   *Office Management Series*, 1924–1941. Originally published by the
            American Management Association. New York: Kraus Reprint
            Corporation.
Page, E.D.
    1906   The new science of business: making an office efficient. *World's
            Work* 12(June):7682–7684.
Pell, O.
    1937   *The Office Worker—Labor's Side of the Ledger.* New York: League for
            Industrial Democracy.
Previts, G.J., and B.D. Merino
    1979   *A History of Accounting in America: An Historical Integration of the
            Cultural Significance of Accounting.* New York: John Wiley & Sons.
Rhode Island Working Women
    1981   Oral History Project. Unpublished transcripts. Rhode Island
            Working Women, Providence.
Rotella, E.J.
    1977   Women's Labor Force Participation and the Growth of Clerical
            Employment in the United States, 1870–1930. Unpublished Ph.D.
            dissertation. Department of Economics, University of Pennsylva-
            nia.
Soma, J.T.
    1976   *The Computer Industry: An Economic-Legal Analysis of Its Technology
            and Growth.* Lexington, Mass.: Lexington Books, D.C. Heath.

Strom, S.H.
1983 Challenging "woman's place": feminism, the left, and industrial unionism in the 1930s. *Feminist Studies* (Summer)8:359–386.
1985 "We're no Kitty Foyles": organizing office workers for the CIO. Pp. 206–234 in Ruth Milkman, ed., *Women, Work and Protest.* New York: Routledge and Kegan Paul.
U.S. Department of Labor
1939 *Dictionary of Occupational Titles.* Washington, D.C.: U.S. Government Printing Office.
Weiss, J.
1978 Educating for Clerical Work: A History of Commercial Education in the United States since 1850. Ed.D. dissertation. Harvard Graduate School of Education.
Women's Bureau, U.S. Department of Labor
1942 Office work and office workers in Philadelphia in 1940. *Women's Bureau Bulletin* 188-5. Washington, D.C.: U.S. Government Printing Office.

New Technology and Office Tradition: The Not-So-Changing World of the Secretary

Mary C. Murphree

THE NEW TECHNOLOGY AND THE SECRETARY

Electronic word and data processing—a multibillion dollar business made possible by the invention and mass production of the microchip—is invading the American office. Few work environments are immune to the temptations of the fast, cheap, and effective automated office equipment now available. Organizations ranging from Fortune 500 corporations, law and accounting firms, public agencies, hospitals, and universities to small businesses and professional partnerships are experimenting with data- and word-processing equipment on a scale scarcely imaginable 10 or even 5 years ago (U.S. Congress, Office of Technology Assessment, 1985).

The emergence of the modern office a century ago, its technological evolution to mid-century, and even its impact on women's employment have been documented by historians (Baker, 1964; Davies, 1982; Oelrich, 1968; Lockwood, 1958). The current phase of technological revolution, particularly its effects on American office workers, calls for further documentation.

This paper examines the impact of office technology on the secretarial occupation. It analyzes how the current revolution in office organization intersects with changes in secretarial attitudes and demographics and with an office culture traditionally based on gender. It argues that the persistence of patrimonial authority in secretary-boss relations, combined with new staffing ratios (when each secretary is assigned to work for more and more bosses), determine—to a far greater extent than technology itself—the work life of the word-processing secretary.

History teaches us that technological change—whether in the form of the steam engine, electricity, or the automobile—never occurs in a vacuum and that its effects on social organization cannot be understood as random or idiosyncratic events. Nor are its costs and benefits shared equally by all members of society. Rather, much of industrial history depends on the interaction of technology with prevailing social, demographic, and political conditions in a particular era. The introduction of word and data processing into the office of the 1980s, and its impact on the secretary, is no exception.

Although there is no one way to define the word "secretary," particularly in this period of transition or "shakeout," I use a definition that relates both to the social characteristics of the job (e.g., the authority or superior-subordinate structure) and to the tasks characteristic of the job (e.g., the division of labor). My focus will be entirely on what I call the "word-processing secretary." This is a clerical person working on a decentralized microcomputer or terminal who is formally assigned as support staff to one or more principals, with whom she is in daily personal contact and for whom she performs some combination of clerical tasks (e.g., text and data entry, editing, filing, copying, or stenography) and administrative or managerial services (e.g., gatekeeping, coordinating, planning, letter drafting). Such a secretary is distinct from a word-processing operator who works at a video display terminal (VDT) in a large, centralized facility and who is exclusively charged with word and data production.[1]

---

[1] Currently, there are no data indicating how many word-processing secretaries versus word-processing operators there are in the United States, nor how many workers use particular types of word-processing equipment. Such distinctions should be made in future data-collection efforts. Companies with word-processing centers continue to employ large numbers of secretaries who work in decentralized settings. An increasing number of companies are moving to decentralize their clerical operations entirely.

The secretarial occupation is the largest and most catholic of women's occupations, employing some 4 million women. Secretaries are widely distributed among industries, professions, and throughout government, in offices of every size, and in towns and metropolitan areas across the United States. Recently, the occupation has experienced tremendous growth, although it has not ridded itself of its traditional sex-stereotyping. Since 1950, secretarial-typist employment has more than tripled. The composition of the secretarial labor force has also changed. Since the 1970s, the number of minority women has increased dramatically; between 1970 and 1980 the number of black women secretaries increased 148 percent, while the number of secretaries of Spanish origin increased 131 percent (U.S. Department of Labor, 1984–1985). And, like the female labor force in general, there are more working mothers, more mothers with preschool children, more single heads of households, and more women who plan to be a part of the paid labor force on a sustained basis.

The secretary's relationship to technology, on which this paper focuses, has also changed significantly. The secretary now interacts with sophisticated, computer-based office systems and electronic typewriters as well as with the familiar telephone, copy machine, and dictaphone.[2]

A wave of publicity heralded the introduction of these systems and may have contributed to raising the expectations of many secretaries. Employers, eager to sell their support staffs on the new equipment, have repeated vendor and media claims and waxed enthusiastic about the benefits that office automation offers

---

[2] Innovations and improvements in office technologies have essentially been incremental since the 1870s (see Strom, this volume). Model after model of typewriters, calculators, dictaphones, telephones, and duplicators have been designed with an end to making them more efficient, less costly, and more marketable. For example, the original beeswax and paraffin "Graphaphone" dictating machine, powered by a sewing machine treadle, was replaced at the turn of the century by a solid wax recording medium with a shaver making it erasable. This in turn was made obsolete by an electronic desk model that appeared in 1936, and that, by World War II, was equipped with a flexible Dictabelt and transistors. Finally, by the 1970s the dictating and transcribing units had been combined into a single small unit; small magnetic cassette tapes were available, and remote "off premises" telephone transmission was developed. Similarly, improvements in carbon paper streamlined early duplicating tasks alongside mimeograph machines and stencils, which went through dozens of design innovations until the entire duplicating market gave way to the photocopying process.

secretaries. Employment agencies and secretarial schools—eager to supply their clients with willing and trainable personnel—have urged secretaries and prospective secretaries to acquire the new skills quickly so that they too can reap the benefits awaiting them in the electronic office. Many secretaries interpret this enthusiasm and encouragement to mean that all office work has become "high tech" and expect that they will be given a chance to do challenging work, sharpen their skills, earn better pay, and move up in their organizations. Preliminary evidence indicates, however, that there is a serious disjuncture between what secretaries have been led to expect from the automated office and what many feel they are actually getting. Particularly at risk in this scenario are minority and older women.

Understanding the effects of office automation on secretaries is difficult for several reasons. First, it is not clear whether supply, declining cost, and marketing of new office technologies are driving the push toward office reorganization or whether factors such as increasing labor costs, a shortage of skilled and willing women clericals, and management fears of clerical unionization are stimulating the demand for office automation (Murphree, 1984b). Second, as pointed out above, the term "secretary" has no generally accepted meaning, but rather is a catch-all word for a person performing a variety of clerical, administrative, and personal tasks (Watstein, 1985). The term "office," moreover, is just as ambiguous and encompasses myriad shapes and forms. There are large offices and small ones, headquarters and branches, public-sector sites and private-sector sites. An office can also have different occupational or industrial cultures: it can be a professional office (e.g., the doctor's office) or a sales office tied to a particular industry (the brokerage office). The information process itself can also take a multitude of forms. For example, hardware and software systems can vary according to how "multifunctional" they are (i.e., the number of tasks they are capable of performing). Systems can also be more or less interactive. They range from highly integrated, advanced information systems to stand-alone micro and personal computers. They may also vary in the extent to which they are "networked" to each other or a larger computer (Spinrad, 1982). Research also indicates that diffusion of the new technology is occurring at a fast but by no means uniform pace (Kelly Services, 1982).

Until very recently, most discussions have focused on the general "goodness" or "badness" of word processing (Murphree, 1984a). Vendors and their partisans extolled its promise—to liberate secretaries and turn them into high-tech managers—while critics feared it would reduce secretaries to robots or extensions of machines, if not eliminate them altogether. These simplistic ideas are being discarded as a growing corpus of research on office automation illuminates its complexities. Experts have now begun to distinguish among different kinds of word-processing arrangements and stress the differential effects these arrangements have upon clericals (Pomfrett et al., 1984; Feldberg and Glenn, 1983). At the crudest level a contrast is drawn between word processing that is centralized in pools, on the one hand, and that which is decentralized to satellite stations, on the other (Johnson et al, 1985; Iacono and Kling, 1984; Murphree, 1984a; Werneke, 1984; Menzies, 1981). In the former, an organization's word-processing functions are all located in a single work site or word-processing center. In decentralized word processing, satellite units are distributed throughout the organization. Inherent in this distinction is a focus on the difference between word-processing "operators," who perform VDT work at the centers under the supervision of a manager, and the word-processing secretaries who concern us here, i.e., secretaries working at satellite VDT terminals in face-to-face relations with principals or bosses to whom they are assigned.

Some research examines the sequential phases of the integration process (Giuliano, 1982; Gery, 1982) and the effect of office automation on different occupational groups (Kanter, 1983; Bjorn-Andersen, 1983). Westin et al. (1985), for example, focus on customer service representatives, data-entry clerks, and clerical-secretarial employees. Bikson and Gutek (1983) analyze the variety of activities and complexities of the tasks performed by different white-collar work groups (including secretaries) who share an information-handling function. Johnson et al. (1985) refine the centralized-decentralized theme by discussing different forms of integration of information processing into organizations and their consequences for organizations. The ergonomic arrangement of different settings has also received attention in the literature. Finally, researchers have attempted to evaluate the success and problems encountered in the use of different staffing arrangements with word-processing equipment (Pomfrett et al., 1984).[3]

This paper develops a focus omitted by other analysts, namely, the strong gender-based authority relations and patrimonial organization through which word-processing secretaries are linked to their superiors, and by which, traditionally, the nature of their tasks, prestige, wage levels, opportunities for mobility, and, hence, job satisfaction have been determined. [4]

The discussion that follows is divided into four sections. Wherever possible, the analysis discusses the experience of minority women, who make up a growing proportion of word-processing users, and of older women secretaries, whose work patterns are subject to the greatest disruption. The first section examines the patrimonial form of social organization that has traditionally characterized secretarial work. The second section discusses the new breed of secretary produced by a changing labor force supply and by women's changing expectations concerning their rewards and rights on the job. The third section explores how technology affects secretarial expectations and experiences in the new office particularly through changes in "staffing ratios" (e.g., private secretaries versus shared secretaries versus team or minipool secretaries). The fourth section argues that patrimony not only persists in the new office, but when combined with new staffing ratios also accounts in important ways for the lack of challenge, responsibility, and opportunity to move up in the job that many secretaries are experiencing. The section ends with a discussion of other variables such as size of office and organization, resources and wealth of the

---

[3] Pomfrett et al. (1984) offer a useful typology of the possible permutations of principal/secretary social organization, as well as a report on the satisfaction and dissatisfaction of the different groups and individuals. They also identify "quality of supervision" as an important variable for operator (read secretarial) satisfaction, especially where pool scenarios are concerned. The study does not deal with gender questions nor with the patrimonial aspects of word-processing secretarial jobs.

[4] My analysis draws heavily on case studies and survey data reported by vendors and by researchers in academia, unions, private research firms, and women's advocate organizations. It also uses interviews and case studies conducted by the author with secretaries in a variety of industries, including law firms, government agencies, universities, and broadcasting. Systematic research, however, on secretarial subtypes (by socioeconomic status, industry, size of firm) does not exist and should become a research priority for policy makers concerned with understanding the changes taking place.

firm, and industry or service in which the firm engages, which may influence changes and rewards in the secretarial occupation. The final section brings together my conclusions.

PATRIMONY IN TRADITIONAL SECRETARIAL WORK

Traditionally the secretarial role has been understood as a support role with the subordinate performing a variety of administrative, clerical, and personal tasks for a superior. For the last century, women have been secretaries while men have been principals. The classic description of this role was provided by Rosabeth M. Kanter (1977) in her pioneering work, *Men and Women of the Corporation*. Focusing on the secretarial role in the structure of a large organization called INDISCO, Kanter analyzed the patrimonial nature of the role relationship between secretaries and their principals. Using Weber's definition of patrimony as a guide, and the "lord-vassal" model as metaphor, she identified three aspects of the traditional boss-secretary relationship: (1) principled arbitrariness (secretaries have no job description but rather are subject to the arbitrary power of a boss who, within limits of fair practice set by "principles" or tradition, can make whatever job request of a secretary he chooses); (2) fealty (an emphasis on loyalty and "the personal" in boss-secretary relations, such that symbolic, emotional, and nonutilitarian rewards become substitutes for economic ones); (3) status contingency (the fact that secretaries derive their status from the rank and power of their bosses). Each impacts in varying degrees on secretarial tasks and on the secretary's access to better pay and mobility.

TRADITIONAL SECRETARIAL TASKS

Secretarial tasks are generally defined by a principal or boss who has a great deal of latitude and personal authority in determining what a secretary does. Typically, a secretary and boss carve out a personal set of procedures and understandings concerning what tasks the secretary will perform. The organization provides only the merest skeleton for the structure of the secretary's job. One boss may delegate challenging and creative work to a secretary. His successor may delegate nothing. The secretary's work is also characterized by a constant flow of orders with no routinized schedule. Typically she must respond "to momentary demands and immediate requests generated on the spot" (Kanter, 1977:79). Traditionally the secretary acts as a kind of "office wife," performing an array of personal and socioemotional services for her boss. These may include listening to his troubles, performing office housekeeping duties, running personal errands outside the office, or even granting sexual favors (Kanter, 1977:79–81).

The secretary must also act as a buffer between the boss and the outside world. This includes acting as a "gatekeeper" (screening calls and visitors), as well as assisting the boss in presenting a certain front to the organization or world. As I wrote about legal secretaries in my 1977 case study (Murphree 1984a:142):

> Essentially skilled "generalists," legal secretaries have traditionally performed a multitude of both simple clerical and house keeping functions and complex administrative and lawyering tasks. Beyond taking shorthand and transcribing items for her boss's signature and beyond acting as his gatekeeper . . . legal secretaries typically might type corporate minutes, draft standard wills or petitions following boiler-plate forms, or check legal citations and references for her attorney. She might also monitor the court calendar or docket, handle the firm's bills and charges, and work with an outside accountant on firm taxes. All this has been in addition to filing, ordering supplies, handling the mail, typing endless copy from draft, collating multiple final copies, and, of course, making coffee. . . .
>
> In keeping with the office-wife role expected of her, the Wall Street legal secretary further has traditionally performed certain supportive and nurturant tasks as well. Covering for an attorney's mistakes, lying about his whereabouts when it is helpful, listening supportively (and in confidence) to his career or family problems, . . . are all important tasks associated with her sex-stereotyped role as handmaiden and confidante.

REWARDS AND CAREER MOBILITY

Secretaries in jobs defined by patrimonial relations are subject to a special set of standards and rewards that, unlike most other occupations in the office, is highly particularistic. By and large secretaries are rewarded for loyalty and devotion to their bosses. In the INDISCO study, for example, Kanter found that secretarial ratings were determined by two main traits or attitudes. One was initiative and enthusiasm, and the other was the secretary's ability to "anticipate and take care of personal needs." They were not necessarily rated for professional skills. Even when the company attempted to standardize the evaluation process, managers often rated secretaries in terms of the quality of their relationships rather than in terms of skills that benefit the organization generally (Kanter, 1977).

A number of recent studies have begun to analyze the skilled but often "invisible" labor that secretaries perform. Too often these skills go unrecognized and undercompensated. Secretaries, for example, perform many highly skilled tasks that require expert social and cognitive judgments and use sophisticated mediating and negotiating techniques that involve great diplomacy (Murphree, 1984; Suchman and Wynn, 1984). As "gatekeepers" they must know when to disturb their managers for telephone calls as well as how to put off the unwanted call diplomatically. In addition to knowing who's who in the manager's world, they must know how to read urgency in the tones of their bosses and their bosses' superiors; how to follow complicated and often poorly explained instructions; and how to negotiate and shepherd projects through the various departments and support services of the organization. These skills, according to Machung (1983), while handsomely rewarded at the executive or managerial level, are undervalued when performed by women labeled as secretaries.

This perception of inequity is increasingly a source of grievance to secretaries. The Consensus Statement of Professional Secretaries International (a nonunion organization) insists that "discretionary judgment, not clerical skills, is the key component of the secretary's productivity." Further it maintains that "[A]ppreciation does not replace compensation." This message is similar to that of "Raises Not Roses" promulgated by District 9 to 5 of the Service Employees International Union.

Secretaries are paid less and have less control and less independent recognition than they might have otherwise. Instead they receive such nonutilitarian rewards as praise, appreciation, prestige, love, or flattery.

Symbolic rewards are also frequent substitutes for promotion. Typically women in secretarial jobs derive their formal rank and pay from the formal rank of their bosses rather than from the skills they utilize or the tasks they perform. A common career path for a secretary traditionally has been to begin as a pool secretary, advance to working for a lower-level manager or divisional officer, and end up as a secretary to a vice president or a president (Kanter, 1977).

In my study of legal secretaries I found two main types of career mobility: vertical and horizontal. Vertical mobility was most commonly achieved by the "pool to partner" route. It also meant moving from the typing pool to working for any attorney, or moving from a junior law partner to a "top partner," or from an associate to a partner. Sometimes it involved moving from a pair of attorneys to a single attorney. Secretaries sometimes moved horizontally within an organization as well. At Law Firm X, where I conducted a case study, this simply meant the secretary changed to an attorney with the same rank as her present boss. For example, through the office grapevine a secretary might learn of a good position opening in the office of an attorney with a reputation for being particularly nice and request permission from the personnel department to transfer laterally to that attorney. Partners' secretaries, however, were usually not permitted to move laterally. Any move they made had to be to a higher-level attorney or out of the firm altogether. Only rarely, however, did any legal secretary move to another service department of the firm, i.e., to the paralegal department, to proofreading, or to the library.

Whatever industry or profession they are tied to, secretaries have generally not moved with any ease into managerial and professional jobs. Moreover, the ladders that do exist are exceedingly short and confining. Research indicates that moving up typically means an easier work load but not necessarily a more challenging one. In many instances the "hardest work," with the most demands and greatest variety of technical requirements, is performed at the lowest secretarial level (Kanter, 1977). Secretaries at the upper levels of INDISCO, for example, had more responsibility in the sense that they took on a few administrative duties (and often their mistakes had greater consequences), but they did not necessarily have the heaviest work loads. This was also true at Firm X, where legal secretaries to junior partners or senior associates had less status and pay but heavier work loads than senior partners' secretaries. Their attorneys—not the senior partners—typically generated the most paperwork in the firm (Murphree, 1981).

CHANGES IN THE SUPPLY OF WOMEN TO
SECRETARIAL JOBS: RISING EXPECTATIONS
AND DECLINING SATISFACTION

For many years women secretaries have shaped their expectations to the patrimonial structure surrounding them. In recent years, however, the workplace expectations of more and more women have soared, creating a striking dissonance between expectations and actual experience—a dissonance exacerbated by new office technology.

In the late 1970s, Daniel Yankelovich (1979) focused attention on the growing "psychology of entitlements" characterizing American workers, female as well as male. Workers increasingly demand rights and rewards at work that they did not consider due them in the past. Women, while generally satisfied with less than men (Gutek and Bikson, 1985), are nonetheless an important part of this movement. According to Rosabeth Kanter, since the 1960s women in the nonprofessional rank and file have lobbied with a new legitimacy for an extension of their basic civil rights into the workplace and have demanded equity, discretion, and greater employee control (Kanter, 1977).[5] Many are questioning their subordinate place in organizational hierarchies as nurturant "office wives," servants, and sex objects. At the same time they are seeking recognition for their "invisible labor" and their role as important players on the office team.

Accompanying this drive for entitlements has been an observable decline in the overall satisfaction of working women, especially secretaries. As early as 1977 women were reporting a gap between what they expected from their jobs and what they felt they were getting. The Quality of Employment Survey, for example, reported a decline of some 25 points in the mean job satisfaction

---

[5] There is a wide range as to what different workers mean by their "rights." At the most radical level, the rights issue focuses on access to real power for subordinates, namely, access to the resources of the organization, or what a union organizer in Terkel's *American Dreams: Lost and Found* (1981) called "profits and say-so." Worker rights may also involve "freedom from hierarchy" (Blauner, 1966; Presthus, 1978) and the opening up of an organization's opportunity system to any qualified workers (Kanter, 1977). In most instances, however, the rights discussed involve such specifics as the right to pay equity or privacy, the right to participate in decisions involving departmental production, or the right to more control by the worker over his or her immediate work tasks and environment.

score of secretaries between 1969 and 1977 (Quinn and Staines, 1979; Staines, 1979).

A 1975 study by the U.S. Department of State examined the morale of its secretaries at home and abroad. It found over half of the 845 respondents to be dissatisfied with their careers. The most frequent criticisms concerned a lack of status and recognition, as well as a lack of responsible and interesting work (i.e., respondents were assigned work that made too few demands on their skills, felt overqualified for their present assignments, and thought themselves able to do the work of their superiors) (U.S. Department of State, 1975:iii–v). A later study by the National Commission on Working Women (1979) surveyed the perceptions, problems, and prospects at work of some 20,399 secretaries and typists— self-selected as respondents from the readership of a variety of national women's magazines. It too found widespread perception of underutilization, limited advancement opportunities, and low pay.

Grandjean and Taylor (1980) examined sources of job satisfaction of 231 secretaries, stenographers, and typists in a federal agency. The items rated most important to secretarial job satisfaction were the opportunity to advance, do quality work, and have responsibility. The importance placed on advancement and responsibility, however, contrasts markedly with the actual satisfaction secretaries expressed regarding the opportunity to achieve them.

Over the last few years, the combination of increasing expectations and declining satisfaction has increased political activism among many women clericals. Organizations of secretaries, including Working Women, 9 to 5, and Professional Secretaries International, all provide secretaries with an institutional base from which to advocate better pay, greater respect on and off the job, more opportunity to perform interesting and challenging work, and an opportunity to advance in their careers. In addition, these associations seek to repudiate the stigma that became attached to the occupation in the 1970s when being "just a secretary" was often seen as an inferior occupation compared to the many nontraditional occupations some women began to enter. Organizations such as the Women's Bureau of the U.S. Department of Labor, The Business and Professional Women's Foundation, the commissions on the Status of Women, the Displaced Homemaker's Network, the National Commission on Working Women, and many women's centers in educational institutions and community-based organizations throughout the country have also taken up the secretary's cause. Unions have been active as well. The Coalition of Labor Union Women serves as the research hub for national unions interested in organizing secretaries. In 1980 the National Association of Office Workers joined with the Service and Industrial Employees Union to form District 9 to 5.

The media's changing attitude toward working women in general supplements institutional support for secretaries. Television, newspapers, magazines, and movies sensitive to their buying power publicize the needs and wants of working women, including secretaries. Television serials, movies, and documentaries have taken up such issues as sexual harassment, day care, pension and pay problems, and health and safety rights.

Contemporary studies—as I will show in the balance of the paper—continue to show disparities between secretarial expectations and experiences, especially as they pertain to specific factors. Moreover, the new breed of secretary does not encounter a static workplace. Her expectations are soaring at the same historical moment that offices are being transformed by automation.

THE NEW OFFICE ENVIRONMENT

WORD PROCESSING: THE CORE TECHNOLOGY

From the perspective of most secretaries, word processing is a handy technology and a welcome tool for getting the job done. Secretaries generally report that they like the new automated equipment and they are optimistic about what it can do for them (Westin et al., 1985; Johnson et al., 1985; Professional Secretaries International and the Minolta Corp., 1984; 9 to 5, National Association of Working Women, 1984; Honeywell Inc., 1983; Bikson and Gutek, 1983). In a national survey conducted by a major vendor, 86 percent of the secretaries reported being satisfied to very satisfied with their automated equipment (Honeywell Inc., 1983). About 9 out of 10 secretaries agreed that this equipment speeded up their routine chores, made their job easier, and improved the flow of work through the office. At least three-quarters agreed that the equipment allowed secretaries to get more done each day, improved the quality of their work, and freed their time for more interesting and challenging tasks (Honeywell Inc., 1983).

Two other vendor-sponsored surveys (Westin et al., 1985; Professional Secretaries International and the Minolta Corp., 1984), as well as a large union-sponsored survey (9 to 5, National Association of Working Women, 1984), also found that favorable attitudes were widespread. Sixty-eight percent of the respondents of the 9 to 5 Working Women Education Stress Survey reported that using VDTs made their jobs more interesting and enjoyable, and 88 percent of the members of Professional Secretaries International said they liked using automated equipment. (See also Bikson and Gutek, 1983). More important, none reportedly are eager to return to the typewriter (Pomfrett et al., 1984).

The problems associated with the quality of secretarial employment in automated offices have much more to do with organizational factors, including the design of new jobs, the way in which word processing is introduced, and general working conditions, than with the equipment itself. Iacono and Kling (1984) recently pointed out that, while most workers accept innovation as normal and are highly pleased with new technologies, they are also very frustrated with the conditions under which they use them:

> Women, who are most adversely affected by technological change, are rarely dissatisfied or hostile toward their machine. However, clerical workers are much more frequently dissatisfied with the working conditions that accompany new technologies.

The objectionable conditions most commonly reported by secretaries involve a multitude of practical factors: lack of privacy, storage, and desk top space; noise; poor equipment maintenance; inadequate access to software consultants (Johnson et al., 1985); poorly written manuals; and low functionality of systems (Johnson, 1984; Bikson and Gutek, 1983). Secretaries also object to being excluded from the process of deciding how to automate the office; they resent not being consulted about what kinds of equipment to buy for their offices or about whether and how their jobs should be redesigned. They also want to take part in evaluating how well an office system works. For example, secretaries resent having to master a particular system thrust on them, only to have that system replaced with an entirely different one—all without input or evaluation from themselves, the primary users. While deeply aggravating, these are short-term problems that in theory could be solved.

A more difficult problem lies in the area of secretaries' long-term expectations. The introduction of word processing has raised these expectations: secretaries anticipate that the new systems and associated skills will give them access to more challenging work, create opportunities for advancement in their organizations, and lead to more money and higher status. Sharing in these expectations are large numbers of minority women, especially blacks and Hispanics. In the 1970s women benefited from new opportunities, many of them made possible by equal opportunity legislation and affirmative action regulations in the 1960s. Different groups of women, however, benefited in different ways. In the last decade, for example, large numbers of white, educated women who formerly looked to secretarial work as an appropriate career have moved into professional and managerial positions. Their exodus, together with a staggering increase in secretarial jobs, opened up many clerical positions to minority women, who had traditionally been forced by discrimination to work at lower-paying, lower-status factory and domestic jobs. In 1970 there were approximately 155,000 black and Hispanic secretaries; by 1980 that number had more than doubled to 374,000. Secretarial and clerical positions have also become available to less-educated white women whose level of schooling would previously have disqualified them (Women's Bureau, U.S. Department of Labor, 1985). These new groups, however, bring to their work a set of rising expectations characteristic of American working women generally, and, moreover, they are looking to the new technology to provide them with even greater opportunities.

Commentators, including employers and policy makers, have made much of the claim that secretarial work is a step up for many women in that it offers them better wages, a cleaner work environment, greater status outside the workplace, and a chance to get dressed up and mix with white-collar professionals (Murphree, 1981; Crozier, 1964; Mills, 1956). Implicit in this analysis, however, is the assumption that expectations are static—e.g., that minority women, by virtue of the relative improvement in their status and wages that secretarial jobs bring compared with most service and domestic work, will remain forever grateful and content in these jobs. More recent research suggests that these clericals respond to new incentives and seek to grow in their jobs just as other employees do. My own field studies and much anecdotal material suggests that once a certain "mastery" of word processing is attained, most word-processing secretaries—whatever their race or ethnic group—tend to seek greater compensation for new skills acquired, the opportunity to improve those skills even more, and a chance to advance in their organizations.

In theory, new information-processing technology affords secretaries opportunities to perform a wide variety of interesting tasks ranging from high-level information-processing functions (e.g., numeric data manipulation, including spreadsheets and financial analysis; planning and project management; and programming and form development) (Goldfield et al., 1985; Hirschhorn, 1984) to a multitude of lower-level tasks such as filling in forms or keying in text and data supplied by someone else (Bikson and Gutek, 1983; Schrage, 1984). The list below enumerates the range of tasks. Recent research, however, indicates that secretaries—while using more skills than ever before—are nonetheless performing few of the higher-level, autonomous information-processing tasks sophisticated computer systems make available to them (Bikson and Gutek, 1983; Gutek and Bikson, 1985). This, as the following sections show, occurs because of the dominance of new staffing ratios in offices where private secretaries are shared among principals or are obliged to work as specialists in minipools and because of the persistence of patrimony in secretarial work, in particular the still-operative stereotypes of the appropriate division of labor between principals and secretaries.

SECRETARIAL SHARING AND MINIPOOLS:
NEW STAFFING RATIOS IN THE AUTOMATED OFFICE

Office economics, in particular the costs generated by investment in computers and concerns about labor overhead, are pushing many managers—in a trend predicted by Mills (1956) and Braverman (1974)—to continue their efforts to reduce the number of private secretaries in their organizations by decoupling secretaries and executives. Two observations, in fact, about word-processing secretaries stand out in office after office today. First, while some word-processing secretaries are assigned to work for one person, far more work for two, three, or more principals in varying degrees of intimacy.[6] Second, authority over the secretary is increasingly "shared" between a number of different bosses, be they several

---

[6] Mills (1956) referred to the pool concept in *White Collar*. Until recently, systematic data on secretarial job design in decentralized groups has been unavailable. However, a new study by Pullman and Szymanski (1986) for The Private Industry Council of New York City presents a useful cross-sectional analysis of clerical workers in the banking, insurance, and legal industries and the increased staffing ratios found there.

Tasks of the Word-Processing Secretary

Administrative and para-professional tasks
Answer letters and inquiries (including electronic mail)
Drafting letters and documents for boss's signature
Electronic calendaring and time management
Arranging conferences and meetings, including teleconferencing
Planning and project management
Project follow-through and cleanup
Spreadsheets and financial management
Research
Inventory control
Personnel records (time and attendance logs)

Diplomatic and social tasks
Gatekeeping and buffering
Receiving visitors or incoming calls
Scheduling appointments for boss
Gathering information and gossip about organization
Shepherding projects through bureaucracy
Acting as sounding board for boss
Advising boss

Clerical tasks
Placing telephone calls
Making restaurant reservations
Making travel arrangements
Photocopying
Stenography
Taking minutes or notes at meetings
Proofreading
Maintaining files of paper copies
Distributing/sending out mail

Clerical tasks--computer-based
Text and data inputting
Own (drafting)
Others (copying; transcribing from dictaphone)
Formatting and graphics
Using judgment
Only as instructed
Text and data-editing
Own (editing and correcting)
Others (making editorial changes and corrections as instructed)
File management
Develop own system using judgment
Use predesigned system with preassigned and standardized file name
Proofreading, using spelling and grammar programs
Budgeting space on disks

Maintenance and housekeeping tasks--computer-based
Changing ribbons
Changing print wheels
Hand-feeding printer with paper or otherwise controlling paper input
Gathering printed output
Stocking and fitting computer supplies
Fetching or ordering supplies

Maintenance and housekeeping tasks--non-computer-based
   Getting coffee, ordering food
   Cleaning, straightening, and dusting
   Setting up conference rooms

Personal and quasi-personal tasks
   Financial management (e.g., preparing tax material, paying bills for
      boss, keeping securities or insurance records for boss)
   Carrying out club and social organization commitments of a clerical
      nature for boss (e.g., alumni mailing)
   Gift buying/private errands

executives or an executive and the organization's personnel department.

Essentially the job of every word-processing secretary can be analyzed in terms of the number and configuration of principals assigned to that secretary, i.e., the staffing ratio. In some Wall Street law firms and many other large organizations, two different secretary-to-boss configurations are predominant: shared word-processing arrangements and minipool or team arrangements.

The Shared Secretary

A common arrangement now found in many offices is the shared word-processing secretary. A secretary is assigned to work on a daily basis for two or more principals. This arrangement bears such names as the "two on one" or "three on one" plan.[7] In the Honeywell Inc. (1983) study, for example, 36 percent of all the secretaries interviewed worked for two or three managers, while nearly 20 percent worked for four or more managers. Ratios can range from 2 principals per secretary, such as found in a small architectural firm or doctor's office, to 20 or 30 principals per secretary, such as found in many high-tech engineering firms (Honeywell Inc., 1983).

Knowing how many bosses the word-processing secretary has can provide important clues to understanding the scope and quality of the secretary's job. Exploratory research suggests that word-processing secretaries who are shared perform a more restricted

---

[7] This is not to say that the private secretary has disappeared in the automated office. In almost every office, one can find examples of the private word-processing secretary working for a single executive or manager. In personnel parlance this is known as the "one-on-one plan."

set of tasks than secretaries who work for only one boss, regardless of how sophisticated their particular word-processing system may be. In large part this is due to the demands made on the secretary's time by a stable of bosses for routine typing, data-entry, and editing chores. The bulk of the shared word-processing secretary's work is often made up of text inputting and routine editing. She must also perform the many traditional gatekeeping and "office wife" functions. As a result there is little time, with even the most sophisticated system, for her to undertake high-level tasks such as project management, accounting, electronic calendaring, or developing a data base or file management system.

Unrealistic expectations about the capabilities of new equipment further limit the shared secretary's work. Most people associate "high-demand, low-control jobs" with centralized data- and word-processing work (Karasek, 1979; 9 to 5, 1984). But these problems can be found just as readily in decentralized scenarios.

Dazzled by the speed and multiple text-editing features of word processing, many bosses in decentralized settings see the machine, rather than the secretary, as the production unit (U.S. Department of Labor, 1984–1985). They give their secretaries sloppier-than-usual first drafts, many more revisions to make, and less time in which to correct the material (Zimmerman, 1983). For shared secretaries the need to speed up tends to be worse the larger the number of principals they serve. Challenge in these jobs, therefore, comes not from the intrinsic complexities of the tasks, but rather from one's ability to keep up with a demanding work load generated by many bosses.

Pomfrett et al. (1984), for example, describe a work situation where only two secretaries now perform all the office's word-processing work. They report that the two secretaries felt they were spending more time doing word processing and associated tasks than they had previously spent at typing in the precomputer office, with a reduction in task variety and hence work satisfaction.

In addition, managers continue to vie with one another for a secretary's time—just as they did in the precomputer office, and pull rank and status with her to get their work done first and fastest. The secretary frequently gets caught in the middle between two principals, and must stop working on one job to accommodate the higher-ranking principal.

The Minipool Secretary

Many companies are using new office technologies as a vehicle to reorganize their secretaries into small decentralized pools. Although such pools existed in the precomputer office for years, they are considered by some management consultants today to be the latest trend in reorganizing office work.

These small work groups bear names such as teams, clusters, or minipools. Their attraction to managers is that they maximize the use of every secretary's time and eliminate some of the "costs, inefficiencies, and inequities of the social office" that Mills (1956) and Kanter (1977) described. For example, the private and shared systems limit, to an extent, whom a secretary must take work from and cast a patrimonial glow around boss-secretary relations. In contrast, the team or minipool secretary—at least in principle—is available to work for any principal. (Some of the greatest uproars in the traditional office have involved an executive asking someone else's secretary to do work for him.)

From the perspective of the secretary seeking challenge, variety, and control over her work, minipools can be a boon insofar as they cut down on the favoritism or prima donna syndrome. They also create a setting for secretaries to work out a division of labor among themselves, such as who will specialize in what tasks (e.g., text editing, gatekeeping, maintenance) and how jobs will be rotated among different staff members. They allow for group support in learning new software techniques and, for secretaries attached to highly specialized teams, an opportunity to hone their skills (e.g., gain proficiency at creating glossaries and "plombing" a software program or a system in great depth).

Decentralized pools, however, can create some very real problems for those secretaries who find their new jobs enlarged but not enriched. Too often they are very high stress, heavy work load environments. More important, however, they are frequently coordinated by a senior secretary or supervisor who is answerable to a distant personnel department. While such a person can benefit the work group by running interference between the secretaries and the managers, she often becomes a co-supervisor alongside the set of executives the pool serves. This arrangement frequently results in the secretaries not being sure who is boss, who to please most, or whose evaluation counts most. Many end up trying to please both the coordinator and the more powerful managers attached to their pool. Such supervisory ambiguity is characteristic of pool work of any kind in that it mixes a kind of bureaucratic authority with old-fashioned patrimonial authority (Murphree, 1981). Like so much else that characterizes today's office, it is independent of any technology and can be found in both high-tech and low-tech offices.

The trend toward minipools and secretarial sharing is likely to affect different groups of women in different ways. White, middle-class women are likely to move into the private secretarial jobs or be promoted to the team supervisor jobs. Minority women are likely to move into lower-level shared or pool jobs.

THE PERSISTENCE OF PATRIMONY
IN THE NEW OFFICE

THE NEW TASKS

Many patrimonial aspects of the traditional office persist in the newly automated one. Kanter (1977) points out that high-challenge jobs in secretarial work have generally resulted from a manager's largess or the secretary's ability to persuade him to assign her such jobs. In automated offices dominated by a patrimonial ethos, in which secretarial work is decentralized, the division of labor between secretary and boss continues to be negotiated in a similar way.

Just as in the precomputer office, many secretaries working in automated offices are kept busy accomplishing a host of lower-level clerical and administrative tasks. For example, in the traditional office the secretary did all the typing; in the automated office she continues to do most of it—depending upon how resistant her boss is to keyboards. (Indeed, managers' resistance to word and data processing has been blamed on their disdain for typing, hence the euphemism, "keyboarding.") As one analyst put it, women type, men keyboard.[8]

Secretaries, particularly private or executive secretaries who have a professional orientation to their work, continue to feel

---

[8] Bikson and Gutek (1983) found a high keyboarding rate for the managers, administrators, and text- and data-oriented professionals in their study. They caution, however, that the organizations they studied were early adopters of new technology and hence not necessarily representative of office work groups generally.

capable of performing far more demanding and responsible tasks in the new office than their male managers are willing to give them. Half of the managers in the Honeywell study reported wasting more than 10 percent of their time on activities such as supervision of minor tasks and composing routine correspondence, memos, or reports. These same managers, however, say they do not delegate these "time-wasting" tasks to their secretaries either because the nature of the task makes it impossible or because their secretaries are too busy. The secretaries disagree. Only one in four secretaries say they are too busy to take on extra duties. Furthermore, 4 in 10 report that their managers see no need to delegate work to them. The study also points out the divergent viewpoints held by secretaries and managers as to what makes an office more productive. Secretaries were twice as likely as their managers to say that more of a team relationship between managers and their secretaries would improve office productivity, with managers twice as likely as their secretaries to feel that "more automated equipment" was the answer (Honeywell Inc., 1983).

Even in organizations where word processing is highly integrated and executives work "on line" a great deal, secretaries and principals do quite different tasks (Johnson, 1984). And, just as in the traditional office, it is the principals who perform most of the creative and rewarding tasks, namely, those demanding high levels of verbal skill, discretion, responsibility, and decision making, such as writing original material, manipulating financial programs, or creating project management systems (Bikson and Gutek, 1983). In many instances, for example, I witnessed executives passing documents that had been generated on a home computer to their secretary for entry and text editing on the office system.

An Omni group study suggests that executives are delegating these tasks to their secretaries out of boredom. According to the director of the study, Tech Trends '85: Inside the American Office, "personal computing tends to glamorize clerical work, and managers have begun to realize that."

Many systems, for example, are designed in such a way that there is little or no room for secretarial input. Computerized file management programs, for example, allow users to create, access, and store data in computers—tasks that can involve varying degrees of computer expertise and cognitive skill. In "high-challenge" situations, secretaries are given a great deal of discretion in file management. They can create their own file management program or customize an off-the-shelf program to fit their particular needs. Frequently, however, the word-processing secretary is required to mark up files or retrieve them using schemas predetermined and programmed by others. Similarly, text editing can vary in the amount of discretion and creativity allowed the secretary. Few secretaries are allowed to function as true editors, using their conceptual and verbal skills to rework the writing of a principal.

The word-processing secretary is inheriting a good deal of the new hardware maintenance tasks as well, in particular, supervising the printer. Keeping it supplied with paper, changing ribbons, and tearing off output are all tasks falling in the secretary's domain.

Inadequate training and time to experiment with new functions present other stumbling blocks to secretaries seeking challenging work in the automated office. Too frequently, secretaries receive little or no training in system functions (U.S. Department of Labor, 1986) and thus lack the background to experiment with new programs such as project planning or spreadsheet software.

Career Opportunities

Women secretaries have long expressed a desire for greater career mobility and opportunity to advance in their organizations (Grandjean and Taylor, 1980; National Commission on Working Women, 1979; Schrank and Riley, 1976; U.S. Department of State, 1975). The sweeping changes in office organization that often accompany automation offer employers an opportunity to improve women's access to higher-level professional and managerial jobs. An important attraction for secretaries of acquiring and honing computer skills has been the belief that such skills would facilitate their entry into higher-level occupations. (Honeywell Inc., 1983; Kelly Services, 1982; Verbatim Corp., 1982).

Contrary to the promise of many vendors and schools offering word-processing instruction, however, preliminary research indicates that clerical women are increasingly frustrated with the opportunity for advancement offered them in the "office of the future." Many are reporting uncertainty as to whether word processing per se should be viewed as a clerical, a technical, or a professional occupation (Verbatim Corp., 1982). In its survey of some 900 women working in VDT occupations, the Educational Fund for Individual Rights found that nearly a third of the female clericals felt discriminated against in terms of the promotional and career path opportunities they received compared to men in their organization. In an employer survey of a large, highly automated customer-service organization reported on by the same researchers, two-thirds of the women clericals said they were not satisfied with their chances for advancement (Westin et al., 1985). Similar numbers were obtained in a 1983 study of professional secretaries (Professional Secretaries International and the Minolta Corp., 1984): 49 percent of the secretaries said they were dissatisfied with the opportunity for advancement offered by their jobs, with 22 percent being "very dissatisfied." In the same survey approximately two-thirds of the secretaries felt there were limitations to advancement for secretaries in their company.

A review of study research conducted for the National Academy of Sciences (Werneke, 1984) focuses specifically on the nexus between technology and women's occupational mobility and links women's blocked mobility and their low pay to occupational segregation and the fact that women are locking into lower-level computer jobs.

A concern of many researchers, in fact, is the eventual elimination of many of the professional and managerial jobs into which women have moved over the last decade as a result of affirmative action efforts. New data indicate a trend toward employers using attrition and retrenchment to reduce the number of recently created lower-level management positions through a last in, first out policy (Applebaum, 1984, Kraft, 1985). The social reorganization and new staffing ratios being adopted by many offices when automating may, however, not only cut women off from upper-level jobs but reduce their access to secretarial jobs by eliminating many typists and clerk positions. These "bridge positions" traditionally have offered women—most recently, minority women—an important entree into higher-paid secretarial work (Noyelle, this volume). For years, entry-level typists have aspired to move up into private secretarial or, more recently, administrative assistant jobs (Watstein, 1985). From there, as Kanter (1977) points out, mobility has traditionally been contingent on either the upward mobility of the boss or on a kind of horizontal mobility, with the secretary moving from firm to firm in search of a higher-paying job in a more prestigious firm or industry.

To the extent that more and more private secretarial slots are phased out and secretaries are shared or pooled, organizational career ladders will become even shorter. This could be a particular problem for minority women. In one Wall Street law firm, the private secretaries' slots are being eliminated through attrition. Secretaries who leave or retire are not replaced. All new secretarial recruits—a large percentage of whom are minority women from a local community college—are hired with the clear understanding that as long as they are with the firm they will be "team secretaries" and should not expect to be promoted to "private secretary." As such they will work in a pool with three other secretaries for nine attorneys. At a salary of $400 per week these terms are easy for the new young recruits to accept. According to the firm's director of personnel, however, problems do eventually arise. Typically these team secretaries, after a couple of years on the job, will come to her seeking raises because they are not permitted to move up to work for partners and their skills on the office's very advanced word-processing system have greatly increased.[9]

Hirschhorn, however, in a concept paper, suggests that a different scenario is occurring in the automated office. He posits that because a shift is taking place whereby office workers do more "negotiating" on their jobs than "taking orders," three "para-professions" may emerge from "the increasingly obsolete secretarial role." These are the para-publisher, the para-librarian, and the para-manager. The first supervises the document production process; the second supervises file and index management, with particular emphasis on cross-referencing; and the third prepares budgets, monitors master-calendar preparations, and maintains "control system data bases," such as productivity and time records (Hirschhorn, 1984:1).

In Hirschhorn's view this development is likely to move secretaries into the professional and managerial ranks. In his words: "The para-publisher, once a secretary, can become a manager of an in-house publishing unit. The technology capitalizes his or her innate skills." He also points out, however, that "the person who cannot achieve para-professional status cannot hope to rise from filing clerk to receptionist to secretary" and cites the dangers this poses for "poor, uneducated or miseducated people," which could

---

[9] Some law firms and academic departments are experimenting with building career mobility into their teams by creating supervisory slots for "captains" or coordinators. The number of these slots, however, is very limited and is not likely to compensate for the old career route of "pool to partner" or typist to departmental secretary.

disproportionately be minorities or older women excluded from the training process (Hirschhorn, 1984).

Minority secretaries also often have a problem of another kind in moving up. Tora Bikson of the Rand Corporation reports in a private communication that the status of a work group—what she calls its "organizational niche"—is a powerful indicator of the goodness and badness of women's opportunities in an organization (see also Gutek and Bikson, 1985). Minorities frequently are attached to the least prestigious divisions or departments of an organization. Their superiors, often minority males, have the poorest access to the resources or power structure of the organizations and consequently lack the ability to promote their female subordinates in any meaningful way. These departments also often have the poorest access to up-to-date equipment, and hence, these secretaries have the least opportunity to acquire those computer skills that would make them the most promotable. They may also be the first unit of an organization to experience budget cuts and, hence, the need for secretarial sharing or minipools.

Minorities may be disadvantaged by the electronic office in other ways. Electronic telecommunications technology makes it possible for employers to move clerical work away from geographical locations such as inner cities to other locations, such as suburban and rural areas, thus depriving minorities of jobs (Nelson, 1984; Baran and Teegarden, 1983). Another threat is posed by the continuing transfer of clerical jobs out of the United States to cheaper, usually third-world, labor forces (U.S. Congress, Office of Technology Assessment, 1985).

COMPENSATION AND SKILLS

Wages and Upskilling

The issue of equitable wages for secretaries has been of growing importance over the last decade (U.S. Department of Labor, 1986; Professional Secretaries International, 1984). A great many secretaries feel undervalued and underpaid. They resent not being paid for the skills they use, both their traditionally "invisible" gatekeeping (diplomacy) skills and their new computer-based skills.

According to a study by Professional Secretaries International (1984), pay for secretaries has been based mainly on seniority. The length of time with an employer, in fact, has more impact on salary than skills, education, or even job title. The next most influential factor affecting the secretary's salary is the title of her boss, followed by scope of the business (regional, national, international); employer's pay policy (whether it pays high, average, or low salaries to all employees); and finally, the number of employees at the work location (the more employees, the higher the salary). The lack of a high school diploma costs a secretary approximately $2,500 a year, while having a master's degree adds only $1,500 to the average annual salary. Experience also counts for little. New secretaries earn only $1,000 a year less than those with 20 years of experience. Titles also count for very little. A move up to a higher title such as "executive assistant" or "senior secretary" counts for only about $1,000 a year per step up.

With the advent of word processing, the definable skills of the traditional secretary (e.g., typing, filing, shorthand, and gatekeeping) have now been expanded to include data handling, text editing, and other technical computer skills. As a result, the issue of equitable pay for secretarial workers has taken on a new relevance. According to a study by Kelly Services, 88 percent of all secretaries believe that learning as much as possible about using word processing will help them increase their salaries. Half, in fact, believe it to be very influential (Kelly Services, 1984). In many offices, however, skill upgrading has not resulted in greater compensation.

In most instances word-processing skills exceed those needed to operate a typewriter. Text editing and formatting, for example, both demand a degree of knowledge of software and hardware logic. On-line file management demands a blend of cognitive and conceptual skills in addition to computer logic. For example, to set up a workable file management system (e.g., affix appropriate labels to a file, assign key words), secretaries must have a "knowledge of context" that realistically reflects the goals of the boss and the organization as well as the capabilities of the office computer system.

Many secretaries, moreover, are taking on training responsibilities and acting as informal teachers and instructors to other secretaries and to managers and executives on how to use the new equipment (Kanter, 1983). Too often these instructional efforts are taken for granted, and the secretary is not paid for her special knowledge.

Many employers (and some secretaries) believe that the on-the-job training on new equipment is a sufficient substitute for additional pay (Women's Bureau, U.S. Department of Labor, 1985). Most secretaries, however, want to see their new computer skills reflected in their paychecks and argue their case through organizations such as Professional Secretaries International and The Working Women's Education Fund.

In a recent poll of 1,250 secretaries, almost 90 percent believed their computer skills should earn them higher pay. However, the same survey reports that 58.1 percent feel that their computer skills had not earned them a higher salary (Fusselman, 1986). Thirty-five percent of the secretaries interviewed in the Panasonic Study, in fact, cited "insufficient pay" as a source of their greatest job stress. In the Kelly survey only 30 percent of the word-processing secretaries interviewed reported receiving pay increases as a result of their word-processing skills. The Educational Fund for Individual Rights also found "a strong minority"—perhaps 25–35 percent of the women VDT users it studied—expressing concern about fairness of the pay they were receiving. These attitudes were particularly strong among clericals, including secretaries, under 30 years of age. (This is also the group, according to the Kelly study, most likely to receive a pay increase as a result of developing new word-processing skills [Kelly Services, 1982].)

It is essential that research be undertaken that tracks the types of skills used in different word-processing jobs and how currently these skills relate to wages. Secretaries in private, shared, and team jobs perform very different constellations of tasks and hence are likely to use a different collection of skills. Individuals working in the same kind of word-processing job may vary greatly among one another in expertise. Two secretaries can have very different abilities in exploiting a sophisticated word-processing program like Wordstar© or Xywrite©. They may differ in the number of commands they know, knowledge of when a command should be used, understanding of the computer's operating system, ability to save space on files, and ability to program the machine to take shortcuts or customize it to their needs. Developing a fair and equitable formula for evaluating word-processing and secretarial skills is an essential job still to be done.

OTHER VARIABLES AFFECTING CHANGE

Altered staffing ratios and the authority structure are only some of the organizational variables affecting change in the secretary's job. Other important variables include the size of the office, the kind of industry or profession (legal secretary, medical secretary, bank secretary, etc.), and the resources and wealth of the office or work group.

Office Size

Office size has always had an impact on secretarial work. Secretaries working in small offices have always been spared the costs of extreme specialization. Most have great variety in their jobs as "Jills" of all trades. Their work includes typing, housekeeping, research, inventory control, and accounting. Caste distinctions tend to be played down, with work relations warmer and more family-like and rules and regulations kept to a minimum (Murphree, 1981; Litwak and Figueira, 1968).

Secretaries in small offices nevertheless generally forgo the perks of larger establishments. Large firms often tend to have good back-up services (e.g., duplicating departments, mail and messenger services, canteens in which to make coffee and wash the pot) and higher salary scales. Just as important, large organizations tend to be financially sounder. As one secretary in a very large law firm pointed out to me: "They've got cash at the end of the month; their check is good!" Large organizations also afford a certain panache or status by association that reflects on any employee in her life outside the office, however modest her status at work. ("I can read about our clients in the *New York Times*.")

Computerization is making dramatic inroads in small offices (U.S. Congress, Office of Technological Assessment, 1985). The impact of automation in small offices alters few of these differences. Its impact, however, is not well defined.[10] There are indications that secretaries in small offices may be in a better position to be delegated higher-level computer tasks, such as setting up a computerized billing system or some other administrative or managerial software packages. For example, many small law firms

---

[10] Unfortunately, we have little systematic research on small-office automation and its effect on secretaries. Such research is essential since small business generates the bulk of new clerical jobs in the United States today, and more and more secretaries are likely to find jobs there.

cannot afford customized packages, and the task of adapting a retail software package falls to the legal secretary with initiative.

Moreover, while salaries of word-processing secretaries in small offices are likely to remain lower than those of secretaries in large organizations, the opportunity in small firms to broaden one's skills may put the small-office secretary in a better position to advance into higher-paying jobs, depending on the industry in which she works.

Industrial Variation

Secretarial jobs, before and after the introduction of the computer, have tended to vary in significant ways by industry and profession. Want ads routinely promote secretarial jobs by advertising different industrial or professional cultures. Secretarial jobs in broadcasting are considered glamour jobs; law and publishing are portrayed as intellectual and dignified; medicine is for the secretary who wants to help people.

It is, in fact, true that the service or product put out by a company will have an effect on the secretary's tasks. Medical secretaries, brokerage secretaries, and academic secretaries, for example, tend to have more client contact than do large-firm legal secretaries.

Research, however, indicates that secretaries who work in the professions, while generally better paid (academia is the exception), have the shortest career ladders and least opportunity for mobility into management. In an earlier piece (Murphree, 1981), I distinguished between professional or caste bureaucracies and class bureaucracies. In the former (e.g., law and accounting firms), mobility is based on credentials, and hence beyond the reach of the secretary. In the latter (e.g., brokerage houses and some manufacturing firms), initiative, savvy, and salesmanship are highly valued, and secretaries have a better chance for advancement. Secretaries in the caste-like Wall Street law firms are, by definition, barred from moving into any professional jobs, except for two or three supervisory jobs in personnel or as "leaders" or coordinators of a clerical team.

Public versus private sector is another variable that may affect the nature of change in secretarial work in the automated office. Public sector secretaries are more likely to be protected by unions than are secretaries in the private sector. Increasingly, contract bargaining includes discussions of the impact of technology on office workers. Negotiating points can include job security, wage increases for word- and data-processing skills learned, ergonomic improvements, and job design standards.

Resources and Wealth of Office

The quality of secretarial jobs has always varied according to the resources and wealth of the organization. This is no less true in the automated office. Wealthier firms are the most likely to spend extra dollars for upgrading the ergonomics of the office, i.e., improving lighting and air quality, purchasing the proper chairs and desks, and keeping the equipment in top-notch condition. They are also the most likely to preserve the private secretarial role. Secretaries give status to a boss, and this is important in many offices. It is not clear—despite vendor claims—that a terminal on the boss's desk can replace the prestige of having a secretary. More likely, those who can afford to maximize their status will have both a terminal and a secretary. Most law firms, for example, have maintained private or shared secretaries as long as the bottom line has permitted.

Poor firms or economically shaky firms (or poor departments), on the other hand, are the most likely to attempt to cut costs by not replacing secretaries who leave. They may also be more likely to implement secretarial sharing or minipools in their office when word processing is brought in. They are also the least likely to give extra pay to secretaries who work for a large number of bosses and who have very heavy work loads.

CONCLUSION

In this paper I have stressed the importance of examining the social context in which office automation is occurring in order to determine its effects on secretaries. I have also pointed out the importance of examining the differential effects automation can have on various "at risk" groups of women office workers, particularly black and Hispanic women, who come into offices with different work histories and backgrounds but who have—more than many managers are prepared to acknowledge—the same expectations and needs for growth and advancement as their coworkers.

Key factors in my analysis have included gender relations at work, especially the persistence of a strong patrimonial tradition in boss-secretary relations, and variation in staffing ratio (private, shared, and pool secretaries), which are found in the contemporary office. These can either mitigate or exacerbate traditional social relations between bosses and word-processing secretaries in important ways.

My focus, which considers office automation from the perspective of the word-processing secretary, suggests hypotheses about where it is likely to succeed and to fail. Crucial to its success or failure are the rising expectations working women bring to their jobs and the limited extent to which these expectations are being met. It appears that too often word-processing secretaries are led to expect more from the new technology than it can realistically deliver, given the strong traditions that continue to shape office organization. The trend toward secretarial sharing and certain pool-like arrangements, along with a lack of training, make it impossible for many secretaries to learn and perform the more challenging high-tech tasks technology in principle permits. The persistence of patrimony in certain word-processing settings continues to require secretaries to negotiate their job tasks just as they always have.

Mobility and access to real career ladders continue to be a problem. In the new, as in the traditional, office, favoritism and manipulation of a boss is more likely to produce a move upward to a professional position than any reorganization of career ladders that is technology-driven or management-inspired. Moreover, secretaries shuttled from private secretarial status into slots as shared secretaries or into strict minipools lose access to even the short-ladder career routes (e.g., pool to executive) that were formerly available.

Wages and salary increases for skills acquired may prove to be the biggest problem of all. Word-processing secretaries may have to work "smarter" and "harder" and learn new skills just to maintain their jobs and current pay. This is a source of frustration for many women who look for incentives to "get on the word-processing bandwagon" and contribute to office productivity.

The dearth of data on the subject should not be minimized. The occupation of secretary has reached a critical juncture in office history. Yet, analysis of it and its incumbents currently must be based on exploratory case study material and crude preliminary survey data. Lacking more reliable data, I am restricted in this paper to presenting a series of hypotheses.

My inquiry suggests a troubling relationship between women's experiences in the new office and their expectations, at least in the typical case in which office automation is experienced as an invasion of VDT terminals in a piecemeal and unsystematic fashion. Many traditional tasks and rules remain. But there is also a troubling trend toward eliminating some secretarial functions. The trend of word processing by professionals, in which authors or bosses handle everything from the generation of ideas to the generation of finished texts, may be growing.

What then becomes of the secretary? What are the consequences of these changes for secretarial job design, wages, working conditions, and mobility? What jobs, if any, can minority women move into? What happens to older secretaries? What jobs for women office workers will continue to exist?

It is imperative to get answers to these kinds of questions. Careful, systematic research on those pace-setting high-tech environments that have moved beyond pools or secretarial sharing to a basic redivision of labor may furnish clues to what the nation's largest women's occupation can expect.

REFERENCES

Appelbaum, Eileen
    1984   Technology and the Redesign of Work in the Insurance Industry. Project Report No. 84-A22. Institute for Research on Educational Finance and Governance, School of Education, Stanford University.
Austin, William M., and Lawrence C. Drake, Jr.
    1985   Office automation. *Occupation Outlook Quarterly* Spring:16–19.
Baker, Elizabeth F.
    1964   *Technology and Women's Work.* New York: Columbia University Press.
Baran, Barbara, and Suzanne Teegarden
    1983   Women's Labor in the Office of the Future, Changes in the Occupational Structure of the Insurance Industry. Paper Prepared for the Conference on Women and Structural Transformation. New Brunswick, N.J.: Rutgers University (November).
Benston, Margaret Lowe
    1983   For women, the chips are down. Pp. 44–54 in Jan Zimmerman, ed., *The Technological Woman.* New York: Praeger.
Bikson, Tora K., and Barbara A. Gutek
    1983   Advanced Office Systems: An Empirical Look at Utilization and Satisfaction. Santa Monica, Calif.: Rand Corporation Publication Series.
Bjorn-Andersen, Niels
    1983   The changing roles of secretaries and clerks. In *New Office Technology: Human and Organizational Aspects.* London: Pinter.

Blauner, Robert
1966 Work satisfaction and industrial trends in modern society. In R.
Bendix and S. Lipset, eds., *Class, Status and Power*. New York: Free
Press.
Braverman, Harry
1974 *Labor and Monopoly Capital*. New York: Monthly Review Press.
Crozier, Michel
1964 *The Bureaucratic Phenomenon*. Chicago: University of Chicago
Press.
Data-Pro Newsbriefs
1985 Technology and Compensation. In *Data-Pro NewsBriefs*, Automated
Office Management 8(1):1–2.
Davies, Margery W.
1982 *Woman's Place Is at the Typewriter: Office Work and Office Workers,
1870–1930*. Philadelphia: Temple University.
Driscoll, James W.
1979 People and the automated office. *Datamation* (November):106–112.
1982 How to humanize office automation. *Office, Technology and People*
1:167–176.
Duff, Thomas B., and Patricia A. Merrier
1984 Secretaries: caught in the past? *Management World* (October):9–11.
Feldberg, Roslyn L., and Evelyn Nakano Glenn
1983 Technology and work degradation: effects of office automation on
women clerical workers. Ch. 4 in Joan Rothchild, ed., *Machina
Ex Dea: Feminist Perspectives on Technology*. New York: Pergamon
Press.
Form, William, and David B. McMillen
1983 Women, Men, & Machines. *Work and Occupations* 10(2):147–178.
Fusselman, Kay
1986 Do computer skills mean higher pay, better jobs? *The Secretary*
(June/July):14–23.
Gery, Gloria J.
1982 Office technology: creating receptivity among executives and professionals. *National Productivity Review* (Spring):204–216.
Giuliano, Vincent E.
1982 The mechanization of office work. *Scientific American* 247(3):148–
164.
Glenn, Evelyn Nakano, and Roslyn L. Feldberg
1977 Degraded and deskilled: the proletarian of clerical work. *Social
Problems* 25(1):52–64.
Goldfield, Randy J., et al.
1985 Office technology: advancing or retreating? *The Secretary* (Novem-
ber/December):5–6.
Grandjean, Burke, and Patricia Taylor
1980 Job satisfaction among female clerical workers. *Sociology of Work
and Occupations* 7(1):33–53.
Gregory, Judith, and Karen Nussbaum
1982 Race against time: automation of the office. *Office, Technology, and
People* 1(2–3):197–236.

Gutek, Barbara, and Tora K. Bikson
  1985   Differential experiences of men and women in computerized offices. *Sex Roles* 13(3,4):123–136.
Gutek, Barbara A.
  1983   Women's work in the office of the future. Pp. 159–168 in Jan Zimmerman, ed., *The Technological Woman.* New York: Praeger.
Hirschhorn, Larry
  1984   Office Automation and the Entry Level Job: A Concept Paper. Management and Behavioral Science Center, Wharton School, University of Pennsylvania.
Honeywell Inc.
  1983   National Survey on Office Automation and the Workplace, a National Survey of Managers and Secretaries. Minneapolis, Minn.
Iacono, Suzanne, and Rob Kling
  1984   Changing Office Technologies and the Transformation of Clerical Work: A Historical Perspective. Working Draft #9D, Public Policy Research Organization, University of California, Irvine.
Johnson, Bonnie McDaniel
  1985   Organizational Design of Word Processing from Typewriter to Integrated Office Systems. American Federation of Information Processing Societies, Inc. Office Automation Conference (February).
  1984   *Getting the Job Done.* Glenview, Ill.: Scott, Foresman.
Johnson, Bonnie McDaniel, et al.
  1985   Innovation in Office Systems Implementation. National Science Foundation, Report No. 8110791, Washington, D.C.
Kanter, Rosabeth M.
  1977   *Men and Women of the Corporation.* New York: Basic Books.
  1983   Office automation and people: a new dimension white paper, prepared for Honeywell Inc., Minneapolis, Minn.
Karasek, Robert
  1979   Job demands, job decision latitude and mental strain: implications for job redesign. *Administrative Science Quarterly* 24:285–308.
Kelly Services
  1982   The Kelly Report on People in the Electronic Office. Survey conducted by Research & Forecast, Inc., New York.
  1984   Kelly Report on People in the Electronic Office, Vols. I, II, and III. Public Relations Department, Detroit, Mich.
Kraft, Philip
  1985   A review of empirical studies of the consequences of technological change on work and workers in the United States. Pp. 117–150 in *Technology and Employment Effects*, Interim Report of the Panel on Technology and Women's Employment, Committee on Women's Employment and Related Social Issues, National Research Council. Washington, D.C.: National Academy Press.
Litwak, Eugene, and Josefina Figueira
  1968   Technological innovation and theoretical functions of primary groups and bureaucratic structures. *American Journal of Sociology* 73:468–481.

Lockwood, David
    1958   *The Blackcoated Worker.* London: George Allen & Unwin Ltd.
Machung, Anne
    1983   From Psyche to Technic: The Politics of Office Work. Ph.D. disser-
            tation. Department of Political Science, University of Wisconsin,
            Madison.
Marschall, Daniel, and Judith Gregory, eds.
    1983   *Office Automation: Jekyll or Hyde?* Cleveland, Ohio: Working
            Women's Education Fund.
Menzies, Heather
    1981   *Women and the Chip: Case Studies of the Effects of Informatics on Em-
            ployment in Canada.* Montreal, Canada: The Institute for Research
            in Public Policy.
Mills, C. Wright
    1956   *White Collar.* New York: Oxford University Press.
Murphree, Mary C.
    1981   Rationalization and Satisfaction in Clerical Work: A Case Study
            of Wall Street Legal Secretaries. Ph.D. dissertation. Department
            of Sociology, Columbia University.
    1984a   Brave new office: the changing role of the legal secretary. Pp.
            140–159 in K. Sacks and D. Remy, eds., *My Troubles Are Going
            to Have Trouble with Me: Everyday Trials and Triumphs of Women
            Workers.* New Brunswick, N.J.: Rutgers University Press.
    1984b   Management Discovers Women: The Reorganization of Clerical
            Workers in the 1980's. Paper presented at the Sixth Berkshire
            Conference on the History of Women. Smith College, June 1–3.
National Commission on Working Women
    1979   National Survey of Working Women: Perceptions, Problems, and
            Prospects. Washington, D.C. June.
9 to 5, National Association of Working Women
    1984   The 9 to 5 National Survey on Women and Stress.   National
            Association of Working Women, Cleveland, Ohio.
Nelson, Kristin Louise
    1984   Back-Offices and Female Labor Markets: Office Suburbanization
            in the San Francisco Bay Area. Ph.D. dissertation. Department
            of Geography, University of California, Berkeley.
Oelrich, Elizabeth S.
    1968   The Position of the Female Secretary in the U.S. from 1900 through
            1967: An Historical Study. Ph.D. dissertation. University of North
            Dakota.
Otos, Sally, and Ellen Levy
    1983   Pp. 149–158 in Jan Zimmerman, ed., *The Technological Woman.* New
            York: Praeger.
Pomfrett, S.M., et al.
    1984   Proceedings of the 1st IFIP Conference on Human-Computer In-
            teraction. *Interact* 2:357–363.
Presthus, Robert
    1978   *The Organizational Society.* Revised edition. New York: St. Martin's
            Press.

Professional Secretaries International
1984   Secretaries. . . Who Earns What? And Why? Kansas City, Mo.: PSI Research and Educational Foundation.
1983   Consensus Statement. Secretary Speakout '83. Boston, Mass.
1981   Consensus Statement. Secretary Speakout '81. San Francisco, Calif.
Professional Secretaries International and the Minolta Corp.
1984   *The Evolving Role of the Secretary in the Information Age.* Survey sponsored by Minolta Corp., in cooperation with Professional Secretaries International Research and Educational Foundation. Kansas City, Mo.
Pullman, Cydney, and Sharon Szymanski
1986   The Impact of Technology on Clerical Worker Skills in the Banking, Insurance and Legal Industries in New York City: Implications for Training. A Study for the Private Industry Council of New York City, The Labor Institute. August.
Quinn, Robert P., and Graham L. Staines
1979   *The 1977 Quality of Employment Survey.* Ann Arbor, Mich.: ISR, Survey Research Center, University of Michigan.
Rothschild, Joan, ed.
1983   *Machina ex dea: Feminist Perspectives on Technology.* New York: Pergamon.
Salmans, Sandra
1982   The debate over the electronic office. *New York Times Magazine,* November 14, pp. 131–137, 157–158.
Schlefer, Jonathan
1983   Office automation and bureaucracy. *Technology Review* (July):32–40.
Schrage, Michael
1984   PCs may redefine secretaries' jobs, *Washington Post,* "Washington Business," December 17.
Schrank, Harris T., and J.W. Riley, Jr.
1976   Women in work organizations. Pp. 82–101 in Juanita Kreps, ed., *Women and the American Economy.* Englewood Cliffs, N.J.: Prentice-Hall.
Scott, Joan W.
1982   The mechanization of women's work. *Scientific American* 247(3): 166–187.
Spinrad, R.J.
1982   Office automation. *Science* 215:808–813.
Staines, Graham L.
1979   Is worker dissatisfaction rising? *Challenge* (May–June):38–45.
Suchman, Lucy, and Eleanor Wynn
1984   Procedures and problems in the office. In *Technology and People.* Amsterdam: Elsevier.
Terkel, Studs
1981   *American Dreams: Lost and Found.* New York: Balantine.
The Professional Survey on Secretarial Stress
1986   Survey sponsored by Panasonic Industrial Co. and Professional Secretaries International. *The Secretary* (March):10–21.
U.S. Congress, Office of Technology Assessment
1985   *Automation of America's Offices,* Washington, D.C.: Government Printing Office, OTA-CIT-287, December.

U.S. Department of Labor
1984– *Occupational Outlook Handbook,* Washington, D.C.: U.S. Government
1985 Printing Office.
U.S. Department of State
1975 Secretarial Task Force Report. Washington, D.C.: U.S. Govern-
ment Printing Office.
Verbatim Corp.
1982 Office Workers' Views and Perceptions of New Technology in the
Workplace. Survey conducted by Group Attitudes Corp., New
York.
Watstein, Esther
1985 Administrative assistant. Just another title? *Biz* 16(1):4–9.
Werneke, Diane
1984 Microelectronics and Working Women: A Literature Summary.
Committee on Employment and Related Social Issues, National
Research Council, Washington, D.C.
Westin, Alan F., et al.
1985 *The Changing Workplace: A Guide to Managing the People, Organiza-
tional and Regulatory Aspects of Office Technology.* White Plains, N.Y.:
Knowledge Industry Publications, Inc.
Women's Bureau
1986 Women, Clerical Work, and Office Automation: Issues for Re-
search. Report of a conference co-sponsored by the Women's Bu-
reau and the Panel on Technology and Women's Employment,
National Research Council. Washington, D.C.: U.S. Government
Printing Office.
1985 Women and Office Automation: Issues for the Decade Ahead.
Washington, D.C.: U.S. Government Printing Office.
Yankelovich, Daniel
1979 Work, values, and the new breed. In C. Kerr and J. Rosow, eds.,
Work in America, The Decade Ahead. New York: Van Nostrand.
Zimmerman, Jan, ed.
1983 *The Technological Woman.* New York: Praeger.

Integrated Circuits/Segregated Labor: Women in Computer-Related Occupations and High-Tech Industries

MYRA H. STROBER and CAROLYN L. ARNOLD

We are just beginning to see the repercussions in all of our lives of the technological feat of fitting the electronic wiring and switches of what was a room-sized computer in 1946 onto a less than fingernail-sized piece of silicon and metal by the end of the 1970s. This silicon chip is the core of a technological revolution, the result of many attempts over a century to produce a "computing machine" that is small, fast, and cheap. Now, as the chips and, thus, the computers they make possible get smaller, faster, and cheaper, their applications in both old and new products are spawning a new high-technology industry. We see changes in a multitude of workplaces and homes, the expansion of opportunities in existing industries and occupations, and the creation of new

The authors would like to thank Deborah Thresher for her excellent preliminary research on this topic. An earlier version of this paper was given at the annual meeting of the American Educational Research Association, New Orleans, April 25, 1984, and benefited from comments by Russell Rumberger. We also received helpful comments from Francine Blau and Philip Kraft on the version presented at the National Academy of Sciences on February 28–March 1, 1985.

136

industries and occupations that were not even imagined just a few years ago.

The occupations most involved in the computer revolution are engineers, computer scientists/systems analysts, programmers, electronic technicians, computer operators, and data-entry workers; these occupations are expanding both within the computer industry and in other industries as well. In addition, the computer industry provides new opportunities for managers, clerical workers, and production workers. Traditionally women have been sharply segregated into different occupations from men and have been paid less than men (Gross, 1968; Lloyd and Neimi, 1979; Blau and Hendricks, 1979; O'Neill, 1983; Bielby and Baron, 1984; Strober, 1984; Treiman and Hartmann, 1981). This study poses several questions. Are there better opportunities for gender integration and earnings equity in these new occupations that are growing rapidly, are exhibiting labor shortages, and are supposedly not locked into past traditions and stereotypes? Are there better opportunities for gender integration and pay equity in high-technology (high-tech) industries? What does the growth of these occupations imply for women's employment?

This paper is divided into four sections. The first discusses the details of the occupations we analyze. The second section uses published data as well as the 1/1000 Public Use Samples (P.U.S.) from the 1970 and 1980 U.S. Censuses to look at how women are faring in the six major computer-related occupations and in high-tech industries. In the third section, the 1980 published data and the 1980 P.U.S. are used to examine the relative earnings of men and women in three computer-related occupations in high-tech and non-high-tech industries. In the fourth section, we discuss our findings and their implications.

In brief, we found that although high tech in general and computer occupations in particular are often seen as the great equalizers, especially for those with higher education, in fact, there is considerable gender segregation in both high-tech industries and computer-related occupations in all industries; there is also considerable male-female earnings differentiation. We suggest that one possible cause of the earnings differentiation is that men and women in computer occupations are not employed equally across industries; women tend to be employed more frequently in the lower-paying end-user industries.[1]

COMPUTER-RELATED OCCUPATIONS

DESCRIPTIONS OF OCCUPATIONS

The development of semiconductors, computers, and computer languages spawned several new occupations and expanded several others. There are six major computer-related occupation groups—engineers, computer specialists, engineering and science technicians, production workers, computer operators, and data-entry operators. For three of these groups (engineers, engineering and science technicians, and production workers), we have restricted the analysis to those employed in the computer industry. For the other three groups (computer specialists, computer operators, and data-entry operators), we have examined employment in all industries. The following descriptions of the occupations in these groups are based on definitions in the *Standard Occupational Classification Manual, 1980* (U.S. Department of Commerce, 1980), California Employment Development Department publications (ABAG, 1981), and interviews with workers and employment counselors.

Engineers

Engineers design hardware for computers, including the electronic circuits. The largest group of engineers is electrical engineers, but mechanical and industrial engineers also work in the computer industry. Sometimes they incorporate software designs into the circuits. Engineering is the highest-status and highest-paid computer-related occupation, with engineers generally having at least a B.S. degree in engineering; many have advanced degrees.

---

[1] We define "end-user" industries as those that use the products of the computer industry and make only minor changes to the products to accommodate their needs, rather than making basic new developments in these products. The companies developing computers and/or their software are part of the computer industry. The companies in all other industries, which will use these computers and/or software, are part of end-user industries. It is true that even within the computer industry the administrative divisions of the companies are end-users of computers. However, census data do not permit us to make such fine distinctions within industries, and we are interested here mainly in any broad differences between industries.

Computer Specialists

As we look beyond designing hardware to designing software, the sets of instructions that tell the computer which operations to perform, we encounter the *computer specialist* occupations. While computer engineers tend to be employed largely by computer companies, computer specialists are employed in virtually every major industry group. These jobs involve a hierarchy of tasks that used to be done by one person with the title of computer programmer.

When the first computer was unveiled in 1946 (it was room-sized because the circuits were made with glass vacuum tubes), the engineers who designed it thought that the main task of arranging the circuits had been done, and that giving instructions to the computer to perform calculations would be a simple clerical task. So they hired people who usually do clerical tasks—women. In this case the women were recent college graduates with math backgrounds. However, these women found that in order to get the computer to do calculations, they (the programmers) had to know all about the design of the circuits and the way those circuits worked in the computer; they had to tell the computer not only *what* to do, but *how* to do it. The simple operation of performing calculations (in this case for Navy shell trajectories) became a high-level task that involved a knowledge of logic, mathematics, and electronic circuits. These women programmed the necessary calculations and went on to do others. However, those who watched the programming process began to realize that programming was a high-level, challenging, and creative occupation. As the occupation grew, it became largely male (Kraft, 1979).

Ironically, some programming today is akin to the type of clerical job that computer designers (mistakenly) thought it would be in the late 1940s. Over time, with the development of higher-level languages (closer to human languages)[2] and more routine applications, programming tasks that were previously highly skilled, highly paid, and concentrated among highly educated workers have been broken down into more routine tasks and distributed among less-skilled workers. Kraft (1977) has suggested that, as this "deskilling" has occurred, it is women who have moved into

---

[2] Note that higher-level languages are closer to human languages and hence are easier to use in programming. Thus, paradoxically, "higher"-level languages require lower skill and have lower prestige associated with their use.

the less-skilled jobs.[3] Greenbaum (1979) found that the lowest-level programming jobs were disproportionately occupied by racial and ethnic minorities.

This history of the developing hierarchy in computer programming is reflected in the designations given by the Bureau of the Census to the computer specialist occupations. In 1960 and 1970, computer specialists, including programmers, were included in the professional category. By 1980, the Census put the three-digit occupational category of computer scientists/systems analysts in the professional category and the three-digit category of computer programmers in the technical category.

The following descriptions attempt to capture the current hierarchy and educational requirements among computer specialists. Some workers in these occupations do not have formal credentials, having been trained or self-taught on the job. These job titles and descriptions continue to change and overlap.

Computer scientists and some systems analysts work with engineers to design the overall hardware and software systems and sometimes know just as much about the hardware, although their training is more concentrated in the logic and mathematical models of computer systems, rather than on electronic principles. They also develop new languages to be used by other programmers. Generally, they have an M.S. or Ph.D. in computer science (CS) or electrical engineering (EE) or both (CS/EE).

Computer systems analysts conceptualize and plan how a business or industrial task, such as automating a payroll or an assembly line, will be solved by computerization. Systems analysts do not write the programs but make flow charts to show the subtasks that need to be done by people and computers and their sequence and timing.

Computer programmers are often promoted into systems analysts positions because these positions represent higher-level skills, responsibility, and pay than do programming positions. If systems analysts were not previously programmers, their education is either in business or data processing. There is a debate in this field about whether systems analysts need programming skills or not.

---

[3] Braverman (1974) originally identified and labeled this process as the "degradation of work." It soon became known as "deskilling."

Systems programmers maintain and modify operating systems—systems of programs that coordinate all the hardware in a particular computer so it will run according to certain high-level languages. They are also responsible for updating the high-level software on the system in their particular company. They generally require a B.S., M.S., or Ph.D. in CS, EE, or math.

Programmer/analysts update operating systems and write programs that tailor the computer's uses to each individual workplace. Although ready-made software is available for many purposes, most firms need programmers to modify or write programs that reflect their own computing needs. These programmers need to know both operating systems and high-level languages. Education requirements are a B.A. in related subjects with some programming experience, a B.S. in CS, or an M.B.A.

Software engineers, as some programmers are increasingly called, design and write programs in high-level languages specifically for certain computers. These programs, often called packages, are sold with the computer to make it easier for nonprogrammers to use. Packages can include such items as games, accounting programs, and instructional programs. Producing these programs requires the creativity to conceptualize and design new ways to use the computer. People writing these software packages require a good knowledge of the language used to program the software and good ideas about marketable packages. Acquiring knowledge of programming and having creative ideas are more important for job success than are educational degrees. Consequently, a range of people, from high school students to Ph.D.s, are designing and writing software.

Programmers, sometimes called coders or applications programmers, are mainly translators. They translate instructions for a certain application in one language into the programming language that their particular computer will use to produce the same results. The job category itself encompasses a range of skill and creativity from routine coding of sections of an application program to a task more like a programmer/analyst, depending on their industry or firm. These jobs can be done with less than a B.S. in CS. However, if those with a B.S. degree are available, employers often prefer to hire them.

Engineering and Science Technicians

A third major group of computer-related workers is *engineering and science technicians*. This group is found in the computer industry and is mainly made up of engineering technicians trained in electronics, although there are also some science technicians working within the industry. The electronic technicians have enough specialized knowledge of electronics to be able to construct, test, and repair the circuitry and components of computers that the engineers design and to understand engineering specifications and problems. Although they do not do original design work, they operationalize designs, test them, and then advise engineers on possible modifications. They work both in research design and in production to test and troubleshoot both new and existing products. Also included in the engineering technician category are drafters, who, using both manual and computer-assisted drafting tools, make drawings of the circuit boards and components that the engineers design. The standard degrees are the 2-year associate of arts (A.A.) or associate of science (A.S.) for an engineering or science technician and an A.A. in drafting for a drafter.

Computer Operators

The fourth computer-related occupational group is *computer operators*. They are employed in all industries. Computer operators run the external operation of the computer; ensure that the computer receives the programs and data; and coordinate disks, tapes, and printing connections to the computer, either manually or by supervising automated systems. This occupation ranges from active high-level interactions with the programs to routinized supervision of automated systems. It is sometimes an entry-level job leading to low-level programming. Education needed is simple knowledge of the equipment from a short training course and/or from experience. The occupation is rapidly being deskilled as more of its functions become automated.

Data-Entry Operators

Data-entry operators, the fifth computer-related occupation, put information into a form that can be read by a computer. This information used to be keypunched onto cards but is now almost always put onto tapes or disks from terminals. The operators, who basically type numbers and letters into a terminal, require training in typing. They are also employed in all industries.

Production Workers

The sixth major computer-related occupation is *production worker*. While many of the production jobs are similar to those in other industries, the following jobs are unique to semiconductor and computer production. There are generally no specific educational requirements for these jobs, although people with some knowledge of electronics are generally preferred. Often hazardous chemicals are used in the production process.

Semiconductor processors put materials through chemical and mechanical processes to create semiconductor integrated circuits on chips. They work either manually or, as these tasks become mechanized, with processing machines.

Semiconductor assemblers assemble chips into wired devices which become the complete integrated circuit. This includes bonding wires to circuits, a task which is done under a microscope, and cleaning the circuits with chemicals.

Electronic assemblers assemble the integrated circuits and other electronic components into a frame that becomes the finished product (e.g., a computer). Electronic assemblers can be promoted to *electronic testers*, who test chips, boards, and components as they go through assembly, or *electronic inspectors*, who examine the components for errors and specification requirements.

A skilled occupation that is sometimes part of production and sometimes part of customer service is *data-processing repair*, which involves installing and repairing data-processing machinery in offices and on production lines. This job category includes a range of workers from electronic mechanics to assembly and wiring technicians.

There are also, of course, managerial, professional/technical, sales, clerical, and service occupations within the computer industry. These jobs tend to be similar to such jobs in other industries.

GENDER SEGREGATION

COMPUTER-RELATED OCCUPATIONS

In this section we begin the analysis of gender segregation by examining trends in total employment and women's employment in computer-related occupations. Table 1 presents data both for occupations that are computer related regardless of their industry (computer specialists, computer operators, data-entry operators, and data-processing repairers) and for occupations that are computer related only when found in computer industries (engineers, engineering and science technicians, and most production workers). As Table 1 shows, between 1970 and 1980, employment in computer-related occupations grew about 80 percent—from about 1.5 million to 2.4 million. However, although the growth of these occupations is widely heralded, it is important to note that they represented only 2.0 percent of all employment in 1970, and 2.5 percent in 1980. (Among all women workers, those in computer occupations represented 2.3 percent of employment in 1970 and 2.9 percent in 1980. The corresponding percentages among men workers were 1.8 percent in 1970 and 2.2 percent in 1980.)

This growth took place in the context of increasing participation in the labor force by women. In 1970, women were 38 percent of the U.S. labor force; by 1980, they were 43 percent. However, in both those years, women's representation in computer-related occupations was either considerably below or considerably above their representation in the labor force as a whole, depending on the specific occupation.

Despite the fact that the computer-related occupations are of relatively recent origin, they are already remarkably segregated by gender. In 1970, women were 2 percent of all engineers in the computer industry; in 1980, that figure had risen to only 5 percent. Thus, in the highest-paid, highest-prestige computer-related occupation, women are virtually absent.

Among computer specialists in all industries, the situation is somewhat better, although women are still below their proportion in the overall work force. In 1970, women were 15 percent of all computer scientists/systems analysts. This occupation more than doubled from 1970 to 1980 (from 93,000 to 201,000), but by 1980, women were still only 22 percent. Among programmers, the proportion of women also increased, but they were also still underrepresented. The number of programmers almost doubled (from 161,000 to 313,000), and the proportion of women grew from 23 percent in 1970 to 31 percent in 1980.

Women were better represented among engineering and science technicians in the computer industry than among engineers, but were less well represented than among computer specialists.

TABLE 1 Total and Women's Employment in Computer-Related Occupations, 1970 and 1980

Occupation	1970		1980	
	Number	Percent Women	Number	Percent Women
Total employed in labor force	76,553,599	38	97,639,355	43
Total employed in computer- related occupations	1,497,683	--	2,424,240	--
Engineers[a]	90,626	2	125,055	5
Electrical/electronic engineers	47,004	2	67,320	4
Computer specialists	254,537	20	513,863	28
Computer scientists/systems analysts	93,200	15	200,684	22
Computer programmers	161,337	23	313,179	31
Engineering and science technicians[a]	58,292	11	90,990	17
Electronic technicians	31,454	11	60,299	15
Drafters	16,963	7	16,726	16
Computer operators	117,222	29	408,475	59
Data-entry operators	272,570	90	378,094	92
Production workers[a]	680,299	46	872,345	49
Operatives, fabricators, transporters, and laborers	519,221	58	591,091	58
Assemblers	158,191	74	208,284	72
Electronic assemblers	--	--	55,879	77
Data-processing repairers[b]	24,137	3	35,418	88
Percent of total employed labor force in computer-related occupations	1970		1980	
	2.0		2.5	

NOTE: Computer-related occupations are defined in Appendix B.

[a]Employment data for these occupations are only for the computer industry defined as two three-digit industries: Electronic Computing Equipment (SIC Codes 1970:189; 1980:322) and Electrical Machinery, Equipment, and Supplies, not elsewhere classified, including semiconductors (SIC Codes 1970:208; 1980:342). Data for all other occupations are for all industries.

[b]Workers not in the computer industry; data-processing repairers in the computer industry are included in "Production workers" above: 6,707 in 1970 and 11,208 in 1980. Women also accounted for 3 and 8 percent, respectively in 1970 and 1980, for these repairers.

SOURCE: 1970 data, Bureau of the Census (1972:Table 8); 1980 data, Bureau of the Census (1984:Tables 1 and 4).

In 1970 in the computer industry, women were 11 percent of engineering and science technicians; in 1980 they represented 17 percent. They were similarly represented among electronic/electrical technicians—11 percent in 1970 and 15 percent in 1980. As drafters, women did less well in 1970 than other technicians—only 7 percent were women—but did better in 1980, when 16 percent were women.

Initially, there was no clear indication as to which gender would be assigned to the occupation of computer operator. In 1960, when there were only 2,000 computer operators, women held 65 percent of the jobs (Dicesare, 1975). Between 1960 and 1970, the jobs in this occupation increased more than 50-fold, to 117,000. More of these new jobs were filled by men than by women so that in 1970, women were only 29 percent of all computer operators. In the period from 1970 to 1980, however, while the occupation increased fourfold, to 408,000, more of the new additions to the occupation were women, so that in 1980, women were 59 percent of all computer operators.

Like most clerical occupations, data entry is preponderantly female. In 1970 women were 90 percent of data-entry operators. Between 1970 and 1980 the occupation became even more segregated so that by 1980 women represented 92 percent of such operators.

Of all production workers in the computer industry, women were only slightly over their representation in the labor force as a whole: 46 percent in 1970 and 49 percent in 1980. However, when we look more closely at the less-skilled production occupations, women's representation is much higher. Of all the operators, fabricators, laborers, and transportation workers, a group which includes the semiconductor processors and assemblers and all other lower-level production workers in the computer industry, women represented 58 percent in both 1970 and 1980. Among assemblers, a subset of operatives, women were about 73 percent in 1970 and 1980. Of electronic assemblers, a group identified only in 1980, women were an even higher proportion: 77 percent.[4] However, in the occupation "data-processing machine repairers," we find again the extraordinary gender segregation we often see in technical occupations: women held 3 percent of these jobs in 1970 and 8 percent in 1980.

In Table 2 we present the difference between the percentage of women in the total labor force and the percentage of women in each computer-related occupation listed in Table 1. This difference represents a rough measure of occupational segregation. If we compare the data for 1970 and 1980 we find that except for

---

[4] In Silicon Valley in 1981, 40 percent of women assemblers were ethnic minorities (Rogers and Larsen, 1984). This production occupation is even more segregated abroad (Grossman, 1980).

TABLE 2   Underrepresentation of Women in Computer-Related Occupations

Occupation	Index 1970	1980
Engineers	36	38
Electrical/electronic engineers	36	39
Computer specialists	18	15
Computer scientists/systems analysts	23	21
Computer programmers	15	12
Engineering and science technicians[a]	27	26
Electronic technicians	27	28
Drafters	31	27
Computer operators	9	-16
Data-entry operators	-52	-49
Production workers[a]	-8	-6
Operatives, fabricators, transporters, and laborers	-20	-15
Assemblers	-36	-29
Electronic assemblers	--	-34
Data-processing repairers[b]	35	35

NOTE: Data from Table 1. The index is defined as the difference between percent women in total labor force and percent women in each computer-related occupation. Computer-related occupations are defined in Appendix B.

[a]Same as Table 1.
[b]Same as Table 1.

computer operators, the level of segregation was approximately the same for the 2 years.

Table 3 presents total employment and women's employment for the computer industry and for computer-related occupations in all other industries. These totals show the number of people who are involved in developing, maintaining, or supporting the production of computers in the computer industry, plus those working in occupations that were created as a result of the computer revolution.

Between 1970 and 1980, *combined* employment in the computer industry and computer-related occupations grew about 60 percent—from about 1.8 million to 2.9 million. Still, they represented only 2.4 percent of all employment in 1970 and 3.0 percent in 1980. (Among all women workers, those in the computer industry and computer occupations represented 2.7 percent of employment in 1970 and 3.4 percent in 1980. The corresponding percentages among men workers were 2.3 percent in 1970 and 2.8

TABLE 3 Total and Women's Employment in the Computer Industry and in Computer-Related Occupations in All Industries, 1970 and 1980

Industry or Occupation	1970 Number Employed	1970 Percent Women	1980 Number Employed	1980 Percent Women
Total employed in labor force	76,553,599	38	97,639,355	43
Total employed in computer industry[a] and computer-related occupations[b] in all other industries	1,805,481	43	2,940,891	48
Total in computer industry[a]	1,173,866	38	1,685,461	41
Executives, managers, and administrators	66,043	6	181,362	11
Professional/technical	229,017	9	321,185	12
Sales	19,093	7	38,447	15
Administrative support and clerical	158,276	66	243,693	70
Services	21,138	19	27,728	20
Production	680,299	46	873,046	49
Total in computer-related occupations[b] in all other industries[c]	631,615	--	1,255,430	--
Computer scientists/systems analysts	81,794	15	174,299	23
Computer programmers	146,565	23	282,673	32
Computer operators	112,646	30	394,421	59
Data-entry operators	266,473	90	368,619	92
Data-processing repairers	24,137	3	35,418	8

149

	1970	1980
Percent of total employed labor force in computer industry and computer-related occupations in all other industries	2.4	3.0

[a]Computer Industry defined as two three-digit industries: Electronic Computing Equipment Manufacturing (SIC Codes 1970:189; 1980:322) and Electrical Machinery, Equipment, and Supplies, not elsewhere classified (including semiconductors) (SIC Codes 1970:208; 1980:342). Although an effort has been made by the authors to achieve consistency, these occupational categories do not include precisely the same occupations in 1970 and 1980, so the percentage of women in each category should be interpreted as the percentage of women in that category as it was defined in each year rather than directly comparing the percentages between years. However, the total employed in the computer industry for each year includes all occupations, so these percentages can be directly compared. For the computer industry data, a detailed listing of the occupational categories used here for 1970 and 1980 is available from the authors.
[b]Computer-related occupations are defined in Appendix B.
[c]Calculated by subtracting number employed in these occupations in the computer industry from number employed in all industries.

SOURCE: 1970 data, Bureau of the Census (1972:Table 8); 1980 data, Bureau of the Census (1984:Tables 1 and 4).

percent in 1980.) Although there appear to be changes between 1970 and 1980 in the percentage of women in the occupations listed in Table 3, changes in occupational definitions during the 10-year period were such that the categories cannot be reliably compared.

GENDER, RACE, AND ETHNIC DISTRIBUTION IN FOUR COMPUTER-RELATED OCCUPATIONS

If we look more closely at the four computer-related occupations that are present in all industries—computer scientists/systems analysts, computer programmers, and data-entry operators—we can see how women and men in the three largest racial and ethnic groups are represented. Table 4 shows that in the employed labor force as a whole, white men are 50 percent of the workers, white women are 36 percent, black men are 4.8 percent, black women are 4.8 percent, and other racial groups make up 8.4 percent of the workers. Men and women of Spanish origin, who can be of any race, represent 3 and 2 percent of the workers, respectively.

In the occupations of computer scientist, systems analyst, and computer programmer, women of all groups and minority men are underrepresented compared to their representation in the labor force as a whole, while white men are overrepresented. Within each racial and ethnic group, men are better-represented than women.

Among computer scientists/systems analysts, the highest paid of these four occupations, white men hold 71.3 percent of the jobs, which is much higher than their representation of 50 percent in the labor force. White women occupy 19.5 percent of the jobs, only half as high as their representation in the labor force. Black men are less represented in this occupation than in the labor force (3 percent versus 4.8 percent). Black women's representation is even poorer, 1.7 percent in computer scientists/systems analysts versus 4.8 percent in the labor force. People of other races are only about half as well represented in this occupation as in the labor force. Like black men, the representation of men of Spanish origin is just over half that of their presence in the labor force (1.8 versus 3 percent). Women of Spanish origin are virtually unrepresented; they are only 0.1 percent of computer scientists/systems analysts, though they are 2 percent of the labor force.

Among computer programmers, the next lower paying occupation, white men are still overrepresented, and the other groups

TABLE 4 Employment Distribution by Race, Spanish Origin, and Gender, Total Labor Force and Four Computer-Related Occupations, 1980 (in percent)

Race, Origin, and Gender	Total Labor Force (N = 97,639,355)	Computer Scientists/ Systems Analysts (N = 200,684)	Computer Programmers (N = 313,179)	Computer Operators (N = 408,475)	Data-Entry Operators (N = 378,094)
White					
Men	50.0	71.3	62.2	33.9	5.7
Women	36.0	19.5	26.5	49.5	71.3
Black					
Men	4.8	3.0	3.1	4.7	1.1
Women	4.8	1.7	2.5	6.9	15.1
Other races	8.4	4.5	5.7	5.0	6.8
Total	100.0	100.0	100.0	100.0	100.0
Spanish origin					
Men	3.0	1.8	1.9	2.4	0.1
Women	2.0	0.1	0.1	2.8	5.7
Not of Spanish origin	95.0	98.1	98.0	94.2	94.8
Total	100.0	100.0	100.0	99.4	100.6

NOTES: Not all columns total 100.0 due to errors in rounding. Persons of Spanish origin can be of any race.

SOURCE: Bureau of the Census (1984:Table 1).

are still underrepresented, but somewhat less so. White men are overrepresented by 12 percentage points (62.2 percent versus 50 percent) and white women are underrepresented by 10 percentage points (26.5 percent versus 36 percent). Black men's representation is still about 3 percent, but black women's representation has increased to 2.5 percent. However, both percentages are below their share of the labor force. Other racial groups have also increased their representation, but it is still below their labor force representation. Men and women of Spanish origin have virtually the same representation among computer programmers as among computer scientists/systems analysts—1.9 and 0.1 percent, respectively.

This situation changes and in some cases reverses itself in the lower-paying occupation of computer operator. White men are now only one-third of the workers, 16 percentage points *less* than in the labor force, and white women are now half of the workers, 14 percentage points *above* their representation. Black men's representation is about the same as in the labor force, and black women's representation is higher among computer operators (6.9 percent) than in the labor force (4.8 percent). People of other racial groups are still underrepresented, however. Men of Spanish origin have a representation among computer operators below their labor force percentage, while the percentage of women of Spanish origin is above their percentage in the labor force. Thus, in this lower-paid computer occupation, white and black women and women of Spanish origin are overrepresented, and white men are underrepresented, while the percentage of black men and men of Spanish origin reflects their percentage in the labor force as a whole.

When we look at the lowest-paid computer occupation of data-entry operator, a clerical occupation, we see that all women's representation is dramatically higher and all men's representation is dramatically lower than for the other occupations listed in Table 4. White women are 71 percent of data-entry operators, twice their labor force representation. Black women and women of Spanish origin are represented in this occupation with a frequency three times greater than their representation in the labor force—15 and 6 percent, respectively.

Like gender, race and ethnicity of workers in computer occupations is associated with pay and status of the occupation. The higher status and pay of an occupation, the more white men are overrepresented and the more minority men and all women are underrepresented. In occupations with lower pay and status, the presence of white men drops to much below their percentage of the labor force, the percentage of women of all races becomes higher than their labor force percentage, and the percentage of minority men approaches their labor force representation. In an occupation that is clerical, women's representation doubles and triples above their labor force percentage, and men virtually disappear.

HIGH-TECH INDUSTRIES

This section looks at how women are faring not just in computer-related occupations but in the group of industries known as "high tech," of which the computer industry is one part. We are interested in whether the computer industry and other high-tech industries, because they are growing rapidly and are relatively new, are, therefore, perhaps less gender stereotyped and more hospitable to women than are non-high-tech industries.

The Bureau of Labor Statistics recently reviewed all current definitions of high-tech industries and developed a range of definitions based on three factors (Riche et al., 1983:51): "(1) the utilization of scientific and technical workers, (2) expenditures for research and development, and (3) the nature of the product of the industry."

Different combinations of these factors produced three groups of high-tech industries, from the least-inclusive definition with 6 three-digit industries, to the most-inclusive definition with 48 three-digit industries. In some respects, the most intuitively appealing definitions of high-tech industries are the least inclusive (drugs; office, computing, and accounting machines; electronic components and accessories; miscellaneous electrical machinery; aircraft and parts; and guided missiles and space vehicles). However, the P.U.S. 1/1000 sample of employment in these six industries is too small for the kinds of analyses we wish to do. Thus, we use as our definition of high-tech industries the middle group of 28 three-digit industries: 26 manufacturing industries (including computers and semiconductors) with a proportion of technologically oriented workers equal to or greater than the average for all manufacturing industries and a ratio of R&D expenditure to sales close to or above the average for all industries, and 2 nonmanufacturing industries that provide technical support to high-tech

TABLE 5 Number Employed in High-Tech Industries as Percentage of Employed
Labor Force, 1970 and 1980

| | 1970 | | 1980 | |
	Number Employed	Percent of All Employed	Number Employed	Percent of All Employed
All workers	4,557,000	6.5	6,060,000	6.4
All women	1,254,000	5.0	2,026,000	5.1
All men	3,303,000	7.4	4,034,000	7.4

NOTE: See Appendix A for definition of high-tech industries.

SOURCE: Calculated by authors from U.S. Census (1/1000 P.U.S. Tape, 1970 and
1980).

manufacturing industries (computer and data-processing services,
and research and development laboratories) (Riche et al., 1983). A
list of the industries designated as high tech appears in Appendix
A.

Although employment in high-tech industries grew over the
1970–1980 decade from 4.6 million to 6.1 million, these industries
employed only about 6.5 percent of all employed workers, about
5 percent of all women workers and about 7.4 percent of men
workers. Table 5 presents these employment trends for high-tech
industries.

We find also that these industries are no less segregated by
gender than are other industries and, in fact, may be even more
so. Table 6 shows that in both 1970 and 1980, most men in high-
tech industries were in management, professional/technical work,
or production, while most women were in clerical work or production. Compared to women in non-high-tech industries, women in
high-tech industries are less likely to be in managerial and profes-
sional/technical jobs and are much more likely to be in production
work. High-tech industries provide more low-status occupations to
women, as a group, than do non-high-tech industries. By contrast,
men in high-tech industries are more likely to be in managerial or
professional/technical positions than are men in non-high-tech industries.

TABLE 6 Percentage of Men and Women Employed in High-Tech Industries and
Non-High-Tech Industries, 1970 and 1980

Occupation	High-Tech Industries		Non-High-Tech Industries	
	Men	Women	Men	Women
1970				
Number (thousands)				
Total	3,195	1,205	39,357	23,676
Percentage distribution				
Managers	10	3	13	5
Professional and technical	27	6	12	16
Sales	3	<1	8	10
Clerical	8	36	7	33
Services	2	1	8	20
Production	48	55	37	14
Other (farm and transportation)	2	<1	14	1
1980				
Number (thousands)				
Total	4,034	2,206	50,263	37,729
Percentage distribution				
Managers	14	6	13	8
Professional and technical	26	10	13	18
Sales	3	1	10	11
Clerical	8	35	7	31
Services	3	2	9	18
Production	44	46	36	11
Other (farm and transportation)	3	1	12	2

NOTE: See Appendix A for definition of high tech and non-high tech.
Occupational categories were adjusted for consistency between 1970 and
1980 by the authors; a detailed listing of the categories is available
from the authors.

SOURCE: Calculated by authors from U.S. Census (1/1000 P.U.S. Tape, 1970
and 1980).

ANALYSIS OF RELATIVE EARNINGS OF WOMEN AND
MEN IN THREE COMPUTER-RELATED OCCUPATIONS

UNCORRECTED EARNINGS DIFFERENTIALS

To examine salary differences between women and men we
analyze three computer-related occupations where a sufficient
number of jobs (at least 20 percent) are held by the "minority gender"—computer scientists/systems analysts, computer programmers, and computer operators.[5] We find that even when
women are employed in the same occupations as men, they do not
receive the same pay.

We used two sources to calculate the gender differential in
pay—the published census reports, where the only available measure was the mean annual earnings, and the census P.U.S. samples, where we could calculate the median hourly earnings. With
each source, for the years available, we calculated the ratio of
the women's earnings to men's earnings for each of these three
occupations in all industries combined. As each source has both
advantages and disadvantages, we present data from both.

The advantage of using the published census reports is that
they are more accurate than the samples. The disadvantages are
that only the mean annual earnings are available for 1980, and the
mean is a poor estimate of average earnings since it is so influenced
by a few high values. In addition, since the median was used as
an estimate for most of the comparable occupations in 1970, the
2 years could not be compared, except in the combined category
of computer specialist. Another disadvantage is that the use of
annual earnings precludes controlling for part-time or part-year
workers.

The advantages of using the census samples are that we could
calculate the median—the most accurate estimate for average
earnings—for each occupation and year and could control for part-
time and part-year workers by calculating the hourly earnings.[6]

---

[5] Although production workers also qualified under the criterion, we did
not study them, because they are only "computer related" if they are in the
computer industry, and isolating that industry would have created too small
a sample. In addition, we wanted to compare computer-related occupations
across industries, and computer-related production workers by definition are
not included in other industries.

[6] Hourly earnings were calculated by dividing each person's yearly salary
(from the year prior to the census year) by the number of weeks worked (in

The disadvantage is that the estimates were subject to large standard errors.

Interestingly, the two sources of income data produced similar and consistent results. Table 7 contains the uncorrected gender differentials in pay, based on the published census data. In the first two columns are the numbers (in thousands) of total employees (men and women) in each occupation in 1970 and 1980. The second two columns show percentages of all employees who were women in each year. The next four columns show, for the years it was available, the mean annual earnings of men in that occupation and the ratio of women's mean annual earnings to men's earnings. This ratio is the gender differential in pay for each occupation, with no controls for education or experience.

For the combined computer specialist occupations, the uncorrected ratio of women's to men's mean annual earnings was 0.71 in 1970 and 0.72 in 1980. This constancy of the ratio is noteworthy, as employment more than doubled over the 10-year period and the proportion of women in these occupations increased by 40 percent.

In 1980, the uncorrected ratio of women's to men's mean annual earnings was available for the three occupations. For both computer scientists/systems analysts and computer programmers, the ratios were 0.73. For computer operators the ratio was 0.65. Since these were not corrected for part-time or part-year workers, we would expect the ratio estimates that did have these corrections to be somewhat higher, and they were.

Table 8 contains the gender differentials in pay based on the P.U.S. samples, corrected for part-time and part-year workers but not for education or experience. In the first two columns are the sample numbers of men and women employed in each occupation in 1970 and 1980. These numbers are the samples upon which the earnings estimates are based. The second four columns show, for each year, the median hourly earnings of men in the occupation and the ratio of women's median hourly earnings to men's earnings.

For the occupation computer scientist/systems analyst, the ratio of women's to men's median hourly earnings was 0.75 in 1970 and 0.74 in 1980. Again, such constancy is noteworthy since

---

the year prior to the census) and dividing that by the hours they worked in an average week. Because the data are based on the respondents' estimate of the average hours worked, the data are subject to possible errors.

TABLE 7 Employment and Annual Earnings for Men and Women in Three Computer-Related Occupations in All Industries, 1970 and 1980

Occupation	Total Number Employed (thousands)		Percent Women Employed		Mean Annual Earnings					
					Men's Earnings		F/M Earnings Ratio			
	1970	1980	1970	1980	1970	1980	1970	1980		
Computer specialists	254,537	513,863	20	28	$11,004	$20,090	0.71	0.72		
Computer scientists/ systems analysts	93,200	200,684	15	22	n.a.	23,405	n.a.	0.73		
Computer programmers	161,377	313,179	23	31	n.a.	17,967	n.a.	0.73		
Computer operators	117,222	408,475	29	59	n.a.	14,203	n.a.	0.65		

NOTE: See Appendix B for the definition of computer-related occupations.

SOURCE: 1970 data, Bureau of the Census (1972:Table 8); 1980 data, Bureau of the Census (1984:Table 1).

TABLE 8 Employment and Hourly Earnings for Men and Women in Three
Computer-Related Occupations in All Industries, 1970 and 1980

| Occupation | Total Number Employed (sample size) | | Median Hourly Earnings | | | |
| | | | Men's Earnings | | F/M Earnings Ratio | |
	1970	1980	1970	1980	1970	1980
Computer scientists/ systems analysts	105	199	$5.17	$10.19	0.75	0.74
Computer programmers	155	312	4.10	8.12	0.85	0.83
Computer operators	106	456	3.15	6.38	0.63	0.69

NOTE: See Appendix B for the definition of computer-related occupations. For
1980, computer operators included computer equipment operator supervisors.

SOURCE: Calculated by authors from U.S. Census (1/1000 P.U.S. Tape, 1970 and
1980).

employment more than doubled over the decade. It is also interesting that correcting for part-time and part-year workers does
not increase this differential to much above the estimate from the
published data for computer specialists.

Among programmers, there was still a gender differential after
correcting for part-time and part-year workers, although the gap
was smaller than that for computer scientists and systems analysts.
The ratio of women's to men's median hourly earnings was 0.85
in 1970 and 0.83 in 1980—again, remarkably constant given the
more than doubling of employment in the occupation.

For computer operators there was a rise in the differential with
the correction for part-time and part-year workers. In 1970, when
women had only 29 percent of the jobs, the female/male ratio of
median hourly earnings was 0.63. By 1980, the gender division
of labor had reversed and women dominated the occupation, with
59 percent of all the jobs. Still, the earnings ratio was 0.69, quite
close to what it had been 10 years earlier.

Although the sources are based on different measures and
samples, they both show that women earn substantially less than
men in these three occupations and that these ratios do not change
much over time. Clearly, earnings equity is not an automatic result
of the existence or the growth of these occupations.

Despite the fact that women earn less than men in computer programming and computer science/systems analysis, professional computer-related occupations are financially attractive for women. Relative to what professional women earn in other occupations requiring similar years of educational attainment, computer programming and systems analysts positions enable women to earn at the top of the female earnings hierarchy. Table 9 shows that for women in 1981, computer systems analysts was the second highest paying occupation and computer programming the seventeenth highest. In both of these occupations, women earned more on average than they did in secondary school teaching (Rytina, 1982), despite the fact that in 1980 the mean educational attainment was only 15.75 years for women systems analysts and only 14.88 years for women computer programmers. For women secondary school teachers, the mean educational attainment was 16.43 years in 1980 (according to P.U.S.).

EARNINGS REGRESSIONS

Earnings differentials between women and men in the same occupations are in part a result of differences between women's and men's human capital and productivity and in part a result of wage discrimination (lower payment to women even after human capital and productivity have been held constant). To what extent is wage discrimination against women present in the relatively new computer occupations? Does employment in a high-tech industry lessen wage discrimination within the computer occupations? In order to answer these questions, we ran OLS (ordinary least squares) regressions for the three computer-related occupations in 1970 and 1980 on the natural log of hourly earnings using the P.U.S. samples. The independent variables we used to proxy human capital and productivity were determined by the availability of data. The census 1/1000 P.U.S. reports age, years of education, and gender but not years of work experience, type of degree, or field of college major. We used AGE and AGE^2 as continuous variables. We divided years of education into six categories, reflecting the fact that number of years of education affects one's position in the labor market in a discontinuous fashion. The categories are: eight years or less; some high school; high school graduate; some college; college graduate; and more than a college

TABLE 9 Occupations with Highest Median Weekly Earnings for Women
Employed Full Time in Wage and Salary Work, 1981 Annual Averages

Occupational Title[a]	Female Earnings[b]
Operations and systems researchers and analysts	$422
Computer systems analysts	420
Lawyers	407
Physicians, dentists, and related practitioners	401
Social scientists	391
Teachers, college and university	389
Postal clerks	382
Engineers	371
Ticket, station and express agents	370
School administrators, elementary and secondary	363
Life and physical scientists	357
Health administrators	357
Public administration officials and administrators, not elsewhere classified	337
Vocational and educational counselors	336
Registered nurses	331
Personnel and labor relations workers	330
Computer programmers	329
Editors and reporters	324
Secondary schoolteachers	321
Librarians	318

[a]Occupations listed are those in which female employment was 50,000 or more in 1981.
[b]Excludes earnings from self-employment.

SOURCE: Rytina (1982), based on Current Population Survey data.

degree. The category "some college" was the reference group and was omitted from the regression.

These variables have some serious deficiencies as indicators of education and productivity. Although age is often used as a proxy for work experience, a component of human capital, age is less likely correlated with years in the labor force for women than it is for men, and is, therefore, a less than satisfactory proxy for experience. Level of education, although frequently used as a measure of human capital and productivity, says nothing about the quality or type of education. Because our controls for human capital and productivity are problematic, the gender variable is a poor measure of discrimination.[7] We use age and level of education as control variables only because we have no others; we have traded off poor human capital proxies for the relatively large samples of these three occupations which the Census provides.

In addition to human capital variables, the regressions have two dummy variables: GENDER (equal to one for women) and HTECHIND (equal to one for those employed in a high-tech industry). Race and ethnicity could not be included as variables because the number of minorities in the P.U.S. sample was too small. The combined effects of the human capital variables and the two dummy variables, GENDER and HTECHIND, on salary were tested in an additive model.[8]

For computer scientists/systems analysts in 1970, age, gender, education, and industry type explained 20 percent of the variance in the log of hourly earnings (see Table 10); however, only having a college degree and older age were significantly related to earnings. By 1980, only 10 percent of the variance was explained by these four factors. Age and a college degree still significantly *increased* earnings, but gender less significantly *decreased* earnings. Holding the other variables constant, having a B.A. or B.S. increased one's salary by 27 percent, while being a woman decreased it by 20 percent. The drop in explained variance suggests that by 1980 other unmeasured factors were beginning to affect salaries for this occupation. Being in a high-tech industry was not significantly related to earnings for computer scientists/systems analysts.

For computer programmers, we saw a more dramatic trend. In 1970, age, education, gender, and industry explained almost none of the variance. However, by 1980, 20 percent of the variance was explained by these factors, and all but industry type were significantly related to earnings. Age and having a B.A./B.S. or more than a B.A./B.S. significantly *increased* earnings, while gender, somewhat less significantly, *decreased* earnings. The changes in the effects of age and education may reflect the formalization

---

[7] See Strober and Reagan (1982) for a discussion of the problems of using regression techniques to measure discrimination.

[8] We also ran regressions with the education and high-tech variables interacted with gender, testing a multiplicative model. No interactions were significant in 1980, the few interaction terms that were significant in 1970 could have been so by chance, and most residuals in the additive model were acceptable. Thus, we followed the usual statistical practice of reporting the more parsimonious model (Chatterjee and Price, 1977:78–85).

TABLE 10 Earnings Regressions for Computer Scientists/Systems Analysts, Computer Programmers, and Computer Operators, 1970 and 1980

| Variable | Computer Scientists/Systems Analysts | | |
	Mean	(S.D.)	B
1970			
Ln. of hourly earnings	1.7	(0.44)	
Education: up to 8 years	0.01	(0.10)	0.53
Some high school	0.02	(0.14)	-0.23
High school	0.29	(0.45)	-0.05
BA or BS	0.23	(0.42)	0.26**
More than BA/BS	0.22	(0.42)	0.15
Age_2	34.69	(9.77)	0.07***
Age^2	1,297.66	(797.95)	-0.006**
Gender (= 1 if female)	0.14	(0.35)	-0.07
High-tech industry	0.29	(0.45)	0.13
Constant	0.02		
N	105.0		
Adjusted R^2	.20		
1980			
Ln. of hourly earnings	2.16	(0.63)	
Education: up to 8 years	0	(0)	
Some high school	0.01	(0.07)	0.21
High school	0.13	(0.33)	0.14
BA or BS	0.31	(0.46)	0.27**
More than BA/BS	0.27	(0.45)	0.15
Age_2	34.58	(8.39)	0.09**
Age^2	1,265.98	(637.18)	-0.001**
Gender (= 1 if female)	0.25	(0.43)	-0.20*
High-tech industry	0.44	(0.50)	0.06
Constant	0.10		
N	199.0		
Adjusted R^2	.10		

| Variable | Computer Programmers | | |
	Mean	(S.D.)	B
1970			
Ln. of hourly earnings	1.30	(0.79)	
Education: up to 8 years	0.0	(0)	
Some high school	0.02	(0.14)	0.29
High school	0.23	(0.42)	0.09
BA or BS	0.37	(0.49)	0.07
More than BA/BS	0.07	(0.26)	0.04
Age_2	29.65	(8.05)	0.04
Age^2	943.52	(568.57)	-0.0002
Gender (= 1 if female)	0.32	(0.47)	-0.16
High tech industry	0.36	(0.48)	0.05
Constant	0.50		
N	155.0		
Adjusted R^2	-.01		
1980			
Ln. of hourly earnings	2.01	(0.57)	
Education: up to 8 years	0.0	(0)	
Some high school	0.02	(0.15)	-0.16

TABLE 10 (continued)

Variable	Computer Programmers		
	Mean	(S.D.)	B
High school	0.17	(0.38)	-0.006
BA or BS	0.31	(0.46)	0.22***
More than BA/BS	0.15	(0.36)	0.24***
Age_2	32.28	(8.76)	0.10***
Age^2	1,118.15	(656.98)	-0.001***
Gender (= 1 if female)	0.29	(0.45)	-0.12*
High tech industry	0.32	(0.47)	0.04
Constant	-0.13		
N	312.0		
Adjusted R^2	.20		

Variable	Computer Operators		
	Mean	(S.D.)	B
1970			
Ln. of hourly earnings	1.16	(0.67)	
Education: up to 8 years	0.01	(0.10)	-0.14
Some high school	0.07	(0.25)	-0.12
High school	0.53	(0.50)	0.02
BA or BS	0.01	(0.10)	0.77
More than BA/BS	0.01	(0.10)	0.12
Age_2	28.80	(9.40)	0.04
Age^2	917.07	(675.91)	-0.0004
Gender (= 1 if female)	0.21	(0.41)	-0.70***
High-tech industry	0.25	(0.43)	-0.10
Constant	0.51		
N	106.0		
Adjusted R^2	.16		
1980			
Ln. of hourly earnings	1.70	(0.58)	
Education: up to 8 years	0.01	(0.10)	0.01
Some high school	0.04	(0.19)	-0.16
High school	0.48	(0.50)	-0.01
BA or BS	0.11	(0.31)	0.04
More than BA/BS	0.02	(0.15)	0.09
Age_2	32.08	(10.77)	0.06***
Age^2	1,145.03	(812.62)	-0.001***
Gender (= 1 if female)	0.53	(0.50)	-0.27***
High-tech industry	0.20	(0.40)	0.18***
Constant	0.59		
N	456.0		
Adjusted R^2	.20		

* $p < .10$.
** $p < .05$.
*** $p < .01$.

NOTE: See Appendix B for the definition of computer-related occupations. For 1980, computer operators included computer equipment operator supervisors.

SOURCE: Calculated by authors from U.S. Census (1/1000 P.U.S. Tapes, samples for 1970 and 1980).

of qualifications for this occupation; whereas earlier, people with diverse education and experience were recruited and trained into it, by 1980 there were more formalized career ladders and more institutional training in the field. The beginning of an effect based on gender suggests that some differences based on gender may also have been in the process of becoming institutionalized. For programmers, being in a high-tech industry did not appear to affect salaries when other variables were held constant. It may be that for both computer programmers and computer scientists/systems analysts, it is employment in the computer industry specifically, rather than in high-tech industries in general, that has a positive effect on salary.

Computer operators show a different pattern. For both 1970 and 1980, 16–20 percent of the variance was explained by age, education, gender, and industry. Being a woman decreased one's salary significantly in both years. In 1970, gender was the only significant variable in the regression; being female, all other variables held constant resulted in a 50 percent decrease in salary.[9] By 1980, higher age and working in a high-tech industry also contributed significantly to higher earnings, but education was still not significant. In 1980, the effect of gender on salary, while still highly significant, was much smaller (27 percent) than it had been in 1970. These results reflect that this occupation has few educational requirements, that training takes place largely on the job, and that jobs in high-tech industries pay more. However, it also points out that women with the same education and age are still paid less than men, and that this was true both when the occupation was predominantly male (in 1970) and when it was predominantly female (in 1980).

---

[9] When the log of earnings is the dependent variable, the coefficient (b) on an independent variable is *approximately* the percentage effect of a unit change in that variable on the dependent variable. That approximation is worse the larger the absolute size of b. The *exact* effect is e^{b-1}. The only coefficient on gender that was large enough for the exact effect to be appreciably different from the approximate effect was for computer operators in 1970: $e^{-.70-1} = -.50$.

A Closer Look at Earnings and
Employment Differences by Industry

How does the labor market operate to pay men and women differentially even when they are in the same occupation and are similar with respect to age and level of education? In her book on clerical employment, Blau (1977) reports that often women and men in the same occupation in the same city earn different salaries because they work for different firms—women for low-wage firms and men for high-wage firms. It may be that, analogously, women and men in computer occupations earn different salaries in part because they work in different industries—men in high-paying industries and women in lower-paying "end-user" industries.

These differences may not have shown up in the reported regressions because the industry dummy variable divided industries into only two groups, high tech and non-high tech. Unfortunately, the P.U.S. sample sizes in each industry are too small to include major industry groups as variables in the reported regressions. However, Table 11, based on the census publication, *Occupation by Industry*, shows that within these three computer-related occupations in 1980, women and men are not employed in equal proportions across major industry groups.

In the first column of Table 11, we find the estimated number of total employees (men and women) in each occupation by industry. The second column contains the percentage of women in the occupation for each industry. The third column shows the men's mean annual earnings in the occupation by industry. In the fourth column we have calculated the ratio of the women's mean annual earnings to men's mean annual earnings for each industry. The first row of each occupation contains these data for all industries combined. The second row isolates these data for part of the computer industry, based on the census three-digit industry category, "Electronic Computing Equipment Manufacturing." The remaining rows show the data in the major two-digit industry groups. Several industry groups (agriculture, forestry, and fishing; mining; construction; personal services; and entertainment and recreation) have been removed from the analysis altogether, because they employ so few persons in computer-related occupations.

As shown in Table 11, women are 22.3 percent of computer scientists/systems analysts in all industries, but only 14.9 percent

of computer scientists in electronic computing equipment manufacturing. Among the major industry groups listed in Table 11,
the percentage of women employed ranges from 16.9 percent in
mining to 35.6 percent in finance, insurance, and real estate. For
all industries, the men's mean annual earnings for computer scien-
tists/systems analysts is $23,405; earnings figures are not available
for electronic computing equipment manufacturing. Among major industry groups, men's mean annual earnings range from a
low of $20,296 in professional and related sciences to a high of
$26,031 in mining. Note that in mining, where the percent women
employed is lowest, men's earnings are highest; conversely, where
the percent women employed is highest (in finance, insurance, and
real estate) men's earnings are the second lowest.

To examine the relationship between the percent women and
men's mean annual earnings across major industry groups we
computed a rank correlation coefficient. For computer scien-
tists/systems analysts the rank correlation coefficient is −.95,
significant at the 99 percent confidence level. However, because
the sample sizes are relatively small, we also computed the rank
correlation coefficient, taking into account the standard errors
of the percentages and means.[10] The corrected rank correlation
coefficient is −.68, not significant at the 95 percent confidence
level.

The ratio of female/male (F/M) earnings for computer sci-
entist/systems analyst is 0.73 for all industries and ranges from
0.69 in manufacturing to 0.82 in transportation, communications,
and public utilities. The data do not suggest a relationship across
industries between F/M earnings and percent women or between
F/M and men's mean annual earnings, mainly because of the lack
of wide variation in the F/M earnings ratio.

---

[10] The standard errors for the percentages were calculated from Table B or
the formula below the table in Appendix C in *Occupation by Industry* (Bureau
of the Census, 1972, 1984). This was multiplied by 1.2, the appropriate
design effect factor for a cross-tabulation of industries and occupations, as
shown in Table C of Appendix C. A 95 percent confidence interval was
created by calculating two standard errors on either side of the estimate. The
standard errors for means were calculated using the formula in Appendix
C, page C-2, for standard errors of means. The variances needed in that
formula were not provided by the Census, so a conservative guess was used
of a standard deviation equal to 5,000 for all salary distributions. This
was squared to produce the estimated variance. A 95 percent confidence
interval was created by calculating two standard errors on either side of the
estimate.

TABLE 11 Employment and Earnings in Three Computer-Related Occupations for All
Industries, Electronic Computing Equipment Manufacturing, and in Selected Major
Industry Groups, 1980

Occupation	Total Employment	Percent Women	Men's Mean Annual Earnings	F/M Earnings Ratio
Computer Scientists/ Systems Analysts				
All industries	200,684	22.3	$23,405	0.73
Electronic computing equipment manufacturing	22,129	14.9	n.a.	n.a.
Mining	2,159	16.9	26,031	0.77
Construction	1,500	22.3	22,661	0.70
Manufacturing	65,606	17.5	24,093	0.69
Transportation, communications, and public utilities	12,947	26.8	23,812	0.82
Wholesale trade	8,953	21.4	22,840	0.80
Retail trade	5,336	26.5	22,195	0.71
Finance, insurance, and real estate	18,051	35.6	21,381	0.78
Business services	46,384	19.9	23,288	0.74
Professional and related services	15,241	28.4	20,296	0.68
Public administration	23,415	24.4	24,991	0.75
Computer Programmers				
All industries	313,179	31.1	$17,967	0.73
Electronic computing equipment manufacturing	22,702	22.0	n.a.	n.a.
Mining	3,171	32.5	19,455	0.76
Construction	2,802	34.8	17,275	0.69
Manufacturing	93,010	26.5	19,037	0.75
Transportation, communications, and public utilities	22,537	34.9	19,704	0.78
Wholesale trade	11,477	32.1	18,064	0.67
Retail trade	10,052	33.6	16,400	0.73
Finance, insurance, and real estate	39,749	36.6	16,774	0.77
Business services	63,423	28.0	17,826	0.72
Professional and related services	35,352	34.3	12,353	0.83
Public administration	29,635	35.9	18,868	0.74
Computer Operators				
All industries	408,475	59.0	$14,203	0.65
Electronic computing equipment manufacturing	7,175	46.6	n.a.	n.a.

TABLE 11 (continued)

Occupation	Total Employment	Percent Women	Men's Mean Annual Earnings	Earnings Ratio
Mining	4,647	42.9	16,041	0.63
Construction	5,758	68.8	14,833	0.67
Manufacturing	98,886	55.3	16,079	0.63
Transportation, communications, and public utilities	35,852	56.7	17,067	0.69
Wholesale trade	30,876	73.2	14,213	0.64
Retail trade	26,140	67.4	13,026	0.62
Finance, insurance, and real estate	63,660	57.3	12,878	0.66
Business services	43,697	45.8	13,010	0.65
Professional and related services	54,466	67.2	10,024	0.80
Public administration	39,185	59.3	15,237	0.65

NOTE: Computer-related occupations are defined in Appendix B. The Electronic-Computing Equipment Manufacturing Industry is defined as Census Industry Code 322 in 1980.

SOURCE: Bureau of the Census (1984:Tables 1 and 2).

Among computer programmers, women are 31.1 percent of employees in all industries but only 22.0 percent in electronic computing equipment manufacturing. As in the case of computer scientists/systems analysts, women are more likely to be employed in end-user industries. Across major industry groups, the percent women employed ranges from 26.5 in manufacturing (which includes the manufacturing of electronic computing equipment) to 36.6 percent in finance, insurance, and real estate. Men's mean annual earnings are $17,967 for all industries; among major industry groups, they range from a low of $12,353 in professional and related services to a high of $19,704 in transportation, communications, and public utilities. However, unlike the situation for computer scientists/systems analysts, neither the uncorrected nor the corrected (for standard error) rank correlation coefficient shows a significant relationship between percent women's and men's mean annual earnings.

The ratio of F/M earnings for programmers does not vary across major industry groups. The ratio for all industries is 0.73;

for all but one major industry group, the F/M earnings ratio is within a few percentage points of the mean. However, in professional and related services the ratio is 0.83. It is interesting that in this industry men's earnings are the lowest for all of the industries listed.

Among computer operators, women are 59.0 percent of those employed in all industries, but only 46.6 percent of those employed in the manufacture of electronic computing equipment. As in the case of computer scientists/systems analysts and computer programmers, women computer operators are more likely to be employed in end-user industries than in the computer manufacturing industry. Among major industry groups, the percentage of women employed ranged from a low of 42.9 percent in mining to a high of 73.2 in wholesale trade.

Men's mean annual earnings were $14,203 for all industries and ranged from a low of $10,024 in professional and related services to a high of $17,067 in transportation, communications, and public utilities. There is no systematic relationship between men's mean annual earnings and percentage of women in the industry.

The ratio of F/M earnings for computer operators was 0.65 for all industries. As in the case of the other two occupations discussed, the F/M earnings ratio did not vary much across industries. The only "outlier" was in the professional and related services industry where the ratio was 0.80. And, as in the case of computer programmers, this industry had both the highest F/M earnings ratio and the lowest men's mean annual earnings.

Our data suggest that in computer occupations, women are more likely to be found in end-user industries than in the computer manufacturing industry itself. In some occupations, particularly computer scientists/systems analysts, women also may more likely be found in industries where men are lower paid.[11] However, it is not possible at this point to test this hypothesis definitively. If we were to disaggregate industry groups further, the sample sizes would become even smaller and the standard errors would rise accordingly.

---

[11] Kraft and Dubnoff found similar results in a 1982 survey of "software specialists" in Boston. They found women concentrated in the "worst paying industries" (Kraft and Dubnoff, 1983).

CONCLUSIONS

FINDINGS

1. Although computer-related occupations are of recent origin, they are not gender-neutral. The computer field was sired by the fields of mathematics and engineering, and the newly born prestigious and technical jobs quickly took on the gender designation of the parent fields. Computer engineering and electronic technical work employ very few women. On the other hand, data entry, which quickly took on the characteristics of clerical work, became a virtually exclusive female preserve. Production work, too, is preponderantly female (see Table 1).

Computer programmers were female when the occupation first emerged, but very shortly after the computer was introduced, men began to fill the emerging jobs. Although women have increased their representation in the jobs of both programmer and analyst, women remain less than a third of the incumbents of these occupations. While the occupation of computer operator did not seem immediately to be gender typed, in that it was preponderantly female in 1960 and male in 1970, it was becoming preponderantly female again by 1980.

2. When the difference between the percentage of women in the total labor force and the percentage of women in each computer-related occupation is used as a measure of occupational segregation, the level of segregation was approximately the same in 1970 and 1980, except for computer operators (see Table 2).

3. Among four computer-related occupations found in all industries—computer scientists/systems analysts, computer programmers, computer operators, and data-entry operators—the higher the status and pay of the occupation, the more white men were overrepresented, compared with their representation in the labor force as a whole, and the more minority men and women of all racial and ethnic groups were underrepresented. In occupations with much lower pay and status, the presence of white men dropped to much below their percentage in the labor force, the percentage of women of all racial and ethnic groups became much higher than their percentage of the labor force, and the percentage of minority men approached their labor force representation (see Table 4).

4. Within high-tech industries, most men were in production, professional/technical, or managerial occupations, while most women were in production or clerical occupations. Women and men were equally likely to be in production occupations. However, men were more likely to be in managerial and professional/technical occupations in high-tech industries than in non-high-tech industries; women fared worse in these occupations in high-tech industries than in other industries (see Table 6).

5. Within the occupations of computer scientists/systems analysts, computer programmers, and computer operators, women's mean annual earnings and women's median hourly earnings were less than those of men. In addition, the ratios of women's to men's earnings generally remained constant between 1970 and 1980 (see Tables 7 and 8).

6. Within the three occupations analyzed, women's hourly earnings were generally less than those of men, even after age, level of education, and high-tech versus non-high-tech industry were held constant (see Table 10).

7. Women employed as systems analysts, programmers, and computer operators were more likely to be found in end-user industries than in the computer manufacturing industry itself. Within the three computer-related occupations, women were paid less than men no matter in what industry they were employed (see Table 11). We found some evidence that in several occupations, particularly computer scientists/systems analysts, women may be more likely to be found in industries where men are lower paid. However, this hypothesis has not been tested definitively here and requires further investigation.

These findings dispel the myth that high tech is automatically a great equalizer. High tech may produce integrated circuits, but it does not necessarily produce an integrated work force or eliminate the female/male earnings differential.

DISCUSSION

Although a detailed explanation of the implications of these findings is beyond the scope of this paper, it is likely that the explanations can be found in the discussions of gender segregation and earnings differentials commonly found in the literature (see Blau and Jusenius, 1976; Cain, 1976; Amsden, 1980; Sokoloff,

1980; Strober, 1984; Reskin, 1984; and Reskin and Hartmann, 1986). These theories focus on women's own behavior, on employer discrimination, and on the interactions of labor markets and gender relations in society. However, to devise the various types of policies that are required to change existing patterns of gender segregation and earnings differentials for the computer industry and computer-related occupations reported here, more research on the dynamics of each aspect of gender segregation is needed. More detailed research on the differences in women's employment between and within industries and between and within firms would identify the bottlenecks preventing the gender integration of occupations. Attention needs to be given to the processes by which women are allocated and/or allocate themselves into the lower-paid occupations and industries. This involves investigating how employers structure and define occupations and career ladders and distribute skilled job applicants and workers in ways that result in gender-segregated occupations and industries. Research also needs to be done on the degree to which technologically trained women (and some men) self-select out of certain occupations or industries because a certain definition or culture for the occupation or industry precludes respect for the participation of people with different work styles or cultures.

Some explanations have been advanced for women's low representation among the specialized computer-related occupations. For example, DeBoer (1984) argues that women are still more likely than men to exclude themselves from advanced math and science training: even when women in high school and college science perform at a higher level than their male classmates, they have a higher drop-out rate. He proposes that teachers in secondary and postsecondary education make special efforts to acknowledge the skills of talented women.

Hacker's work (1981), however, suggests that merely encouraging women may not be sufficient to change their educational decisions, since women's decisions to exclude themselves from technical fields may be related in part to a dislike of the fields' "culture." Hacker, based on research at a technical institute, argues that there is a "culture of engineering" that includes an extension of the profession's formal objectification and control of the natural world to an informal objectification of women.

It may be that a distaste for being part of the "engineering culture" also leads technically trained women to exclude themselves from certain sectors of the computer industry. If an engineering culture appears most strongly in those sectors and industries of the computer field that are at the technological forefront and most competitive technologically, then it may be that those sectors and industries are the least appealing to women. However, it may not be accidental that these sectors have the strongest engineering culture. In terms of Strober's theory (1984), men who work in these intellectually challenging and highly lucrative sectors may acquire the habits of the "engineering culture" in part precisely to keep women out.

The work style and work pressures in the most technologically competitive sectors of the computer industry may also keep many women out. While firms in all industries must remain competitive with similar firms, the computer industry, a new industry with a steady stream of technological breakthroughs, has some unique pressures: to make and increase profits in a competitive nonoligopolistic environment, stay on the technological forefront, and stay ahead of not only young and old domestic companies but their Japanese counterparts as well. These financial and technological pressures are intensified as each firm tries to survive and succeed before the industry "shakes down." There is much pressure on workers in the computer industry to maintain high levels of productivity, including overtime work and other forms of commitment to the success of the firm. Women who want to succeed have to put in long, hard hours of work, and this may be a barrier for women (and men) who are trying to balance their home and work lives.

We have presented evidence of gender segregation of the high-tech industries and highly technical computer occupations. At the same time we have called for research-assisted strategies to end these observed patterns of occupational inequity. While we encourage women to enter these computer-related fields, we need to disseminate the findings of studies such as this one. This will make women aware of the channeling that leads them into less-prestigious, lower-paying occupations or "end-user" industries within high-tech fields and help them develop strategies to counteract this channeling. At the same time this research can be used to assist in developing policies to make occupations and workplaces more welcoming to both genders and more compatible with satisfying personal and family lives.

REFERENCES

ABAG (Association of Bay Area Governments)
  1981   Silicon Valley and beyond: high technology growth for the San Francisco Bay Area. *Working Papers on the Region's Economy,* 2. Berkeley, Calif.
Amsden, Alice H.
  1980   Introduction. Pp. 11–38 in Alice H. Amsden, ed., *The Economics of Women and Work.* New York: St. Martin's Press.
Bielby, William T., and James N. Baron
  1984   A woman's place is with other women: sex segregation within organizations. Pp. 27–55 in *Sex Segregation in the Workplace: Trends, Explanations and Remedies.* Committee on Women's Employment and Related Social Issues. Commission on Behavioral and Social Sciences and Education, National Research Council. Washington, D.C.: National Academy Press.
Blau, Francine D.
  1977   *Equal Pay in the Office.* Lexington, Mass.: D.C. Heath.
Blau, Francine D., and Wallace E. Hendricks
  1979   Occupational segregation by sex: trends and prospects. *The Journal of Human Resources* 14:197–210.
Blau, Francine D., and Carol Jusenius
  1976   Economists' approaches to sex segregation in the labor market: an appraisal. Pp. 181–199 in Martha Blaxall and Barbara B. Reagan, eds., *Women and the Workplace: The Implications of Occupational Segregation.* Chicago: University of Chicago Press.
Braverman, Harry
  1974   *Labor and Monopoly Capital.* New York: Monthly Review Press.
Bureau of the Census
  1971   *Census of Population: 1970. Alphabetical Index of Industries and Occupations.* U.S. Goverment Printing Office. Washington, D.C.: U.S. Department of Commerce.
  1972   *Census of Population: 1970. Occupation by Industry.* Final Report PC(2)-76. U.S. Government Printing Office. Washington, D.C.: U.S. Department of Commerce.
  1982   *Census of Population: 1980. Classified Index of Industries and Occupations,* Final edition. U.S. Government Printing Office. Washington, D.C.: U.S. Department of Commerce.
  1983   *Data User News* 18(June):8–9.
  1984   *Census of Population and Housing: 1980. Subject Report, Occupation by Industry.* PC80-2-7c. U.S. Government Printing Office. Washington, D.C.: U.S. Department of Commerce.
Cain, Glen G.
  1976   The challenge of segmented labor market theories to orthodox theory: a survey. *Journal of Economic Literature* 14(December):1215–1257.
Chatterjee, Samprit, and Bertram Price
  1977   *Regression by Example.* New York: Wiley and Sons,
DeBoer, George E.
  1984   *Factors Affecting the Science Participation and Performance of Women*

in High School and College. Hamilton, N.Y.: Colgate University, Department of Education.

Dicesare, Constance Bogh
1975   Changes in the occupational structure of U.S. jobs. *Monthly Labor Review* 98(March):24–34.

Greenbaum, Joan M.
1979   *In the Name of Efficiency: Management Theory and Shopfloor Practice in Data Processing Work.* Philadelphia: Temple University Press.

Gross, Edward.
1968   Plus ça change...? The sexual structure of occupations over time. *Social Problems* 16:198–208.

Grossman, Rachael
1980   Women's place in the integrated circuit. *Radical America* 14(January/February):29–49.

Hacker, Sally L.
1981   The culture of engineering: woman, workplace, and machine. *Women's Studies International Quarterly* 4(3):341–353.

Kraft, Philip
1977   *Programmers and Managers.* New York: Springer-Verlag.
1979   The industrialization of computer programming: from programming to software production. Pp. 1–17 in Andrew Zimbalist, ed., *Case Studies in the Labor Process.* New York: Monthly Review Press.

Kraft, Philip, and Steven Dubnoff
1983   Software workers survey. *Computer World* XVII(November 14):3–13.

Lloyd, Cynthia B., and Beth T. Neimi
1979   *The Economics of Sex Differentials.* New York: Columbia University Press.

O'Neill, June
1983   The Determinants and Wage Effects of Occupational Segregation. Project Report. Washington, D.C.: The Urban Institute.

Reskin, Barbara F., ed.
1984   *Sex Segregation in the Workplace: Trends, Explanations, Remedies.* Committee on Women's Employment and Related Social Issues. Commission on Behavioral and Social Sciences and Education, National Research Council. Washington, D.C.: National Academy Press.

Reskin, Barbara F., and Heidi I. Hartmann, eds.
1986   *Women's Work, Men's Work: Sex Segregation on the Job.* Committee on Women's Employment and Related Social Issues. Commission on Behavioral and Social Sciences and Education, National Research Council. Washington, D.C.: National Academy Press.

Riche, Richard W., Daniel E. Heckers, and John U. Burgan
1983   High technology today and tomorrow: a small slice of the employment pie. *Monthly Labor Review* 106(November):50–59.

Rogers, Everett M., and Judith K. Larsen
1984   *Silicon Valley Fever.* New York: Basic Books.

Rytina, Nancy F.
1982   Earnings of men and women: a look at specific occupations. *Monthly Labor Review* 105(April):25–31.

Sokoloff, Natalie J.
　1980　*Between Money and Love: The Dialectics of Women's Home and Market Work.* New York: Praeger.
Strober, Myra H.
　1984　Toward a general theory of occupational sex segregation: the case of public school teaching. Pp. 144–156 in Barbara F. Reskin, ed., *Sex Segregation in the Workplace: Trends, Explorations, Remedies.* Washington, D.C.: National Academy Press.
Strober, Myra H., and Barbara B. Reagan
　1982　Sense and nonsense in measuring employment discrimination in higher education. Unpublished paper.
Treiman, Donald J., and Heidi I. Hartmann, eds.
　1981　*Women, Work, and Wages: Equal Pay for Jobs of Equal Value.* Washington, D.C.: National Academy Press.
U.S. Department of Commerce, Office of Federal Statistical Policy and Standards
　1980　*Standard Occupational Classification Manual.*

APPENDIX A: INDUSTRIES WITHIN MAJOR INDUSTRY GROUPS, BY HIGH-TECH AND NON-HIGH-TECH CATEGORIES

Industrial categories that comprise the high-tech sector definition used here are based on those designated Group III in Riche et al., 1983. This is a moderately inclusive definition containing 27 three-digit SIC industries and 1 four-digit SIC industry. Census Industry Codes which most closely matched these SIC codes were used to designate high-tech industries in the 1970 and 1980 Census Public Use Sample tapes. The Census Codes each include from one to several SIC industries, and some Riche-designated high-tech SIC industries are grouped with non-high-tech SIC industries, so it is not possible to perfectly match the Riche Group III list using census data. Below are listed the census industrial categories that were designated for this study as high tech and non-high tech. For the high-tech industries, 1970 and 1980 Census Industrial Codes are shown in parentheses, with the 1970 code first followed by the 1980 code (Bureau of the Census, 1971, 1982).

HIGH-TECHNOLOGY INDUSTRY GROUPS (HIGH TECH)

Durable Manufacturing

Ordnance (258;248); engines and turbines (177;310); office and accounting machines (188;321); electronic computing equipment

(189;322); radio, television, and communication equipment (207; 341); electrical machinery, equipment, and supplies, n.e.c. (208; 342); aircraft and parts (227;352); scientific and controlling instruments (239;371); optical and health services supplies (247;372); photographic equipment and supplies (248;380).

NONDURABLE MANUFACTURING

Industrial and miscellaneous chemicals (281 and 368;192); plastics, synthetics, and resins (348 and 349;180); drugs and medicines (357;181); soaps and cosmetics (358;182); paints, varnishes, and related products (359;190); agricultural chemicals (367;191); not specified chemicals and allied products (1970;369); petroleum refining (377;200); miscellaneous petroleum and coal products (1970;378).

BUSINESS AND REPAIR SERVICES

Commercial research, development, and testing labs (729;730); computer programming or computer and data-processing services (739;740).

NON-HIGH-TECHNOLOGY INDUSTRY GROUPS (NON-HIGH-TECH)

DURABLE MANUFACTURING

Lumber, furniture, stone, clay, and glass products, other metal industries, cutlery, handtools, hardware, other machinery, household appliances, transportation equipment, clocks, toys, sporting goods.

NONDURABLE MANUFACTURING

Food, tobacco, textile, apparel, paper, printing, rubber, leather products.

BUSINESS AND REPAIR SERVICES

Advertising, buildings services, personnel supply, business management and consulting, detective and protective services, business services, automotive services and repair, electrical repair, miscellaneous repair.

AGRICULTURE, FORESTRY, AND FISHERIES

Agricultural production, crops; agricultural production, livestock; agricultural services; horticultural services; forestry; fisheries; fishing, hunting, and trapping.

MINING

Metal mining; coal mining; crude petroleum and natural gas extractions; nonmetallic mining and quarrying, except fuel.

CONSTRUCTION

General building contractors; general contractors, except building; special trade contractors; nonspecified construction.

TRANSPORTATION, COMMUNICATION, AND PUBLIC UTILITIES

Rail, bus, taxi, truck services, warehouses, U.S. Postal Service, water and air transportation, pipelines, miscellaneous transportation services, radio, television, telephone, telegraph, electricity, gas, steam, water supplies, and sanitary services.

WHOLESALE TRADE

All wholesale trade of durable and nondurable goods, including sale of high-tech products.

RETAIL TRADE

All retail outlets for durable and nondurable goods, including sale of high-tech products.

Finance, Insurance, and Real Estate

Banking, savings and loans, credit agencies, securities and investment, insurance, real estate and real estate insurance and law offices.

Professional and Other Services

Offices of doctors, dentists, chiropractors, optometrists, and other health practitioners and services; hospitals, nursing, and personal care services; legal services; elementary and secondary schools; colleges and universities; business, trade, and vocational schools; libraries; educational services; job training and vocational rehabilitation; child care services; residential care; social services; museums; art galleries; zoos; religious and membership organizations; engineering, architectural, and surveying services; accounting, auditing, and bookkeeping services; and noncommercial educational and scientific research.

Public Administration

Offices of chief executive and legislative bodies and their advisory and interdepartmental committees and commissions; government civil rights and civil service commissions; offices providing support services for government such as accounting, personnel, purchasing and supply; courts; police protection; correctional institutions; fire protection; government legal counsel; public finance; tax and monetary policy; administration of educational programs; public health, social, manpower, and income maintenance programs; veterans' affairs; environmental protection; housing and urban development programs; regulatory agencies; national security; and international agencies.

APPENDIX B: COMPUTER-RELATED OCCUPATIONS

We define computer-related occupations using the following detailed occupation categories and codes from the 1970 and 1980 U.S. censuses:

Census Occupation Categories	Census Occupation Codes	
	1970	*1980*
Engineers	006-023	044-059
Electrical/electronic engineer	012	055
Computer specialists	003-005	064,229
Computer scientist/systems		
analyst	004-005	064
Computer programmers	003	229
Engineers and science technicians	150-162	213-217,
Electrical/electronic		223-225
engineering technicians	153	213
Drafters	152	217
Computer operators		
(includes computer and peripheral		
equipment operators)	343	308,309
Data-entry operators	345	385
Production workers[a]		
(includes crafts, precision		
production, operatives,		
transportation, laborers,		
and farm occupations)	401-824	473-889
Electronic assemblers		
(a category in 1980 only)		
within precision production	–	683
Data-processing repairers		
Within precision production	475	525

Operatives, fabricators, transportation, and laborers[a] Within production (excludes farm, crafts, and precision production. Not precisely the same occupations in each year.)	601-785	703-889
Assemblers Within operatives	602	785

---

[a] There were changes in occupational coding and categorizing between the 1970 and 1980 Censuses (Bureau of the Census, 1983), which affected the occupations included in large occupational categories such as "Production Workers" and "Operatives, Fabricators, Transportation, and Laborers." The category of "Production Workers" as defined here is so large that the occupations included are identical except for three which are included in 1970 and not in 1980: decorators and window dressers (1970 code 425); inspectors, n.e.c. (1970 code 452); and conductors and motormen, urban rail transit (1970 code 704). Since few of these workers would be in the computer industry, we do not feel that this affects the results. However, the category of "Operatives, Fabricators, Transportation, and Laborers" does differ significantly between the years, and therefore the data presented for 1970 and 1980 are not strictly comparable.

Part III

Technology and Trends in Women's Employment

Women's Employment and Technological Change: A Historical Perspective

CLAUDIA GOLDIN

The impact of technological change on female employment is an issue in two parts: that relating to all workers and that just to women. Technological change, in concert with the demand for output, is the driving force for all employment in the long run, and determines total employment, the share of employment in each sector of the economy, and the share of output received by labor. Female workers, however, have characteristics that distinguish them from their male counterparts and that cause them to be differentially affected by technological change.

Among the distinctive characteristics of the female labor force are the lower participation rates of women as compared with those of men. Because of this difference the supply of women to the labor market is more responsive to changes in earnings and occupational opportunities. Related to this point is that women, on average, have less labor market experience than men, and their lower degree of seniority might make them more vulnerable to rapid technological change. It is also the case, however, that women have less training specific to a particular technology and might be less at risk of losing income from changes in the production process. For various reasons women work in certain sectors and occupations more than in others. To the extent that certain sectors, industries, or occupations are "female intensive," technical changes that increase employment in these areas relative to others will have positive employment effects for women.

The precise employment impact of technological change, either on an individual sector or on the national economy, is a rather complicated affair. There are no a priori reasons to believe that technological change will reduce employment in any particular sector; its precise role is empirical in nature and is explored below. In addition, long-run and short-run effects may differ. In the long run, technological change alters the relative size of different sectors and the female intensity of the labor force in these sectors. We can assume, in the long run, that the economy adjusts to the various shocks imposed on it by technological change, returning eventually to the natural rate of unemployment. But over the short run there are displacement effects, involving retraining and geographical mobility. Because the focus here is on historical changes over an extensive period of time, only the long-run effects are considered in detail.

The conclusions of this research are many. Over the long run, technological advances, proxied by a measure called total factor productivity, have been positively associated with the female intensity of a sector; that is, female-intensive sectors have had greater advances in technology. But sectors having the greatest advances in technology did not necessarily experience the largest expansion in employment. Technological changes associated with a greater division of labor, both in the early part of the nineteenth century in manufacturing and in clerical work a half century later, fostered the employment of relatively unskilled workers, especially women. Technological changes embodied in individuals, particularly advances in education, have provided the greatest impetus to the employment of women in the more recent period, most often in sectors undergoing general technological change.

Without knowing the precise reasons for the expansion and evolution of the female labor force in general over the last two centuries it is difficult to ascribe a portion of it to technological change. But it is clear that advances in manufacturing in the nineteenth century increased the relative productivity of females to males (and children to adults) by substituting machinery and inanimate power for human strength. Such technological change frequently led to the substitution of capital and unskilled labor for skilled (artisanal) labor, a factor substitution that is rather different from that observed later in the twentieth century.

It is equally difficult to ascribe a portion of the changes in the sectoral distribution of labor in general over the last two centuries to technological change biased in favor of particular sectors. But it is clear that the relative decline in agriculture throughout the period and the rise of the tertiary (service) sector in the first decades of this century were instrumental in changing employment opportunities for women. Not all women's employment changed in the same direction in response to these movements. Black women, who have always been disproportionately employed in agriculture and domestic service, experienced decreases in employment with sectoral shifts that occurred early in this century, but these declines did not necessarily entail decreased well-being. In the most recent period, black women's employment, along with employment of white women, has been greatly affected by educational advances.

This paper explores various aspects of technological change and women's employment in the United States from 1800 to the present. I begin with a discussion of conceptual issues regarding technological change and then consider the evidence on female employment over the last two centuries. Four aspects of the topic are then detailed: (1) the correlation over time and in cross-section between technological change and the proportion of a sector or an industry's labor force that is female; (2) the role of educational change in altering the employment of women; (3) changes in the organization of work; and (4) the relative wages of females to males, a ratio measuring what is commonly termed the "gender gap." The focus is entirely on changes in technology outside the home, thus omitting changes in household production and contraceptive technology.

One way of integrating the topics in this paper is to partition changes in the proportion of the total labor force that is composed of women, F/L, into that portion due to changes within sectors and that part due to the changing distribution of the labor force across sectors. Thus,

$$d(F/L) = \Sigma_i[d(F_i/L_i)](L_i/L) + \Sigma_i(F_i/L_i)d(L_i/L), \tag{1}$$

where F = the female labor force ($F = \Sigma F_i$), L = the total labor force ($L = \Sigma L_i$), and i denotes sector or industry i. The change in the proportion of the labor force that is female is divided into two sources, and each can be studied in terms of the impact technological change has on it. The first is the impact of technological change on changes in the female intensity of a sector or an industry (F_i/L_i) times the relative importance of that sector or industry in total employment. The second is the impact of technological change on sectoral shares (L_i/L) times the female intensity of that sector or industry. Each of these sources is discussed below.[1]

TECHNOLOGICAL CHANGE AND EMPLOYMENT: A THEORETICAL FRAMEWORK

To clarify the economist's conceptualization of technological change (see Mansfield, 1969; Rosenberg, 1972; Stoneman, 1983), let me offer this brief description. Technology is knowledge, and technological change is an increase in knowledge measured as an increase in output for a given quantity of inputs or, equivalently, a decrease in inputs required to produce a given amount of output. Technological change is identified with technological advance; all agents, in firms, sectors, and the economy as a whole, can reject any technological change that decreases outputs or increases the costs of production. One generally thinks of technological change as altering the demand for a particular factor, such as labor; it can also alter the set of prices and wages in the economy. The employment effects of technological change are complicated by the impacts such price changes have on the demands for input and output. Even a labor-saving technological change can result in an increase in the demand for labor if the quantity of output demanded increases sufficiently because of a lower price or a higher quality of output. Further, a technological change that is neutral in its effects on the various inputs can alter the economy's demand for labor if it tends to increase demand for outputs produced by relatively less labor-intensive sectors (or less intensive in the use of a particular type of labor—women, blacks, skilled, unskilled).

Production occurs when one combines particular inputs in some manner. Denoting the output as Q and the inputs as K

---

[1] One can add another source, the increase in the female labor force participation rate, by scaling each source. One can scale, for example, the female intensity of each sector by expressing it as an index in relationship to the female intensity of the economy as a whole. This index is used in the empirical work below.

(capital) and L (labor), Q = f(K,L) is a production function. The theoretical framework economists use to study technological change can be condensed by considering a particular production function known as Cobb-Douglas. This production function is a geometrically weighted average of the inputs multiplied by a constant term, T:

$$Q = TK^{\alpha}L^{(1-\alpha)}. \tag{2}$$

In the case shown, the exponents of the two inputs, K and L, sum to one, which ensures the characteristic of constant returns to scale (a proportional increase in the inputs will increase the output proportionally). The constant term, T, indicates the degree to which the same input levels lead to greater output. Thus, the change in T is the measure of technical change, when the outputs and the inputs are measured properly. T is known as total factor productivity, and changes in T are known as total factor productivity (technological) change. Various types of technological change are absorbed in the constant term T.

Technological change can be disembodied or embodied in a particular factor. Technological change can be disembodied in the sense that it does not require the inputs to change in any noticeable manner. One can think of a disembodied technological change as some increase in general knowledge that allows an increase in output for the same quantity of physical inputs. Embodied technological change is more easily conceptualized than is disembodied. When technological change is embodied in a piece of capital equipment we usually think of the new input as having a particular vintage, with later ones being the most efficient. When technological change is embodied in labor, we generally think of labor as being more skilled, more educated, healthier, and so on. We can measure inputs in physical terms, as in hours of labor or persons, or we can measure inputs in efficiency units, as in an education-weighted index of person-hours. When one is able to measure inputs in these efficiency units, one can more easily distinguish between technological change that is embodied and disembodied. This procedure is required for understanding precisely the sources of technological change and the impacts on women workers.

In the Cobb-Douglas production function, if either K or L is multiplied by some amount λ, we would not be able to discern empirically its impact on output (Q) from a change in the constant term T. Thus the Cobb-Douglas form does not distinguish between disembodied change that augments K from that which augments L. Furthermore, if the inputs are measured in physical terms, rather than in their efficiency units, and if their efficiency units expand (because of technological change that is embodied in labor or capital) while the physical units stay constant, we would not be able to distinguish the impact on Q from a disembodied technological change.

In the analysis that follows, I explore the impact of technical change on the employment of women across various sectors of the economy and within the manufacturing sector from 1890 to the present. The measure of technical change used is the rate of change in total factor productivity. Recall that total factor productivity indicates the degree to which more output is produced for a given level of inputs. Assume that the production technology can be represented by a Cobb-Douglas production function, given in Equation 2. When Equation 2 is expressed in rate-of-change form, where an asterisk (*) over a variable indicates its time derivative, the rate of change in total factor productivity is given by

$$\overset{*}{T} = \overset{*}{Q} - \alpha\overset{*}{K} - (1 - \alpha)\overset{*}{L}. \tag{3}$$

In other words, the rate of change in total factor productivity (read, in technology) is given by the rate of change in the output minus a weighted average of the rates of change of the inputs. The definition of technological change summarized in this manner—that it is measured by how much output increases above and beyond increases in the inputs—is very intuitive.

The measurement of the inputs and the outputs pose certain difficulties. The outputs and the inputs ought to be measured in physical units rather than in value terms. The procedure is ordinarily not possible, and one generally weights outputs by prices. Thus cars become the value of cars or value added in the automobile sector. The inputs themselves are normally measured in conventional or physical terms (for example, hours of labor) rather than in efficiency units. Thus part of total factor productivity will be attributable to the increased efficiency of the factors (for example, from increased education, skills, or health), and disembodied and embodied technological change are not distinguished. The rates of change of the inputs are weighted by the exponents, and to get estimates of the exponents one must appeal to economic theory. Under conditions of equilibrium in the factor (input) markets and competition, the exponents will be the shares of the factors in national income. These data are easily located for even long periods of time.

Standard measures of total factor productivity exist for various sectors and industries in the extensive work of Kendrick (1961, 1973, 1983). One aspect of technological change that is necessarily hidden in the use of this methodology is factor bias. To explore issues of biased technological change requires a more flexible functional form than Cobb-Douglas, and some estimates of factor bias using the translog production function are discussed below.

TRENDS IN FEMALE EMPLOYMENT: 1800 TO 1980

It is instructive to review the historical record regarding the labor market involvement of women in the United States before examining the impact of technological change. Data on the occupations of women were first collected in 1860, but the printed tabulations were aggregated at the state level and provide little detail by age and other characteristics. Marital status was not requested by the U.S. Census of Population until 1880. Readily available labor force data dictate that the period under study begins with 1890. The period before 1890, particularly that from 1832 to 1880, is explored with materials from the manufacturing censuses, which necessarily include only a portion of the labor force.

Although substantial change in the conventionally measured female labor force has only recently surfaced, it has been rooted in a longer history of economic transition. Increases in education during the first three decades of this century and the related increase in the tertiary sector, particularly clerical occupations, were instrumental in the post-World War II increase in participation rates of women. The data on manufacturing labor force participation rates indicate the importance of early factory development in the employment of young women, particularly in the New England and Middle Atlantic regions. These points are more fully developed below.

Labor force data for the aggregate female population together with data by race, marital status, and nativity are given in Table 1. The overall trend for the aggregate from 1890 to 1980 is upward, but most of the movement comes from increases in the participation rate of married women, particularly after 1950. The increase is most apparent for white married women. Before turning to a more detailed exploration of the data for white women, those for black women must be given more careful attention.

The labor force participation of black women across all marital statuses and ages (with the exception of single young women) has always been higher than that for white women. Several factors account for these differences (see Goldin, 1977, for a review and an exploration of the role of slavery). The lower family incomes of black Americans throughout the period are responsible for much of the difference that appears in Table 1, as are the rural, southern location of the black labor force in general and the crops produced in the South, especially cotton.

The geographical location of black women, their greater participation rate early on, and their occupational structure make the analysis of the effects of technological change on their employment different from that for white women. In 1910, for example, fully 95 percent of all employed black women were in just two occupational groupings—agriculture and domestic and personal service; the comparable figures for white women were 43 percent for native born and 27 percent for native born of foreign parentage. In 1940 77 percent of black working women were found in these two occupational groupings; in 1980 the figure was under 30 percent. Despite dissimilarities between the black and white female labor forces, various changes in the economy, such as increases in education and the rise of the clerical sector, have had strong impacts on both.

The participation rate of young single women across the entire United States rose until around 1920, when it reached a plateau at about the 0.40 level. Participation rates for this group varied significantly by geographical location. The daughters of native-born white parents in urban areas in 1890, for example, experienced a participation rate of 0.43, almost twice the aggregate level for that group. These data suggest that the labor force participation rate for the entire population of young single women converged by 1920

TABLE 1 Female Labor Force Participation Rates by Marital Status, Race, and Nativity, 1890-1980

	≥16 years old		≥15 years old					≥16 years old	
	1890	1900ᵃ	1920	1930	1940	1950	1960	1970	1980
Total	18.9	20.6	23.7	24.8	25.8	29.0	34.5	42.6	51.5
Totalᵇ	19.0	n.a.	n.a.	n.a.	n.a.	n.a.	n.a.	n.a.	55.4
Married	4.6	5.6	9.0	11.7	13.8	21.6	30.7	40.8	(49.2)
Single	40.5	43.5	46.4	50.5	45.5	46.3	42.9	53.0	61.5
White	16.3	17.9	21.6	23.7	24.5	28.1	33.7	41.9	(49.4)
Married	2.5	3.2	6.5	9.8	12.5	20.7	29.8	39.7	49.3
Single	38.4	41.5	45.0	48.7	45.9	47.5	43.9	54.5	64.2
Nonwhite	39.7	43.2	43.1	43.3	37.6	37.1	41.7	48.5	(53.3)
Married	22.5	26.0	32.5	33.2	27.3	31.8	40.6	52.5	59.0
Single	59.5	60.5	58.8	52.1	41.9	36.1	35.8	43.6	49.4
Foreign born	19.8	n.a.	n.a.	19.1	n.a.	n.a.	n.a.	n.a.	n.a.
Married	3.0	n.a.	n.a.	8.5	n.a.	n.a.	n.a.	n.a.	n.a.
Single	70.8	n.a.	n.a.	73.8	n.a.	n.a.	n.a.	n.a.	n.a.

ᵃThe 1910 labor force figures have been omitted because of the overcount of the agricultural labor force in that year.
ᵇAdjusted for unemployment by subtracting out the unemployed and calculated for 15- to 64-year-olds for 1890 and for 16- to 64-year-olds for 1980.

SOURCE: Goldin (1977). The 1980 data are from the Current Population Survey. Numbers in parentheses are decennial census figures.

on the rate experienced by the urban native-born group as early as 1890. The data for the 1832 to 1880 period demonstrate that wherever manufacturing activity spread, labor force participation rates of young single women rose, and the elasticity of supply of this labor force was rather high.

Despite the apparent stability in the percentage of single urban women in the labor force over the twentieth century, there was substantial variation in the activities of the approximately 60 percent who were not employed. In 1890 young women not in the labor force were overwhelmingly occupied "at home," ostensibly helping their mothers. Data for 1900 indicate that about two-thirds of the young women not in the labor force were also not in school, and were listed in the census as being at home. With the increase in high school education, the percentage at home dropped rapidly over the early twentieth century to less than one-tenth by 1930. The increase in formal education exactly offset the decline in time devoted to home production by young single women.

Participation rates of married women did not expand to any great extent until the 1920s. Also in contrast to the experience of young single women, participation rates for married women did not vary significantly by region or by industrial development. Although the 1920s marked the first discernible increase, it was only after 1950 that the employment of married women rose rapidly, first for women over age 35 and later for those under 35 years (see also Easterlin, 1980).

As part of a larger study of women's changing economic roles, I have prepared a matrix of cross-section and time-series labor force participation rates by marital status, age, race, and national origin from 1890 to the present. Figure 1 is part of this larger matrix and summarizes the expansion of the labor force participation of white (native-born) married women, born from 1866 to 1955. (Comparable data for black women are discussed below.) Each set of solid (or dashed) lines represents the participation rate of a particular birth cohort, tracing its market role as it matures. Cross-sectional data can also be read from this figure by connecting the relevant points on the cohort lines; for example, the data for 1970 are given by the top set of dotted lines.

Although several qualifications[2] should be kept in mind in interpreting the data in Figure 1, they make a more or less transparent statement: for every cohort born since 1866, participation in the labor force has increased within marriage, at least to about age 55. Despite the generally held notion that married women universally have experienced interruptions in their work careers, the majority who entered the labor force at mid-life had not experienced labor force work since they were single, if even at that time. (Note that because the data are given only for married women, one cannot observe the participation rates of these women when they were single.) The notion of interrupted work careers as the norm has arisen, in part, from the pattern of double-peaked labor force participation characteristic of cross-sectional data for women's work experiences in many contemporary developed nations. This pattern emerged in the United States in 1950 and is illustrated by the top dotted line in Figure 1, giving participation rates for the cross-section of married women in 1970.

Of most importance with regard to the issue of technology and women's employment is the variation in the increases for various cohorts. These variations indicate period effects, and technological change is likely to have been more important in some periods than in others. Cohorts born around 1900 achieved a considerably higher labor force participation rate than those born previously. Similarly, cohorts born after 1945 had substantially increased participation rates. All other cohorts, to be sure, contributed to the expansion of the female labor force participation rate, but the cohorts mentioned appear to have gone far beyond the trend line.

---

[2] The qualifications are (1) while the data are for native-born white married (spouse present) women, there is heterogeneity in other respects: women enter the data when they marry, and thus the data are contaminated by selection bias if people who marry late or who are widowed early have different labor force participation rates; (2) intermittency of participation is disguised in these data and depends on the aggregate rate of labor turnover for married women; (3) there are numerous definitional issues, particularly the change in 1940 from the "gainful worker" to the "labor force" construct and the omission in the early period of many women working on farms and in the home (Goldin, 1987, addresses these issues); and (4) the 10-year intervals mask certain changes, particularly those at the early ages. Related to this consideration is that the data concern only married women; participation rates for young single women are considerably higher than are those for young married women, particularly before the 1960s.

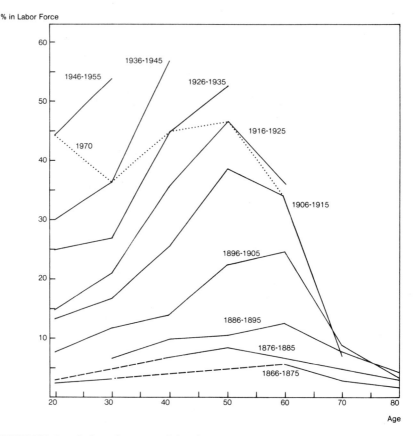

FIGURE 1   Labor force participation rates of cohorts of white married women, born 1866 to 1955, for the entire United States. Notes: Dashed lines denote missing data. Data for 1890 to 1920 are for native-born women with native-born parents. Dotted line is 1970 cross-section. Source: Derived from population census data. Data appendix on request from author.

Similar data for black women have been compiled and reinforce the finding from the aggregated data in Table 1 that black married women's participation rates have always been substantially higher than those for white women. But beginning with the cohort born around 1910, black married women have also had large increases in participation rates. Unlike the data for this cohort of white women, however, those for black women increase only for ages over 40. It is with the cohorts born around 1930 that increases in participation rates across the life cycle occur. These findings complement those for white women. Even though the cohorts affected tend to be different, the underlying reasons for the expansions in these two labor forces are similar. Educational advances occurred at different times for each group, and the findings for each reinforce the importance of increases in education for women as a whole.

The evidence that has been compiled for the period before 1890, for which the aggregate data are either entirely absent or lacking in detail, indicate that wherever significant industrial development occurred, labor force participation rates for young women rose. Furthermore, participation rates in industrial areas were extremely high even as early as the 1830s. Although the data are fragile at best for the period before 1860, estimates of a "manufacturing labor force participation rate" for young females in five northeastern states have been computed and are given in Table 2. The estimates must also be interpreted in light of the severe undercounting of manufacturing firms in the 1832 data for all states but Massachusetts. The 1832 manufacturing participation rate estimates, ranging across states from 12 to 27 percent, indicate that the manufacturing sector attracted a substantial portion of the population of young women in the Northeast. In the early industrializing state of Massachusetts, where the reporting was most complete, one-third of all young females were employed in the manufacturing sector by 1850, if not before. This level roughly equalled that prevailing in 1880.

Given that some young women were employed in alternative pursuits such as domestic service and teaching, the crude manufacturing labor force participation rates indicate that a high proportion of single women in New England had been drawn into the market economy by the 1830s. Comparable evidence on female labor force participation before 1832 is not available, but the levels implied by the 1830s data were most likely achieved quite rapidly, because opportunities for the employment of females were limited prior to industrial development.

TABLE 2 The Manufacturing Employment of Females as a Percentage of 10-
[or 15-] to 29-Year-Olds in Five States, 1832-1880

State	1832	1837	1850	1860	1870	1880[a]
Connecticut	[11.6][b]		22.6	23.1	18.4 [19.1]	28.5 [33.7]
Massachusetts	27.1[b,c] [18.7]	40.2[c] [29.7]	32.9	28.4	36.7 [44.0]	32.8 [39.5]
New Hampshire	11.6[b,c] [10.5]		20.1	22.0	21.7 [26.6]	28.1 [36.6]
New York			8.0	6.8	9.2 [10.8]	15.3 [18.7]
Rhode Island	26.6[b] [24.6]		26.5	33.3	48.7 [53.9]	40.9 [45.0]
Percentage of U.S. total female manufacturing in five states			70.3	62.9	60.7 [61.3]	56.5 [57.7]

[a]Children were allocated between boys and girls as given by the 1880
population figures for children in manufacturing employment by states.
The bracketed figures express the number of females employed in
manufacturing as a percentage of those 15 to 29 years old in the population.
[b]The returns for Rhode Island listed women and female children separately.
The Massachusetts and New Hampshire returns did not, and the estimates
assume that 45 percent of all working children were female. The bracketed
figures give the employment of adult women as a percentage of those 15 to
29 years old. The Connecticut estimate is only for adult women as a
percentage of those 15 to 29 years old. In all cases, the population
figures for 1832 are for white females only.
[c]The estimates include women in home workshop employment, mainly palm
leaf hats and straw hats, bonnets, and braids; the bracketed figures exclude
them.

SOURCE: Goldin and Sokoloff (1982:Table 8).

TOTAL FACTOR PRODUCTIVITY AND
FEMALE EMPLOYMENT

TECHNICAL CHANGE AND FEMALE INTENSITY

Cross-section and time series data on female employment for 1890 to 1980 are presented in Table 3 in two ways: as a percentage of the sector or industry labor force that is female and as an index, which divides the industry percentage by the percentage for the entire economy. The index is the more appropriate indicator of change over time and measures the extent to which particular sectors and industries expand their female employment at a rate greater than the national average.

The information contained in Table 3 is easily summarized. Most sectors and industries have been either male- or female-intensive for the entire century under consideration, although several have undergone shifts in labor force composition. Farming, mining, transportation, construction, and public utilities, among the sectors, have been male intensive.[3] Lumber, furniture, chemicals, petroleum, stone, metals, machinery, and transportation, among the manufacturing industries, have been male-intensive. Large shifts in the composition of the labor force have occurred in the communications, professional, and clerical sectors.

How has the index of female intensity for the economy's sectors and industries been affected by changes in total factor productivity, the measure of technological change used in this analysis?[4] The answer can be found in Table 4, which presents the results of a pooled cross-section, time series regression in which the dependent variable is the relative proportion of the labor force in a sector, at time t, that is female (given by the index in Table 3). The explanatory variables in the regressions are total factor productivity change (TFP), lagged by 5 to 10 years; sector and industry

---

[3] Male and female intensities are defined here in terms of whether the index (times 100) is less than or greater than 100.

[4] The data on total factor productivity are discussed in several volumes by Kendrick (1961, 1973, 1983). Total factor productivity data have been computed for the private sector, and those for the service sector join together three major but disparate occupational groups—professionals, clerical workers, and domestic workers. Thus the professional, clerical, and domestic occupations cannot be included, and only the private sector can be considered. The omission of services from the analysis is unfortunate because of the preponderance of women in these three areas of employment.

TABLE 3 Female Employment as a Percentage of the Labor Force (and as an Index) of the Private Domestic Economy's Sectors and Manufacturing Industries, 1890–1980

Major Industrial Sector	Female Employment as a Percentage of the Sector's Labor Force and as an Index									
	1890	1900	1910	1920	1930	1940	1950	1960	1970	1980
Agriculture	7.9 (45.8)	9.1 (49.6)	7.9 (41.7)	9.2 (45.0)	8.0 (36.5)	5.8 (23.3)	8.5 (30.6)	10.0 (30.4)	11.2 (29.4)	18.5 (43.4)
Mining	0.1 (0.7)	0.2 (1.0)	0.1 (0.6)	0.3 (1.3)	0.1 (0.4)	1.1 (4.5)	2.5 (8.8)	4.6 (14.2)	7.9 (20.9)	11.8 (27.8)
Transportation	0.2 (0.9)	0.7 (3.6)	0.7 (3.5)	0.8 (3.7)	0.8 (3.4)	3.4 (13.8)	*	*	*	*
Communications and public utilities	14.4 (83.8)	25.1 (137.4)	25.1 (132.3)	43.3 (211.7)	56.0 (254.7)	53.0 (214.8)	*	*	*	*
Construction	*	*	*	*	*	*	2.7 (9.8)	3.8 (11.5)	5.8 (15.3)	7.9 (18.5)
Rail transportation	*	*	*	*	*	*	5.2 (18.7)	5.6 (17.0)	7.1 (18.8)	7.6 (17.9)
Transportation (excluding rail)	*	*	*	*	*	*	7.1 (25.6)	9.2 (27.9)	16.4 (43.1)	21.7 (51.1)
Communications	*	*	*	*	*	*	57.4 (205.9)	52.3 (159.4)	48.8 (128.4)	46.4 (108.9)
Public utilities	*	*	*	*	*	*	12.1 (43.4)	12.2 (37.3)	13.0 (34.2)	16.8 (39.5)
Trade	*	*	*	*	*	*	34.0 (122.0)	37.7 (114.8)	38.0 (99.8)	43.0 (101.1)

Finance and insurance	*	*	*	*	*	*	44.5 (161.4)	49.5 (150.8)	53.1 (139.6)	61.5 (144.4)
Real estate	*	*	*	*	*	*	29.9 (107.4)	33.2 (101.2)	37.7 (99.1)	46.6 (109.4)
Manufacturing	9.0 (110.4)	19.2 (104.8)	17.0 (89.7)	15.0 (73.5)	15.7 (71.7)	22.0 (89.1)	25.0 (89.5)	25.8 (78.7)	29.0 (76.2)	32.5 (76.3)

Two-digit SIC Manufacturing Industries

Female Employment as a Percentage of the Industry's Labor Force

Foods	20.2	21.0	29.5	29.7	24.9	29.7	24.4	26.8	30.0	32.3
Beverages	0.8	1.3	1.9	1.1	2.2	*	*	*	*	*
Tobacco	31.9	39.3	46.5	58.9	67.2	65.0	53.5	48.3	41.4	37.2
Textiles	40.8	41.4	51.0	47.6	45.7	43.0	42.8	44.8	47.0	48.2
Apparel	60.2	65.2	62.6	63.7	68.1	73.3	70.4	74.9	77.9	78.6
Lumber	0.7	0.6	0.6	0.1	0.9	1.5	4.6	5.7	10.3	14.5
Furniture	4.8	3.9	2.6	8.3	6.5	11.7	15.6	17.8	26.7	31.1
Paper	39.9	34.6	32.9	24.5	25.4	24.3	23.7	22.0	22.7	24.5
Printing	17.5	21.5	22.4	24.0	16.7	23.8	25.0	26.7	32.2	41.2
Chemical	15.9	13.2	14.2	10.7	8.7	16.0	19.8	19.5	23.0	28.2
Petroleum	0.0	0.0	0.0	0.1	0.4	1.5	11.5	12.3	14.4	16.7
Rubber	48.8	36.8	16.4	11.9	19.2	24.8	26.6	28.2	32.1	33.8
Leather	21.0	23.2	24.8	30.2	34.2	40.3	44.0	49.7	57.4	60.4
Stone	1.4	2.6	3.5	7.2	7.6	11.9	17.2	16.6	19.4	23.8
Primary metal	0.0	0.5	0.3	0.8	1.8	2.9	6.5	7.3	9.3	13.3
Fabricated metal	3.3	5.6	10.8	11.0	13.8	16.8	17.4	17.7	19.3	22.7
Machinery	0.8	0.5	1.8	3.1	2.6	7.4	13.4	13.9	17.0	21.7
Electrical machinery	16.8	15.3	22.7	22.9	28.5	32.6	33.6	35.4	39.5	43.3
Transportation	0.5	0.6	0.5	1.6	2.6	6.0	11.5	12.5	14.0	19.1

TABLE 3 (continued)

Two-digit SIC Manufacturing Industries	Female Employment as a Percentage of the Industry's Labor Force									
	1890	1900	1910	1920	1930	1940	1950	1960	1970	1980
Residual services										
Professional	26.3	37.0	42.9	46.8	46.9	/55.8	57.7	60.2	63.5	66.5
Domestic	87.8	69.6	67.3	54.3	64.2	/71.7	66.5	72.0	71.7	70.3
Clerical	14.1	25.4	34.4	45.8	49.4	*	*	*	*	*
Entire United States	17.2	18.3	19.2	20.4	22.0	24.7	27.9	32.8	38.0	42.6

NOTES: The labor force is defined as those 10 years old and over for 1890 and 1900 and as those 14 years and over for 1910 to 1980. Experienced civilian labor used for 1950 to 1980.

After 1940 Beverages are included in the Food Industry.

The professional category includes educational services publicly provided.

Domestic includes personal services.

The index is defined as the percentage of the sector's labor force that is female divided by the percentage of the national labor force that is female multiplied by 100. It measures the female intensity of a sector relative to the national average.

A slash within a series (/) indicates a change in definition and noncomparability over time. An asterisk (*) indicates that the series does not exist for that year.

SOURCES: All but manufacturing detail, 1890 to 1980 Censuses of Population. Manufacturing detail for 1890 to 1930, Censuses of Manufacturing. The two-digit SIC groupings were approximated using only those industries with more than 15,000 employees in the earlier years and more than 25,000 in the later years.

TABLE 4 Explaining an Index of Female Employment Across Sectors and Industries, 1890 to 1980

Dependent Variable: Index of Female Employment (in year t)[a]	Estimation 1[b]		Estimation 2[b]	
Constant	0.789	(7.94)	0.805	(10.86)
Total Factor Productivity (TFP) change at time $(t-i)$, $5 < i < 10$ years	0.0234	(1.74)	-0.0317	(1.31)
Time, years from 1900	-0.0020	(1.59)	0.0007	(0.91)
Sector and industry dummies				
Farm	-0.298	(1.38)	-0.431	(5.33)
Mine	-0.496	(3.11)	-0.709	(9.98)
Transportation (before 1940)	-0.762	(1.92)	-0.843	(6.95)
Communications and public utilities (before 1940)	0.853	(1.62)	0.762	(5.03)
Construction	-0.463	(2.56)	-0.718	(9.38)
Rail	-0.427	(1.58)	-0.683	(7.34)
Transportation (non-RR)	-0.298	(1.36)	-0.533	(6.50)
Communications	0.032	(0.05)	-0.282	(1.65)
Public utilities	-0.242	(0.92)	-0.518	(5.56)
Trade	0.403	(0.95)	0.141	(1.11)
Finance	0.836	(4.38)	0.579	(7.40)
Real estate	0.398	(1.40)	0.131	(1.35)
Food	0.482	(2.25)		
Apparel	1.981	(7.50)		
Textiles	1.291	(5.39)		
Interactions with TFP				
Farm	*		*	
Mine	*		*	
Transportation	*		0.065	(1.60)
Communications and public utilities	*		0.174	(3.87)
Construction	*		*	
Rail	*		0.032	(1.01)
Transportation (non-RR)	*		0.068	(1.77)
Communications	0.149	(1.22)	0.218	(5.38)
Public utilities	*		0.039	(1.36)
Trade	*		*	
Finance	*		0.071	(1.61)
Real estate	*		0.056	(1.01)
Food	-0.085	(1.15)		
Apparel	*			
Textiles	-0.131	(1.90)		
Number of observations	328		107	
R^2	.60		.97	

NOTES: Absolute values of 't'-statistics are in parentheses. Ordinary least-squares estimation used. An asterisk (*) indicates coefficient is insignificant at even unconventional levels of significance testing. Manufacturing is the omitted sector in both estimations; two-digit industries other than food, apparel, and textiles are omitted from Estimation 1.

[a]The index is defined in the note to Table 3.
[b]See text for discussion.

SOURCE: Calculated by the author based on data from Table 3 and Kendrick (1961, 1973, and 1983).

dummies; a time trend; and interactions between TFP and the dummy variables. The estimation indicates that female intensity has increased with increases in total factor productivity—where technological advances have been greatest, women's employment share relative to the average has increased the most.

Estimation 1, which includes all sectors and all industries within manufacturing, indicates that each percentage point increase in total factor productivity increases the index by 0.0234. (The mean of the index is 0.794, and the mean of the change in total factor productivity is 2.19.[5]) Estimation 2 excludes the 19 detailed two-digit SIC manufacturing industries, reducing the number of observations from 328 to 107. While the coefficient on the change in total factor productivity is negative (-0.0317, but not very statistically significant), the interaction terms with the various sectors suggest strong positive net effects. The coefficients on the interactions with transportation (before 1940); communications and public utilities (before 1940); and transportation, communications, trade, public utilities, and finance are large enough (and generally statistically significant) to outweigh the negative coefficient on technical change. Only the farm, construction, mine, rail, trade, and real estate sectors appear to have either negative or zero net impacts of changes in total factor productivity on the index. The impact of total factor productivity change on female intensity is different in these sectors than for the economy as a whole, and the reasons in the cases of the farm, construction, mine, and rail sectors seem obvious.

Several qualifications to this analysis must be noted. The relationship between the index and total factor productivity has not been explicitly modeled, and the analysis should be viewed as one that is exploratory rather than one of hypothesis testing.[6] Total

---

[5] The index would have a mean of 1.0 if all sectors were included, because the index is merely the female intensity of a sector at time t divided by the female intensity of the economy's labor force at time t. The private service and the government sectors have been excluded because of the lack of total factor productivity data; taken together these sectors have an index greater than 1.0.

[6] Kendrick (1983:44) regressed changes in total factor productivity on variables that included the proportion of the sector's labor force that was female, for the cross-section 1966 to 1979. The size of the coefficient on the percentage female is in the range of those in Table 4 (although note the reversal of the causality). Kendrick's motivation, it should be noted, was to

factor productivity (read technological) change is implicitly assumed to be independent of the female intensity of a sector's labor force, but it may not have been. More female-intensive sectors may have had higher levels of total factor productivity change because of lower unionization and less-specific human capital, among other influences that might reduce resistance to technological advance. Several variables that might be included in the analysis, such as the education and the skills of the labor force and the level of unionization, have not been. In addition, the total factor productivity measure of technological change is constructed as a residual, and as such it can measure more than the change in output for constant inputs. It may unintentionally measure changes in the inputs that are not observed.[7] Leaving this source of potential bias aside, the findings from the estimation indicate that sectors that have increased total factor productivity more than average

---

study the determinants of technological change rather than to understand its impact.

[7] The labor force is measured by a weighted average of hours of work, where the weights are based on labor compensation (see Kendrick, 1961, Appendix A for further details). As the labor force increases because more women enter it, the measure will increase less than a labor force increase because men entered. The lower average compensation of women accounts for the difference. But if the lower compensation of women does not entirely reflect lower productivity, the labor force measure will be biased downward. Sectors and industries increasing their labor force by adding women will appear more productive in terms of the total factor productivity index, because their labor force will be increasing by less than their output even if there had been no change in technology. A related bias concerns the efficiency units of labor. Increases in education for society as a whole have had impacts on the labor force that differ for males and females. Certain occupations, it appears, enable workers to substitute training acquired off the job for that traditionally acquired on the job, and women, whose life-cycle labor force participation is more discontinuous and shorter than that of men, have tended to enter such occupations. Thus, as the average educational attainment of the population has increased, women have become a higher proportion of the labor force in certain sectors, such as those employing clerical workers. More highly educated workers will increase the measure of total factor productivity, because only the number of laborers or the hours of labor input, and not the quality-adjusted labor input, is used. Thus a positive correlation between the index and the measure of technological change can occur. This possible bias can be accounted for by including the mean level of education of the work force in each sector. Such data exist only for relatively recent periods of time.

tend to have more female-intensive methods of production.[8] The
result stems primarily from the correlation found in the cross-
sections, rather than from a positive relationship between total
factor productivity change and female intensity in time series for
given sectors. Indeed, the female-intensity indices of most of the
sectors and industries are relatively constant.

Why might there be a positive correlation between the index
of female intensity and the change in total factor productivity?
It is possible that the most innovative sectors require flexible
labor forces, and that the female labor force, being less unionized
and less experienced, has been more amenable and receptive to
change in work organization. It may also be the case that total
factor productivity change is correlated with an increase in the
proportion of the labor force that is less skilled.[9] The degree
to which technological change increases or decreases a portion
of the labor force is probably dependent on the degree to which
the capital employed is a relative substitute or complement to
that type of labor. Technological change in the clerical sector,
in manufacturing earlier in this century, and in communications
may well have involved the substitution of relatively unskilled
for skilled labor, but other evidence suggests that skilled labor
has more recently become a relative complement to capital in
the economy as a whole (see, for example, the evidence cited in
Williamson and Lindert, 1980).

What does the positive correlation between changes in total
factor productivity and the relative female intensity of a sector

---

[8] Manufacturing data for the early nineteenth century confirm the positive
correlation between the proportion of females in an industry and the rate of
technological change found here. From 1820 to 1850, total factor productivity
change was greatest in cotton textiles, hats, tanning, and wool and mixed
textiles. All but tanning was a female-intensive industry. Total factor
productivity change was the lowest in liquors, flour milling, and tobacco.
Only the tobacco industry, among the three, hired female employees. (Indexes
of total factor productivity for 1820 to 1860 were produced by Kenneth
Sokoloff as part of Sokoloff [1984] and were made available to me by the
author.) The evidence on factor bias is more mixed (Cain and Paterson,
1986). The industries with the greatest labor-saving technical change from
1850 to 1919 were apparel, rubber, leather, and metals (both primary and
fabricated). The female intensities of the labor forces in these industries were
diverse and did not change much over the 70-year period.

[9] Kendrick does find a positive correlation between the proportion of the
labor force consisting of production workers and the change in total factor
productivity.

or an industry imply about the impact of technological change on female employment? That female-intensive sectors have been those experiencing the greatest technological advances does not necessarily mean that these sectors have had the greatest increases in employment. Indeed, the opposite could have occurred.

The regression analysis examined the first portion of Equation 1, the impact on an index of female intensity of a sector or industry. The second part of that equation concerns the impact on total employment. Equations similar to those in Table 4 (but not presented here) have been estimated for the entire labor force, where the dependent variable was some function of the proportion of total employment in a particular sector. The dependent variable was expressed as the percentage, the change in the percentage, or the percent change in the percentage. In almost all estimations the dependent variable was negatively related to total factor productivity in the preceding decade. That is, sectors with higher productivity growth had a smaller increase in their employment share or a smaller share or a smaller proportional increase in the share. Simply put, employment growth was negatively associated with technological advance. The agricultural sector had the largest impact on the regression and, in at least one variant of the estimation, was responsible for the entire effect. Agriculture experienced relatively small increases in total factor productivity until the mid-twentieth century when its technological advance was among the greatest in the economy. It has also been a sector of rapidly reduced employment. The example of agriculture is a reminder that the income and price elasticities of demand, which are only implicit in this simple analysis, are driving many of the results.

It does appear to be the case that more female-intensive sectors have generally had expanded employment relative to all others because of less, and not greater, technological advance. That is, among the female-intensive sectors, those with the least technological change grew the most in employment. Services are a well-known example, although it has also been claimed that total factor productivity measures do an imperfect job of capturing technological advance in this diverse sector (National Research Council, 1979). On balance, the role of technological change in the total employment picture is less one of encouraging the expansion of female-intensive sectors as it is one of allowing the reduction in the employment of the single largest sector early in this century, that of agricultural production.

EDUCATION AND THE CHANGING EMPLOYMENT OF WOMEN

The expansion of knowledge, termed technological advance here, is frequently embodied in a factor and expands it when the factor is expressed in efficiency units.[10] Measures of total factor productivity do not ordinarily use efficiency units, and embodied technological change is then necessarily included in the residual measure of technological change. Denison (1962, 1974), among others, has computed the portion of the residual due to increases in education. From 1929 to 1957 real national income rose at 2.93 percent average annually. Labor, land, and capital, conventionally measured, accounted for 1.43 percentage points, with the residual measure of technological change equal to 1.50. Of this 1.50, almost one-half, or 0.67 percentage points, was due to the augmentation of labor in the form of increased education.

In the American case, educational advances for males and females have paralleled each other, but the impact on the occupational structure and labor force participation of women has probably been greater. I turn first to the data on educational change and then to the impact on employment and occupations.

The two lines in Figure 2 give, from left to right, median years of schooling for female cohorts born from 1876 to 1952 and the percentage with 4 or more years of college. The data on median years of schooling clearly show a sharp rise in the educational attainment of young American women beginning approximately with the cohorts born between 1900 and 1910. During a very brief period, the median female increased her years of education by one-third, from about 9 to 12 years. The rapid rise in years of schooling was a product of the well-known increase in high school education, with these individuals leaving school from 1915 to 1928.

---

[10] Inputs are generally measured in physical units, such as labor hours. To express a factor in efficiency units means that one measures, in some manner, the degree to which the factor is skilled or educated, for example. One method of doing this is to use a weighting scheme for, say, education. Years of education are valued using earnings at some date to form an index, and as the labor force becomes more educated its value rises.

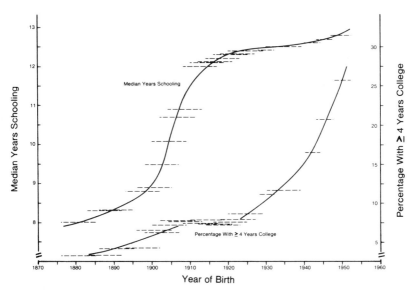

FIGURE 2   Educational attainment for cohorts of white women born from
1876 to 1952. Note: Horizontal lines indicate the width of the birth cohorts
for which data on educational attainment are given. Source: Bureau of the
Census, *Current Population Reports*, Series P-20 for years 1940, 1947, 1962,
1966, 1968, 1970, 1972, 1974, 1977.

After the initial schooling increase with the cohorts born from
1900 to 1910, median years of education have increased only gradually, with the exception of the most recent cohorts. Change in their
educational attainment can be seen more clearly with reference to
the graph in the far right of Figure 2, which gives the percentage
of women with 4 or more years of college. That indicator has
increased most rapidly with cohorts born after 1940.

The employment effects of increased education can be seen
by comparing the educational data with those on cohort labor
force participation in Figure 1. It is not at all coincidental that
the cohorts experiencing the greatest increases in participation
rates over their lifetimes were those with the greatest increase
in education when young. The cohort born from 1900 to 1910
achieved an educational transformation in high school completion
rates; it was precisely this cohort that experienced substantial
increases in its labor force participation both during its early years
and even more so during the 1950s when it was 40 to 50 years old.
Although Figure 1 does not show the labor force participation

rate of single women, the cohort born around 1910 also achieved a high rate of labor force participation when single, even though it had an increased educational attainment. It was able to achieve this both by spending considerably less time "at home," as the census termed those individuals not at school and not having an occupation.

The data on education in Figure 2 are for the white female population. Increases for the black female population have been greater than those for the female population as a whole, beginning with cohorts born around 1900. Cohorts of black women born in 1900 had, on average, three years less schooling than their white counterparts; cohorts born around 1950 had one-half year less schooling (Smith, 1984). The large increase in high school completion evident from Figure 2 for white women was achieved about two decades later for black women. Thus, differential rates of educational attainment might explain some of the differences pointed out earlier in labor force participation rates between black and white married women.

How did educational change in the first three decades of this century affect the job opportunities of young women, and how did it later affect their labor force participation when married? Occupational data arranged by cohort suggest that young women with increased education moved into the clerical sector and, relatively, out of manufacturing employment in 1930 and 1950; and other data indicate that women, who in the 1920s and 1930s were employed in such occupations, had a higher probability of remaining in or reentering the labor force when older (Goldin, 1986b). Table 5 gives various occupational distributions by age for 1930 to 1950, where the group described varies somewhat over time because of definitional changes in the census. Despite this complication, it is clear that the percentage of women in the clerical sector is lowest for those birth cohorts having the least amount of education, with the latter variable given by the data in Figure 2. Cohorts born after 1900 increased their percentages in the clerical sector from about 13 to 24 percent for married women in 1930 and from 17 to 23 percent for all marital statuses in 1950. Micro-level data from 1940 demonstrate that educational levels above high school substantially increased earnings in clerical-sector jobs (Goldin, 1984), and in general, occupations in the clerical sector have had employees with relatively high levels of education.

TABLE 5 Percentage of the Female Labor Force Employed in the Clerical (and sales) Sector, 1930-1950 by Birth Cohort

Demographic Group	Birth Cohorts					
	1916-1922	1911-1915	1906-1910	1896-1905	1886-1895	1885- and earlier
1930 Married, native white			26.9	24.0	13.3	6.7
1930 Single, native white		26.1	35.6			
1940 Married, white[a]		35.5	36.4	34.2	28.8	19.5
1940 Married, white, urban[b]		42.4	43.0	39.6	31.9	21.4
	1926-1930	1921-1925	1916-1920	1906-1915	1896-1905	1891-1895	1886-1890
1950, All marital statuses, white	48.9	39.7	30.3	26.4	23.1	17.3	14.0

[a]Married, husband present. Employment away from home and not on public emergency works.
[b]Married, husband present, in cities with more than 100,000 persons.

SOURCE: U.S. Censuses of Population, 1930-1950.

Thus, increased educational standards for all Americans during the first few decades of this century expanded the employment of women at that time and later, as cohorts with increased education aged. Furthermore, the increase in educational attainment with the cohorts born after 1940 to 1945 is easily correlated with substantially higher labor force participation in the most recent decades. The influence of increased education on labor force participation can also be observed in cross-sectional analysis. Almost all labor supply studies find positive coefficients on education in participation or hours equations (see, for example, the studies in Smith, 1980). The reasons for this positive cross-sectional relationship are a bit different from those offered here. Education augments wages, and labor supply increases with the wage, holding income constant or giving a relatively small income effect. The relationship for the time series analysis concerns the shift in occupations from those requiring on-the-job training to those for which off-the-job training is a good substitute.

CHANGES IN WORK ORGANIZATION

Technological change also encompasses alterations in work organization that enhance productivity. During the first half of the

nineteenth century the employment of young women in the manufacturing regions of America greatly expanded both in industries
that were mechanized, such as textiles, and in those that were not,
such as boots and shoes, paper, and clothing (Goldin and Sokoloff,
1982; Sokoloff, 1984). In the mechanized industries, part of the
increased scale of firms and the increased employment of women
was due to technological change involving new and improved types
of capital equipment. But even in these industries, and certainly
in the nonmechanized ones, much of the increased employment of
women was attributable to an increase in the division of labor and
thus to changes in the organization of work in nascent factories.
Changes external to the firm, such as improved transportation of
goods, better-integrated labor markets, and more efficient capital markets, enabled firms to increase their scale of operations,
and thus benefit from the increased division of labor and achieve
greater efficiency.

Within manufacturing, there have been wide differences in the
organization of work for female and male employees. In 1890, for
example, 47 percent of all female manufacturing operatives were
paid by the piece, but only 13 percent of the males were. Females
were therefore 3.5 times as likely to be employed on piece rates
than were males. Furthermore, piece-rate payment almost always
prevailed when males and females occupied the same position in
the same firm. Examples from the textile industry are instructive.
In only one out of the six predominantly male occupations in
cotton textiles was payment generally made by the piece, but
among four, in which both men and women were found, only one
was paid by time. Also, males, but not females, were frequently
employed in teams and by the method of inside contracting, by
which independent contractors organized labor within a firm.

Goldin (1986a) explores the role of monitoring and supervisory
costs in the adoption of different methods of work organization for
male and female manufacturing employees. Firm-level data on
supervisory costs and the numbers of male and female workers
in piece and time rate positions suggest that differences in the
costs of supervision influenced the form of work organization. In
factories, male workers were more often paid time-based wages
rather than piece rates and employed on teams because their time
on the job was generally longer than that of females and thus they
required less supervision. The ability of manufacturing enterprises
both to use a technology with an intricate division of labor and to

monitor the output of workers therefore fostered the employment of females.

The existence of monitoring and supervisory costs can also explain the transformation of occupations in the clerical sector that were "feminized" rapidly from 1900 to 1920. It has frequently been claimed that this feminization was the result of technological changes, such as the mechanization of the office. But was the feminization of the office a function of the reduced level of skill required with the division of office work into tasks or was it a function of a reduced level of supervision needed to elicit some level of output?

In the early history of the modern office various tasks were paid by the piece. Typewriters in the Graton and Knight Manufacturing Company, for example, were equipped with cyclometers; "240 depressions of the typewriter keys or space bar [were] equivalent to one point . . . 600 points [were] considered base production and each point produced in excess [was] allowed for at the rate of one and one-half cents a point" (Coyle, 1928:23–24). But piece rates did not prevail in this sector, and their decline was a tribute to the ability of employers to pretest employees whose training in commercial and high school courses was completed before job entry.

Monitoring in the office became even simpler and cheaper than in the factory. Employers divided workers into homogeneous groups and paid each a set day rate. Standardization enabled employers to screen workers prior to employment. Thus, it appears that women began to be employed in the clerical sector when its jobs could be more finely divided, as had occurred a full century before in manufacturing, and its output more cheaply monitored. (See Rotella, 1981, for an analysis of clerical employment that stresses human capital aspects of the mechanization and feminization of the office.)

RELATIVE EARNINGS OF FEMALES TO MALES, 1815 TO 1982

The degree to which technological change is biased within sectors or industries and the degree to which even neutral technological change occurs in particular sectors or industries alters the relative earnings of inputs, such as capital and labor or male and female labor. Such impacts can be ignored when only one sector or one industry is at issue, but not when the entire economy is being

considered. Changes in female earnings alter female employment
because their labor supply function is elastic. How have the earnings of females changed relative to those of males over the course of
American history, and what role has been played by technological
change?

Table 6 and Figure 3 give the ratio of female to male earnings
for the manufacturing sector from 1820 to 1970 and for all sectors
from 1890 to 1982. The relative wage of females to males was
fairly low in the northeastern states prior to industrialization but
rose quickly wherever manufacturing activity spread (Goldin and
Sokoloff, 1982, 1984). Around 1815 the ratio of female to male
wages in agriculture and domestic activities was 0.288 and rose to
about 0.303 to 0.371 among manufacturing establishments at the
inception of industrialization in the United States in 1820. By 1832
the average ratio in manufacturing was about 0.44, and it continued to rise to 0.50 in the northeastern states by 1850. Nationwide
the ratio rose slowly to about the year 1885, when it reached its
1970 value of approximately 0.56. Early industrialization, therefore, increased the relative wage of females to males by almost 50
percent, and in the briefest of periods, a mere two decades, the
gender gap in manufacturing and domestic employment narrowed
by 15 percentage points.

The ratio of female to male full-time earnings for the entire
population increased from 0.463 to 0.603 over the period 1890 to
1970, using the series constructed from earnings in six sectors. The
increase over time is somewhat greater when earnings are adjusted
for hours of work among full-time employees, from 0.498 to 0.657.
The gender gap has remained relatively constant over the period
since 1950, with the exception of an initial decline in the ratio
and a rise beginning in about 1980. The recent rise appears to
be substantial in magnitude, and if the explanations in Goldin
(1986b) and Smith and Ward (1984) are correct it will continue
for some time.

Goldin (1986b) and Smith and Ward (1984) present data on
the life cycle labor force experience of the working population of
women, which indicates that working women's labor market experience has not increased substantially, if at all, during the period
from 1950 to the present. The increase in the labor force participation rate of women was substantial enough that new labor force
entrants pulled down the average labor market experience accumulated by those already employed. Because wages are computed

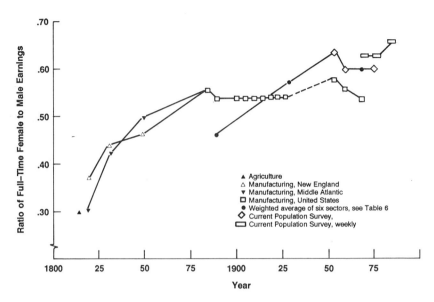

FIGURE 3   The gender gap in historical perspective: the manufacturing sector and the entire United States, 1815 to 1982. Sources: see Table 6 and O'Neill (1985).

only for those in the labor force, an increase in the relatively inexperienced will prevent the average earnings of women from rising relative to those of men, all other things being equal. This scenario is coming to a close, however. As more and more women have entered the labor force, new entrants are a smaller percentage of the working population of women, and the lesser experience of these new entrants has a far smaller effect. Thus the experience of the working population of women has begun to increase, and with it the relative earnings of women. The same explanation holds for the educational attainment of the working population of women. Working women in each cohort have always been among the more educated. Therefore, as more and more women have entered the ranks of the employed, the average education of working women in each cohort has declined. This process, too, has come to an end, and the educational attainment of the working population of women is now increasing faster than that of men.

What accounted for the decrease in the gender gap over the past century? Various studies have shown that earnings within occupational groupings have increased for females relative to those

TABLE 6 Wage Ratios for Males and Females in Manufacturing Employment, 1815 to 1970, and Across All Occupations, 1890 to 1982

Agriculture
  1815   0.29
Manufacturing
  1820[a]   0.37-0.30
  1832[a]   0.44-0.43
  1850[a]   0.46-0.50
  1885   0.559
  1890   0.539

			Full Time	
	Full Time	Actual	Weekly	Hourly
1899	0.535	0.536		
1904	0.536	0.535		
1909	0.536	0.537		
1914	0.535	0.534	0.568	0.592
1920			0.559	0.645
1921	0.536	0.536	0.617	0.653
1922			0.612	0.677
1923	0.535	0.536	0.607	0.672
1924			0.593	0.664
1925	0.536	0.536	0.592	0.657
1926			0.585	0.662
1927			0.597	0.652
1928			0.573	0.645
1929			0.575	0.637
1930			0.578	0.635
1931			0.612	0.621
1932			0.653	0.618
1933			0.661	0.656
1934			0.688	0.704
1935			0.653	0.700

	Manufacturing		All Occupations (median earnings)		Constructed from Six Sectors
	Full Time	Total	Actual	Adjusted for Hours	
1890					0.463
1930					0.556
1939	0.539	0.513	0.581		
1950		0.537			
1951		0.532			
1952		0.558			
1953		0.512			
1954		0.497			
1955	0.580	0.526	0.639	0.689	
1956	0.583	0.515	0.639	0.690	
1957	0.554	0.496	0.633	0.680	
1958	0.570	0.477	0.630	0.677	
1959	0.580		0.613	0.664	

TABLE 6 (continued)

	Manufacturing		All Occupations (median earnings)		Constructed from Six Sectors
	Full Time	Total	Actual	Adjusted for Hours	
1960	0.559		0.608	0.663	
1961	0.534		0.594	0.647	
1962	0.557		0.595	0.652	
1963	0.544		0.596	0.654	
1964	0.547		0.596	0.659	
1965	0.532		0.600	0.666	
1966	0.524		0.580	0.646	
1967	0.563		0.578	0.639	
1968	0.549		0.582	0.644	
1969	0.544		0.605	0.669	
1970	0.540		0.594	0.655	0.603
1971			0.595	0.653	
1972			0.579	0.636	
1973			0.566	0.627	
1974			0.572	0.627	
1975			0.588	0.633	
1976			0.602	0.666	
1977			0.589	0.648	
1978			0.600	0.658	
1979			0.596	0.656	
1980			0.602	0.646	
1981			0.592	0.646	
1982			0.617	0.672	

NOTE: Except where noted these ratios are based on mean earnings of full-time year-round employees.

[a]The range is for New England and the Middle Atlantic.

SOURCES: This series has been compiled by the author from a variety of sources. See Goldin (1986c) for details. Data for All Occupations category from O'Neill (1985:Table 1).

for males, particularly in the clerical and professional sectors. Furthermore, the skill differential across all occupations narrowed considerably after 1940 (Keat, 1960). Thus, relative earnings for females to males have increased within occupations, and this factor has been of overwhelming importance in accounting for the increase in the earnings ratio over time. It appears that the occupational distribution mattered far less than earnings within occupations in determining the overall earnings ratio of females to males (Goldin, 1986c; Polachek, 1984). This finding is particularly noteworthy, since it is generally presumed that the occupational distribution is the primary determinant of the gap between male and female earnings.

The degree to which the occupational distribution matters in determining the aggregate ratio of female to male earnings involves constructing two hypothetical cases. In one, all women have the occupational distribution of men, but their earnings for each occupation remain the same. In the other, counterfactual world, all men have the occupational distribution of the women but have the earnings for each occupation that they ordinarily have. There are then three (or more) measures of the percentage of the earnings gap that is explained by occupations; one minus this measure gives the difference in pay within occupations. The three measures include the two from the hypothetical cases and a third which averages the first two.

This technique has been used by Polachek (1984) and Treiman and Hartmann (1981). One problem with it is that the answer depends on how many occupations are used. Polachek uses 195 occupations and finds that somewhat more than 10 percent of the earnings gap is explained by occupational differences; Treiman and Hartmann use 222 occupations and find that somewhere between 11 and 19 percent of the gap is explained. Neither of these measures seems particularly large. But when the number of occupations rises to 479, more is explained. If the first of the counterfactual worlds is used (and this seems to be the one that makes the most sense in this context), then 19 percent of the pay gap is explained; the second counterfactual world leads to 41 percent being explained.[11] Even 19 percent seems rather low. Furthermore, it is not clear whether it would be useful to increase the

---

[11] Note that these numbers differ from those cited in early printings of Treiman and Hartmann (1981:Table 9), which were in error.

number of occupations in the analysis beyond 222. The issue of the optimal or correct number of occupations to use is still very much unexplored.[12]

Technological change narrowed the gender gap during the period of early industrialization, when the use of new forms of capital equipment and work organization raised the relative productivity of females and the young. The increase in the manufacturing sector, which was relatively female intensive, also served to raise the overall ratio of female to male earnings. But changes in the earnings ratio after the first half of the nineteenth century are more complicated. Employment effects of technical change combined with differing demand, income elasticities expanded certain sectors and contracted others, and the increase in education raised the relative earnings of females within occupational groups.

The large increase in female labor force participation over the last 30 years has meant that recent labor market entrants have had substantially less job training than have previous participants. Entrants have, until recently, also had less education than the average female population. Therefore, the average wages of the working population of women as a whole have been depressed by the wages of the new entrants, even though the wages of prior participants have been rising. In a period of rising labor force participation, a stable ratio of female to male earnings does not necessarily indicate an absence of economic and social progress for women.

CONCLUDING REMARKS

Technological advances have altered the employment of women in the following ways throughout American history:

1. Increases in total factor productivity across sectors from 1890 to 1980 have been positively associated with an index of the female intensity of the labor force, but total employment of both males and females has not necessarily been positively related to technological advance.

---

[12] One procedure would be to assess the cross-elasticity of substitution among occupations for individuals. Such a procedure would be similar to that used in antitrust cases in deciding what the market is for a particular good, and thus what the definition of a good is. As a general rule, one does not want to disaggregate occupations so finely that occupation itself is an exact proxy for earnings.

2. Increases in education have been positively associated with increases in female labor force participation and may be the single most important factor in altering the shape of participation rates for married women during their life cycles.

3. Changes in work organization, in particular an enhanced division of labor in manufacturing from 1820 and in the clerical sector from around 1900, have increased the demand for female employees.

4. Relative earnings for females to males rose after 1820 and continued to rise to about 1930 or 1940. The aggregate ratio was virtually constant from 1950 to 1980, but has risen during the past half decade. The ratio for manufacturing employment has remained virtually constant since about 1885. Changes in technology seem to be the most likely reason for the initial advance, and changes in the experience and education of the working population of women appear to have been responsible for much of the recent rise.

The secular increase in female employment in America has owed much to the relative growth of particular sectors in the economy, such as those employing clerical and professional workers, and to the decline of others, such as agriculture. Further work will have to perform the major task of separating the role of technological change from those of demand and income elasticities in altering the sectoral distribution of labor.

REFERENCES

Cain, Louis P., and Donald G. Paterson
    1986   Biased technical change, scale, and factor substitution in American
            industry, 1850–1919. *Journal of Economic History* 56(March):153–
            164.
Coyle, Grace
    1928   *Present Trends in the Clerical Occupations.* New York: The Woman's
            Press.
Denison, Edward F.
    1962   The Sources of Economic Growth in the United States and the
            Alternatives Before Us. Supplementary Paper 13. New York: Com-
            mittee for Economic Development.
    1974   *Accounting for United States Economic Growth. 1929 to 1969.* Washing-
            ton, D.C.: The Brookings Institution.
Easterlin, Richard
    1980   *Birth and Fortune: The Impact of Numbers on Personal Welfare.* New
            York: Basic Books.

Goldin, Claudia
1987 The female labor force and American economic growth, 1890 to 1980. Ch. 10 in S.L. Engerman and R. Gallman, eds., *Long-Term Trends in the American Economy*. Chicago: University of Chicago Press.
1986a Monitoring and occupational segregation by sex: a historical analysis. *Journal of Labor Economics* 4(January):1–27.
1986b Life-Cycle Labor Force Participation of Married Women: Historical Evidence and Implications, University of Pennsylvania. Revised version of National Bureau of Economic Research Working Paper #1251. Cambridge, Mass. December.
1986c The Earnings Gap Between Male and Female Workers: An Historical Perspective. National Bureau of Economic Research Working Paper #1888. Cambridge, Mass. April.
1984 The historical evolution of female earnings functions and occupations. *Explorations in Economic History* 21(January):1–27.
1983 The changing economic role of women: a quantitative approach. *Journal of Interdisciplinary History* 13(Spring):707–733.
1977 Female labor force participation: the origin of black and white differences, 1870 to 1880. *Journal of Economic History* 37(March):87–108.
Goldin, Claudia, and Kenneth Sokoloff
1982 Women, children, and industrialization in the early republic: evidence from the manufacturing censuses. *Journal of Economic History* 42(December):741–774.
1984 The relative productivity hypothesis of industrialization: the American case, 1820 to 1850. *The Quarterly Journal of Economics* 44(August):461–487.
Keat, Paul G.
1960 Long run changes in occupational wage structure, 1900–1956. *Journal of Political Economy* 68(December):584–600.
Kendrick, John W.
1961 *Productivity Trends in the United States*. National Bureau of Economic Research. Princeton: Princeton University Press.
1973 *Postwar Productivity Trends in the United States, 1948–1969*. National Bureau of Economic Research. New York: Columbia University Press.
1983 *Interindustry Differences in Productivity Growth*. Washington, D.C.: American Enterprise Institute.
Mansfield, Edwin
1969 *The Economics of Technological Change*. New York: Norton.
National Research Council
1979 *Measurement and Interpretation of Productivity*. Report of the Panel to Review Productivity Statistics, Committee on National Statistics. Washington, D.C.: National Academy of Sciences.
O'Neill, June
1985 The trend in the male-female wage gap in the United States, *Journal of Labor Economics* 2(January, Suppl.):49–70.
Polachek, Solomon William
1984 Women in the economy: perspectives on gender inequality. Pp. 34–53 in U.S. Commission on Civil Rights, *Comparable Worth: Issues*

for the 80's. Vol. 1. A consultation held June 6–7. U.S. Government Printing Office 1984-524-379. Washington, D.C.: U.S. Commission on Civil Rights.

Rosenberg, Nathan
　　1972　*Technology and American Economic Growth.* New York: Harper & Row.

Rotella, Elyce
　　1981　*From Home to Office: U.S. Women at Work, 1870–1930.* Ann Arbor: UMI Press.

Smith, James, ed.
　　1980　*Female Labor Supply: Theory and Estimation.* Princeton: Princeton University Press.

Smith, James
　　1984　Race and human capital. *American Economic Review* 74 (September):685–698.

Smith, James, and Michael Ward
　　1984　*Women's Wages and Work in the Twentieth Century.* Santa Monica, Calif.: Rand.

Sokoloff, Kenneth
　　1984　Was the transition from the artisanal shop to the nonmechanized factory associated with gains in efficiency? Evidence from the U.S. Manufacturing Censuses of 1820 and 1850. *Explorations in Economic History* 21(October):351–382.

Stoneman, Paul
　　1983　*The Economic Analysis of Technological Change.* Oxford, England: Oxford University Press.

Treiman, Donald J., and Heidi I. Hartmann, eds.
　　1981　*Women, Work, and Wages: Equal Pay for Jobs of Equal Value.* Washington, D.C.: National Academy Press.

Williamson, Jeffrey, and Peter Lindert
　　1980　*American Inequality: A Macroeconomic History.* New York: Academic Press.

Recent Trends in Clerical Employment: The Impact of Technological Change

H. ALLAN HUNT and TIMOTHY L. HUNT

THE GROWTH OF CLERICAL AND FEMALE EMPLOYMENT

Clerical jobs are the largest single occupational group in the economy; they are also one of the most diverse. Generally people associate the traditional office occupations with the term "clerical." Indeed, secretaries, typists, stenographers, file clerks, office machine operators, and receptionists do make up a large proportion of all clerical workers. But bookkeepers and bank tellers are also clerical workers according to the Bureau of the Census, as are bill collectors, insurance adjusters, postal carriers, factory expediters, and most enumerators and interviewers.

The tremendous growth in the number of clerical workers in the United States is well known, but the true magnitude of this expansion cannot be appreciated without comparing it to the growth in total employment. Figure 1 shows that the proportion

Facts and observations presented in this document are the sole responsibility of the authors. The viewpoints do not necessarily represent positions of the W.E. Upjohn Institute for Employment Research.

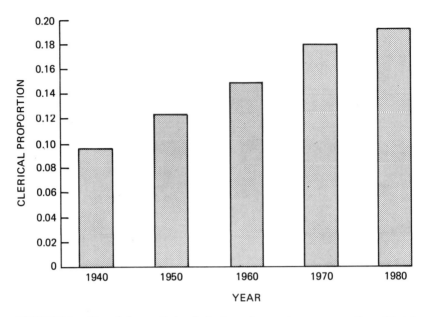

FIGURE 1   Decadal growth in clerical employment as a proportion of total employment, 1940–1980. Source: Hunt and Hunt (1986); based on 1940–1980 census data.

of clerical workers in total employment has doubled in the last 40 years, from just under 1 employee in 10 in 1940 to 1 in 5 by 1980. However, the general recessionary conditions of the last 5 years combined with developments of the last 10 years or so in office technology raise one of the most puzzling questions about future employment: Will this trend continue?

Those who are convinced that this trend cannot continue and may reverse itself base their predictions primarily on the introduction to the office of microprocessor-based technologies. The incredible reductions in the cost of computing power, combined with the reductions in bulk made possible by microprocessor technology, may possibly constitute a revolutionary technical development. And there has been an apparent reduction in the rate of increase in the proportion of clerical workers. As Figure 1 indicates, while the clerical proportion rose almost linearly from 1940 to 1970, a slight reduction in the rate of increase occurred between 1970 and 1980. Is this the beginning of the end of clerical employment growth? If so, what will be the impact on women workers?

Clerical jobs are also female jobs. Is it a coincidence that the expansion of clerical employment occurred simultaneously with the expansion of female labor force participation rates? To what extent have female job opportunities been linked to the expansion of the clerical work force? The overwhelming majority of clerical workers are in fact female, and this is even more true today than it was 30 years ago: from just over 60 percent female in 1950, the proportion grew to nearly 80 percent by 1980. Indeed, not only are clerical workers increasingly women but women are increasingly clerical workers. Between 1950 and 1980, the proportion of women workers who worked in clerical jobs grew from about 27 percent to over 35 percent. Thus, the sex segregation of clerical occupations appears to have been increasing, although there was very little increase in the proportion of females employed as clerical workers between 1970 and 1980.[1] The participation rate for men in clerical work was only 7.6 percent in 1980. Clearly, females are much more likely than males to work as clerical workers and clerical work has increased in importance as a source of employment for women.

This paper reviews trends in clerical employment over the last 30 years and seeks evidence of the impact of changes in process technology on those trends. It also assesses prospects for the future of clerical employment. The next section reviews clerical employment trends from 1950 to 1980 by decade, as well as annual employment changes.[2] Because this period encompasses the first computer revolution, the introduction of mainframe computers to the office, and the beginnings of the microcomputer age, the review can be interpreted as a search for the employment effects of technological change. If changing office technologies displaced large numbers of clerical workers during the first computer revolution, the evidence should be in the employment record of the 1960s and 1970s. Similarly, if the current office technologies threaten clerical jobs, some evidence of this should be found in the employment figures of the early 1980s.

The following section of the paper discusses the determinants of clerical employment in the broadest sense. The influence of industry occupational structure and industry employment trends

---

[1] See Reskin and Hartmann (1985) for a discussion of sex segregation on the job.

[2] A much more thorough review of existing data is provided by Hunt and Hunt (1986:Ch. 2 and 3).

on clerical employment totals are examined. The aggregate change in clerical employment from 1972 to 1982 is decomposed into portions attributable to general economic growth, changes in the sectoral composition of the economy, and changes in occupational staffing patterns. Evidence of the direct impact of technological change on office employment levels is sought for the finance and insurance industry, reputedly the most advanced user of office automation systems.

This paper does not try to assess the influence of other important factors that will determine future labor market outcomes for clerical workers. In particular, there is no consideration of future supply issues. If female labor force participation rates continue to rise as they have in the past, the issue of job creation for women will be of even greater significance. On the other hand, if women increase their penetration of nontraditional female occupations, the number of females seeking clerical positions in the future may decline. Whether men are more likely to begin to look to clerical positions for career opportunities in the future presumably depends on labor market developments for clericals, as well as the job outlook in more traditional male occupations.[3] Clearly these considerations are crucial to understanding whether the supply and demand of clerical workers will be in approximate balance in the labor market of the future, but these questions are beyond the scope of the present effort. We seek only to illuminate past trends in clerical employment and investigate the causes behind those trends. Throughout the analysis we strive to develop an understanding of the employment implications of technological change for clerical workers. In a concluding section, we draw on these findings and on a review of existing forecasts of clerical employment to narrow the range of uncertainty about the probable future impact of technological change on the demand for clerical employment.

A CLOSER LOOK AT CLERICAL EMPLOYMENT TRENDS

EMPLOYMENT FROM 1950 TO 1980, DECENNIAL CENSUS DATA

Table 1 reports the best derivable estimates of detailed clerical employment on a consistent basis across the 1950 to 1980

---

[3] Many of these issues are addressed by Hartmann, Kraut, and Tilly (1986).

time span. These figures are based on data from the decennial censuses, and although they are far from perfect, everything that can be done has been done to maximize the consistency of the estimates and minimize the distortions introduced by the measurement system and changes in it.[4] Table 1 shows that there were just over 19 million clerical workers employed in 1980 in 42 separate clerical occupations ranging from secretary, the largest, to tabulating machine operator, the smallest. There were more than 4 million secretaries employed in 1980; they represented just over

---

[4] Because these data have been adjusted rather extensively for consistency, the figures reported here do not correspond exactly with census figures from other sources. Comparisons of occupational data among decennial censuses are complicated, first, because the data came from a sample of all census respondents (though the numbers are very large by normal sampling standards), and second, because the measuring rod, the occupational classification system, changes between censuses. In 1950, occupational employment was tabulated in 12 major groups and 469 detailed occupational categories. In 1960, the same 12 major groups contained 494 detailed occupations; in 1970 there were only 417 detailed occupations but still accumulated into 12 major occupational groups. The overall changes in the classification system can be regarded as relatively minor over this period, although with regard to individual occupations, major distortions can occur when an occupational category is added or deleted. In 1980, however, the magnitude of the differences in the occupational coding system are enormous: 503 detailed occupations, which have been reshuffled into 13 new major groups. For example, cashiers, who have previously been classified as clerical workers, are reclassified as sales workers; 1.65 million workers are thereby moved from one major occupational group to another. For the first time, there is a fundamental lack of consistency at the major occupational group level between adjacent census observations. To convert all occupational employment numbers to a consistent basis, the classification system of 1970 was chosen as the standard upon the advice of the Bureau of the Census. The comparison between 1960 and 1970 employment in terms of the 1970 classification was readily available from the Bureau (Bureau of the Census, 1972:Table 221, and Priebe et al., 1972). The 1950 census employment could not be converted directly into 1970 categories, and were first reclassified into 1960 terms, using Technical Paper No. 18; then those numbers were converted to the 1970 basis using Priebe et al. (1972). The 1980 data were converted to the 1970 basis using preliminary unpublished results from the Census Bureau. It requires a painstaking effort to bridge from one decennial census to the next in this manner, and the accuracy of the results is uncertain. All of the reclassification work is done on the basis of sample results. The reclassified employment figures are thus subject both to the original sampling error in estimating occupational employment and the secondary sampling error involved in the reclassification study. These issues are discussed more fully in Hunt and Hunt (1986:Ch. 2).

TABLE 1 Employment in Clerical Occupations, 1950 to 1980, Ranked by Level of Employment in 1980

Occupational Title	Employment				Annual Percent Change
	1950	1960	1970	1980	
Total employment	57,178,206	64,639,256	76,553,599	97,639,355	
Clerical workers	6,875,546	9,575,247	13,856,074	19,119,280	
Secretaries	1,005,968	1,539,017	2,875,826	4,058,182	4.8
Not specified clerical workers	1,185,906	1,610,020	862,394	1,880,102	1.5
Bookkeepers	744,053	973,224	1,633,490	1,804,374	3.0
Cashiers	252,252	510,179	884,531	1,654,151	6.5
Miscellaneous clerical workers	253,633	328,399	506,677	1,163,635	5.2
Typists	60,534	547,923	1,041,804	799,561	9.0
Stock clerks and storekeepers	274,089	384,115	482,259	580,979	2.5
Receptionists	77,965	164,446	323,552	536,963	6.6
Shipping and receiving clerks	323,785	325,307	400,890	483,183	1.3
Bank tellers	66,944	139,477	265,197	476,233	6.8
Estimators and investigators, n.e.c.	112,469	171,901	282,074	442,553	4.7
Counter clerks, except food	96,313	127,630	243,697	398,029	4.8
Computer and peripheral equipment operators	868	2,023	124,684	391,909	22.6
Keypunch operators	75,091	169,000	290,119	382,118	5.6
Clerical supervisors, n.e.c.	44,348	56,887	119,887	340,946	7.0
Expediters and production controllers	123,277	151,191	217,107	329,621	3.3
File clerks	118,211	152,160	382,578	316,419	3.3
Postal clerks	216,164	242,872	321,263	315,111	1.3
Telephone operators	363,472	374,495	433,739	314,674	-0.5
Statistical clerks	109,956	143,922	265,431	297,939	3.4
Mail carriers, Post Office	164,851	203,116	268,612	258,966	1.5
Payroll and timekeeping clerks	65,697	112,901	165,815	218,387	4.1

Occupation				
Teachers' aides, except school monitors	6,105	17,804	139,790	207,391	12.5
Mail handlers, except Post Office	53,563	67,300	133,839	182,223	4.2
Insurance adjusters, examiners, and investigators	33,061	58,726	102,043	159,124	5.4
Ticket, station, and express agents	69,807	76,994	104,285	152,841	2.6
Library attendants and assistants	16,235	38,203	133,911	140,808	7.5
Billing clerks	32,357	45,254	112,876	117,943	4.4
Stenographers	429,424	283,486	136,197	91,593	-5.0
Enumerators and interviewers	85,013	118,723	68,697	88,712	0.1
Dispatchers and starters, vehicle	33,746	49,205	63,699	87,622	3.2
Messengers and office helpers	111,508	61,303	61,050	82,225	-1.0
Collectors, bill and account	25,395	34,229	54,728	76,982	3.8
Meter readers, utility	40,696	39,712	35,144	41,407	0.1
Real estate appraisers	11,754	15,822	22,735	41,343	4.3
Office machine operators, n.e.c.	9,788	21,352	38,669	39,864	4.8
Bookkeeping and billing machine operators	26,610	53,914	67,341	37,200	1.1
Weighers	80,915	44,548	41,410	29,717	-3.3
Proofreaders	12,708	17,171	29,940	27,321	2.6
Clerical assistants, social welfare	0	0	1,279	24,128	n.a.
Duplicating machine operators	5,520	14,392	21,682	17,971	4.0
Calculating machine operators	19,176	38,903	37,153	17,881	-0.2
Telegraph operators	34,811	21,064	13,052	7,604	-4.9
Tabulating machine operators	9,725	26,937	8,685	3,345	-3.5

NOTE: n.e.c. = not elsewhere classified.

SOURCE: Decennial Census. Data were adjusted for consistency by the authors.

4 percent of total employment and 21 percent of clerical employment in that year. The second largest category was bookkeepers, with about 1.8 million employed, followed by cashiers, with 1.7 million. The only other clerical occupation that has approached 1 million employees is typists.

Together, these "big four" clerical occupations accounted for 8.5 million jobs, or about 45 percent of all clerical employment in 1980. These same four occupations accounted for only 27 percent of clerical employment in 1950; all four of these occupations have grown substantially in employment during the last 30 years. On the other end of the scale in terms of size, there were only about 3,300 tabulating machine operators and about 7,600 telegraph operators employed in 1980. These occupations have been declining for some years, as have the next two smallest occupations, duplicating machine operators and calculating machine operators. Each of these occupations has been adversely impacted by changes in technology.

When these same data for the various occupations are examined in terms of their annual compound rates of change in employment between 1950 and 1980, computer and peripheral equipment operators far exceeded all other clerical occupations in their rate of increase. This occupation has grown from an employment level of 868 persons in 1950 at the dawn of the computer age to nearly 400,000 persons in 1980, an annual rate of growth of over 22 percent. This is the labor market expression of the computer revolution, which began to substantially affect employment levels in computer-related occupations in the 1960s. It is interesting to note that the second fastest growing clerical occupation over the 1950 to 1980 period was teachers' aides: from high tech to high touch in one easy step! The number of teachers' aides increased from 6,000 to over 200,000 in this 30-year period, or about 12 percent per year. The third fastest growing clerical occupation was typists, even though there was actually a 23 percent decline in employment from 1970 to 1980. The phenomenal growth of typists in the 1950s and 1960s was sufficient to offset the recent decline, for an average annual rate of growth of 9 percent when the entire 30-year period is considered. Following in order of rate of growth are library attendants, clerical supervisors, bank tellers, receptionists, and cashiers. Clearly, there is not a high-tech occupation among them, although they have all been impacted in one way or another by technological change as well as many other influences.

There were also a few clerical occupations that showed absolute declines during this 30-year period. The most rapid declines were among stenographers and telegraph operators, declining in employment by about 5 percent annually. Both occupations have been impacted by technology, but not in an obvious way. The telegraph has been all but replaced by superior communications devices, and this has nearly eliminated the jobs of telegraph operators. Improvements in dictation equipment and changing habits of users have spurred the decline in the stenographer occupation. In 1950, there were 2.3 secretaries per stenographer while by 1980 the ratio had risen to 44 to 1.

Fairly rapid declines were also shown by tabulating machine operators and weighers. Actually, the tabulating machine operators would have been the most rapidly retreating if 1960 had been taken as the base year. This occupation provides an excellent example of a technology-specific occupation that experiences rapid growth and then declines. Tabulating machines were very popular in the 1950s for analyzing data on punched paper cards. The number of tabulating machine operators nearly tripled between 1950 and 1960. But data-processing technology moved rapidly beyond the capabilities of tabulating machines, and the number of employees in this occupation has fallen by nearly 90 percent since 1960. Rounding out the declining occupations are messengers and office helpers, calculating machine operators, and telephone operators. All appear to be office-technology-related declines, since the communications and computing capabilities of modern offices have rendered these jobs less essential than in the past.

With the spectacular exception of the computer operator category, the rapid-growth jobs do not show any particular high-technology bent. On the other hand, the declining occupations do seem to offer a technological interpretation, at least in part. Whether this represents a general principle is not clear at this time. What is clear is that the bulk of clerical employment occurs in a few very large, very diffuse occupational titles, such as secretary and bookkeeper. This was more true in 1980 than in 1950. It is possible that one impact of office technology over the last 30 years has been to foster more generality in job title and perhaps in duties, but that cannot be conclusively demonstrated with the data that are currently available.

ANNUAL EMPLOYMENT CHANGES, CURRENT
POPULATION SURVEY DATA

The long-term decennial census data do not seem to demonstrate a widespread impact of technology on clerical occupations, but annual data from the Current Population Survey (CPS) may be more revealing. Figure 2 shows aggregate clerical employment as a proportion of total employment on an annual basis from 1958 to 1984. It clearly shows that the rate of increase of clerical workers relative to all employment was much slower in the 1970s than it was in the 1960s.[5] Even more apparent is the stagnation in the proportion of clerical workers since 1980. Clerical workers did not fare as well in the last recessionary period as they did earlier. It is less certain what the downturn in the clerical proportion in 1984 means. Such a decline has been typical of recovery periods in the past (as in 1976–1977), when the number of production workers rises rapidly to restore the prerecession balance between production and nonproduction workers, including clericals. Whether the trend of the early 1980s is something different is not yet clear. The magnitude of the drop is unprecedented, but that does not prove that the cause is fundamentally different.

A look at recent annual CPS data for detailed occupations may be instructive. Unfortunately, the only time period for which this can be done is the decade from 1972 to 1982. If the microprocessor revolution is going to have catastrophic impacts on clerical employment, it should have become apparent by 1982 when the microcomputer population reached the 1 million unit level (Computer and Business Equipment Manufacturers Association, 1985:87). While this period would seem to be adequate for analysis, it is complicated by the fact that the recession of 1981–1982 occurs right at the end of the period.[6] In addition, because of the smaller sample used by the CPS, some reservation must be expressed about any particular annual observation. More

---

[5] The apparent drop in 1971 should be ignored as it reflects the conversion to new census codes rather than any actual change in clerical employment levels.

[6] It is frustrating to stop the analysis in 1982; however, the massive reorganization of the occupational classification system introduced to the CPS in 1983 (corresponding to the 1980 decennial census reclassification) prevents the development of consistent data for all occupations after 1982.

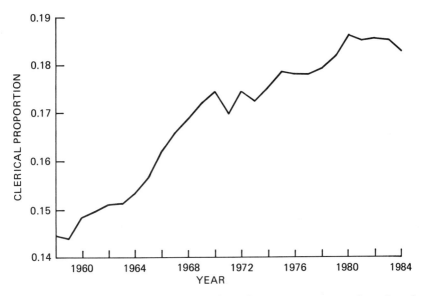

FIGURE 2   Annual changes in clerical employment as a proportion of total employment, 1958–1984. Source: Hunt and Hunt (1986); based on 1958–1984 CPS data.

confidence can be put in trends that emerge over a period of 3 or 4 years.

Table 2 shows the CPS clerical occupations sorted by the annual rate of change over the 1972–1982 decade. As in the decennial data for 1950 to 1980, computer and peripheral equipment operators experienced the most rapid rate of increase of any clerical occupation, although it was only about half the average annual rate shown for the 1950–1980 period. Bank tellers and insurance adjusters, examiners and investigators both edged ahead of teachers' aides in growth rates during the more recent decade. This reflects the falloff in the rate of growth in teachers' aides as employment growth in education as a whole faltered because of funding difficulties and a reduction in the student population.

Other clerical occupations showing relatively rapid growth during the 1972 to 1982 decade include cashiers, estimators and investigators, and receptionists. All three of these occupations involve direct customer contact and probably would fall into the "hard to automate" category. Messengers and office helpers emerge as a relatively rapidly growing clerical occupation in the

TABLE 2 Employment in Clerical Occupations, 1972 to 1982, Ranked by Relative Change, 1972 to 1982

Occupational Title	Employment (in thousands)											Ann. % Chg.
	1972	1973	1974	1975	1976	1977	1978	1979	1980	1981	1982	
Computer and peripheral equipment operators	199	220	251	302	295	311	403	465	535	564	588	11.4
Bank tellers	290	329	356	356	378	416	458	503	542	569	561	6.8
Insurance adjusters, examiners, and investigators	109	114	127	153	159	172	173	178	179	191	200	6.3
Teachers' aides, except school monitors	208	232	253	292	325	326	348	357	391	381	373	6.0
Cashiers	998	1,060	1,127	1,200	1,280	1,354	1,434	1,512	1,592	1,660	1,683	5.4
Estimators and investigators, n.e.c.	350	334	374	389	423	459	460	506	545	540	570	5.0
Receptionists	439	450	465	468	511	542	600	614	644	675	672	4.3
Messengers and office helpers	79	85	77	78	83	95	89	95	98	97	115	3.8
Collectors, bill and account	61	59	64	73	66	73	80	77	81	93	87	3.6
Mail handlers, except Post Office	129	144	148	145	140	149	164	170	168	175	182	3.5
All other clerical workers	1,329	1,331	1,388	1,375	1,444	1,587	1,705	1,818	1,899	1,956	1,871	3.5
Enumerators and interviewers	39	49	53	44	49	55	54	61	87	58	53	3.1
Clerical supervisors, n.e.c.	200	184	231	228	239	229	207	241	245	250	270	3.0
Expediters and production controllers	196	202	201	214	210	219	228	244	238	254	257	2.7
Secretaries	2,964	3,088	3,218	3,281	3,428	3,470	3,646	3,792	3,944	3,917	3,847	2.6
Clerical workers	14,329	14,667	15,199	15,321	15,788	16,372	17,207	17,953	18,473	18,564	18,466	2.6

Keypunch operators	284	255	251	253	279	284	277	279	271	248	364	2.5
Dispatchers and starters, vehicle	86	88	92	93	89	99	99	109	105	115	110	2.5
Bookkeepers	1,592	1,673	1,706	1,709	1,712	1,754	1,861	1,945	1,942	1,961	1,968	2.1
Statistical clerks	301	301	328	331	342	363	384	408	396	370	365	1.9
Payroll and timekeeping clerks	185	200	206	202	211	231	245	241	237	231	224	1.9
Ticket, station, and express agents	130	118	123	138	126	132	131	148	144	148	154	1.7
Counter clerks, except food	331	352	350	331	359	349	383	369	358	360	373	1.2
Shipping and receiving clerks	453	461	469	433	446	474	469	493	515	525	499	1.0
Library attendants and assistants	138	123	135	146	143	144	174	168	155	152	150	0.8
Billing clerks	149	166	158	145	140	157	170	164	165	153	154	0.3
File clerks	274	287	279	268	274	280	279	312	332	315	278	0.1
Mail carriers, Post Office	271	268	268	254	244	244	258	256	247	242	264	-0.3
Stock clerks and storekeepers	513	478	493	479	499	505	516	539	544	528	497	-0.3
Postal clerks	282	303	295	293	291	271	272	264	291	269	271	-0.4
Typists	1,025	1,040	1,046	1,035	995	1,020	1,060	1,038	1,043	1,031	942	-0.8
Telephone operators	394	390	393	348	343	347	317	333	323	308	283	-3.3
Bookkeeping and billing machine operators	69	57	59	60	49	53	47	59	52	49	42	-4.8
Stenographers	125	107	104	101	101	84	96	78	66	74	66	-6.2

NOTE: n.e.c. = not elsewhere classified.

SOURCE: Current Population Survey.

1970s, which is in contrast with their declining employment from 1950 to 1970. The number of bill collectors increased at 3.6 percent annually during the decade, and non-Post Office mail handlers increased at 3.5 percent. No particular pattern emerges from the listing of clerical occupations that grew more rapidly than average during this recent decade.

At the other end of the distribution, the declining occupations, stenographers and telephone operators, are joined by bookkeeping and billing machine operators in rather rapid decline for the 1972 to 1982 period. Small annual declines were registered for typists, postal clerks, mail carriers, and stock clerks and storekeepers. Bookkeeping and billing machine operators are another clerical occupation that may be impacted by the microprocessor revolution. As microcomputers have become more widely distributed, increasing attention has been paid to creating accounting software that will run on the micros. This has undoubtedly impacted the number of bookkeeping machine operators. What is not clear is whether it has reduced the number of people doing bookkeeping work. Since they are not doing it on a special purpose device, it would no longer be appropriate to call them bookkeeping machine operators, however, and the job titles are very likely changed.

Without more careful study of both inputs and outputs of office production, definitive conclusions about the impacts of office technology cannot be drawn. This analysis leaves the impression that office technology cannot be regarded as an important determinant of clerical employment for more than a few occupations. Nonetheless, it is also the case that clerical employment growth has slowed in the last decade.

DETERMINANTS OF CLERICAL EMPLOYMENT

Analysis of the trends in occupational employment indicated that some clerical jobs were growing while others were declining. On an aggregate basis, it was seen that clerical jobs as a whole were becoming relatively more important as a proportion of total jobs in the economy, although that growth slowed in the 1970s. It also appeared that in the recession of 1980–1982 the proportion of clerical jobs did not increase significantly as it has in past recessions. What might be causing those movements?

In the broadest terms possible, employment depends upon the demand for output and the productivity of the workers who produce that output. National output is generally measured by gross national product (GNP), the value of all final goods and services produced in the economy in a year. This simple relationship, although devoid of occupational and industrial content, emphasizes two important points.

First, if one accepts the notion that productivity is more or less fixed in the short run by the technological structure of production, then it should be clear that changes in GNP—aggregate demand in the economy—drive any changes in employment. Many factors affect both the level and rate of growth of GNP, including unforeseen shocks to the economy, such as the energy crises of the 1970s, which at least temporarily disrupt the national economic system, and business cycles, which may vary tremendously in terms of their length and severity. All occupations and industries are adversely affected by the failure of GNP to grow sufficiently; likewise, all occupations and industries tend to benefit from reasonable economic growth.

The second factor that influences employment is productivity. The concern, of course, is that productivity growth will outpace the growth of GNP. During recessionary periods it is not unusual for the lack of jobs to be blamed on labor-saving technology, and office automation is a case in point. However, productivity growth and GNP growth are actually intertwined: productivity gains *allow the possibility* of economic growth. Historically, technological change has not created permanent unemployment for millions of workers; instead it has raised living standards. To be sure, there have been winners and losers in this process, both among firms and individuals, but the net result has been real economic growth. No one can guarantee that history will repeat itself with office automation today, but some appear to be too easily persuaded that history will *not* repeat itself, that office automation and other labor-saving technologies will wipe out millions of jobs.

The demand for labor is a derived demand based upon the demand for the goods or services which that labor produces. The rise and fall of occupations is related to the rise and fall of products and services which are produced in particular industries. Prospects for clerical workers, then, are linked to the prospects of the industries in which they work.

TABLE 3 Employment by Industry, 1982

Industry	Total Industry Employment (thousands)	Percent of Total Employment	Percent of Workers in Industry in Clerical Jobs[a]	Clerical Employment (thousands)	Percent of All Clerical Workers Employed in Industry
Agriculture	3,401	3.4	2.4	83	0.4
Mining	1,028	1.0	12.5	128	0.7
Construction	5,756	5.8	7.8	451	2.4
Durables	11,968	12.0	12.6	1,513	8.2
Nondurables	8,318	8.4	12.9	1,074	5.8
Utilities	6,552	6.6	22.3	1,463	7.9
Wholesale trade	4,120	4.1	20.5	844	4.6
Retail trade	16,638	16.7	17.1	2,840	15.4
Finance	6,270	6.3	43.9	2,750	14.9
Services	30,259	30.4	18.1	5,473	29.7
Public administration	5,218	5.2	35.0	1,827	9.9
Total	99,528	100.0	18.5	18,466	100.0

[a]This percentage is also known as the clerical staffing ratio.

SOURCE: Calculated by the authors from CPS data.

CLERICAL EMPLOYMENT BY INDUSTRY

The relative importance of the various industries in the national employment picture is presented in Table 3, based on CPS data for 1982. By far the most important of the individual one-digit industries is the service sector. It accounts for a little over 30 percent of all employment, almost double the size of the next biggest sector, retail trade. Table 3 also shows the clerical staffing ratio, which indicates how important the clerical jobs are in each of these industries. A staffing ratio for an occupation measures the relative importance of that occupation compared to all others in an industry. The ratio is obtained by dividing employment in that occupation in an industry by total industry employment. (The staffing ratios of all occupations within an industry must sum to one; shown as percents, they must sum to 100.)

According to Table 3, the finance industry shows the highest percentage of clerical workers; nearly 45 percent of all employees in this industry are clerical workers. While not shown in the table, twice as many clerical workers work in finance as any other type of worker. Public administration is also a heavy employer of clerical workers; 35 percent of all jobs in this industry are clerical. It is followed by utilities and wholesale trade, which also utilize heavy proportions (more than 20 percent) of clerical workers to produce their output. However, in neither of these industries are clerical workers as dominant as in finance or public administration. The service industry and retail trade both show between 15 and 20 percent of their total employment in clerical occupations (although their needs for other occupations do not look similar at all). The durable and nondurable manufacturing industries show between 10 and 15 percent of their total employment in clerical occupations (both are the home base of operatives, of course). Last is the construction industry, which employs relatively few clerical workers (but is the dominant user of skilled craft workers in the economy).

Clearly, different industries use very different mixes of occupations to produce their final output. The occupational staffing ratios are relatively unique to each type of production. It is this variation in the staffing ratios between industries that makes trends in industry employment an important influence on the distribution of occupations throughout the economy.

The absolute number of clerical jobs in each of the major industries is also presented in Table 3. About 5.5 million clerical workers can be found in the service industry. Just under 3 million clerical jobs are located in each of two sectors, retail trade and finance. These three sectors combined—services, retail trade, and finance—account for more than 11 million clerical jobs, almost 60 percent of total clerical employment. Clerical workers may be dispersed broadly throughout the national economy, but these three sectors are especially important to total clerical employment.

The 20 most important industrial employers of clerical workers in 1982 are presented in Table 4. These data are from the Bureau of Labor Statistics (BLS) Occupational Employment Statistics (OES) program, which currently collects the most detailed data on occupational employment by industry.[7] The entries in the table are ranked by the number of clerical employees in each industry. The clerical staffing ratios and total employment in each industry are also included. Finally, the percent of total clerical jobs accounted

---

[7] These data provide the historical basis for the staffing ratios in the Bureau of Labor Statistics (BLS) industry-occupation matrix, which is subsequently used as the starting point for the BLS projections of future occupational employment. See BLS (1981).

TABLE 4 Clerical Employment by Industry, 1982

Industry	Total Industry Employment (thousands)	Clerical Employment (thousands)	Clerical Staffing Ratio (percent)	Percentage of Total Clerical Employment	Cumulative Percentage of Total Clerical Employment
State and local government and educational services	13,068	2,512	19.2	13.4	13.4
Miscellaneous retail trade	10,476	2,496	23.8	13.3	26.8
Wholesale trade	5,294	1,531	28.9	8.2	34.9
Banking	1,650	1,180	71.5	6.3	41.2
Federal government	2,739	1,138	41.5	6.1	47.3
Insurance	1,700	911	53.6	4.9	52.2
Miscellaneous business services	3,139	896	28.5	4.8	57.0
Hospitals	4,166	666	16.0	3.6	60.5
Social services, museums, and membership organizations	2,755	587	21.3	3.1	63.7
Credit agencies, security and commodity brokers	1,015	577	56.9	3.1	66.8
Legal and miscellaneous services	1,628	560	34.4	3.0	69.7
Telephone and other communication	1,174	529	45.1	2.8	72.6
Physician and dental offices	1,309	394	30.1	2.1	74.7
Construction	3,913	324	8.3	1.7	76.4
Eating and drinking places	4,781	224	4.7	1.2	77.6
Electric services and gas distribution	792	207	26.2	1.1	78.7
Trucking and warehousing	1,206	199	16.5	1.1	79.8
Miscellaneous printing and publishing	846	192	22.8	1.0	80.8
Real estate	986	188	19.1	1.0	81.8
Miscellaneous personal services	1,219	186	15.3	1.0	82.8

SOURCE: Calculated by the authors, based on data tape from the 1982-1995 OES/BLS occupational employment projections.

for by each of the 20 industries as well as the cumulative total is also reported.

The top 10 industries in terms of clerical employment account for about two-thirds of all clerical employment. The top 20 industries account for over 80 percent of all clerical jobs. Federal, state, and local government sectors are clearly important to clerical employment; jointly they account for more than 3.6 million clerical jobs or almost 20 percent of the total. We can also see the importance of banking and insurance, the two largest sectors within finance in terms of clerical employment. Finally, clerical jobs are important in a variety of service sector industries, from business services to personal services. None of the top 10 clerical employment industries is from the goods-producing sector.

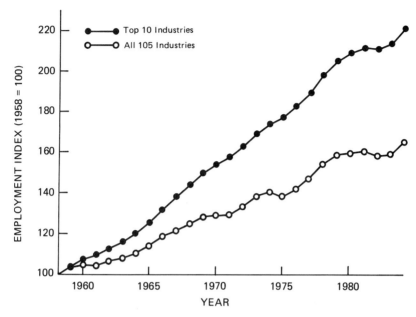

FIGURE 3   Total employment in the top 10 clerical-employing industries, 1958-1984. Source: Hunt and Hunt (1986); based on 1958–1984 BLS data.

Since industry employment is so crucial to occupational employment levels, the trends over the last 27 years in industry employment are presented in Figure 3 and Table 5. Figure 3 aggregates the employment in the top 10 industries, while Table 5 presents the employment trends for each of the 10 industries. The numbers are reported in index number form to make it easier to compare the growth trends. The average growth in employment for all industries is also reported to facilitate comparisons between the particular industry and the average for all industries.

Figure 3 demonstrates a number of important features of the top 10 clerical employment industries. First, these industries have been much less susceptible to the vagaries of the business cycle than all industries. The growth rate of the sum of these 10 sectors has remained positive through two of the three recessions during the period. It was only in 1982, during the worst recession since World War II, that the composite growth rate of these 10 sectors turned negative—and then, barely so. Second, the average growth rate of these 10 industries has clearly outdistanced the all-industry average for the entire 27-year period, but this is mostly because

TABLE 5 Total Industry Employment Growth of Sectors with the Largest Number of Clerical Employees, 1958-1984

Year	State and Local Government	Miscellaneous Retail Trade	Wholesale Trade	Banking	Federal Government	Insurance	Miscellaneous Business Services	Hospitals	Credit Agencies and Commodity Brokers	Social Services and Museums	Top 10 Industries	All Industries
1958	100	100	100	100	100	100	100	100	100	100	100	100
1959	104	103	103	104	102	101	110	106	109	118	104	104
1960	108	98	105	109	104	103	116	113	116	122	108	105
1961	112	105	105	112	104	105	123	120	124	128	109	105
1962	116	107	107	116	107	106	135	126	129	131	113	107
1963	122	109	109	120	108	109	146	134	132	133	116	108
1964	128	112	112	124	107	111	159	143	138	134	120	111
1965	136	116	116	128	109	112	173	149	142	136	126	114
1966	146	121	121	134	117	114	192	156	149	140	132	119
1967	154	124	124	141	124	119	211	171	156	146	138	122
1968	161	128	127	148	125	122	224	182	171	153	144	125
1969	167	133	131	159	126	125	248	195	186	157	150	129
1970	174	136	134	169	125	129	262	205	182	159	154	129
1971	180	139	134	174	123	131	264	213	184	163	158	130
1972	189	144	138	181	123	133	282	218	194	157	163	134
1973	196	149	144	191	122	135	308	226	202	158	169	139
1974	203	149	149	202	124	139	326	238	202	162	174	141
1975	211	148	148	206	125	140	333	250	202	165	178	139
1976	215	153	153	212	125	142	359	260	210	170	183	142
1977	220	158	158	220	124	148	386	271	222	172	190	148
1978	229	165	167	231	126	154	429	280	238	177	199	155
1979	233	168	175	243	127	160	472	287	256	183	206	159
1980	237	167	177	255	131	164	504	303	268	189	210	160
1981	235	168	180	264	127	167	540	320	284	190	212	161
1982	232	166	177	268	125	168	551	332	291	190	212	159
1983	232	169	176	270	126	169	580	334	317	190	215	160
1984	233	177	185	273	127	172	654	329	343	196	222	167

NOTE: 1958 equals 100.

SOURCE: Calculated by the authors, based on data from the BLS input-output industry series.

employment in these sectors does not ordinarily retreat during recessionary periods, but continues to expand.

As Table 5 shows, growth patterns among the top 10 industries have been diverse. Their average growth over the 27-year period was 122 percent; all but one grew faster than the economywide rate of 67 percent. The most robust growth has clearly occurred in miscellaneous business services; hospitals; banking; and credit agencies and security and commodity brokers. The growth in employment in miscellaneous business services is particularly striking, with more than six times as many workers in this sector in 1984 as there were in 1958. This sector provides myriad services to business firms, from accounting to customized computer software to consulting advice. Also striking is the growth rate of employment in hospitals; employment tripled over the period 1958 to 1984. Some of the causes of this growth, such as the aging of the population and the increasing availability of medical insurance for retirees and the indigent through government programs, are well known. In any event, the growth of this sector has not been affected by business cycles and may have even accelerated during the last recessionary period. Surprisingly, however, hospital employment growth slowed in 1983 and actually turned negative in 1984. The recent emphasis on cost containment and the shortening of hospital stays may be having an impact on employment.

It is also clear that the finance sector—especially banking; credit agencies and security and commodity brokers; and insurance—contributed significantly to clerical job growth during these years. All three of these sectors have staffing ratios for clerical workers in excess of 50 percent, the highest of all industries. Insurance employment grew at about the economywide average until about 1974, then began to accelerate, and outdistanced the national economy in job growth thereafter (except for 1984). The growth of employment in banking was consistently higher than that for insurance, nearly tripling from 1958 to 1984.

The slowest growth among the 10 industries with large clerical employment occurred in the federal government. The federal government has not been a source of significant employment growth in the last 20 years; its growth is well below average. State and local government employment, while generally above average in growth, actually declined absolutely during the 1980–1982 recession. By the end of 1984, employment had still not exceeded its peak employment level, achieved in 1980. This is significant because it is the first such decline and sluggish recovery in recent history for the largest single employer of clerical workers among the 105 industries in this analysis.

Of course, the gnawing question is: Will these industries show rapid employment growth in the future? That question cannot be answered at this point. However, the nation is still experiencing a long-run shift from a goods-producing economy to a service-producing economy. Historically, clerical workers have benefited from this shift since service industries employ much higher proportions of clerical workers. Thus, even if staffing ratios begin to fall for clerical workers (because of office automation or other factors), it is still possible for them to grow at or above the average rate for all jobs because they are concentrated in the non-goods-producing sectors. Clerical workers have so far had a fortunate industry mix in their employment pattern.

TECHNOLOGICAL CHANGE AND CLERICAL EMPLOYMENT GROWTH

Because one of the goals of office automation is to improve labor productivity, actual gains in labor productivity may be the best measure of the degree to which this goal is realized. The major problems in attempting to estimate the true gains from office automation are twofold. First, it is impossible to glean from current data any information whatsoever about the relative importance of office automation spending by firm or industry. Investment data are subdivided only into the two broad subcomponents of machinery and equipment and structures. Second, complete data about clerical jobs are not available over time, and no information links workers to the use of equipment. Thus, it is impossible to estimate the productivity gains specifically attributable to clerical workers utilizing various types of electronic office technology.[8]

One simple approach to examining the productivity gains from office automation is to study those sectors that are significant employers of clerical workers and that are also believed to be leaders in office automation. The broad industrial sector of finance and insurance is the recognized leader in the field of office automation,

---

[8] See Hunt and Hunt (1985) for a more detailed discussion of the available data.

and more than one-half of the workers in this sector are clerical workers. Of the 105 detailed industries analyzed in this paper, the finance and insurance sector is composed of three of these industries: banking, insurance, and credit agencies and security and commodity brokers. Thus, if office automation improves productivity, these three industries are logical candidates to demonstrate the effects of such gains.

Figure 4 reports the productivity gains for banking, insurance, and credit agencies and security and commodity brokers for the period 1958–1983.[9] The data are reported in index number form to better depict the percentage changes in productivity from year to year. The productivity trend for all private nonfarm employment is reported as well to facilitate a comparison of these industries with the aggregate. Surprisingly, Figure 4 reveals no discernible trend that can be attributed to office automation. The productivity gains in banking, insurance, and credit agencies and security and commodity brokers have all tended historically to lag behind the average for private nonfarm employment. In fact, productivity for credit agencies and security and commodity brokers was very slightly lower in 1983 than in 1958, and productivity deteriorated absolutely in insurance after 1977. Since 1981, banking productivity has improved relative to all private nonfarm productivity, but the improvement is hardly revolutionary, especially given that banking productivity declined from 1979 to 1981.

It should be emphasized that these are *not* measures of the productivity gains for clerical workers nor can these gains be attributed to office automation. They are industry-wide measures for output gains due to *all* improvements across all employees. All that can be fairly concluded is that there is nothing in the aggregate industry data to support the notion that office automation has engendered significant overall productivity gains in these three industries.

Have these industries been investing in office automation? Although office automation expenditures are not reported separately, Figure 5 reports, in index number form, real investment spending per employee for the financial industries. The data are for finance

---

[9] The gross output in constant dollar terms and employment measures are defined in Bureau of Labor Statistics, 1979; the data utilized here are from an unpublished update (April 1985).

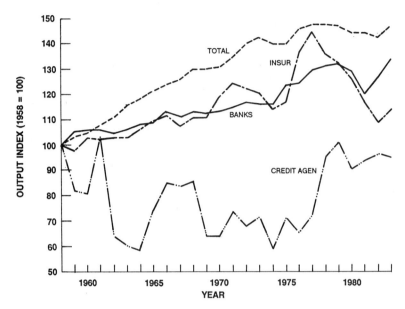

FIGURE 4 Productivity gains in terms of output per hour for banking, insurance, and credit agencies, 1958–1983. Source: Based on unpublished data provided by BLS, April 8, 1985.

and insurance firms, the smallest level of industrial detail available for such investment data (Seskin and Sullivan, 1985). Once again, the totals for private nonfarm employment are also shown for comparison. In contrast to the lack of any "takeoff" evident in the productivity data for finance and insurance, the investment data in Figure 5 clearly indicate much higher than average investment trends in finance and insurance after 1966–1967. In fact, investment per employee virtually exploded, growing a little more than five times the average for all private nonfarm employment after 1966–1967.[10]

Although there is no doubt that the finance and insurance industries are investing heavily in new capital equipment, it is less certain that they are investing in office automation. What can be concluded is that the dramatic growth in investment in finance and insurance has not resulted in measurable labor productivity gains to date. One explanation of this puzzling situation is that the aggregate industry data may be flawed, but given such pronounced

---

[10] Historically, absolute investment per employee in finance and insurance has tended to be much less than the average for all nonfarm private industries.

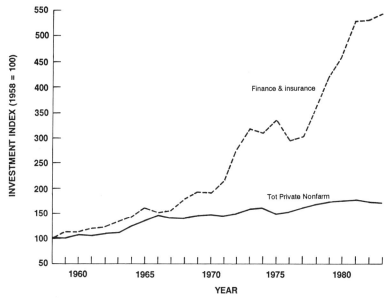

FIGURE 5   Real investment spending per employee for finance and insurance firms, 1958–1983. Source: Based on unpublished data provided by BLS, April 8, 1985.

investment growth in finance and insurance over such a long period of time, it is difficult to believe that the productivity data are so flawed that they would not register at least the beginning of a new trend, if one were actually occurring.[11]

The lack of productivity increase shown in the aggregate data is borne out to some extent by other sources. Although formal case studies of the economic impacts of office automation are generally lacking,[12] there is fragmentary information that casts doubt on the most wildly optimistic productivity claims of advocates of

---

[11]   There are serious concerns about the quality of the aggregate data (see Hunt and Hunt, 1985). BLS has constructed special productivity indexes in banking, measuring output as services rendered and labor input as actual hours worked. The overall result, 1967–1980, is that productivity growth in banking remains very slightly below the national average for all nonfarm businesses (Brand and Duke, 1982).

[12]   Salerno (1985) and Strassman (1985) concur in the paucity of studies. For a review of a considerable literature about the sociological impacts of office automation, see Attewell and Rule (1984). From the economists' perspective, this literature is lacking in a systematic treatment of output, capital input, prices of outputs and inputs, and other economic variables.

office automation. First, a number of recent books (Bailey et al., 1985; Diebold, 1985; and Katzan, 1982) designed to be guides for managers interested in improving productivity through office automation contain surprisingly few references to the actual experiences of firms or to the productivity gains that managers can reasonably hope to achieve with office automation. For instance, Katzan includes an entire chapter on word processing, but provides no hint about the likely potential productivity gains.

Second, Paul Strassman, an executive and office automation specialist with Xerox, in a recent assessment (1985) of the technology with which he has been associated for over 20 years, eschews the current focus on hardware. Although he is optimistic about the potential productivity gains from computers and information technology generally, he stresses that the hardware is less relevant than the people using it. In fact, he suggests (1985:159) that the growth rates in office automation investment of the early 1980s are unsustainable unless that investment produces demonstrable returns. Strassman finds little evidence of such returns currently:

> The preliminary findings of my research raise doubts about the assumptions which managements in the businesses I have sampled so far must have made when they increased their computer-technology budgets in pursuit of improved productivity.

Strassman thinks the payoff will come when management focuses on strategic goals and the people who will accomplish those goals, rather than on the methods to achieve those goals.

Third, a recent study points to the hidden costs of adoption of information technology, costs so large that productivity gains do not occur. Researchers King and Kraemer (1981) contend that, while the cost of hardware is falling, the total cost of electronic computing is rising rapidly (1981:102): "Software procurement, software maintenance, and data management and computing management, are all becoming increasingly expensive." Furthermore, because many of the non-hardware costs tend to be hidden from normal accounting procedures used to justify implementation, these costs do not necessarily affect the implementation decision itself—although they would adversely impact the firm's actual operating results. New positions and even departments are springing up in firms to evaluate software, perform system maintenance, coordinate among different users, etc. Firms often find that "off-the-shelf" software is unsatisfactory for their computing needs, necessitating significant investment in software programming.

As electronic computing becomes more widespread in firms through the adoption of personal computers, King and Kraemer (1981:101) believe it will become increasingly difficult for management to track these costs. Users at all levels dedicate some portion of their time to routine maintenance tasks. Worse, some may even develop a personal interest in the technology that diverts them from other work. According to King and Kraemer management seldom knows the ongoing costs of training, normal system maintenance, or unplanned downtime that are in fact incurred because of the firm's utilization of information technologies. They cite a variety of other studies and fragmentary data, which appear to indicate that the annual costs for system maintenance run at least 20 percent of the cost of the development of the system itself, and may even be much higher. They think the costs due to breakdowns may be particularly significant in highly integrated systems. According to King and Kraemer (1981:107),

> when systems become integrated and units become more interdependent in a real-time sense, problems in one system or unit can literally stop progress in others simply by disruption of the *process* of interaction. As integration increases, interdependency increases. Together, these two phenomena result in increased costs.

Fourth, International Data Corporation (IDC), which may be the information industry's largest market research and consulting firm, has repeatedly stressed that the labor productivity gains from office automation fall far short of justifying the purchase of the equipment. According to IDC (1984, 1983, 1982), the direct labor savings attributable to an office automation project over a 5-year period usually amount to no more than one-half the cost of implementation of the system. IDC states that this rule of thumb does not include the training costs of implementing office automation. However, it also does not include any improvements in the quality of the output of offices. IDC concludes that the quality improvements justify the adoption of office automation. Even some computer vendors are not emphasizing cost savings *per se* in their attempts to sell office automation. A booklet about cost justification that Wang Laboratories makes available to potential customers stresses the complexity of the cost justification process for office automation. One of the premises of the booklet (Wang Laboratories, Inc., 1985:3) is that information technology systems are fundamentally "different from other kinds of capital equipment investments and should be treated differently with regard to cost justification." In the six examples of firms that have successfully cost-justified their systems included in the booklet, the emphasis in all cases is on improvements in quality rather than on direct cost savings.

In general, these sources indicate little improvement in productivity overall (Katzan, Strassman), higher costs of installation and operation (King and Kraemer), or quality rather than quantity improvements (IDC and Wang). Still other reasons why office automation may not have a significant impact on productivity include its limited spread to date, weaknesses in its technical capabilities, and its role in making production more information intensive.

First, one of the most obvious reasons that office automation may not have created measurable productivity gains industry-wide is that the diffusion of the technology may not have proceeded nearly as far as implied by the popular media. According to a national random survey by Honeywell Inc. (1983) of 1,264 general office secretaries employed in information-intensive establishments with 100 or more employees, office automation equipment is not yet in widespread use in most offices. Fewer than one-half of the secretaries reported having access to an electronic memory typewriter/word processor/personal computer in the general office area in which they work; less than one-fourth possessed any of this equipment at their individual workstation (1983:III-5). Almost none of the secretaries reported having direct access to electronic mail, computerized scheduling, or computerized filing, while about 15 percent said that such equipment was located somewhere in the office area (1983:III-5). The limited use of automation found is especially surprising because the survey was limited to large establishments in information-intensive industries, exactly where one would expect to find office automation in place.

Second, office automation may not be producing the promised productivity gains, because technical constraints inherent in the current technology reduce its effectiveness. Word processors may not be that much different from their earlier nonelectronic predecessors; both are tools used to accomplish standard office functions. More advanced devices and appropriate methods may be necessary to bring about more significant changes in production methods. There also appear to be severe hardware and software compatibility problems across computer systems, which limit applications. Electronic mail, for example, is currently limited by system incompatibilities. Even when direct communications systems are installed, for example, in the form of a local area network, it will likely still be a relatively primitive system. It may not be possible to use the local area network to access the large data bases on the firm's mainframe computer. It may not be possible to transmit graphics via the network. While it may be possible to access a user who is not on the local area network, the procedure may be too tedious and cumbersome to be truly useful in the transmission of serious business messages. In short, the allowable traffic on the local area network may be very structured and severely limited by the available hardware and software. The office with instantaneous access to any data base around the world and total communications flexibility still lies somewhere in the future.

Many writers have compared this stage in the evolution of computers with that of automobiles in the 1920s. The technology for automobiles had already been firmly established by that date. What was needed, however, were the highways which would make it possible to effectively utilize the technology. According to this analogy, computers now need "pathways" to effectively communicate across dissimilar hardware and software systems before it will be possible to realize their full potential.

The third reason that office automation may not be having an impact on productivity is that much of what we term office automation is not being purchased as labor-saving process technology at all. A deepening of capital may be occurring as products and services become more information intensive and new products and services are developed. Office automation may represent simply additional capital support for office workers rather than capital substitution for labor.

In part, this is a restatement of the quality argument presented earlier. Office automation may be seen as a means to ensure a firm's competitive survival by providing improved access to data and feedback. Aside from the question of whether electronic office technology saves labor time directly, there is no doubt that it permits more adequate analytical support for decision making, timely answers to customer inquiries, more rapid tracking of sales data allowing better inventory control, and many other gains in quality. Those who have utilized electronic spreadsheet software know that it results in a whole new world of opportunities for tabular and graphical analyses. The availability of personal computers taps hidden computing needs that executives always had but that could not be satisfied previously because of insufficient staff or time available to do so on the firm's mainframe computer. The diffusion of the newer and smaller micros is eliminating this roadblock. Managers are simply taking advantage of the lower marginal cost of computing by utilizing it in new and different ways. This result is compounded by the difficulty of adequately measuring output from an office; it is extremely difficult to know how much the new technologies have added to the bottom line of the firm. In particular, changes in quality are especially difficult to measure.

In summary, this review of the technological influences on clerical employment has been relatively unsatisfying. There are no general time series data about office automation spending by industry or about the application of devices by individual occupations. The analysis of overall productivity gains in finance and insurance did not provide any evidence that office automation is producing significant productivity gains in that sector despite the fact that real investment spending in finance and insurance has increased rapidly since the late 1960s. Similarly, other sources, citing a variety of explanations, support the notion of an apparent lack of productivity gains from office automation to date. Consequently, it seems likely that productivity gains are not having a major impact on clerical employment trends.

DECOMPOSITION OF CLERICAL EMPLOYMENT CHANGES

Employment change in an occupation can be understood as resulting from three factors: (1) general economic growth, (2) differential rates of industry growth (because each industry uses a different mix of occupations), and (3) the relative importance of each occupation within each industry, which can be thought of as the intensity of use of a particular occupation (or the occupational staffing ratio introduced above). The above discussion focused on industry growth rates and the impact of office automation on the intensity of use of clerical workers. If the net effect of office automation is the displacement of clerical jobs, over time clerical staffing ratios will fall. In the following discussion, an analytical tool is used to summarize the effects of all three factors. Using the mathematical technique of decomposition, occupational employment changes can be artificially separated into their three components.

The decomposition methodology provides another, more systematic opportunity to assess the technological influence of office automation on clerical jobs. In general, changing staffing ratios are probably the most visible manifestation of the *specific* effects of technological change on occupational employment. For example, the staffing ratios for computer-related occupations have risen in many industries over time because of the dramatic increases in the use of computers. On the other hand, the staffing ratios for stenographers have been falling over a long period of time because of the adoption of dictation equipment, a technological change that reduces the need for stenographers.[13]

The mathematical decomposition technique holds some of the factors constant over time while allowing others to vary. For example, the effects of a change in staffing ratios on clerical employment during a particular time period can be determined by comparing current clerical employment with simulated employment levels obtained by holding staffing ratios constant at their original levels but using current industry employment as the multiplier. In other words the simulated clerical employment level uses the "correct" industry levels—actual current employment in these industries— but the "wrong" staffing ratios—those that existed at the start of the period. Thus, the difference between actual current clerical employment and simulated employment indicates the extent to which the change can be attributed to staffing ratio changes.[14] While one may presume that these changes are due to technological change, the mathematical decomposition of occupational employment growth is not an explanation of cause and effect; many complex economic and noneconomic forces lie behind the numbers revealed by the technique.

---

[13] It should be emphasized that staffing ratios may change for reasons other than the use of innovations, such as organizational change, job title change with no change in job content, or others. Any time an individual occupational staffing ratio changes, all of the remaining staffing ratios in that industry will change as well. (This occurs because the sum of the staffing ratios in an industry must equal one.) For example, if a particular industry was very successful in automating production worker jobs, perhaps by using robots, then the *relative* importance of other jobs such as clericals, professionals, etc. will increase.

[14] A more technical description of the decomposition is provided in Hunt and Hunt (1986:Ch. 4).

TABLE 6 Clerical Employment Growth by Industry, 1972-1982

| | Clerical Employment Changes | | | |
| | 1972 Employ- ment (000's) | 1982 Employ- ment (000's) | Change in Employ- ment 1972- 1982 (000's) | Change in Employ- ment 1972- 1982 (%) |
Industry				
Agriculture	48	83	35	72.9
Mining	59	128	69	116.9
Construction	362	451	89	24.6
Durables	1,352	1,513	161	11.9
Nondurables	1,040	1,074	34	3.3
Utilities	1,307	1,463	156	11.9
Wholesale trade	684	844	160	23.4
Retail trade	2,099	2,840	741	35.3
Finance	2,007	2,750	743	37.0
Services	3,691	5,473	1,782	48.3
Public administration	1,678	1,827	149	8.9
Total	14,326	18,446	4,120	28.8

Decomposition of Clerical Employment Changes, 1972-1982

| | Absolute Changes (in thousands) Due to: | | | Percent of Employment Changes Due to: | | |
Industry	Aggregate Economic Growth	Differential Rates of Industry Growth	Staffing Ratio Changes	Aggregate Economic Growth	Differential Rates of Industry Growth	Staffing Ratio Changes
Agriculture	10	-11	36	21.1	-22.9	75.0
Mining	12	29	28	21.1	49.1	47.5
Construction	77	-44	56	21.1	-12.1	15.5
Durables	286	-244	119	21.1	-18.0	8.8
Nondurables	220	-222	36	21.1	-21.3	3.5
Utilities	276	-23	-97	21.1	-1.8	-7.4
Wholesale trade	145	86	-71	21.1	12.6	-10.4
Retail trade	444	45	252	21.1	2.1	12.0
Finance	424	457	-138	21.1	22.8	-6.9
Services	781	605	396	21.1	16.4	10.7
Public admin.	355	-53	-153	21.1	-3.2	-9.1
Total	3,029	625	466	21.1	4.4	3.2

NOTES: Totals and percentages may not add exactly due to rounding. Percentages based on 1972 employment.

SOURCE: Calculated by the authors, based on data from the Current Population Survey.

The results of the decomposition for the major occupational group of clerical workers are presented in Table 6. One-digit industries and occupations are used in this analysis, based on CPS data, because the sample is far too small to provide *both* industrial and occupational detail below that level. The time period for the analysis, 1972–1982, is selected because that is the only recent time span for which consistent data are available. From 1972 to 1982 the number of clerical jobs increased by just over 4 million for a 28.8 percent gain over 1972 employment levels. During that same time span total employment increased by 21.1 percent. Clerical jobs grew faster than the average for all jobs, which also means that clerical jobs were becoming relatively more important in the national economy.

The bottom row in Table 6 indicates that the bulk of all new clerical jobs, a little more than 3 million, were added as a consequence of the overall growth of the economy; another 625,000 clerical jobs were added because clerical workers were more prevalent in industries that were growing faster than the average for all industries (the factor labeled differential rates of industry growth in the table); finally, 466,000 clerical jobs were added because of increasing staffing ratios for clerical jobs; that amounts to 3.3 percent of the 1972 employment level for clerical workers. This does not mean that staffing ratios in all industries were increasing for clerical occupations, but rather that the net effect across all industries was positive. Neither changing staffing ratios nor differential rates of industry growth, however, were major contributors to clerical employment growth in the 10 years from 1972 to 1982, although both factors were modestly positive during the period.

An examination of the data for each industry shows that staffing ratios for clerical jobs are actually *falling* in a number of industries. Most interesting are the results for the finance sector, as noted above probably the biggest user of office automation to date. The finance sector has been a rapidly growing sector as indicated by the 37 percent overall growth rate of clerical jobs in that sector versus the 28.8 percent growth rate for all clerical jobs. Thus, the effects of falling staffing ratios, which would have reduced jobs in this sector by 6.9 percent from 1972 employment levels, were more than recovered by the fast growth of the industry itself. However, if the industry had not expanded so rapidly, there would have been actual reductions in employment of clerical workers in the finance sector.

Staffing ratios for clerical jobs have also been falling in three other important industries—utilities, wholesale trade, and public administration. The decline in public administration may not be due primarily to office automation. Except in the postal service, which has automated the mail-sorting operation, government has not been in the forefront in adopting automation. Government was one of the slowest-growing sectors during this time period. Perhaps government administrators, when faced with tight budgets and rising demands for services, economized more on clerical jobs than other positions. It is not easy to provide an adequate explanation of the fall in staffing ratios for public administration or the other industries. It is possible that they are linked to office automation. Clearly, more study of these trends is called for.

It is possible that office automation is raising the productivity of clerical workers, contributing to the falling staffing ratios in those sectors, and thereby negatively impacting clerical jobs. It is puzzling that the aggregate productivity data for finance and insurance showed below-average productivity growth for the sector as a whole, yet the decomposition analysis showed declining staffing ratios for clerical jobs within finance and insurance. Many unanswered questions remain about the causes of employment trends for clericals in sectors such as finance and insurance.

The changing composition of industries has tended to favor clerical jobs, but the influence of industry mix was only moderately positive during the 1970s, and some sectors that are heavy employers of clericals have recently experienced much slower growth or even absolute declines in total employment. This is particularly true for hospitals, and state and local government, the latter of which is the largest single employer of clericals. Even though other sectors, notably services, will likely continue to be fast growing, there is no strong reason to think that industry mix will play a more significant role in the future employment outlook for clerical workers; it may well play a less-significant role.

Most importantly, this analysis reveals that economic growth is by far the most important factor in determining clerical employment. Economic growth accounted for three-fourths of the clerical jobs created. Yet this factor may be in the process of becoming less favorable to clerical employment. In the past, clerical employment continued to grow when the economy as a whole experienced a recession. In the last recession, however, clerical jobs failed to grow. They may be becoming more like other jobs in their sensitivity to general economic conditions.

CONCLUSION

Clerical employment has grown rapidly in the last 40 years or so, but many factors suggest that the growth of clerical jobs has slowed significantly. Clerical workers have had a favorable industry mix in their employment pattern, benefiting from the shift toward finance and other service-related industries because those industries employ much higher proportions of clerical workers. Furthermore, the relative importance of clerical jobs has tended to rise within industries. Thus, in the past all the factors have tended to be positive and the result has been spectacular growth in clerical employment. Given the rapid growth in clerical jobs over the last 30 years or so, it appears reasonable to conclude that many goods and services have been becoming more and more information intensive per unit of output over time. This has tended to boost clerical employment.

However, it is clear that the rate of growth of clerical jobs slowed during the last decade. Clericals did not benefit from the last recession as they have in earlier recessions, nor are some of the sectors that are important employers of clericals growing as fast as they once were. Finally, although office automation may not be producing a revolution, it should at least contribute to the slowing of employment growth in these occupations in the future.

Changing staffing ratios, probably the most visible manifestation of the *specific* effects of technological change on occupational employment, had a *moderately* positive effect on the employment growth of clerical workers from 1972 to 1982, creating about 450,000 new clerical jobs (compared to about 3 million created by aggregate economic growth and 600,000 by the concentration of clerical workers in rapidly growing industries). Although the net effect of changing staffing ratios on clerical employment was modestly positive across all industries, there were a few sectors, notably finance, where the effect was negative. This is taken as evidence of the adverse impact of technological change on clerical employment. Investment in this sector has been dramatically higher than the historical average for that sector for the last 15 years, but measured industry-wide productivity gains in finance and insurance do not support the thesis that office automation is having a significant impact. This lack of measured productivity results remains a puzzle. Nevertheless, future employment may well be impacted by the capital buildup in this and other sectors that have traditionally been large employers of clerical workers.

A LOOK TOWARD THE FUTURE

It is, of course, risky to attempt to predict what might happen to clerical employment in the future, but the changes that lie behind the trends noted above provide some clues, as do recent forecasts made by the Bureau of Labor Statistics (BLS) and other researchers. These will not be fully reviewed here, but their major conclusions are summarized as part of our assessment of the likely future for clerical employment. (For a more complete discussion see Hunt and Hunt, 1986.)

The BLS occupational projections represent the most important effort of the federal government to anticipate future needs for specific occupations. The BLS methodology is based on a modeling framework that accounts for many economic variables. The resulting occupational projections are not necessarily superior to others, but they do have the advantage of being produced in a comprehensive and reasonably consistent manner. Other forecasts of clerical employment growth are not nearly as comprehensive as that of the BLS. For example, Leontief and Duchin (1986) of New York University analyze the impacts of computer automation on employment from 1963 to 2000. Their research is limited to certain specified computer technologies and does not consider other productivity-enhancing technologies or any other source of productivity growth. Roessner et al. (1985) of the Georgia Institute of Technology, examines clerical jobs in two industries, banking and insurance. Finally, Drennan (1983) of Columbia University looks at clerical employment in six industries. His projection methodology utilizes extrapolation of historical trends after accounting for the effects of the 1980–1982 recession.

The BLS anticipates near average growth for clerical jobs. Between 1982 and 1995, BLS anticipates an average growth in employment of 28.1 percent. Growth in employment of clerical occupations is anticipated to be 26.5 percent. The effect of differential rates of industry growth is expected to be slightly positive at 1.6 percent (smaller than their contribution between 1972 and 1982). The effect of changing staffing ratios is expected to be negative at minus 3.1 percent. In fact, all the existing forecasts of employment in clerical occupations are unanimous in predicting that staffing ratios for clerical jobs will decline in the years ahead, presumably because of office automation. The fall in staffing ratios anticipated by BLS is modest compared with other predictions.

Still, it is significant that the only turnaround from historical trends anticipated by BLS at the major occupational group level due to changing staffing ratios is that for clerical workers. At least through 1982, the decomposition analysis discussed earlier showed that the staffing ratios for clerical jobs were rising, whereas the BLS forecast (base year 1982) and other forecasts expect that this trend will be reversed in the years ahead.

Growth rates forecast by BLS for 95 specific clerical occupations range from a positive 76.1 percent to minus 20 percent. The range in the portion due to clerical staffing ratio changes is from plus 38.4 percent to minus 55.6 percent. Clearly, though the effect of BLS's staffing ratio for clerical workers is negative overall, BLS expects many positive staffing effects for clerical workers as well. The fastest-growing clerical jobs are expected to be computer operators, claims adjusters, insurance checkers, peripheral EDP equipment operators, telephone ad takers, claims clerks, and credit authorizers. All are expected to have staffing ratio impacts equivalent to increases in employment levels of 20 percent or more. Besides the obvious technological impacts of computers on this list, it may be important to note that many of these occupations require the worker to interact in some way with the customer who is being served. That may provide a clue as to why BLS thinks secretaries will not decline in importance, or perhaps why cashiers are the 10th fastest-growing occupation, with a 48.2 percent growth rate. Again a world of both high tech and high touch is anticipated.

Roessner et al., Drennan, and Leontief and Duchin all conclude that office automation will have a much greater negative impact on clerical jobs than the BLS predicts, with Leontief-Duchin and Roessner et al. predicting absolute declines in clerical employment within the next decade. Roessner et al. is particularly pointed about his concerns regarding the BLS methodology and forecasts, while Drennan's projections appear to be nearer the BLS position. We find the studies of Leontief and Duchin and Roessner et al. to be seriously flawed for serving policy needs; we think that Leontief-Duchin and Roessner et al. are unduly pessimistic about the outlook for clerical jobs.

There are a variety of reasons that support our contention. First, although Leontief-Duchin use the BLS forecast for demand for goods and services, they predict revolutionary change in the process technology by which those goods and services will be produced. The revolution in office automation is assumed to leave the demand side of the marketplace unchanged. But that is not the way a complex, dynamic market economy operates. If office automation were adopted rapidly, it would change the relative costs of production for those goods and services that are intensive users of office automation. Those lower production costs will generate lower prices. Since office work is concentrated in the service sector, where demand growth has been above average, there is every reason to think that both the lower prices and income growth over time will generate additional demand. This scenario is even more plausible when one realizes that the product markets themselves are not static. So the new electronic office technologies may provide the impetus for the development of entirely new goods and services. Industry interrelationships may change or scale economies may be so significant that they fuel the development of a mass market that heretofore was undreamed of. In our opinion it is inappropriate to fix demand or the growth of demand and then assume a revolutionary change on the supply side of the market. Obviously, such a partial analysis can create false impressions about the true impacts of office automation.

Second, it appears that none of these other studies account for the tendency of output to become more information intensive over time. Yet this is a process that has been occurring for some time. The production recipes for many different goods and services today require more information processing than yesterday. This is not simply a function of the changing composition of demand but relates to the ingredients for a standard unit of output. To the extent that this trend continues in the future, it implies that office automation may have less impact on clerical employment levels than anticipated by some researchers.

Third, it should be mentioned that office automation is likely to lower the marginal cost of some new types of work so much that the required labor needed to produce that work rises by more than the labor-saving impact of the new techniques themselves. The common example is redrafts of documents with word processing. The probability that this will occur may be enhanced by our inability to measure output from offices in the first place. This type of new work or rework is explicitly rejected by Leontief-Duchin, and perhaps implicitly by Roessner et al.

Fourth, these studies do not account for the fact that the new technologies must be cost-effective and relatively reliable for widespread application. The technologies may appear to be cost-less, producing quantum leaps in productivity for the users. Yet there are purchase costs, installation costs, and ongoing costs that must be accounted for. The ongoing costs include system maintenance, software development, and training, among others. The cost of unscheduled downtime may become increasingly significant with more integrated systems.

Finally, Leontief-Duchin and Roessner et al. appear to us to be truly overoptimistic technologically, both in terms of what office automation equipment can do and in the speed of diffusion of that equipment. Leontief-Duchin assume that word processors alone will produce productivity gains for typists and secretaries of 500 percent. Yet this assumption is based upon a short, anonymous trade journal article that is five times more optimistic than the other articles which Leontief-Duchin reference. Roessner et al., on the other hand, emphasizes the potential for two breakthrough technologies, voice input and artificial intelligence. He assumes that innovations will occur in these technologies in the next few years, that they will be successfully marketed, and that they will dramatically reduce clerical employment in banking and insurance during the 1990s.

Our major complaint with the technological assumptions of both Leontief-Duchin and Roessner et al. is not that they may be technically wrong, although there is ample reason to question them, but that the level of uncertainty about the technical forecasts is so great that no one should seriously want to base policy decisions on them. Artificial intelligence, for example, is a technology that has been touted since the 1950s as a major breakthrough. Perhaps we will always be overoptimistic about new technologies; it seems to be part of the human condition. But that is no justification to shape public policy based on our dreams of the future. Suffice it to say that we are unconvinced that technology will evolve as far or as fast as Leontief-Duchin and Roessner et al. predict. This is the kind of analysis that leads to the fear that we will experience massive technological unemployment at some point in the future. Various analysts have been predicting such an event at least since the dawn of the industrial age. Somehow the employment apocalypse is always just ahead, yet fortunately we never quite reach it.

Because of the uncertainties about future demand and the capabilities of future technologies, we would encourage a focus on shorter-range occupational forecasting, exactly the opposite approach being suggested by Leontief-Duchin and Roessner et al. Roessner et al. argues that public policy makers need a longer time period for planning. But, if technological change is occurring faster today, then it is becoming even more impossible to develop long-run employment forecasts. Surely it is folly to think that we can peer 15 to 20 years into the future and see the detailed occupational and industrial structure of this nation. In fact, we think that the current BLS efforts, which produce about a 10-year planning horizon, tax existing forecasting abilities to the limit.[15]

What has this review shown for the future of clerical jobs? First, we think the pessimists who claim that these jobs will either stop growing absolutely or actually decline are wrong. The forces of economic growth, the shift toward services, and the current limitations of office automation technologies all argue strongly against this scenario. However, it is clear that the historical rate of growth of clerical jobs has slowed. Clericals did not benefit from the last recession as they have in earlier recessions, nor are some of the sectors that are important employers of clericals growing as fast as they once were. Finally, office automation is likely to at least contribute to the slowing of employment growth in these occupations in the future. We think that the overall growth of clerical jobs in the future will be average to slightly below average. There is broad agreement among forecasts that clerical jobs will not continue their rapid growth of the past few decades. The recent slowdown in the growth of clerical jobs is very likely permanent.

We find no persuasive evidence, however, that there will be a significant decline in the absolute number of clerical jobs. The forecasts of declining clerical employment are based on overoptimistic expectations of technological improvements or exaggerated productivity claims on behalf of existing technology. In our opinion, current office technology offers significant improvements in product quality and modest improvements in productivity. There

---

[15] We also think BLS should be more open about their handling of technological change in their forecasts. Like the other forecasters discussed here, BLS should reveal the basis for its judgments concerning technological change.

is as yet no empirical evidence of an office productivity revolution that will displace significant numbers of clerical workers. The growth of computer-related clerical positions will continue to be strong. Office automation is not sufficiently advanced at this point to slow the growth of these jobs.

Many factors will contribute to the continued, if slower, job growth of clericals in the future. Chief among these is the simple fact that clericals are so diffused in the national economy. Moreover, to the extent that clerical jobs are concentrated in particular industries, it has been in industries growing faster than average. Even if the growth rate of some of these slows, as it has in some financial industries for example, others, such as services, are likely to continue to grow at above average rates. Therefore, even allowing for negative employment impacts from office automation, the growth of this large, diverse, and diffused major occupational group should not be much below the average growth for all occupations for the next decade.

Many commentators believe that back-office clerical jobs will disapppear. We do not think this is likely. An analogy to manufacturing may be useful. Automation has not caused the total elimination of production workers in manufacturing, but these jobs have not been increasing in absolute terms for 40 years either. Like most of the forecasts discussed, we think the back-office jobs are more threatened by automation than other positions. They share with production workers a routinization of tasks, which tends to support automation. This will not necessarily lead to their demise, but their growth will be well below average.

A good example of the limits of technological change is provided by bank tellers. The growth of this occupation has slowed in recent years. The future growth prospects for bank tellers appear to be directly tied to the public's acceptance of automatic teller machines. But these machines today are used mostly for withdrawals and cannot handle nonroutine transactions. They cannot be thought of as a substitute for a fully staffed bank. Furthermore, it is difficult to know if and when the public will be willing to break the human link in making banking transactions.

Secretaries fall somewhere between the back-office jobs and those positions that involve considerable customer interface. Therefore, secretarial employment growth may slow but will not stop. We think that the growth of secretaries will be average to below average, but the absolute number of these jobs will definitely increase. Secretarial positions require a variety of skills and many are generalist in nature; they are more difficult to eliminate with automation. A variety of skills helps to ensure that the automation of any one of these skills leaves the job intact. It seems clear that secretaries of the future will require an even greater variety of skills and will utilize much more capital equipment.

Computer technology is still not ready to tackle the unstructured situations where humans excel. Clerical positions that involve direct interface with customers or co-workers are likely to experience at least average growth. The office of the future will require both "high tech" and "high touch" occupations.

REFERENCES

Attewell, Paul, and James Rule
    1984   Computing and organizations: what we know and what we don't know. *Communications of the ACM* (December):1184–1192.
Bailey, Andrew D., James H. Gerlach, and Andrew B. Winston
    1985   *Office Systems, Technology and Organizations.* Reston, Va.: Reston Publishing Company.
Brand, Horst, and John Duke
    1982   Productivity in banking: computers spur the advance. *Monthly Labor Review* (December):19–27.
Bureau of the Census
    1972   *1970 Census of Population, Detailed Characteristics, United States Summary.* PC(1)-D(1). Washington, D.C.: U.S. Department of Commerce.
Bureau of Labor Statistics
    1981   *The National Industry-Occupation Matrix, 1970, 1978, and Projected 1990.* Bulletin 2086. Washington, D.C.: U.S. Department of Labor.
    1979   *Time Series Data for Input-Output Industries: Output, Price, and Employment.* Bulletin 2018. Washington, D.C.: U.S. Department of Labor. March.
Computer and Business Equipment Manufacturers Association
    1985   *The Computer and Business Equipment Industry Marketing Data Book.* Washington, D.C.: Computer and Business Equipment Manufacturers Association.
Diebold, John
    1985   *Managing Information: The Challenge and the Opportunity.* New York: AMACOM.
Drennan, Matthew P.
    1983   Implications of Computer and Communications Technology for Less Skilled Service Employment Opportunities. Final report prepared for the Employment and Training Administration. Washington, D.C.: U.S. Department of Labor.
Hartmann, Heidi I., Robert E. Kraut, and Louise A. Tilly, eds.
    1986   *Computer Chips and Paper Clips: Technology and Women's Employment.* Vol. I. Washington, D.C.: National Academy Press.

Honeywell Inc.
1983 *Office Automation and the Workplace: A National Survey.* Minneapolis, Minn.: Honeywell Inc.
Hunt, H. Allan, and Timothy L. Hunt
1986 *Clerical Employment and Technological Change.* Kalamazoo, Mich.: W.E. Upjohn Institute for Employment Research.
Hunt, Timothy L., and H. Allan Hunt
1985 An Assessment of Data Sources to Study the Employment Effects of Technological Change. Pp. 1–116 in *Technological Employment Effects: Interim Report.* Panel on Technology and Women's Employment, Committee on Women's Employment and Related Social Issues. National Research Council. Washington, D.C.: National Academy Press.
International Data Corporation
1982 Information systems for tomorrow's office. *Fortune* (October 18): 17–81.
1983 Office systems for the eighties: automation and the bottom line. *Fortune* (October 3):89–162.
1984 Information systems for tomorrow's office. *Fortune* (October 15): 99–138.
Katzan, Harry, Jr.
1982 *Office Automation: A Manager's Guide.* New York: American Management Associations.
King, John L., and Kenneth L. Kraemer
1981 Cost as a social impact of information technology. Pp. 93–129 in Mitchell L. Moss, ed., *Telecommunications and Productivity.* Reading, Mass.: Addison-Wesley.
Leontief, Wassily, and Faye Duchin
1986 The Future Impact of Automation on Workers. New York: Oxford University Press.
Priebe, John A., Joan Heinkel, and Stanley Greene
1972 1970 Occupation and Industry Classification Systems in Terms of their 1960 Occupation and Industry Elements. Technical Paper No. 26. Washington, D.C.: Bureau of the Census, U.S. Department of Commerce. July.
Reskin, Barbara F., and Heidi I. Hartmann, eds.
1985 *Women's Work, Men's Work: Sex Segregation on the Job.* Washington, D.C.: National Academy Press.
Roessner, J. David, Robert M. Mason, Alan L. Porter, Frederick A. Rossini, A. Perry Schwartz, and Keith R. Nelms
1985 The Impact of Office Automation on Clerical Employment, 1985–2000: Forecasting Techniques and Plausible Futures in Banking and Insurance. Westport, Conn.: Quorum Books.
Salerno, Lynn M.
1985 What happened to the computer revolution? *Harvard Business Review* (November–December):129–138.
Seskin, Eugene P., and David P. Sullivan
1985 Revised estimates of new plant and equipment expenditures in the United States, 1947–1983. *Survey of Current Business* (February): 16–27.

Strassman, Paul A.
 1985   *Information Payoff: The Transformation of Work in the Electronic Age.*
         New York: Free Press.
Wang Laboratories, Inc.
 1985   *Issues in Information Processing: Cost Justification.* Lowell, Mass.:
         Wang Laboratories, Inc.

BIBLIOGRAPHY

Administrative Management
 1978   The many cases for WP. *Administrative Management* (April):70–71.
Bureau of the Census
 1982   *1980 Census of Population: Classified Index of Industries and Occupations.*
         Washington, D.C.: U.S. Department of Commerce.
Business Week
 1985   The computer slump. *Business Week* (June 24):74–81.
Downing, Hazel
 1980   Word Processors and the Oppression of Women. Pp. 275–288
         in Tom Forester, ed., *The Microelectronics Revolution.* Cambridge,
         Mass.: MIT Press.
Employment and Training Administration
 1977   *Dictionary of Occupational Titles.* 4th ed. Washington, D.C.: U.S.
         Department of Labor.
Gold, Bela
 1981   Robotics, programmable automation and increasing competitive-
         ness. Pp. 91–117 in *Exploratory Workshop on the Social Impacts of
         Robotics: Summary and Issues.* Office of Technology Assessment,
         Congress of the United States. Washington, D.C.: U.S. Govern-
         ment Printing Office.
Karan, Mary A.
 1982   Word processing: when it doesn't work. *Computer World* (March):
         16.
Klein, Deborah P.
 1984   Occupational employment statistics for 1972–82. *Employment and
         Earnings* (January):13.
Kutscher, Ronald E.
 1982   New economic projections through 1990—an overview. Pp. 1–9 in
         Economic Projections to 1990. Washington, D.C.: U.S. Department
         of Labor.
Miller, Ann, Donald J. Treiman, Pamela S. Cain, and Patricia A. Roos, eds.
 1980   *Work, Jobs, and Occupations: A Critical Review of the "Dictionary of
         Occupational Titles."* Washington, D.C.: National Academy Press.
Murphree, Mary
 1981   Rationalization and Satisfaction in Clerical Work: A Case Study
         of Wall Street Legal Secretaries. Ph.D. dissertation. Columbia
         University, New York.
Office of Economic Growth and Employment Projections
 1981   Projected Occupational Staffing Patterns of Industries. OES Tech-
         nical Paper Number 2. Washington, D.C.: U.S. Department of
         Labor.

Office of Technology Assessment
    1984   *Effects of Information Technology on Financial Services Systems.* Washington, D.C.: Congress of the United States.

Silvestri, George T., John M. Lukasiewicz, and Marcus E. Einstein
    1983   Occupational employment projections through 1995. *Monthly Labor Review* (November):37–49.

Stanford Research Institute
    1984   Drop in business demand for personal computers. *The SRI Journal* (May):4–5.

Winston, Patrick H.
    1985   The AI business: a perspective. *Manufacturing Engineering* (March).

Restructuring Work:
Temporary, Part-Time, and At-Home
Employment

EILEEN APPELBAUM

This paper examines the extent to which women participate in alternative work schedules and the relation of such arrangements to the implementation and diffusion of computer-based technologies. Alternative work schedules include temporary work, part-time work, multiple jobholding, and at-home work. Each of these employment strategies predates the introduction of high-technology products and production processes; this paper attempts to identify the particular impact of developments in technology on the changing extent of these work schedules. This is not an easy task for two reasons. First, while mainframe computers have been in use since the early 1960s, it is only in the last few years that computer-based technologies have altered the nature of the work process and the way in which work is organized. Second, employment data by occupation and industry, even when they are available, are rarely disaggregated to the extent required for a definitive analysis of the effects of technological change on work schedules. At best, we can hope to find some trace of the impact of technological change on the work options available to women. A limited number of informal interviews have been conducted in order to obtain information to supplement the published data, especially with regard

268

to the relative importance of technological change in influencing the work schedules of women.

The paper is organized as follows: the next section briefly discusses the transformation of internal and external labor markets, changes in the opportunity structure facing women who work, and the effects of technological change. The following sections discuss temporary employment, part-time employment, multiple jobholding, and at-home work. The final section draws some preliminary conclusions and implications from the available information.

THE TRANSFORMATION OF LABOR MARKETS

To a large extent, increased use of alternative work schedules can be explained by developments over the last decade and a half that have reduced the importance and undermined the existence of internal labor markets. These developments include the spread of microprocessor-based technologies, increased emphasis on reducing labor costs, and the growth of higher education. Companies have adopted human resource strategies that increase their flexibility in deploying their work forces. For workers, nearly 6 million of whom are currently employed part-time involuntarily, this has meant increasing difficulty in obtaining the security, fringe benefits, and wages associated with permanent, full-time employment.

TECHNOLOGY AND INTERNAL LABOR MARKETS

The new microprocessor-based technologies currently being implemented have the dual effect of reducing unit labor requirements and reorganizing the labor process. Their effect on worker skills and occupational mobility depend critically on strategic decisions by firms with respect to how they are implemented. At the micro level, the crucial issue is job design. Computer and communication technologies allow for considerable flexibility in the design of the worker/machine interface and the associated skill requirements of jobs (discussed at length by Albin, 1984). At the macro level the pattern of technical development that results from job design choices will have its major impact on the functioning of internal labor markets. In the last half century, internal labor markets, through on-the-job training and promotion along well-defined job ladders, have generated significant numbers of working class jobs paying middle-class wages. Though women and blacks were systematically excluded from these job ladders and often consigned to dead-end work in jobs in the secondary labor market, internal labor markets did provide avenues of upward mobility for many white male workers, thus contributing substantially to the large size of the American middle class. Preliminary evidence suggests that the pattern of implementation of the new production technologies will reduce the importance of these internal labor markets, with, in my view, potentially serious implications for the broader institutional and social framework of society.

Familiarity with the intrinsic capabilities of the new technologies suggests that they are most efficiently utilized when they are deployed so that tasks are integrated, job content is complex, and decision making is decentralized (see, for example, Hirschhorn, 1984). Implemented in this way the technologies would lead to increased employment opportunities for skilled and educated workers. Work would be highly adaptive with numerous opportunities for learning by doing and for related improvements in productivity, and both the private and social returns to formal education would increase. Initially, however, implementation of these technologies in the United States has often followed the older pattern associated with Taylorism—specialization and fragmentation of work. Despite the technology's capability for integrating work processes, computers and telecommunications are sometimes used to fragment work still further as the production process is uncoupled and the stages physically dispersed. Another aspect of computer-based technologies is that they automate the routine aspects of skilled technical and professional work as well as less skilled clerical work. In the process, these technologies eliminate both entry-level positions and the jobs that traditionally formed the rungs of career ladders from semiskilled to skilled work. Natural learning sequences are disrupted and the possibility of learning more complex tasks on the job diminishes.

Thus, I would argue that by-products of the implementation of computer and communications technologies include the disruption of natural learning sequences, a decline in the importance of job ladders and internal labor markets for nonprofessional employees, the resulting weakening in internal labor market structures, and the attendant reduction in occupational mobility for ordinary workers. It would be a mistake, however, to attribute all changes in the organization of work that undermine internal labor markets to the direct effects of the way in which technological change is implemented. Other forces, some of them indirectly related to technology, are at work here as well.

POISED FOR CONTRACTION

Internal labor markets play a special role in meeting the needs of companies that are poised for expansion: they guarantee that the company has workers already in the pipeline at every skill level ready to move up the job ladder should an increase in demand for the company's products warrant increases in production. Under these conditions, assistant managers are not an unnecessary and costly layer of bureaucracy; rather, they are a pool of workers, loyal to the company, steeped in its culture, and possessing the requisite skills to assume the position of manager should the company decide to open additional branch operations. The cost of having such workers on the payroll does not appear excessive when weighed against the costs of quickly recruiting, hiring, and training such workers from outside the firm in order to respond to market opportunities in a timely manner.

Today, however, companies are poised for contraction—anticipating a loss of markets or market share or a decline in unit labor requirements as the labor-saving potential of office automation technologies are realized. In this context, a pipeline filled with workers ready to move up appears to the company to be an unjustifiable expense rather than an investment in its future. A situation in which the competitive position of U.S. industry has declined as a result of the combined effects of an overvalued dollar and the movement of capital into export zones established in cheap labor areas of the world and in which even domestic markets are increasingly subject to foreign penetration dictates that firms develop a lean profile. Deregulation and increased competition among financial institutions and changes in federal payments to hospitals have unleashed powerful pressures for cost containment in these industries as well. Add to this the indirect role played by technological change. Firms that expect a drop in unit labor requirements do not need a pipeline filled with workers expecting to advance. Moreover, with technology in flux, skills learned today at company expense are likely to become obsolete before they are ever used. It becomes clear to a company that a labor process organized to provide a substantial number of nonprofessional workers with successive jobs in which skills are upgraded through on-the-job training or employer-sponsored training programs has become obsolete. While appropriate for the conditions of the 1950s and 1960s, it appears wasteful and costly in the 1980s.

Moreover, a decreasing reliance on internal labor markets and on-the-job training to provide business with skilled workers has been facilitated by the growth of higher education (see Noyelle, this volume). By 1980, nearly one-fourth of those between 25 and 29 years of age had 4 or more years of college education compared with about 10 percent in 1960. Firms have shifted to outside hiring to fill administrative, professional, and managerial positions that until recently would have been filled from within. In the process, they have used formal credentials to create significant barriers to entry into these occupations and have required workers to obtain vocational skills through formal schooling and higher education. Traditional internal ladders are being disbanded, and the earlier link between occupational mobility and training provided within the industry or firm has been weakened.

Though these are recent developments, evidence is accumulating that firms are adjusting to technology and these changes in their environment by reorganizing on a core and ring basis, holding to a minimum the number of workers who can expect to have a future with the company and for whom the company is willing to provide health and life insurance and retirement benefits—these workers make up the stable core, while other workers constitute an ever-changing ring. Flexibility in meeting staffing needs and the ability to retrench quickly increasingly take precedence over the desire for a loyal, well-trained work force and low turnover rates. Firms are experimenting with ways to shift the costs of fringe benefits and the risks associated with a cyclical downturn or a labor-saving advance in technology to their workers. Strategies include the use of part-time workers, temporary employees, and contract labor. This is a major reason for the explosive growth in temporary work and subcontracting during the last few years.

IMPLICATIONS FOR WOMEN WORKERS

The occupational changes brought about by office automation technologies and the desire of many companies for immediate reductions in employment have direct implications for career mobility for women within organizations. Internal labor markets—with their opportunities for promotion and career advancement—have only recently been opened to women, often as a result of successful enforcement of equal employment opportunity laws. These internal job ladders have played a significant role in enabling capable and ambitious clerical workers in industries such as insurance and, to a lesser extent, retail sales, to work their way up through lower-level supervisory or para-professional jobs into management or professional positions. The weakening of internal labor markets is closing off opportunities for advancement for women that have only recently become available.

The outcome for women is complex. In the last decade, firms have begun to rely less on internal job markets to provide formal and informal training for lower-level employees and, instead, to externalize training. Professional and managerial employees are trained in colleges and business schools and then recruited directly into upper-level positions. Even the more-skilled clerical jobs are filled not through promotion from the typing or word-processing pool but from the ranks of community college and vocational school graduates. One effect of office automation technologies is that the skills required of clerical workers in diverse industries are becoming more homogeneous. There is considerable overlap in the skills required of directory assistance operators, customer service representatives, travel agents, library assistants, classified advertisement takers, and so on. The replacement of on-the-job training and occupational mobility within firms by extended formal schooling and job mobility through the external labor market increases the probability that socioeconomic conditions will limit access to training and hence to better jobs. The picture that emerges is one of continuing advancement opportunities for professional women, increased opportunities for lateral moves among firms but no upward mobility for skilled clerical or sales workers, and severely curtailed opportunities for employment or promotion for women in traditional clerical jobs.

The erosion of internal labor markets has weakened the claim of clerical workers to the protections and benefits afforded by permanent full-time employment. Firms have relied on office automation technologies to facilitate their use of clerical temporary workers and home workers. Women workers have, thus, been affected disproportionately by these changes to date, though the logic of organizing the labor market on a core and buffer basis suggests that other occupations and workers, many of them men, will be affected.

TEMPORARY EMPLOYMENT

Of the four alternative work schedules examined in this paper, temporary employment has shown the most dramatic changes since the 1970s. Temporary employment in the United States is booming. According to the Bureau of Labor Statistics, employment growth in the temporary help services industry has averaged 11 percent a year over the last 13 years, compared with a 2.1 percent growth rate for nonagricultural jobs throughout the economy (Collins, 1985). In December 1984 the industry placed 665,400 workers a day in temporary positions (*Employment and Earnings* 32(1), 1985:Table B-2). These figures do not include the growing number of employers who are hiring workers on a temporary basis directly, without requiring the services of a temporary help agency. The U.S. Office of Personnel Management, for example, reports that the federal government filled 244,692 jobs with temporary workers in 1984 (data provided by Mary Ann Madison, Office of Technology Assessment), and the number is expected to increase sharply as a result of new regulations governing the employment of temporary workers, which took effect in January 1985. The new rules allow "temporary" jobs, which, unlike permanent jobs, carry no medical or retirement benefits other than social security, to be extended to higher skill categories and to last up to 4 years. These developments in federal employment mirror changes already under way in the private sector.

FORCES DRIVING THE GROWTH OF TEMPORARY WORK

Sam Sacco, executive vice president of the National Association of Temporary Services, observes that employment is increasingly being organized on a "ring and core basis with temporary employment acting as a buffer for the economy" (telephone interview, February 1, 1985). Thus federal officials publicly welcomed the new rules on temporary employment because having more temporary employees without civil service protection will make it easier for them to adjust the size of the work force. They expect to be able to use the temporary workers as a cushion to protect permanent employees from being laid off first.

Another major force behind the growth of temporary employment—the fundamental reason for its expansion according to Audrey Freedman, a labor economist for the Conference Board—is the desire of firms to contain costs. As Freedman put it, "What the companies are doing is organizing so they don't have to pay for vacations, holidays, health benefits, or pensions. In addition, they don't have to allocate money for training and for promotion" (quoted in Collins, 1985:B1). The savings can be large, and some firms are now building temporary work into their employment strategies. According to Sacco, "companies are increasingly pre-planning for the use of temporary workers and budgeting for them at the beginning of the year." For example, Johnson and Johnson Products, a health care supplier that is an affiliate of the Johnson and Johnson Corporation, has built the use of 450 temporary workers during the year into its personnel plans. The company is budgeting $500,000 for temporary clerical workers, secretaries, lab technicians, data-processing clerks, accounting clerks, and computer clerks to be hired through temporary help agencies (Fiamingo, 1984). This use of temporary workers by companies on a preplanned basis, rather than as an expedient for dealing with an unforeseen situation, is a recent development.

Some companies have begun to staff certain of their facilities with temporary help workers. They are staffing mail rooms where there is high turnover, or facilities that have peak periods, with temporaries. Thus, an advertisement from Norrell Temporary Services that appeared in May 1984 issues of *Office Administration and Automation* and of *Office* magazines promises to solve the turnover problem: "Facilities staffing—using temporary employees as a group to tackle routine jobs permanent employees view as unattractive or dull—Norrell guarantees performance by rotating fresh, trained temporary employees into the job before burnout occurs." The approach appears to be attracting business for the temporary help agencies and increasing the number of long-term arrangements. Western Temporary Services of Walnut Creek, California, reports that most of its contracts are for 1 year; some are longer. Good People Office Automation Temporaries in New York City reports that 80 percent of the assignments it receives are for long-term temporaries. A typical long-term assignment for this company involves providing experienced temporary workers to a company changing from manual filing to a records-processing system. The positions this temporary help agency fills usually require 6 months experience, though some positions may require a year (Fiamingo, 1984).

Advances in technology have contributed to the rapid growth of temporary employment. Companies turn to temporary help supply agencies in order to handle temporary increases in work load associated with the conversion from manual to computer-based data management and filing systems. Some businesses are turning to temporary help agencies to obtain workers experienced with office-automation equipment to assist in training their permanent staff. Companies that face a monthly peak load problem in sending updated reports or form letters to customers often turn to temporary help agencies to obtain workers experienced with word processing. In addition, firms that have made substantial investments in dedicated word-processing equipment or in personal computers find that the equipment is too valuable to stand idle when regular employees are ill and hire experienced temporary workers to fill in for employees who are sick.

The nature of temporary work is changing. The temporary help services industry has diversified far beyond the clerical workers who were its mainstay 15 years ago. The industry currently supplies temporary workers in four main areas: office clerical/office automation (OA) operators, medical (with hospital distinguished from nursing home and homemaking services), industrial, and professional. The medical segment is the fastest-growing component of the industry (Gannon, 1984). By 1982, 46.2 percent of employment and 56.6 percent of total receipts were generated in the non-office help components of the industry.

REVENUE AND EMPLOYMENT GROWTH

Between 1977 and 1982, the temporary help services industry grew substantially. According to census data, industry receipts more than doubled from $2.32 billion to $5.14 billion between 1977 and 1982, despite the fact that 1982 was a recession year (see Table 1). Revenue growth continues to be high. The leading temporary services companies, Kelly Services Inc. and Manpower Inc., each had revenue increases of more than 30 percent in 1984, while a temporary agency based in Silicon Valley, Adia Services Inc., had an increase in net income of 98 percent (*Business Week*, 1985). Industry sources report that the temporary help payroll went from $431 million in 1971 to $3.48 billion in 1981, an annual rate of increase in nominal receipts of 24 percent over the decade. Payroll declined somewhat in 1982 because of the recession but

TABLE 1 Size of Temporary Help Supply Services, 1977 and 1982

	1977	1982
Number of establishments		
Total	$ 4,235	$ 6,247
Office help supply		3,324
Other		2,923
Receipts (in thousands)		
Total	2,323,676	5,143,132
Office help supply		2,230,926
Other		2,912,206
Payroll (in thousands)		
Total	n.a.	3,595,609
Office help supply		1,599,217
Other		1,996,392
Employment		
Total	n.a.	470,541
Office help supply		253,167
Other		217,374

SOURCE: Bureau of the Census (1980, 1985).

recovered and reached $5.50 billion in 1984 (National Association of Temporary Services, unpublished data). This is an annual rate of increase in nominal receipts of 16.5 percent, despite the 1982 decline. Since inflation has been much lower in the 1980s than in the 1970s, real growth in recent years has been higher than it was a decade ago. The industry is expected to continue to grow rapidly through the 1980s. According to the U.S. Department of Labor, temporary help services will be the third fastest growing industry during this decade, after computers and health care (Fiamingo, 1984).

Since temporary employment now functions in part as an economic buffer, it is not surprising that employment in the temporary help services industry declines early in a recession and recovers quickly at the beginning of an expansion. Nevertheless, the magnitude of employment growth in this industry during the recovery from the 1981–1982 recession was unexpected. The most accurate employment data are probably the monthly establishment data collected in the Current Population Survey (CPS) and reported in *Employment and Earnings*. These are reported monthly for the temporary help services industry beginning in 1982. Annual average employment in temporary help services in 1983 increased

17.5 percent over the corresponding figure for 1982. For women, temporary employment increased 18.3 percent between 1982 and 1983 (calculated from data in Table 2). By comparison, annual average employment in nonagricultural establishments increased by less than 1 percent between those 2 years, 1.9 percent for women. In June, July, and November of 1983, employment growth in this industry exceeded 10 percent of the number of nonagricultural jobs added in the economy, despite the fact that temporary help services accounted for less than 0.5 percent of total nonagricultural employment in 1982 (calculated from data in Table 2). The rise in annual average employment—that is, the increase in the number of temporary help jobs every year between 1982 and 1983—was equal to 12.6 percent of the number of jobs added in nonagricultural establishments in the first year of the recovery. Employment increases in the industry continued during 1984, but at a more moderate pace. Nearly 86,000 temporary help jobs were added between December 1983 and December 1984. This followed an increase of about 176,000 jobs between December 1982 and December 1983 (see Table 2). Figures on temporary help jobs do not tell the whole story, however. Sacco estimates that while the temporary help services industry filled more than 600,000 jobs per day on average in 1984, the number of people who held a temporary job at some time during the year was about 5 million. *Business Week* reports that the industry's giants, Kelly Services Inc. and Manpower Inc., have more than 800,000 temporary workers on their books (*Business Week*, 1985). It should be remembered that these figures refer only to jobs filled through temporary help agencies. There are no estimates of the number of temporary jobs filled directly by firms.

Increases in temporary work are outweighed by increases in the number of year-round jobs for women. The proportion of women with work experience during the year who worked full time (50 to 52 weeks) increased from 36.9 percent in 1960 to 40.7 percent in 1970, 45.1 percent in 1981, and 48.0 percent in 1983 (Women's Bureau, U.S. Department of Labor, 1983; Bureau of Labor Statistics, unpublished data).

IMPLICATIONS FOR WOMEN WORKERS

Temporary work does not appear to be viewed by most women who do it as a stopgap measure until they can find permanent work.

TABLE 2 Employment in Nonagricultural Establishments and Temporary Help Supply Services, by Sex, 1982 to 1985

Year	Nonagricultural Establishments (thousands)		Temporary Help Supply Services (thousands)	
	Total	Women	Total	Women
Annual average				
1982	89,566	39,052	400.9	255.7
1983	90,138	39,812	471.8	302.9
1984	99,156	41,831	630.8	398.9
1983				
Jan	87,590	38,849	387.2	254.9
Feb	87,598	38,945	379.5	248.5
Mar	88,208	39,225	410.1	266.1
Apr	89,064	39,509	433.6	279.3
May	89,921	39,774	447.9	287.1
June	90,738	39,886	461.1	294.5
July	90,112	39,243	483.4	314.0
Aug	89,842	39,097	498.5	317.4
Sept	91,485	40,237	519.8	328.3
Oct	92,049	40,669	535.1	338.0
Nov	92,406	40,998	534.3	335.6
Dec	92,645	41,316	571.2	370.6
1984				
Jan	91,065	40,590	547.0	352.5
Feb	91,612	40,862	551.6	353.4
Mar	92,234	41,210	575.2	365.4
Apr	93,234	41,390	597.9	379.5
May	94,063	41,584	621.3	392.5
June	95,003	41,735	633.6	394.0
July	94,236	41,966	649.7	406.8
Aug	94,486	42,094	669.8	419.2
Sept	95,358	42,246	685.3	430.0
Oct	95,894	42,441	687.0	432.7
Nov	96,215	43,142	678.0	427.9
Dec	96,308	43,313	675.7	433.2
1985				
Jan	94,628	42,595	644.2	410.8
Feb	94,851	42,785	637.5	402.1

SOURCE: Bureau of Labor Statistics (1984a:Table 309; 1984b:Tables B-2 and B-3; 1985a:Tables B-2 and B-3; 1985c:156).

TABLE 3 Survey Results: Nurses' and Homemakers' Most Important Reason for Working at a Particular Temporary Help Firm (percent)

Reason	Entire Sample (N=1,101)	Registered Nurses or Visiting Nurses (N=262)	Licensed Practical Nurses (N=221)	Nurses' Aides (N=408)	Home- makers (N=210)
Variety in work, that is, frequent changes in assignment	16.6	8.6	13.1	21.5	20.6
A stopgap measure until I can obtain a permanent job	8.2	9.2	8.0	7.2	9.0
Freedom to schedule my work in a flexible manner	60.2	70.3	65.3	55.9	50.8
Employment during school vacation	1.0	0.8	0	0.8	2.6
Other	14.1	10.9	13.6	14.6	16.9

SOURCE: Gannon (1984).

Nor is the appeal of temporary work, as industry spokespeople suggest, the possibility of increased variety in work. A study of a large national firm that hires more than 50,000 health care temporary employees each year found that more than 60 percent of the temporary workers gave freedom to schedule work in a flexible manner as the most important reason for working at a temporary help firm (Gannon, 1984; see Table 3). Less than 17 percent chose temporary work for the variety it provides, and only 8 percent were doing it until they obtained a permanent job. Flexible work schedules are important to many women who have both work and home responsibilities, but these jobs are not widely available. A 1977 American Management Association survey estimated that 12.8 percent of private sector organizations have some kind of flextime program (Women's Bureau, U.S. Department of Labor, 1983:38). Some women are turning to temporary help agencies to arrange flexible work schedules.

The availability of benefits for women doing temporary work varies, though most receive very few. Temporary jobs with the federal government carry no fringe benefits except social security contributions, and most workers hired directly by private-sector firms appear to face the same situation. Workers employed by temporary help agencies are covered by Workers' Compensation according to Sacco, and after a certain number of hours (required hours vary by state) they are eligible for unemployment compensation as well. Some temporary employment agencies offer fringe benefits on a prorated basis. Manpower Temporary Services appears to have one of the better benefits packages. In Philadelphia the agency has a group insurance program for its workers as well as paid vacations, holidays, and a training program to help clerical workers learn to operate automated office equipment (Collins, 1985).

Training for employees of temporary help agencies also varies widely. Some companies provide no training and require 6 months or more of hands-on experience. Good People Office Automation Temporaries in New York City, Word Processors Personnel Service in Menlo Park, Calif., Personnel Pool of America Inc. in Fort Lauderdale, Fla., and Victor Temporary Services of Northbrook, Ill., are in this category. Some companies will provide training to enhance proven skills of experienced workers. Norrell Services Inc. of Atlanta and Western Temporary Services in Walnut Creek, Calif., have such a policy. Several temporary help agencies provide training in word processing and office automation to their clerical workers: Kelly Services of Detroit, which has equipped 360 of their 500 offices to teach basic word-processing operations for a variety of PCs; Olsten Temporary Services of Westbury, N.Y., which provides training at 45 office-automation training centers; and Manpower Temporary Services of Milwaukee, which provides training in word processing and in business applications of personal computers (using IBM PCs). Manpower Temporary Services has 1,050 offices nationwide, and its goal is to have training facilities in all of them (Fiamingo, 1984).

RELATIONSHIP TO NEW TECHNOLOGY

Employers are turning to the use of temporary workers primarily to keep labor costs down and to achieve maximum flexibility in scheduling work. The use of temporary workers reduces labor costs in two ways. Pools of temporary workers function as an employment buffer—available to meet surges in the demand for goods and services and easily dispensed with when demand declines. In addition, temporary workers typically receive few fringe benefits and very little access to job training. The constraints on employers with respect to job assignment, layoffs, hiring and promotion policies, fringe benefits, and retirement benefits that exist as a result of both explicit and implicit contracts between companies and their full-time employees are waived in the case of temporary workers. As a result employers enjoy complete flexibility in scheduling these workers and are free to use them as a buffer or reserve to accommodate increases or declines in demand.

Technology plays only an indirect role in this process. Companies that have invested in costly office-automation equipment are reluctant to have it stand idle. They rely on temporary help agencies for workers experienced with word processing to replace absent workers. High-tech manufacturing firms face seasonal and cyclical variations in the demand for silicon chips and computers. As much as 30 percent of the work force of some Silicon Valley manufacturers are obtained from temporary help agencies. Permanent employment at Apple Computer Inc., for example, is just over 5,400. Employment at Apple rises to 7,000, however, as the company adds 1,600 temporary workers for the Christmas season. Finally, the temporary help service agencies themselves are highly automated and have computerized their rosters of temporary workers. This has increased the number of workers a temporary agency can handle and the number of employer requests to which it can respond. Office automation has expedited the rapid growth of this industry. Thus, while technology has facilitated the expansion of temporary work, cost containment is the driving force behind its rapid growth.

PART-TIME WORK

While most women who work are employed full time, a sizable minority of working women work less than 35 hours a week. In March 1985, 28.9 percent of employed women worked part time, 22.7 percent of them voluntarily choosing shorter hours (*Employment and Earnings* 32(4), 1985:Table A-9). Adult women have frequently sought part-time employment as a means of meeting home and child care responsibilities while contributing to household income. Family and home responsibilities are the most common reasons cited by women for working part time, although this reason has declined in importance since 1960 (Deutermann and Brown, 1978). Economic theory notwithstanding, the choice of part-time employment cannot be assumed in all cases to reflect the preferences of women for fewer hours of work. For women with children, decisions regarding the number of hours of work are severely constrained by the lack of affordable, quality child care. It is currently estimated that there is just one day-care position open for every 10 children who need placement, and that the average cost of day care for 2 children is $4,000 a year (U.S. Commission on Civil Rights, 1983). One study of a national sample of mothers with children under the age of five found that one-fourth of those employed part time felt they were prevented from working more hours by the unavailability of suitable day care (Presser and Baldwin, 1980). On the demand side of the labor market, the growth of part-time employment has paralleled the growth of retail trade and service industries. Of the more than 18 million part-time jobs filled on average in each month of 1984, nearly 13 million were in wholesale and retail trade or in services (*Employment and Earnings* 32(1), 1985:Table 32). Thus, nearly 71 percent of part-time jobs are found in these two industry groupings.

TRENDS IN PART-TIME EMPLOYMENT

The growth of part-time work since 1954, the first year for which data on the number of such workers were collected, is well documented. Using data from the CPS, Deutermann and Brown (1978) found that the number of part-time employees in nonagricultural industries increased at an average annual rate of nearly 4 percent, more than double the rate for full-time workers. As a result, part-time workers increased from 15.4 percent of employed workers in May 1954 to 22.1 percent in May 1977. For women the corresponding increase was from 27.2 percent to 32.6 percent. Since 1977, however, the proportion of workers employed part time has been virtually unchanged, except for the increase in the number working part time for economic reasons during the 1982 recession. Data on part-time employment reported in Table 4, while also derived from the CPS, are not strictly comparable to those reported above because Deutermann and Brown treat those on full-time schedules who work less than 35 hours a week as part-time workers. Among nonagricultural workers, 15.8 percent worked part time in May 1967; 26.9 percent in the case of women workers. By May 1977 these figures had risen to 19.0 percent for part-time employment, 29.9 percent in the case of women workers. The proportion employed part time in May 1978 was again 19.0 percent and was virtually unchanged at 19.5 percent in May 1980 and May 1984 (see Table 4). For women, there has been a slight decrease in the proportion employed part time, from 30.0 percent in May 1978 to 29.6 percent in May 1980 and 28.8 percent in May 1984 (see Table 4).

A more dramatic decline has occurred in the proportion of women working part time voluntarily. At its peak in May 1970, 26.0 percent of employed women worked part time voluntarily, but this figure declined to 24.3 percent in 1980 and 22.7 percent in 1984 and 1985. Corresponding to this, the proportion of employed women working part time because they could not find full-time jobs increased from 2.7 percent in May 1967 to 3.6 percent in May 1970, 4.5 percent in May 1978, 6.1 percent in May 1984, and 6.2 in 1985 (see Table 4). Thus, the proportion of women desiring part-time work is decreasing, and there are currently about 3 million women employed part time who want full-time schedules. Involuntary part-time employment of women increased 300 percent since 1967, while total employment increased by 77 percent.

Monthly figures on part-time employment are only part of the picture. The number of workers who experience some involuntary part-time employment during the year, either because of slack work on their regular jobs or because they can only find part-time work, is much higher than this. In 1983, the last year for which such data are available, the number of workers with some involuntary part-time employment totaled 14.9 million, up from 11.5 million in 1979 (Bureau of Labor Statistics, 1985b:5). Of these, approximately 9 million were women.[1] The public policy interest in part-time work is related to the poor economic position of part-time workers. These workers typically receive few fringe benefits and they earn, on average, only $4.50 an hour compared

---

[1] About 65 percent of part-time workers in 1983 were women. Assuming that this percentage also applies to workers with some involuntary part-time employment during the year, then the number of such women was well over 9 million.

with \$7.80 for full-time workers. Involuntary part-time work is often associated with poverty status. In 1983, 19.1 percent of those with some involuntary part-time employment during the year lived in households with household incomes below the poverty level compared with 13.4 percent in 1979. Among women who maintain families, the proportion of those with some involuntary part-time employment in 1983 whose family income for the year was below the poverty level was 48.0 percent, 62.7 percent in the case of black women (Bureau of Labor Statistics, 1985b:5, 18). In addition to receiving lower pay and benefits, part-time workers are stereotyped as having a low commitment to their jobs and hence they face more difficult career paths. Part-time jobs and the part-time workers who hold them are often viewed as marginal by employers (Rosow and Zager, 1981). An important concern, then, is whether technological conditions are increasing part-time employment.

PART-TIME EMPLOYMENT IN INDUSTRIES AND OCCUPATIONS AFFECTED BY NEW TECHNOLOGIES

Sorting out the effects of technological change on part-time employment is not easy because of the limitations inherent in available data (Hunt and Hunt, 1985). Analytically, one can make the argument that the importance of part-time work in retail trade and services but not in goods-producing industries can be explained by the fact that goods can be produced at an even pace and held in inventories to meet demand, whereas services cannot be inventoried but must be provided on demand. When demand is uneven, or must be met outside the normal working day or on weekends, employers favor part-time employment as a means of fitting the work force to the work load. Moreover, Nollen et al. (1978) found that employers tend to view part-time work as a strategy for reducing labor costs. In part, this is accomplished by substituting part-time workers for overtime work by full-time employees; but part-time employment is also used to reduce labor costs by paying part-time workers less than full-time workers and by excluding them from some or all fringe benefits. However, Nollen and his colleagues found that employers generally hold the view that jobs involving continuous-process technologies are not suited to part-time employment. These include, in particular, jobs in manufacturing industries and employment in supervisory,

TABLE 4 Full-Time and Part-Time Employment of the Civilian Labor Force, Selected Dates, 1967-1984 (in thousands)

Year, Sex, and Employment Status	Full Time	Part Time			Total Labor Force	Percent Part Time
		Involuntary	Voluntary	Total		
May 1967						
Total	61,978	1,573	10,086	11,659	73,637	15.8
Men	42,605	851	3,688	4,539	47,144	9.6
Women	19,373	722	6,398	7,120	26,493	26.9
Voluntary						24.2
Involuntary						2.9
May 1970						
Total	64,413	2,128	11,816	13,944	78,357	17.8
Men	43,700	1,080	4,184	5,264	48,964	10.8
Women	20,713	1,048	7,632	8,680	29,393	29.5
Voluntary						26.0
Involuntary						3.6
May 1977						
Total	72,963	3,237	13,842	17,079	90,042	19.0
Men	47,347	1,564	4,614	6,178	53,525	11.5
Women	25,616	1,673	9,228	10,901	36,517	29.9
Voluntary						25.2
Involuntary						4.7
May 1978						
Total	76,000	3,212	14,639	17,851	93,851	19.0
Men	49,014	1,485	4,812	6,297	55,311	11.4
Women	26,986	1,727	9,827	11,554	38,540	30.0
Voluntary						25.5
Involuntary						4.5

May 1980						
Total	78,776	4,212	14,813	19,025	97,801	19.5
Men	49,240	1,973	4,613	6,586	55,826	11.8
Women	29,536	2,239	10,200	12,439	41,975	29.6
Voluntary						24.3
Involuntary						5.3
May 1982						
Total	79,141	5,808	15,009	20,817	99,958	20.8
Men	49,069	2,956	4,742	7,698	56,767	13.6
Women	30,072	2,852	11,125	13,977	44,049	31.7
Voluntary						25.3
Involuntary						6.4
May 1984						
Total	84,595	5,292	15,209	20,501	105,096	19.5
Men	51,841	2,478	4,742	7,220	59,061	12.2
Women	32,754	2,814	10,467	13,281	46,035	28.8
Voluntary						22.7
Involuntary						6.1
March 1985						
Total	84,758	5,466	15,544	21,010	105,768	19.9
Men	51,357	2,571	4,845	7,416	58,773	12.6
Women	33,401	2,895	10,699	13,594	46,995	28.9
Voluntary						22.7
Involuntary						6.2

SOURCE: Derived from Employment and Earnings (1985a, 1984b, 1982a, 1980, 1978a, 1977a, 1967: Table A-7, A-8, or A-9).

management, and executive occupations where the work to be performed requires continuity. On the other hand, job technologies involving discrete tasks or repetitive, tedious, or stressful work are believed by managers and employers to be particularly well suited to part-time employment.

An implication of this argument is that to the extent that computer and communication technologies are used to fragment work or to unbundle the production process and allow discrete parts of the process to be done at locations remote from one another, opportunities for part-time employment increase. Thus, one would expect part-time employment of professional workers and clerical employment in office industries, such as insurance or public administration, to increase as well. Retrospective data on the work experience of men and women during the year provide an overview of where individuals have found jobs. These data are available for part-time work by industry for all persons with work experience during the year for the period 1975 through 1983. Table 5 reports the proportion of those with work experience who were employed part time for all workers, and separately for men and women, in broad industrial groups likely to be affected by office-automation technologies—finance, insurance, and real estate; business and repair services; other professional services; and public administration. The proportion of workers with part-time employment at some time during the year is, of course, higher than the proportion employed part time during May of that year. It increases from 20.8 percent in 1975 to 22.8 percent in 1983. Most of the increase is in the part-time employment of men. This is not surprising since the technology reduces the importance of continuity in jobs traditionally held by men. Opportunities for free-lance professional work have increased, especially for computer programming specialists. This is reflected, in part, in the growth of part-time employment among self-employed men from under 16 percent in 1975 to more than 21 percent in 1983.

The part-time employment of women with work experience is virtually unchanged between 1975 and 1983 when all nonagricultural employment is considered. This may not be surprising in light of the increased commitment of women to paid work. However, the fact that part-time employment of women in office industries does not show a relative increase, except for the category "other professional services," is unexpected. The part-time employment of women in that industry increased from 28.6 percent

TABLE 5 Part-Time Employment of Men and Women with Work Experience During Year by Selected Industries for Selected Years, 1975-1983

Industry Group	1975 Total with Work Experience (thousands)	1975 Part Time (percent)	1977 Total with Work Experience (thousands)	1977 Part Time (percent)	1979 Total with Work Experience (thousands)	1979 Part Time (percent)	1981 Total with Work Experience (thousands)	1981 Part Time (percent)	1983 Total with Work Experience (thousands)	1983 Part Time (percent)
Nonagricultural industries	97,088	20.8	102,937	21.2	111,070	20.9	112,880	22.2	113,792	22.8
Men	55,113	11.9	57,613	12.2	61,030	12.1	61,698	13.5	61,639	14.3
Women	41,976	32.6	45,325	32.6	50,040	31.6	51,181	32.7	52,152	32.8
Finance, insurance, and real estate	4,748	13.7	5,238	13.9	5,890	15.0	6,238	14.3	6,559	13.7
Men	2,127	9.1	2,236	9.5	2,254	10.2	2,475	11.3	2,665	10.0
Women	2,621	17.4	3,002	17.1	3,637	18.0	3,763	16.3	3,894	16.3
Business and repair services	2,690	23.4	3,221	22.1	3,603	22.0	4,110	22.6	4,887	22.7
Men	1,750	16.5	2,049	14.5	2,212	15.1	2,563	15.5	2,824	16.1
Women	940	36.3	1,172	35.4	1,392	32.9	1,547	34.4	2,063	31.7
Other professional	1,990	20.2	2,214	19.9	2,384	18.6	2,774	18.9	3,191	24.5
Men	1,025	12.4	1,132	11.4	1,209	12.1	1,410	12.7	1,611	11.7
Women	965	28.6	1,082	28.9	1,174	25.3	1,364	25.2	1,580	37.7
Public administration	5,560	10.1	5,649	11.2	6,057	10.7	5,911	11.6	5,407	9.2
Men	3,658	5.1	3,628	5.9	3,770	5.8	3,597	6.2	3,185	5.1
Women	1,903	19.7	2,021	20.6	2,287	18.7	2,314	19.9	2,222	14.9
Self-employed	5,724	25.6	6,402	26.3	7,068	24.9	7,378	29.2	7,668	29.8
Men	4,177	15.7	4,546	16.5	4,863	14.9	5,007	19.2	5,136	20.7
Women	1,546	52.5	1,857	50.3	2,205	46.8	2,371	50.4	2,532	48.1

SOURCE: Bureau of Labor Statistics (1976, 1978b, 1982b) and unpublished data for 1979 and 1983.

to 37.7 percent between 1975 and 1983. In contrast, in finance, insurance, and real estate, it decreased from 17.4 percent to 16.3 percent; in business and repair services it decreased from 36.3 percent to 31.7 percent; and in public administration it decreased from 19.7 percent to 14.9 percent over the same period. If there has been an increase in the number of women doing back-office and other routine processing work on part-time schedules as a result of the computerization of such tasks, it has apparently been offset by declines in the number working part time at other tasks—by the replacement of part-time bank tellers on evenings and weekends by automatic teller machines, for example.

While retrospective data are informative with respect to the work experience of the population, monthly employment data provide a clearer picture of the actual jobs in the economy. Table 6 indicates the percentage of men and women workers in each industry and in the labor force as a whole who are employed part time for 1970, 1980, and 1984. Tables 7 and 8 report the percentage of men and women workers in each occupation who are employed part time for the same time period.[2] Given the standard definition of part-time work—less than 35 hours a week—the data on persons at work do not show an increase in the proportion of women who hold part-time jobs as a result of the implementation of technology. Nor do they show a major restructuring of women's jobs in general, with part-time work for women increasing more rapidly than full-time work. Overall, the proportion of women working less than 34 hours a week declined from 35.0 percent in 1970 to 32.6 percent in 1984, with most of the drop occurring between 1970 and 1980 (see Table 6). In each of the industries most likely to be affected by the adoption of new technology—manufacturing, transportation, and public utilities; finance, insurance, and real estate; business and repair services; other professional services; and public administration—the proportion of women working part time declined during this period. Only in retail trade and personal services did the proportion of women in the industry working part

---

[2] Several points should be kept in mind while interpreting Tables 6, 7, and 8: (1) the tables report data for wage and salary workers only and exclude the self-employed; (2) some jobs which are scheduled for less than 35 hours are full-time jobs; (3) hours are not reported for employed workers who are not at work, so it is impossible to know whether they work less than 35 hours a week. I estimate that about 10 percent of the employed nonagricultural labor force is affected by these caveats.

TABLE 6 Part-Time Employment of Wage and Salary Workers, by Industry and Sex, for 1970, 1980, and 1984 (percent)

| Industry | Employed Part Time (1 to 34 hours per week) | | | | | |
| | 1970 | | 1980 | | 1984 | |
	Men	Women	Men	Women	Men	Women
All industries	18.3	35.0	16.4	33.5	15.9	32.6
Mining	12.5	19.1	8.9	15.1	12.5	19.1
Construction	24.9	34.2	21.0	31.4	19.4	31.9
Manufacturing	13.6	25.2	10.1	19.7	9.2	17.3
Transportation and						
public utilities	14.7	27.8	12.9	22.6	11.5	19.4
Trade	23.1	45.9	23.3	48.5	23.5	47.7
Retail	26.6	47.7	28.4	51.8	28.8	50.9
Finance, insurance,						
and real estate	16.4	26.4	14.3	23.2	12.4	20.1
Service	22.6	37.6	20.9	35.9	19.9	35.7
Business and repair	19.7	39.5	18.5	37.1	17.9	35.2
Personal	20.7	40.4	23.2	42.8	20.9	41.8
Other professional	18.1	33.5	15.5	28.1	12.4	27.0
Public administration	17.8	31.6	14.0	27.8	12.8	23.8

NOTE: Percentages are based on data for wage and salary workers excluding agricultural and private household workers.

SOURCE: Derived from Bureau of Labor Statistics unpublished monthly data; annual averages.

time actually increase, from 47.7 percent to 50.9 percent in retail trade and from 40.4 percent to 41.8 percent in personal services between 1970 and 1984 (see Table 6). The situation for male wage and salary workers is quite similar. The number of part-time jobs in the economy has increased substantially since 1970 but, except for retail trade and personal services, the growth of jobs in which women work less than 35 hours a week has been slower than the growth of full-time jobs.

The data in Table 6 are consistent with the retrospective data in Table 5. Both show declines in the proportions of women working part time in industries affected by office automation— finance, insurance, and real estate; business and repair services; and public administration. Only the "other professional" category registers a divergence, with the retrospective data showing an increase in the last year reported (1983) and persons-at-work data showing a consistent decrease in the part-time employment of

TABLE 7 Part-Time Employment by Occupation and Sex of Worker in 1970, 1980, and 1982

| | Percent Employed Part Time (1 to 34 hours per week) | | | | | |
| | 1970 | | 1980 | | 1982 | |
Occupation	Men	Women	Men	Women	Men	Women
White-collar workers	7.2	24.0	7.8	24.3	8.5	25.5
Professional and technical	6.7	22.8	7.0	21.2	7.5	23.0
Managers and administrators	3.3	13.2	3.8	12.4	4.2	12.3
Sales workers	13.5	48.4	13.3	49.2	14.8	49.5
Clerical workers	11.0	20.9	13.6	23.3	14.6	24.8
Blue-collar workers	9.7	17.6	11.3	19.3	13.8	22.3
Service workers (except private household)	21.7	38.2	27.4	45.0	28.4	47.2

NOTE: Excludes farm occupations and private household workers.

SOURCE: Derived from Bureau of Labor Statistics (January 1971:133; January 1981b:192; January 1983b:170); data are annual averages of monthly data.

TABLE 8 Part-Time Employment by Occupation and Sex of Worker in 1984

| | Percent Employed Part Time (1 to 34 hours per week) | |
Occupation	Men	Women
Managerial, professional	5.7	18.2
Technicians	6.7	20.3
Sales	12.4	43.0
Administrative support, including clerical	11.7	21.0
Service, except household	27.3	46.7
Precision production, craft, and repair	8.3	14.5
Operators	13.9	19.8

NOTE: Nonfarm occupations only. Occupational categories changed in 1983. Data are not comparable to those in Table 8.

SOURCE: Derived from Bureau of Labor Statistics (January 1985a:Table 34); values are annual averages of monthly data.

women. The overall figures for part-time work are also quite similar, with 32.6 percent of the women at work in 1984 working less than 35 hours and 32.8 percent of women with work experience in 1983 having held part-time jobs.

The proportions of men and women working part time in the major occupational groupings are examined in Table 7. The increase in part-time work for men again shows up quite clearly, with the proportion of men working part time increasing in every major occupational category. The largest increase occurred among male clerical workers, where the proportion working part time increased from 11.0 percent to 14.6 percent; among male blue-collar workers, where it increased from 9.7 percent to 13.8 percent; and among male service workers, where it increased from 21.7 percent to 28.4 percent between 1970 and 1982. These occupations also registered the largest increases in the proportion of women working part time. A comparison of Tables 6 and 7 indicates that the increase in the proportion of clerical workers employed part time has not translated into an increase in part-time work in industries such as business services; public administration; and finance, insurance, and real estate. The spread of office automation technologies in these industries has reduced clerical labor requirements per unit of output and, hence, the relative importance of clerical occupations (Appelbaum, 1984).

HOURS OF WORK OF PART-TIME EMPLOYEES

It has been suggested that expected increases in part-time work in office industries do not show up in comparisons of those who work less than 35 hours a week with those who work 35 hours or more because the real change involves a decline in hours for those who work 30 to 34 hours a week and an increase in the proportions working less than 30 hours. Anecdotal evidence indicates that when clerical jobs are moved from central cities to rural or suburban areas, companies cut hours of work substantially, both to attract women whose hours of work are limited by their family responsibilities and to avoid paying these workers the fringe benefits they make available to employees working more than some critical number of hours per week. If true, this suggests that there should be some variation over time in the proportion of part-time employees working 1 to 14 hours, 15 to 29 hours, or 30 to 34 hours per week.

This is, in fact, the case. Perhaps the widely held perception that part-time work for women is increasing arises because the proportion working 15 to 29 hours per week has increased, with most of the change occurring during the decade of the 1970s. The proportion of all working women employed 15 to 29 hours increased from 15.9 percent in 1970 to 17.1 percent in 1980, while the proportion employed 30 to 34 hours decreased from 11.8 percent to 9.9 percent. The change can be seen more clearly if only women working less than 34 hours are considered. Among women working part time, the proportion employed 15 to 29 hours increased from 45.5 percent in 1970 to 51.0 percent in 1980 and 52.0 percent in 1984. The proportion working 30 to 34 hours decreased from 33.6 percent to 29.5 percent over the same time period (see Table 9).

Among women working part time, increases in the proportions working 15 to 29 hours were registered in every industry affected by new technology—manufacturing, transportation, and public utilities; finance, insurance, and real estate; business and repair services; other professional services; and public administration. Simultaneously, the proportion of women working 30 to 34 hours declined in every affected industry (Table 9). A few of these industries registered declines in the proportion of women working 1 to 14 hours as well. Manufacturing, transportation, and public utilities; finance, insurance, and real estate; and public administration showed increases in this category between 1970 and 1980. However, the proportion working fewer than 15 hours in finance, insurance, and real estate and in public administration has declined since 1980. Most of the decline in very short hours (1 to 14 hours) occurred in retail trade and services.

Thus, while the proportion of part-time jobs in many industries has declined since 1970 when the conventional definition of part-time work—less than 34 hours a week—is employed, a different picture emerges when jobs employing women 15 to 29 hours a week are considered. This is where the continued growth of short-hour work is evident, particularly in industries affected by office automation. It seems likely that jobs in which the usual work week is 30 to 34 hours either are full-time jobs or are considered quite close to full-time work both by the women who hold them and the companies that employ them. Hence, the shift in part-time work to jobs in which the work week is 15 to 29 hours probably represents an increase in jobs without the protections and benefits

TABLE 9 Percentage Distribution of Part-Time Women Workers Across Hours per Week Worked for Major Industry Groups in 1970, 1980, and 1984

Industry	Hours per week: 1970				Hours per week: 1980				Hours per week: 1984			
	1-14	15-29	30-34	1-35[a]	1-14	15-29	30-34	1-35[a]	1-14	15-29	30-34	1-35[a]
All industries	21.0	45.5	33.6	100.0	19.3	51.0	29.6	100.0	18.5	52.0	29.5	100.0
Mining	14.2	28.6	57.1	100.0	16.7	50.0	33.3	100.0	9.5	52.3	38.0	100.0
Construction	29.8	43.3	26.9	100.0	23.8	45.6	31.2	100.0	23.6	50.7	25.7	100.0
Manufacturing	10.1	36.2	53.7	100.0	11.2	42.0	46.8	100.0	12.8	42.6	44.6	100.0
Transportation and public utilities	14.7	46.3	38.9	100.0	15.5	52.7	31.8	100.0	18.6	46.9	34.5	100.0
Trade	24.3	52.0	23.7	100.0	20.6	56.7	22.7	100.0	17.9	58.1	23.9	100.0
Retail	24.6	52.8	22.6	100.0	20.8	57.1	22.1	100.0	17.9	58.4	23.7	100.0
Finance, insurance, and real estate	14.2	43.1	42.7	100.0	14.8	50.1	35.1	100.0	13.9	49.5	36.6	100.0
Service	24.9	46.2	28.9	100.0	21.6	50.1	28.2	100.0	21.0	50.7	28.3	100.0
Business and repair	24.0	43.3	32.7	100.0	20.6	53.5	25.9	100.0	21.4	51.5	27.1	100.0
Personal	21.7	50.2	28.1	100.0	20.2	50.2	29.6	100.0	18.9	51.4	29.7	100.0
Other professional	27.1	44.7	28.2	100.0	22.1	52.3	25.6	100.0	22.6	50.5	26.9	100.0
Public administration	14.7	34.7	50.6	100.0	16.7	39.5	43.7	100.0	12.4	40.8	46.8	100.0

NOTE: Percentages are based on data for wage and salary workers excluding agricultural and private household workers.

[a]Numbers may not add to 100.0 due to rounding.

SOURCE: Derived from Bureau of Labor Statistics unpublished monthly data; annual averages.

associated with full-time work and a worsening of employment opportunities for women.

MULTIPLE JOBHOLDING

During the 1970s both the number and the proportion of women holding more than one job increased substantially. For women without a husband present, the increase was even more dramatic. By May 1980, the most recent year for which data are available, 1.5 million women were multiple jobholders (Taylor and Sekscenski, 1981). Thus, 3.8 percent of employed women were moonlighting in 1980 compared with 2.0 percent early in the 1960s and 2.2 percent in 1970 (see Table 10). Dual jobholding was lower for married women, with 3.4 percent of employed married women holding more than one job, and higher for women who had sole or principle responsibility for their own support. Among employed never-married single women, 3.9 percent held more than one job in 1980, while among those who were separated, divorced, or widowed, 4.6 percent were dual jobholders (Taylor and Sekscenski, 1981). The proportion of multiple jobholders who are women more than doubled over the 1970s, from 16 percent in 1970 to 33 percent in 1980. These changes have been reported as "consistent with the increased proportion of women in the total work force" (Women's Bureau, U.S. Department of Labor, 1983:38). In fact, the number of women in the labor force increased 44 percent between March 1970 and March 1980 (Women's Bureau, U.S. Department of Labor, 1983:Table I-8), while the number of women who are multiple jobholders increased 144 percent during those years (see Table 10). Thus, multiple jobholding has become an increasingly important phenomenon among women.

The growth in multiple jobholding occurred mainly among white women. The proportion of black women holding more than one job was 2.2 percent in 1969, 2.0 percent in 1979, and 2.6 percent in 1980 (Sekscenski, 1980; Taylor and Sekscenski, 1981). But black women were more likely than white to report that economic reasons—meeting regular expenses or paying off debts— were their main motivation for moonlighting. Nearly three-fifths of black women, but only two-fifths of white women, gave this as their main reason for working two jobs. Overall, about 42 percent of women hold multiple jobs for economic reasons compared with

TABLE 10 Multiple Jobholding Rates for All Workers, Men, and Women, Selected
Years, May 1970 to May 1980

Year	Total Employed (thousands)	All Multiple Jobholders (thousands)	Female Multiple Jobholders (thousands)	Women as Percent of All Multiple Jobholders	Multiple Jobholding Rate		
					All	Men	Women
1970	78,358	4,048	636	16	5.2	7.0	2.2
1974	85,786	3,889	867	22	4.5	5.8	2.6
1976	87,278	3,948	911	23	4.5	5.8	2.6
1977	90,482	4,558	1,241	27	5.0	6.2	3.4
1978	93,904	4,493	1,281	29	4.8	5.8	3.3
1979	96,327	4,724	1,407	30	4.9	5.9	3.5
1980	96,809	4,759	1,549	33	4.9	5.8	3.8

SOURCES: Brown (1978), Rosenfeld (1979), Sekscenski (1980), and Taylor and
Sekscenski (1981).

35 percent of the men (Sekscenski, 1980; Taylor and Sekscenski,
1981).

The increase in multiple jobholding appears to be related to
the increase in the number of women who have primary economic
responsibility for themselves and/or their families and to the difficulty of meeting this responsibility while working at a part-time
job. Part-time workers in 1981 averaged 19.0 hours per week, 46
percent of the hours worked by full-time workers. Their earnings,
however, averaged only 28 percent of those of full-time workers.
Among part-time clerical workers, most of whom are women, the
average work week was 50 percent of full-time hours, while earnings were 38 percent of full-time earnings (Mellon and Stamos,
1982:Table 5). These figures have remained virtually unchanged
during the last few years. Women working part-time in the third
quarter of 1984 still earned 38 percent of what women who worked
full time earned (*Employment and Earnings* 32(1), 1985:Tables
A-73 and A-74). Almost half of all women who were multiple jobholders held two part-time jobs. In contrast, less than one-fifth of
men who held more than one job had two part-time jobs. About 82
percent of the men who were multiple jobholders had at least one
full-time job, compared with 54 percent of the women (Sekscenski,
1980; Taylor and Sekscenski, 1981).

The relationship of multiple jobholding to technology is tenu-
ous at best. Some companies, particularly in manufacturing, have

added non-day shifts of part-time and full-time workers in order to recover the costs of sophisticated new equipment more rapidly, both because the equipment is more costly, and because it is expected to become obsolete more quickly (ILO Symposium, 1978). This has probably had the effect of increasing women's opportunities for multiple jobholding somewhat. One study found that one-fifth or more of women in operative occupations worked non-day shifts. However, the study also found that most occupations in which women work non-day shifts are unrelated to the use of new kinds of equipment. These include nurses and other health workers; cashiers; and women working in cleaning, food, personal, and protective services (Presser, 1984:Table 4).

AT-HOME WORK

While cottage industry and at-home work for women has a long history in the United States, telecommuting or electronic at-home work is a very recent innovation.[3] As recently as 1981, only 11 companies that employed workers at home on terminals or word processors could be identified (Pratt, 1984). Partly because it is so new, it affects the smallest number of workers of any of the alternative work styles in which women can be found. Its potential, however, is quite large. Elisabeth Allison of Data Resources, Inc., estimates that there are currently 15 million jobs that could be done at home; Jack Nilles of the University of Southern California predicts that within a decade 5 million white-collar workers could be working mainly at home (*Business Week*, 1982).

The growth of telecommuting—defined by Nilles as "a total or partial substitution of the daily commute by communication via a computer terminal" (Pratt, 1984:1–2)—has been rapid, but the number of people involved is still small. *Business Week* (1982) estimates that there were 35 home worker programs for white-collar workers in 1982, involving perhaps 600 workers. Larger estimates put the number of workers employed as telecommuters at 10,000, though Nilles reports that no more than 1,000 of these were full-time telecommuters (Kingston, 1983). The most recent estimate is that there are about 250 companies with approximately 10,000

---

[3] This section is based in part on the paper, "A Sociological Review of Telecommuting," by Maureen Martella, a graduate student at Temple University.

employees working at home using computer technologies. Between 20 and 30 of them—including New York Telephone, American Express, Walgreens, and McDonalds—are planning to expand their programs (Chin, 1984).

DISTINCTIONS BETWEEN CLERICAL AND PROFESSIONAL AT-HOME WORK

While telecommuting is a recent phenomenon, and still not large, it has some very noticeable characteristics. It is already quite clear that there are important differences between clerical and professional electronic home work. Companies are adopting telecommuter programs for professional employees to meet shortages of skilled personnel, such as computer programmers and analysts, or to attract or retain skilled workers whose family or personal situation places constraints on the amount of time they can spend in an office. The Travelers Insurance Company, for example, has an experimental home work project that enables highly skilled data-processing employees to do most of their work at home, spending between half a day and two days a week at the office. According to an executive at Travelers, "The experiment is designed to help employees who have unique computer skills meet family and other responsibilities. It serves Travelers' business requirements by helping us keep top performers on the job who might otherwise drop out of our workforce temporarily, or even leave permanently" (Mortenson, 1983:112). Time frames for completing work and supervision of professional telecommuters are often based on "mutual trust and respect" (Olson, 1983a:185).

The situation for clerical workers is much different. They are more likely to be paid piece rates, less likely to receive fringe benefits, and are sometimes required to pay rent for the equipment they need to do the work. Thus, the Blue Cross Cottage Keying Program in Washington, D.C., pays its home workers 16 cents per completed insurance claim. The women receive no benefits and must deduct their own taxes, and in addition they are required to pay $95 every 2 weeks to rent the terminals they use (Chin, 1984; *Business Week*, 1982). Supervision of off-site clerical workers is viewed as a problem by management. Companies deal with this problem by giving clerical telecommuters discrete tasks that have definite beginning and ending points and that can easily be measured and by paying piece rates. The 46 home office workers interviewed by Pratt (1984) were critical of the poor organization of their work by the companies employing them, which they felt reduced their earnings.

Claims examiner is a skilled clerical position that California Western States Life Insurance Company now fills with home workers hired as independent contractors. The company provides computer terminals linked by telephone lines to the company's data-processing center to the claims examiners. The claims examiners are independent contractors who are paid on a piece-rate basis. They rent terminals from the company for $50 per month and furnish their own supplies and equipment. The company is able to spot check the work of its at-home examiners as claims payments are entered into the data system. "The task of auditing and managing the at-home examiners is simplified by having all their work instantly accessible in the home office via the computer system. The average at-home claims examiner represents more than $1,000 in reduced costs to the company each month" (Mortenson, 1983:114).

Clerical home work is attractive to firms because of its potential for reducing labor costs. The strategies adopted are a cause for concern to organizations such as 9 to 5, the National Association of Working Women, which opposes electronic home work because it shifts overhead costs, including machinery rental, to employees; it reduces hourly wages by switching to piece rates; it shifts costs of health and life insurance and social security and retirement income to individual workers; and it provides employers with workers whom they can easily release (Gregory, 1983). Productivity is also an issue. Home workers, professional as well as clerical, have reported working during, outside of, and in addition to normal business hours and have complained about the pressures on them to work overly long hours (Kingston, 1983; Pratt, 1984). And 9 to 5 is concerned that employers are "experimenting with productivity measures . . . to develop benchmarks as leverage to increase pressures and intensify control over the main office work force" (Gregory, 1983).

Though there are little data available on the productivity effects of teleworking, corporate experiments with electronic home work indicate that it results in productivity increases among both clerical and managerial teleworkers (Kraut, 1985). In reviewing the evidence from these pilot projects, one researcher tentatively concluded that "the productivity gains associated with telework are probably the result of highly motivated, volunteer workers putting in more time on their jobs when they were working at home than when they were working in a conventional office. The gains may not be sustained with more general use of teleworking by less-motivated workers who have no choice but to work at home" (Kraut, 1985:6).

ADVANTAGES OF TELEWORKING

The major advantages of electronic home work to employers have already been discussed. In the case of managerial and professional employees, firms turn to home work in order to retain or attract qualified workers with skills that are in short supply— computer programmers and other skilled data-processing employees, for example. Firms undertake clerical home work to reduce labor costs. This is often accomplished by setting piece-work rates so that the employee receives no compensation for time spent setting up work, collecting work, delivering work, discussing work with supervisors, or for difficulties encountered and time lost in completing it satisfactorily. The limited data available suggest that while professional home workers are usually permanent, full-time employees receiving full salaries and benefits, clerical home workers are rarely in this position. Instead they are usually part-time employees earning hourly wages or piece rates with reduced fringe benefits or no benefits at all (Olson, 1983b). The costs shifted from companies to workers as a result of the reduction in fringe benefits, especially health insurance, can be substantial. In addition, as in the case of temporary workers, firms have substantial flexibility in scheduling home workers to meet high demand and not using them in off-peak periods, without incurring the costs associated with layoffs and unemployment compensation.

In addition, some firms have achieved cost savings by shifting overhead costs and equipment rental to home workers. Workers may be required to lease terminals or maintain their own computers, provide office furniture, install dedicated telephone lines, and pay for higher telephone, heating, cooling, and electricity bills. Finally, as another advantage to companies, if the home work involves the use of a company's mainframe, it can be scheduled during times of low computer utilization. The company realizes savings both from more intense use of computer resources and from a decreased need to expand computer capacity.

The advantages sought by workers who take jobs as electronic home workers include the opportunity to control their own time and a reduction in child care costs. Control over the scheduling of work is an important benefit to some women who are balancing home responsibilities with paid employment. In practice this benefit accrues mainly to professional employees, since professional work is less closely supervised and allows for more freedom in scheduling particular tasks. For some who cannot find affordable quality day care, teleworking may provide the only opportunity to work at all. Another benefit is that home workers save commuting time and expenses as well as outlays for clothing, dry cleaning, and restaurant meals. These savings, however, need to be compared with the costs that companies have shifted to employees working at home in assessing the benefit to home workers. Finally, teleworking increases employment opportunities for those who cannot easily work away from home on a daily basis—the handicapped, the elderly, and, to some extent, mothers of young children.

THE FUTURE OF HOME WORK

Despite its attractiveness to employers, explosive growth in the number of home workers does not seem likely. Substantial institutional and managerial commitment is required to establish a home work program. Employers express strong reservations about the ability to maintain standards and adequately supervise workers (Cole, 1981; Sample, 1981). Professional employees are afraid that working at home will limit their career mobility since visibility remains essential for promotion (Chin, 1984; Olson, 1983). Of Pratt's respondents, no one thought telecommuting was beneficial to his or her career. Women were certain that working at home was detrimental to their careers, but they viewed it as an alternative to dropping out completely (Pratt, 1984). Low wages and lack of job security are critical issues for clerical telecommuters. Finally, federal, state, and local laws and restrictions currently regulating home work are slowing the adoption of telecommuting. These constraints may be weakened if pilot programs prove successful.

Still, given the apparent cost advantages to firms of electronic home work, these reasons do not seem sufficient to explain why teleworking is not more widespread. A perceptive analysis of the lack of substitution of home work for office work is given by Kraut (1985). He argues that the current office structure is highly stable and provides a resistant barrier to the spread of telework because "conventional, 9-to-5 office arrangements support a large number of activities critical to the functioning of any work organization. Radical changes in the conventional office have the potential to disrupt these other activities" (Kraut, 1985:14). Among the activities that Kraut identifies are socialization of new workers to the workplace, transmission of job skills, informal communication and information flows, communication of organizational norms and information collaboration among individuals, structuring of workers' time, and the spatial and temporal segregation of demands of work and family life. In addition, as Kraut observes, employers have ways other than home work of utilizing computer and communications technologies to reduce costs. These include the relocation of back-office work to suburban or foreign locations where cheaper labor is more abundant, as well as the reduction of both production and information workers through productivity increase.

In light of the advantages to organizing clerical and professional work in a more conventional office setting, the potential cost savings associated with teleworking suggests that a steady but not explosive expansion in the still-small trend toward home work is likely to continue. Work at home as an adjunct to work in a conventional office location may increase and may even be encouraged by employers. A 1982 AT&T study found that 30 percent of those employed outside the home brought work home with them (cited in Kraut, 1985). Most of the work done at home did not require sophisticated equipment but was done with telephone, paper, pencil, and calculators. This may change as more households own personal computers and other new technology. The result would be an increase in telework at home as workers with conventional jobs used telecommunications to complete some tasks at home, rather than a rapid increase in electronic home work and the clerical cottage industry.

CONCLUSION

Management's interest in implementing alternative work schedules and using temporary workers, part-time workers, and home workers—especially in clerical occupations—appears to be more closely related to management's desire to reduce labor costs than to the requirements of office automation technologies. Computer and communications technologies do not require that clerical office work be fragmented and the separate stages of the production process be physically dispersed while decision making and the work process continue to be controlled from corporate headquarters. On the contrary, the evidence suggests that the technology is most productive when it is combined with skilled workers who have a knowledge of the overall production process and when it is used to integrate tasks and decentralize decision making (Albin, 1984; Appelbaum, 1984; and Hirschhorn, 1984). Initial training costs are higher when the technology is implemented in this manner, but the potential for productivity gains over the long term are substantially increased (Albin, 1984; Hirschhorn, 1984).

Concern with reducing labor costs and, in some cases, with realizing savings from office automation immediately rather than over a longer time horizon appears to have led some firms to implement alternative work schedules. These schedules function mainly to increase the flexibility of employers in varying hours to meet periods of high demand and, in some instances, to eliminate fringe benefits to employees. Full-time employees in most medium- and large-size firms have won substantial benefits, including paid holidays, vacations, health insurance, life insurance, and pensions (see Table 11). Office automation technology has enabled some firms to rearrange work schedules on some jobs so that hours of work fall below full time and the job no longer carries some or all of the benefits. The savings to companies of shifting health insurance and other costs to employees are substantial. Concern with quantifiable improvements in productivity sometimes leads to the fragmentation of tasks and to the assembly-line pacing of work, factors which also contribute to the use of part-time or temporary workers because jobs have become subdivided. Productivity concerns may, for example, lead to an increase in remote working—clerical employees located in satellite processing centers or in their own homes doing repetitive and easily measured tasks—linked to the firm's central offices via communications lines and with the computer performing the task of electronically reintegrating the work process and producing a finished product.

At the same time, a substantial minority of women workers have expressed a preference for flexible work schedules in order to meet both work and home responsibilities. Flexible full-time schedules are not widely available, and these women have opted

TABLE 11 Percent of Full-Time Employees by Participation in Employee Benefit Programs, Medium and Large Firms, 1983

Employee Benefit Program	All Employees	Professional and Adminis- trative Employees	Technical and Clerical Employees	Production Employees
Paid:				
Holidays	99	99	100	98
Vacations	100	100	100	99
Personal leave	25	31	35	17
Lunch period	11	4	5	17
Rest time	74	58	76	80
Sick leave	67	92	91	42
Sickness and accident insurance	49	29	34	67
Long-term disability insurance	45	66	58	28
Health insurance for employee	96	98	95	96
Health insurance for dependents	93	95	91	92
Life insurance	96	97	95	95
Retirement pension	82	66	84	79

NOTE: Participation is defined as coverage for time off, insurance, or pension plan. Benefits for which the employee must pay the full premium are excluded. Only current employees are counted as participants.

SOURCE: Bureau of Labor Statistics (1984c).

for part-time, temporary, or home work arrangements rather than leave the labor force entirely. But the negative effects of these arrangements on career mobility and/or earnings growth are a concern even to those who choose these options (Pratt, 1984).

There is no evidence of an increased desire for such alternative work styles by women. At-home work, while a discernible trend, involves only a tiny fraction of workers. Temporary work is increasing rapidly at present, but it is not certain that this increase reflects the preferences of women, especially when the initiative comes directly from the employer as in the case of the new federal regulations on temporary work. The increase in temporary help services does appear to represent an effort by women, particularly those who are skilled workers, to achieve flexibility in scheduling work (Gannon, 1984). It should be noted, however, that the increases in home work and temporary help services since 1982 have been more than offset by the decline in voluntary part-time work between May 1982 and March 1985 (see Table 4). This suggests caution in attributing the trends in home work and temporary work to the desires of women.

Alternative work schedules are, however, desired by many employers who see increased flexibility in scheduling workers as an important way to keep labor costs down. Companies that anticipate cyclical slowdowns in business or expect automation to reduce employment needs are staffing at less than full strength even during periods of economic recovery and expansion. Human resource strategies include the use of temporary workers, part-time workers, and home workers to supplement a smaller staff of permanent full-time employees when employment needs are high in order to avoid layoffs later. The cost savings to firms are substantial and include ease in scheduling work and in cutting back employment, as well as savings on fringe benefits and pensions. Often, there are savings from paying part-time workers lower wages or home workers on a piece-rate basis as well.

The reduction of labor costs has been the main driving force behind the development of these work schedules. Nevertheless, office automation technologies have played an important role in encouraging and facilitating their use and women workers have been very much affected by the changes. However, it should be noted that both the analysis of the reasons for alternative work schedules and the growing use of temporary workers in non-office sectors of the economy, such as hospitals and light industry, suggest that men as well as women are finding it more difficult to obtain the benefits of permanent, full-time jobs. The combined growth of involuntary part-time work and temporary employment for both men and women, while small in relation to the total labor force, is nevertheless significant. Concern centers on the fact that these trends may signal a restructuring of employment opportunities and the extension of sub-par working conditions to sectors of the economy where full-time work and benefits have usually prevailed.

REFERENCES

Albin, Peter S.
 1984 Job design within changing patterns of technical development. Pp.
       125–162 in E. Collins and L.D. Tanner, eds., *American Jobs and the
       Changing Industrial Base*. Cambridge, Mass.: Ballinger Publishing
       Company.
Appelbaum, Eileen
 1984 Technology and the Design of Jobs in the Insurance Industry.
       Institute for Research on Educational Finance and Governance,
       Stanford University.
Brown, Scott C.
 1978 Moonlighting increased sharply in 1977, particularly among women.
       Monthly Labor Review 101(1). Reprinted with supplementary tables
       in Bureau of Labor Statistics, *Multiple Job Holders in May 1977*,
       Special Labor Force Report #211. Washington, D.C.: U.S. De-
       partment of Labor
Bureau of Labor Statistics
 1985a *Employment and Earnings* 32 (various issues). Washington, D.C.:
        U.S. Department of Labor.
 1985b *Linking Employment Problems to Economic Status*. Bulletin 2222.
        Washington, D.C.: U.S. Department of Labor.
 1985c *Supplement to Employment and Earnings*, Revised Establishment
        Data. Washington, D.C.: U.S. Department of Labor.
 1984a *Supplement to Employment and Earnings*, Revised Establishment
        Data. Washington, D.C.: U.S. Department of Labor.
 1984b *Employment and Earnings* 31 (various issues). Washington, D.C.:
        U.S. Department of Labor.
 1984c *Employee Benefits in Medium and Large Firms*. Bulletin 2213. Wash-
        ington, D.C.: U.S. Department of Labor.
 1983a *Work Experience of the Population in 1982*. Washington, D.C.: U.S.
        Department of Labor.
 1983b *Employment and Earnings* 30 (various issues). Washington, D.C.:
        U.S. Department of Labor.
 1982a *Employment and Earnings* 29(6). Washington, D.C.: U.S. Depart-
        ment of Labor.
 1982b *Work Experience of the Population in 1981*. Washington, D.C.: U.S.
        Department of Labor.
 1981a *Work Experience of the Population in 1980*. Washington, D.C.: U.S.
        Department of Labor.
 1981b *Employment and Earnings* 28 (various issues). Washington, D.C.:
        U.S. Department of Labor.
 1980   *Employment and Earnings* 27 (various issues). Washington, D.C.:
        U.S. Department of Labor.
 1979a *Employment and Earnings, United States, 1909–78*. Bulletin 1312-11.
        Washington, D.C.: U.S. Department of Labor.
 1979b *Employment and Earnings* 26(6). Washington, D.C.: U.S. Depart-
        ment of Labor.
 1979c *Work Experience of the Population in 1978*. Washington, D.C.: U.S.
        Department of Labor.

1978a   *Employment and Earnings* 25(6). Washington, D.C.: U.S. Department of Labor.

1978b   *Work Experience of the Population in 1977.* Washington, D.C.: U.S. Department of Labor.

1977a   *Employment and Earnings* 24(6). Washington, D.C.: U.S. Department of Labor.

1977b   *Work Experience of the Population in 1976.* Washington, D.C.: U.S. Department of Labor.

1976   *Work Experience of the Population in 1978.* Washington, D.C.: U.S. Department of Labor.

1971   *Employment and Earnings* 17 (various issues). Washington, D.C.: U.S. Department of Labor.

1970   *Employment and Earnings* 16 (various issues). Washington, D.C.: U.S. Department of Labor.

1967   *Employment and Earnings* 13 (various issues). Washington, D.C.: U.S. Department of Labor.

n.d.   Unpublished data from the Current Population Survey, March 1971, 1976, 1981, 1984, and 1985.

n.d.   Unpublished tables on work experience of the population in 1979 and 1983.

Bureau of the Census

1980   *1977 Census of Service Industries,* Geographic Area Studies, United States. Washington, D.C.: U.S. Department of Commerce.

1985   *1982 Census of Service Industries,* Geographic Area Studies, United States. Washington, D.C.: U.S. Department of Commerce.

Business Week

1982   If home is where the worker is. *Business Week* (May 3):66.

1985   Part-time workers: rising numbers, rising discord. *Business Week* (April 1):62–63.

Chin, Kathy

1984   Home is where the job is. *Infoworld* 6(17):28–32.

Cole, Bernard C.

1981   Computing to work. *Interface Age* 6(8):93–95.

Collins, Huntley

1985   Unions decry trend to short-term federal jobs. *Philadelphia Inquirer.* February 5:B1.

Deutermann, William V., Jr., and Scott Campbell Brown

1978   Voluntary part-time workers: a growing part of the labor force. *Monthly Labor Review* 101(6):3–10.

Fiamingo, Josephine

1984   Need a pro? Try temporary help. *Office Administration and Automation* (August):48–55, 68–70.

Gannon, Martin J.

1984   Preferences of temporary workers: time, variety and flexibility. *Monthly Labor Review* 107(8):26–28.

Gregory, Judith

1983   Clerical workers and new office technologies. Pp. 112–114 in *Office Work Stations in the Home.* Board on Telecommunications. Washington, D.C.: National Academy Press.

Hirschhorn, Larry

1984   *Beyond Mechanization.* Cambridge, Mass.: MIT Press.

Hunt, Timothy L., and H. Allan Hunt
  1985   An assessment of data sources to study the employment effects of technological change. Pp. 1–116 in *Technology and Employment Effects*. Interim Report of the Panel on Technology and Women's Employment, Committee on Women's Employment and Related Social Issues, National Research Council. Washington, D.C.: National Academy Press.
ILO Symposium
  1978   *Arrangement of Working Time and Social Problems Connected with Shift Work in Industrialized Countries.* Geneva: International Labour Office.
Kingston, Jane
  1983   Telecommuting: its impact on the home. Pp. 287–300 in H.F. Didsbury, Jr., ed., *The World of Work, Careers and the Future.* Bethesda, Md.: World Future Society.
Kraut, Robert E.
  1985   Predicting the use of technology: the case of telework. In Robert E. Kraut, ed., *Technology and the Transformation in White-Collar Work.* Hillsdale, N.J.: Lawrence Erlbaum.
Leon, Carol, and Robert W. Bednarzik
  1978   A profile of women on part-time schedules. *Monthly Labor Review* 101(10):3–12.
Mellon, Earl F., and George D. Stamos
  1982   Usual weekly earnings: another look at intergroup differences and basic trends. *Monthly Labor Review* 105(4):15–24.
Mortenson, Patricia
  1983   Telecommuting: the company perspective. *Best's Review Property-Casualty Edition* (November):112–114.
Nollen, Stanley D., Brenda B. Eddy, and Virginia H. Martin
  1978   *Permanent Part-Time Employment.* New York: Praeger Special Studies.
Olson, Margarethe H.
  1983a   Remote office work: changing work patterns in space and time. *Communications of the AMC* 26(3):180–190.
  1983b   *Overview of Work-At-Home Trends in the United States.* New York: New York University Center for Research on Information Systems.
Pratt, J.H.
  1984   Home telecommuting: a study of its pioneers. *Technological Forecasting and Social Change* 25:1–14.
Presser, Harriet B.
  1984   Shift Work and the Family. Paper presented at the Population Issues Research Center, Pennsylvania State University.
Presser, Harriet B., and Wendy Baldwin
  1980   Child care as a constraint on employment: prevalence, correlates and bearing on the work and fertility nexus. *American Journal of Sociology* 85(7):1202–1213.
Rosenfeld, Carl
  1979   Multiple jobholding holds steady in 1978. *Monthly Labor Review* 102(2):59–61.

Rosow, Jerome M., and Robert Zager
  1981   *New Work Schedules for a Changing Society.* Scarsdale, N.Y.: Work
          in America Institute, Inc.
Sample, Robert
  1981   Coping with the "work-at-home" trend. *Administrative Management*
          42(8):25–30.
Sekscenski, Edward S.
  1980   Women's share of moonlighting nearly doubles during 1969–1979.
          Monthly Labor Review 103(5):36–39.
Taylor, Daniel, and Edward S. Sekscenski
  1981   Workers on long schedules, single and multiple jobholders. *Monthly
          Labor Review* 104(5):47–53.
U.S. Commission on Civil Rights
  1983   *Disadvantaged Women and Their Children.* Washington, D.C.: U.S.
          Commission on Civil Rights.
Women's Bureau, U.S. Department of Labor
  1983   *Time of Change: 1983 Handbook on Women Workers.* Bulletin 298.
          Washington, D.C.: U.S. Department of Labor.

Part IV

Policy Perspectives

Employer Policies to Enhance the Application of Office System Technology to Clerical Work

ALAN F. WESTIN

SCOPE AND FOCUS

In this paper, I draw on a recently completed study[1] of office automation (OA) experiences at 110 business, government, and

---

Financial support for the study was provided, in part, by IBM, Hewlett-Packard, NCR, OCLI, Control Data Business Advisors, Haworth, Kelly Services, and Northern Telecom. The research design, field work, and project reports were the responsibility of the Educational Fund, and the sponsors are not responsible for any of our judgments or positions. My senior colleagues on the project were Michael A. Baker, Heather A. Schweder, and Sheila Lehman. The first product of the study, *The Changing Workplace: A Guide to Managing the People, Organizational, and Regulatory Aspects of Office Technology* (Westin et al., 1985), was published by Knowledge Industries, 701 Westchester Avenue, White Plains, NY 10604, in April 1985. A second book, *The Office Automation Controversy*, will be published in 1987.

[1] Between April 1982 and June 1984, the Educational Fund for Individual Rights conducted a study of "The Workplace Impact of Using VDTs in the Office." The centerpiece of the research was a program of on-site visits to 110 organizations implementing office system technology. About 60 percent of these were business firms, in the insurance, manufacturing, financial services, media, transportation, retail, utility, distribution, energy, and consumer-services industries. About 40 percent were federal, state, and local government agencies and nonprofit organizations, such as private

nonprofit organizations to explore four issues of concern: (1) how organizations are going about implementation of new office system technologies; (2) how women workers have been responding to these implementation policies, under both favorable and unfavorable circumstances; (3) what policies of "leading edge" organizations hold promise for long-term productivity and job enhancement; and (4) whether favorable adaptations by both workers and managers will likely occur on their own, or rather be enhanced by intervention.

The discussion concentrates on women clerical workers, since clerical work is the area toward which most office system applications have been directed in the past decade. In this kind of work, video display terminals (VDTs) are used most intensively, and for the longest period per day. Women make up over 90 percent of the clerical work force in the offices where the new technologies are being implemented.

One conclusion from the larger study is that there is considerable variation at this point in the policies and procedures that employer organizations are using in implementing office systems technology. We do not share the view that the technology somehow dictates one dominant implementation strategy, or that women clerical workers are encountering one set of "OA (office automation) impacts" wherever VDTs are being installed. In this paper, the focus is on the *quality of work life* and *equality* aspects of applying office systems technology to clerical work where female employees predominate. We did not study the employment-level impacts of office automation, nor the effects on job security or insecurity.

The 110 organizations that were visited on-site for the larger study were *not* a representative sample of corporations, government agencies, or nonprofits. They were chosen primarily on the

---

universities, hospitals, and civic groups. At these sites, we conducted open-ended interviews with over 1,100 end users of VDTs, primarily at the clerical, secretarial, and professional levels, and with over 650 managers and executives. In addition, the project made visits to 15 large vendors of office systems and support equipment; interviewed officials at 40 U.S. labor unions concerned with VDT and OA issues; did a pilot survey and had follow-up meetings with information-system directors in 55 business and government organizations; and interviewed representatives of women's, religious, minority, industry, and user groups concerned with the impact of office technology. We also conducted interviews with 75 employees using VDTs in organizations to which we did not make site visits.

basis of their reputations as "advanced" and "active" users of office systems technology. Many were selected because of a reputation for having "good human resources policies," though this was not a prerequisite for selection. These reputational characteristics were drawn from nominations by vendors, articles in the computer and business press, articles in the personnel and labor relations media, and suggestions from interest groups, OA experts, and academicians. About 10 percent of the sites were union-represented, about evenly divided between private and government employers.

In the course of our site visits, we spoke with approximately 900 women that use VDTs at their jobs. About 15 percent of these women were professional, technical, or managerial employees, and about 85 percent were clerical workers.

Four main types of clerical work were examined: word processing in both centralized and distributed settings; customer-service work via terminal and telephone; intensive data-entry work; and general secretarial functions. Most of the conversations were conducted with individual employees, but about 20 percent took place in small focus groups.

We used a topic checklist for these interviews, made up of neutrally worded questions designed to minimize prompting or forcing of issues.[2] Our questions asked how long the employee had been using a VDT; whether she had done this job previously without a VDT; what kind of training for the machine she had received; what personal involvement, if any, she had had in the process of using office system technology at her job; how the VDT was affecting "her job" and "her work"; whether she had read or heard anything about "VDT issues"; how management supervised her performance; what problems, if any, she had encountered using the VDT and whether she had raised these with management; how

---

[2] We guaranteed employees complete anonymity for their comments, and our interviews were done without supervisors or managers present. As a result, we believe these women clericals were open and candid in their discussion of how they saw VDT uses affecting them, and their responses provided us with valuable reports on the reactions and problems of clerical workers doing intensive VDT work. However, since we did not conduct a representative-sample survey, or use a standardized questionnaire, our interviews do not provide the basis for making statistical statements about national trends, particular industries, or specific occupational groups. Therefore, we feel most comfortable reporting what we found for these 110 organizations, using broad terminology. Our conclusions must therefore be viewed as exploratory rather than representative.

she saw her future at this organization or elsewhere being affected by her VDT skill; and similar broad inquiries.

In addition, I draw in this paper on two other interview sources. In the course of the larger study, we conducted in-depth interviews averaging about 1.5 hours each with 12 white, black, and Hispanic clerical workers in one large metropolitan area, and these have been used for our analysis of women clerical worker life situations, career aspirations, and orientations on "women's issues." We also obtained the transcripts of 10 excellent in-depth interviews with women clericals conducted in 1983 as part of a larger University of Connecticut Labor History project (Asher, 1983). Both sets of interviews probed personal history, education, pre-VDT work experiences, career goals, social and family situations, treatment as women on the job, and other key elements shaping the reaction of these women to the use of VDTs.

OFFICE AUTOMATION AND WOMEN'S ISSUES—EVIDENCE FROM CASE STUDIES

The following are trends among organizations in our field study that relate most directly to the impact of office systems technology trends on women clerical workers (for the detailed data and full-scale discussions of these trends, see our study report, Westin et al., 1985).

Varied Application Among the organizations visited, we did not find the kind of unitary, deterministic application of office systems technology that some social analysts or group spokesmen have asserted to be taking place. Rather, we found significant variations in the design and implementation of VDT clerical work from industry to industry, among individual firms within industries, from division to division, among different local work units, and even among specific types of jobs. In addition, there were often significant variations in how supervisors and unit managers were applying top management "OA policies" to clerical workers. Such diversities affected both the experiences and attitudes of women clerical workers toward the institution of VDTs at their workplaces.

Importance of Overall Human Resource Policy The overall human resources or personnel philosophy of managements at the organizations we visited was the strongest single variable in how the *quality of work life aspects* and the *women's equality issues* of

OA were being perceived and addressed, both in general and as far as clerical work was concerned. We found firms with nearly identical types of clerical operations, work force characteristics, lines of business or government activity, and economic circumstances whose policies toward the two issues of concern in this paper were dramatically different and were perceived as such by women clerical workers we interviewed. (See the profiles of "Great Northern" and "National Services" later in this paper for specific illustrations of this contrast.)

Significant Differences Among Women Attitudes toward VDT work among women clericals interviewed differed as a result of important individual and group characteristics, such as education, social class, race and ethnic status, age and life situation, economic needs, attitude toward "women's issues," experiences with sex discrimination, etc. (This will also be discussed in greater detail later.)

Positive Perceptions of Office Automation Confirming the results of various national office worker surveys conducted in the past 3 to 4 years, a large majority of the clerical women we interviewed (in the 80 to 90 percent range) expressed positive comments about having VDTs to use in their jobs. Specifically, they reported important quantitative and qualitative improvements in their job performance as a result of the new office systems, and they were glad to have VDT skills which they believed would make them more "marketable" for jobs both within and outside the firms for which they were working. Furthermore, even those women clericals who did not like the content of their jobs very much, or who were upset at the manner in which the new technology was introduced at their workplace, did not attribute the problems to "the machine" as such, but rather to the way that their management was structuring jobs or work settings around the new technology.

Problems of Office Technology Implementation Despite their initial positive attitude toward the technology, a majority of clerical women we interviewed reported a combination of significant VDT problems that they wanted their managements to address. (This also parallels the findings of national surveys of VDT use in offices.) Some of these were general problems growing out of how well or poorly VDT technology was applied (ergonomics, job design, computer-based monitoring), while other problems these clericals reported are issues specific to women workers (such as pregnancy concerns from VDT use, pay equity for "women's work," etc.).

Job Reorganization Women clericals in each of the job sectors we examined—data entry, customer service, word processing, and secretarial—were experiencing a significant reshaping of the content of their jobs compared with the way these jobs had been structured in recent decades. However, contrary to some commentaries, we did not find this to be unidirectional in the organizations we studied. Some clerical jobs were increasing in variety, scope, and satisfaction and were perceived so by employees. For example, new capacities to search data bases and to perform complete on-line transactions for customers in banking, utilities, or newspapers were making customer-service work more interesting for these workers. Similarly, graphics capabilities in word processing were enhancing effectiveness and satisfaction in many secretarial operations. We found other clericals had moved into interesting para-professional jobs, in which they were managing information collection and distribution for work teams in their organizations. However, some clericals, such as claims adjusters in insurance firms and back-office workers in financial institutions, were having the skilled and interesting elements of their jobs taken over by software, and these employees found themselves functioning largely as data-entry workers inputting routine customer information. The feelings of women we interviewed were significantly shaped by whether managements were providing task variety and interesting activities in the new VDT jobs, or whether they were providing retraining and new job opportunities for clerical employees for whom straight data-entry work would be an unsatisfactory job. In terms of the physical comfort of women clericals using VDTs, especially operators using terminals for data entry, customer service, and word-processing jobs for more than 5 hours per day, over three-fourths of the organizations we visited during 1982–1984 did not have the majority of their clerical-worker stations in "minimally correct" ergonomic conditions. We defined this as an adjustable chair, an adjustable terminal *or* work surface, and a nonglare work environment (however achieved, with antiglare screen, adjusted workstation illumination, etc.). As a result, a majority of women clericals we interviewed complained of recurring physical discomforts attributable to such weak ergonomic conditions for intensive VDT use.

Women's Labor-Force Experience A strong minority of women clerical employees—perhaps 25 to 35 percent—expressed concern about the fairness of the pay they were receiving for working with VDTs in their jobs and about the discriminatory treatment they felt they were getting in promotional and career path opportunities compared with men at their organizations. These attitudes were stronger among women clericals we interviewed who were under 30 years of age: they were more inclined to expect management to provide such opportunities and were more ready to make an issue of this at their workplaces than older women. However, "women's consciousness" was also present among some older women, especially those who had been employed a long time at their organizations and knew firsthand how men had been systematically preferred over women in key job opportunities.

Role of Popular Opinion and Activism Feelings about "fair treatment" of women in the high-technology office were being stimulated among women we interviewed by the growing critical discussion of these issues by women's activist and mainstream women's groups, the mass media, unions, and major religious bodies. Though worried about the availability of jobs and about voicing complaints in a time of job insecurity, especially at nonunion sites where there is no protection against arbitrary dismissal, a strong minority (about a fourth) of women clericals we interviewed were convinced that only if they spoke up at the workplace would women's concerns about pay equity and fair promotional treatment be addressed by management.

Variations at the Job-Type Level The executives and managers we interviewed described attracting and keeping good employees for *customer service* and *secretarial work,* using VDTs as a major organizational need. In contrast, many managers believed that *data-entry work* would be greatly reduced in the next few years by a combination of optical scanning and direct customer input, or else would be exported to cheap labor service bureaus abroad. Therefore, ensuring job satisfaction for data-entry work seemed to be less important to these managements than for customer service and secretarial work. Although we visited some sites (about 10 percent) in which having a high-turnover, low-paid, and accepting work force for customer service and secretarial activities was the staffing approach taken by top management, this was not the policy we found being consciously pursued by 90 percent of these organizations. At most corporate and nonprofit organizations we visited, considerable attention was being paid to how to balance management interests in cost control and head-count reduction with organizational needs for a highly motivated and effective customer service and secretarial work force.

Managerial Responses to Women's Issues In about three-quarters of the organizations we visited, managements had not, by early 1984, developed direct and responsive strategies for dealing with the women's concerns and interests we cited. In some of these organizations, staff groups had recommended new policies to improve job quality for women clericals, reduce discriminatory effects, or take positive actions to enhance women's opportunities, but these staff groups had not yet been able to persuade top management to implement the policies. In only a fourth of the organizations had top management set clear affirmative action goals for VDT clerical work and had line managers actually begun putting such policies into effect.

Phases in Office Automation Implementation In the first era of OA implementation in the United States, which we would date from 1978 to 1983, vendors stressed productivity and reduction of labor costs and offered few ergonomically designed terminals and workstations. This was partly because they saw no user willingness to pay for such features. At the same time, purchasers of VDTs that we studied saw themselves as struggling to make OA applications work and to achieve the promised productivity benefits; little serious attention was given by most of these managements to ergonomics, employee communication on health and safety issues, or employee involvement. The overall social climate supported such a focus. Despite the presence of occasional stories raising issues of possible adverse health or other harmful effects of "office automation" on employee interests, overall media treatment in the first era was highly positive.

However, 1983–1985 was the transition into a second era of office system utilization in the United States. This was marked by trends such as vendors responding to criticism and greater user consciousness by providing ergonomically sound products and major user-education campaigns; increased internal attention at most sites we visited in 1984 to sound VDT policies and practices; major media attention to VDT concerns; a very active regulatory and legislative debate over VDT interventions throughout the country, in at least 25 states; growing interest by academics and public interest groups in office automation trends and impacts; and a growing concentration on special issues facing women clerical workers doing intensive VDT jobs. Follow-up calls we made in 1985–1986 to sites visited early in the project showed increased attention being paid by these managements to issues of ergonomics, training, employee communication, and other aspects of using VDTs, compared with 1982–1984.

GOOD MANAGEMENT POLICIES AFFECTING CLERICAL WORKERS: *THE GRAPHIC*— A REPRESENTATIVE EXAMPLE

Among the 110 organizations we visited, there were sites at which objective work conditions for VDT use and management policies toward women's equality issues were both quite positive. To illustrate, we selected a medium-sized organization, with several thousand employees, largely because some analysts assume that good VDT policies in the interest of the users are only developed by very large employers, with large staffs and substantial budgets for innovative policy experimentation. While measures of "good user" need to be defined and applied by researchers, I adopt at this point the subjective perceptions of women clericals as the primary basis for terming management policies as "good" for "women's interests."

The Graphic is a nonunion newspaper located in a suburban area. It is technologically advanced, profitable, and highly regarded for both journalistic and business excellence. Adoption of office systems technology has not led to reduced employment in this firm over the past decade, but rather major expansion of business services (such as selling advertising inserts) that have been accomplished through greater productivity and effectiveness by the same-sized work force. *The Graphic* is well regarded locally for its employment of women and minorities, and its turnover rate is very low, compared to other newspapers regionally.

We interviewed about 50 managers, editors, reporters, and administrative and clerical employees at *The Graphic*. Twenty-one of these were women clericals doing VDT-based customer-service work in the classified advertising and circulation departments, selected by us at random from the operators on duty the days we visited the site. The six customer-service operators whose office automation experiences we will describe are representative of female clericals working at *The Graphic* who use a combined VDT and telecommunication system in a 60-person customer-service department. A new VDT system had been selected and was soon to be installed. It has an automated call system that distributes waiting calls to the next available operator, and also allows more detailed customer information to be displayed on the screen and updated by the operator. This department is presently housed in temporary quarters while a new, ergonomically advanced work site is finished. The employees have been in this makeshift area, with standard office desks and chairs, for about 6 months.

The VDT system they operate allows the operator to call up a customer's account history on the screen, consult it while taking orders or handling complaints from a customer on the telephone, and then complete the transaction by keying in an action and updating the customer's file. Work gets extremely heavy at certain peak points in the week, and there are often delays and down periods in the present system that have caused this department to fall behind deadlines.

The women working in this department are mostly in their twenties, though there are some older women and a few men also in the group. About a quarter of the operators are black or Hispanic. The positive experiences of six women clericals follow:

- Norma, a black woman in her twenties, has worked for 4 years in this organization. Before that, she worked in a local graphics shop. She works 6.5 hours a day, 6 days a week on the VDT, and says, "I like it a lot. I like machines, period. It's fun. I'd like to program more, which I did at the other job I had in graphics, while here I just put in codes. It would be more interesting if I could do more programming and this is something that I want to get into. Now we just type a few words in and the computer takes over and does all the rest." Norma attends school at night to study computer programming, an educational program that the employer pays for. She hopes to still be working here in the next few years, but in a job that involves computer programming: "I'd like to be able to do something with programming here, since it is a great place to work." Norma feels her opportunities here as a woman and as a black are very satisfactory, "much better than lots of my friends are finding."

- Alice, a white woman in her mid-twenties, has worked at the VDT since she joined *The Graphic* 3 years ago. At her previous job with a manufacturing company, she also worked on a

VDT, entering orders. Alice comments "I like working on the VDT very much. I like to see what I do come up on a screen right away. The only real problem we have is when the system goes down. Everything comes to a stop. Work backs up." She said management understands the problem and doesn't lean on employees unfairly, and that is what makes the situation acceptable. Although she feels that the "pay could be better" at *The Graphic*, Alice says that the benefits are quite good, which makes a considerable difference. However, Alice also feels that customer-service representatives must cope with a lot of stress in dealing with customers who are sometimes angry and upset. In her last job, she didn't have contact with customers, she just input orders. She feels that dealing with customers and defusing people's anger are skills that ought to draw better pay. If she stays at this job, she will try to raise this issue seriously with management. Her goal is to become a district manager. To do that she must take courses in sales, and she plans to register for them next year. Since she is a parent with a very small child, she must work her education and career plans into her family responsibilities, and sees her advancement as a gradual process. Because she is "very happy" at her job, she says that she doesn't mind this. Alice reported no headaches or backaches and no problems with glare. She said some experts came in to check radiation levels some time ago, and thinks that such radiation checks have been conducted twice in the time she has been with the company. She has heard things about alleged dangers from VDTs on the news but she's not upset ("Oh, there's always something that's being discussed in the newspapers."). But if it was a real problem, she feels her management would know about it and would do the right thing, so she isn't worried.

- Rosa is a Hispanic woman in her mid-thirties who has been at *The Graphic* for 5 years, and went right into VDT work in this department. Previously, she worked for 3 years at a local Social Security office, where she was trained on the VDT and where she handled the issuance of checks for disability insurance. Of her present job, Rosa says "I love computers. But we could do more with the system. I'd like to see it upgraded so we can get more information out of it. . . . I'm looking forward to the challenge and the interest that the new system (which *The Graphic* has on order) will bring. I pick up easily on technological things and so I have no trouble learning and adjusting to a new system." Rosa spends 6 to

7 hours a day on the terminal. She says that she hasn't had one day when she was bored in her work at *The Graphic*. "The work is very diverse here," she notes. "It challenges you and I love talking to people and dealing with the public. I guess I could adjust to doing just one function on the VDT all day, because I adapt easily, but I like the variety of work that we have here." Rosa also feels that *The Graphic* has excellent working conditions and supervision, and enjoys her co-workers. She isn't looking to change her job or to upgrade herself because she feels she's happy with what she's doing. "If you're happy at the job, and the pay isn't bad and the benefits are good, why would you want to change?" Rosa stresses that everybody is coping with the temporarily bad VDT working conditions now without too much complaint, because they know they'll be moving into excellent quarters soon. "We make fun and games out of it; we laugh a lot and talk about how bad things are but nobody really minds it." She's had no backaches, neckaches, or headaches, and has no problem with glare. She has 20-20 vision without glasses and has had no change in her eyes over the 5 years that she's worked on the VDT. "You can always adjust your screen with the contrast; I don't have to do it but if I had any problems I could certainly take advantage of that."

• Pat, a young white woman, has been working at *The Graphic* for a few months, and came directly from high school. She said "They threw me on the machine with a list of codes. You learn pretty quickly in the first 2 days. Another employee sits with you, shows you how to operate the terminal, and answers your questions. It worked fine because we're a small group and we all help one another." Pat says that she does have tiring of the eyes and she's bothered by the fact that her head has to go up and down constantly. "It's very annoying to look at the paper and then look up at the screen," she says, and she hasn't mastered that yet. However, she hasn't talked to other people about it and has not yet found a way to prop up pages on the machine because there's not enough room on the desk. She knows that "the new quarters that we will go into soon will provide better space on the desk to help solve that problem." She mentioned that she has no back, neck, or headache problems. However, she indicated that each terminal is slightly different, and when you move from one terminal to another, you should really do some adjustment. When people don't do that adjustment, she said, they begin to feel a little extra tired from working on a different machine. Pat works

7 hours a day on the terminal. Since she's young and new, she expects to stay at that for some time. She likes the job and likes the people and is very happy with the position that she has. Someday, she says she would like to be a supervisor in this department or become a district manager, though she knows she would have to go back to school for that. Since she just got out of school and was "sick of it," she expects it to be "a while" before she will take courses to enable herself to apply for a district manager's job.

- Florence has been at *The Graphic* for 4 years. She is a black woman who came to the company straight out of high school, and started working on the VDT. She feels that training was very easy: "[The machine] is just like a typewriter and a big TV set." "I'm not crazy over computers," she comments, "but they do make the job more professional." She also says that she likes the status that working on the computer gives her. When she tells her friends she works on a terminal and is hooked into a computer, they regard her as having an interesting job, especially those that are working in low-status service jobs. Florence has no comfort problems and no eye strain. The only problem is that if she works a straight 2- to 3-hour shift, she sometimes gets finger cramps from keyboarding. Florence sees *The Graphic* as being somewhat low in pay but offering good benefits. She mentioned that there is an annual performance review in which management tells you your strong and weak points, your absence level, your relations with other employees and so forth. The managers will tell you about your errors and whether your error rate is okay, but doesn't compare your volumes and rate of work with those of other employees: "I would hate to have something like that on a job; that would bring too much pressure." The thing Florence hates most is when the computer system goes down. However, she feels that management is very understanding when the system is down, and the situation is improving greatly. She likes her job and she likes keeping busy all the time—"I would be bored out of my skull if there wasn't enough work to do."

- Jennifer is a supervisor in this department, and has held that post for the past 4 years. A white woman in her thirties, she joined *The Graphic* 7 years ago, and was trained in-house on the VDT as a customer service clerk. "I really like the VDT, and now I like helping to set up the new terminal system we're putting in." She is thinking about getting further systems education and possibly getting a professional post in *The Graphic's* EDP department. She participated on a task force that developed the new VDT system that *The Graphic* is installing, and liked that participation very much. Jennifer finds supervising VDT work highly challenging. She thinks the pay could be better for operators after the first year, and hopes to get an "upgrade" authorized when the new terminal system comes in. She notes that she "tried installing formal rest breaks a while ago, to relieve back and headache problems, but the employees don't like that. When we get peak work periods they don't take the set breaks, so I told people to get up anytime. If they want a full 15-minute break, they just tell me and I arrange to have their work covered." Jennifer feels worried about radiation and possible effects on pregnant women, and thinks the management should tell the employees more about this "since we're hearing about it all the time. They should give us material to read up on, and answer our questions." She also wants to start an exercise program, and to have more discussion about physical problems and guidance for dealing with them in the training program. She sees herself as a "young professional" in the new field of VDT work, and finds the whole area of technology "exciting to work in."

ELEMENTS OF GOOD USER PRACTICE

Good user practices in office system implementation do not come from printed assembly instructions in boxes housing VDTs, nor do they arise through some kind of accidental serendipity. They will not occur in exploitive or repressive work environments, in the "sweatshop" mold. Good user practices take place *only* when there is an existing structure of management policy and practice committed to organizational excellence and a progressive human resource philosophy, plus a recognition that a particular new activity or problem (in this case, implementing new office system technology) requires mobilization of management attention and organizational resources.

In the real world of competitive business pressures or pressures to reduce budgets in government, this requires recognition by top management of positive "bottom line" incentives to address VDT issues (increased productivity, reduced turnover) or some serious concerns about organizational "exposures" if this is not done (regulatory controls, legal liability, bad labor–management relations, unionization of nonunion work forces, etc.). Sometimes, an organization may be in the midst of a changeover in human resources policies from a traditionalist/authority-centered philosophy to a more participative quality-of-work-life approach. If this is happening—usually because of a change in top management—applying the new human resources philosophy to office automation can be part of the transition process in such an organization.

A CHECKLIST OF GOOD USER POLICIES

At our site visits, we identified 10 basic ongoing policies that companies with good human resource philosophies were adopting to deal effectively with VDT implementation. Such organizations

1. Build employee satisfaction and organizational change requirements into the organization's overall office technology plan and obtain top management commitment to such requirements.

2. Create a task force, coordinating committee, or multifunction group to guide people–technology aspects of office automation.

3. Develop a program of employee involvement in office automation that fits the organizational culture, or use joint union-management committees in union-represented companies, experimenting with different modes of involvement for different work settings.

4. Inventory ergonomic conditions in VDT uses, starting with the most intensive applications and creating a graduated program of ergonomic upgrades to acceptable standards in all facilities.

5. Examine techniques of performance evaluation for VDT work and install "fair work measurement" systems that avoid "Big Brother" monitoring.

6. Monitor health and comfort responses of VDT employees, take measures to reduce problem areas, and have staff keep abreast of external research findings.

7. Conduct employee-centered rather than machine-centered training programs on using VDTs or installing new applications, and hold similar broad-based supervisor/manager training programs on implementing new office systems.

8. Develop continuous employee communication programs covering both positive achievements and uses of the technology and ways to cope with expected problems.

9. Address women's equality and special workplace needs, especially among clerical and professional employees heavily involved with VDTs.

10. Monitor interest group, media, regulatory, and academic developments relating to VDTs, to understand social concerns and proposals being voiced, and to bring the organization into anticipatory compliance with sound standards emerging from such dialog.

Figure 1 identifies the organizational policies that user managements need to consider in their VDT implementation, and the basic employer, employee, and special women's interests that need to be taken into account in such policy making.

JOB SATISFACTION AMONG WOMEN CLERICALS AT *THE GRAPHIC*

Referring back to the vignettes of our representative customer-service operators at *The Graphic*, we can easily identify the sources of the generally high job satisfaction these women conveyed. Management at *The Graphic* had instituted the following:

- Excellent educational benefits for employees to pursue advanced study and good in-house training in advanced VDT applications. This provided women with opportunities for the skills acquisition needed for career advancement, at the employer's expense.

- Clear promotional ladders and structure within the organization, well known to these women and discussed in performance planning sessions. Based on what they could see other women clericals having achieved at *The Graphic*, these women could, if their ambitions, needs, and life situations stimulated them, work toward supervisory posts in their own department, professional jobs in data processing (programming, data analyst), and middle management (district managers).

- Performance evaluation of their VDT work that was considered absolutely fair. Management knew that the systems went down periodically and output was affected. It knew that peak-period commitments needed to be balanced by rest time and at-will breaks. Supervisors did not use machine monitoring to compare one employee's call rates with another's in order to set quotas.

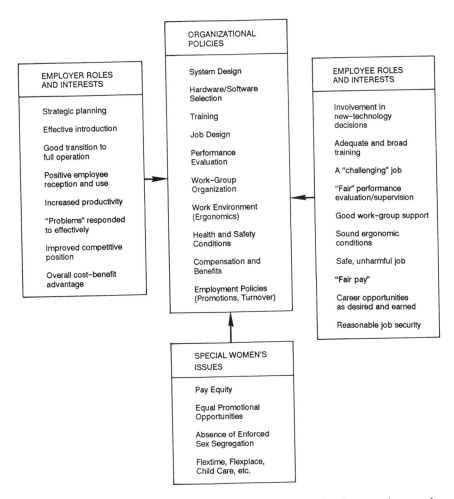

FIGURE 1 Organizational policies for good VDT implementation, and interests to be considered in developing such policies.

• Ergonomics in most of *The Graphic*'s facilities that were very good. At the location where these women worked, conditions were very poor, because temporary space was being used while top-of-the-line ergonomics were being prepared for this unit in new space. Because these women knew that excellent facilities were being prepared for them, and supervisors did not "lean on them" when performance suffered because of poor ergonomic conditions, these employees retained a highly positive attitude toward their employer and their treatment as employees. Employees felt as involved in VDT implementation policies as each wanted to be. They had been given opportunities to test vendor equipment being considered and to give their reactions, and several employees from this unit had volunteered for planning task forces.

• While there had been some educational sessions for employees on health and safety issues in using VDTs, and some literature had been provided, several employees and the supervisor felt more should be forthcoming from management. After our site visit, additional employee communications on these issues were provided by management.

The one significant problem at *The Graphic*, as we reported, was pay. Since customer-service work was primarily being done by women (about 90 percent), this seemed to be heading in the minds of the women we interviewed toward a "pay equity" concern. Because *The Graphic* offered what these women saw as excellent benefits, including education support, the pay question might not become acute. Or it might develop into a real grievance, in which case, based on its overall human resource philosophy, *The Graphic*'s management might be expected to recognize the concern and act on it before it became a deep grievance.

Most important, in terms of identifying model-user practices, what characterized employee–employer relations at *The Graphic* was a condition of basic trust by employees in the good intentions and professional competence of management in the design and implementation of office systems in clerical work. And, business growth and the absence of fears about imminent layoffs provided a solid "floor" to support such employee trust. Taking all these factors together, clerical workers at *The Graphic* were both eager and satisfied users of new office technology. Where there were problems in system design and applications (and there were some, stemming from personal problems in the data-processing management group), or when ergonomics were pursued on an upgrade rather than an all-at-once basis, the basic trust of the clerical work force provided a vital support resource for management.

EXPLOITIVE OR DISCRIMINATORY
TREATMENT OF WOMEN CLERICALS

The sites we visited, as already noted, were weighted in the direction of organizations with positive human resource philosophies and good labor–management relations. Nevertheless, we visited some sites and collected non-site-visit interviews with women clericals in which a pattern of exploitive and discriminatory treatment of women clericals was demonstrated. Here, too, the *advent of office system technology was almost never the source of the poor practices.* These managements had applied harsh personnel practices and engaged in sex discrimination before they had installed VDTs. Now, they were extending their basic approaches into new-technology work settings. The following vignettes, drawn from our interviews and from the Asher (1983) transcripts, illustrate some of the main kinds of practices women clericals are encountering:

- Sheila is a young woman just out of high school who had received basic training in word processing as a course in school. She obtained a job with a small mail-order jewelry firm in a metropolitan area that sells low-cost diamond rings. Five operators verify customer orders, trace invoices, enter refund amounts, and perform similar operations at their VDT keyboards, accessing a customer data base. Their work is monitored by computer printouts and also by surveillance cameras used by this firm, both for security purposes and to watch employee performance. Sheila recalled that "they used the cameras to watch how hard you seemed to be working, when you got up to stretch or take a break, and your 'attitude' at work. It was really a totally monitored place." This woman was not granted the standard raise after 6 months of "probationary" work at minimum wage—even though this was recommended by her supervisor—because the management said "she didn't look like she was working that hard" when they observed her on the camera. She had no access to her own production figures or to those of other employees with which to challenge that judgment, nor were there stated production standards she could rely on even if she had any complaint procedure. She quit in anger and disgust, as did many of the women working in this small shop after their first 6 months. The management saw such a heavy turnover as quite all right, since they had a steady supply of trained VDT operators willing to take "probationary" pay, and the firm did not need operators knowledgeable about the business to do the data-entry work involved. Sheila decided to leave VDT work and is now employed in the food service business.

• Marian worked for 10 years as a customer-service representative for a city government transportation agency in the Northeast. She used the telephone and manual files to handle calls reporting problems on the bus system, in an all-female department. When the agency put in a terminal system, a set of daily production quotas was set by the new male operations manager who took over direction of her unit. Training was weak, and most of the women in the unit had trouble meeting the quotas. Many of the women developed headaches, stomach pains, and muscle pains. Marian developed serious chest pains, and was told by her doctor that it would be "dangerous" for a 55-year-old woman to continue working at a job that was creating such symptoms. When Marian discussed the chest pains with the operations manager, and her feeling that this was caused by the high quotas, he said that "the women will have to keep up or get out." When she tried to appeal his position to higher management, she was told that decisions concerning work quotas were up to unit managers, and maybe "it was time for her to retire." Marian left the agency and now works for a retail store. She feels that she is "a victim of the computer age," but especially because she and her colleagues were women. "I don't think they would get away with that if it was a new garbage truck that was developed, or if the terminal was brought into the accounting department, which is mostly men."

• Claire, 57 years old, is chief clerk in the cash loan surrender department of a large insurance operation run by a national religious organization. After graduating from high school, she entered the Army Air Corps for 2 years (serving in a motor pool in World War II), worked in manufacturing, and later in an office job. She joined the religious organization as a clerk in 1960 and has been there for 20 years. She uses a VDT occasionally for calculating loans and cash-surrender payments, but does not work intensively on the terminal the way other clerks do. Claire is also the president of the local union of the Office and Professional Workers that represents about 300 employees at this company, a post she has held since the early days of the local union, in 1962. Claire sees blatant sex discrimination as the long-time, regular policy of the organization. Men have all the executive and department manager posts; women stay in the clerical ranks. The best EDP job sectors—systems positions—are held by males. Women work alongside men and "are being paid less." When new jobs open up that have higher salaries and status, they are supposed to be open to bidding by all, but a man always gets them. The union has filed sex discrimination complaints with the state commission on human rights, but has lost its cases. Also, this company has been shifting the higher levels of VDT work into jobs that it now classifies as "supervisory work," which takes them out of the union bargaining unit. These jobs also are overwhelmingly filled by males. The union has filed charges contesting this with the National Labor Relations Board (NLRB) and has raised the issue in contract bargaining talks, but has lost there as well. Claire sees this religious body as really conducting a commercial operation—a very big one—but running it under the cover of the religious order, and getting away with discriminatory practices "that it ought to be ashamed of." Claire feels that it runs as a "men's club," and that legal and union actions will be the only way to force change. Some women have been admitted to underwriting and professional jobs, but these have not been promotions for talented clerical women.

It would be easy to multiply these vignettes many times over. What they have in common is that exploitive or discriminatory practices that were followed in pre-VDT work settings are now being applied in the context of VDT-based clerical work.

THE CENTRAL ROLE OF MANAGEMENT PHILOSOPHY: "GREAT NORTHERN" AND "NATIONAL SERVICES"

Policy choices of user managements are key to whether women clericals—or any other VDT users—experience good or bad work and are fairly or unfairly treated at the workplace. To illustrate this concretely, we present anonymous profiles of two large corporations we visited. We will call these "Great Northern" and "National Services" and make only those alterations of fact necessary to prevent recognition of their identities (the profiles are adapted from Westin et al., 1985). Both of these are well-known national firms with successful products and services and currently profitable operations. Neither firm has had any significant sex or race discrimination findings against them by EEO agencies or courts over the past decade. Each is also well regarded in management circles and in general public reputation for its past employee-relations policies.

Between 1982 and 1984, managements enjoyed almost total autonomy in applying office system technology, because there was no state or federal legislation in place and virtually no EEO agency attention to special issues of office technology impact. Less than 10 percent of clerical workers were represented by unions, and even in union-represented workplaces, neither collective bargaining contracts nor grievance systems exercised significant influences over management use of VDTs.

In the Great Northern example we found evidence of sex stereotyping. Sex roles at Great Northern follow strict lines. About 95 percent of the nonexempt workers using VDTs to do customer-service work are women, primarily white. Supervisors of these women are mostly female. At the sales level, the jobs are 95 percent male. At the local-offices level, at which this company's work is primarily done, managers are virtually all male, except for the post of "Personnel Specialist," which has been made into a female-typed position and is mostly occupied by women.

When we interviewed women VDT operators, the absence of career paths into sales and management was often brought up. At Great Northern, about a third of the VDT operators have community college or even 4-year college degrees, and many of them would like to move up into sales and management ranks. There is no path for them to do that now, and their morale is low.

In addition, when we met with women supervisors at Great Northern offices in five states, there was much banter about the "token woman" personnel specialist at their locations, and about the absence of promotional opportunities for these women supervisors into sales or middle-management ranks. "We were the ones that put the new computer system in, worked out its bugs, trained the operators on the CRTs, and made the transition into the automated system succeed. But none of us are considered good enough to go into management. That's the 'boy's preserve.' "

Women supervisors were bitter in their comments on Great Northern's male management. They feel that headquarters people "tap dance around questions" raised by women and that "staff doesn't have much credibility." Nothing is done about the complaint that women are not being allowed into field jobs that are a prerequisite for moving into management posts, nor are women well represented in Great Northern's Management Development Program.

As a result of these policies, women we interviewed see communications between employees and management as poor, and management's basic posture as highly defensive, mostly concerned with averting unionization. There is an "open door" type complaint program at the company, but, as one woman put it, "The doors may be open, but their ears are closed." In some local offices, women told us that the atmosphere was annoying—"women are called 'honey' and 'sweetie' or 'girls,' and the men are very condescending."

Some members of the personnel staff at Great Northern's national headquarters are aware of this situation. In fact, concern over sex stereotyping and lack of affirmative action promotional opportunities for women clericals and supervisors surfaced in one recent employee survey in which two-thirds of women said they weren't satisfied with their chances for advancement. However, when this firm underwent a recent reorganization and a reduction in staff, its sales and management ranks became loaded with men who had seniority, and top management doesn't want to "rock the boat." The alternatives it is considering include having more part-time employees (and getting some men for that work), and accepting a much higher turnover rate among its now dissatisfied female customer-service work force than this company would have accepted in earlier times.

Very few of the upwardly striving women clericals or supervisors that we talked to felt anything would change soon at Great Northern. They like the company, they like the new VDT work, but they feel like second-class citizens in terms of fair treatment as women.

In contrast to Great Northern, when National Services decided to create a large customer-service center for ordering parts and supplies for its manufactured products in an all-VDT system, it set out to improve the work environment. Traditionally, those jobs had been women's work, done by telephone, and there was no shortage of female job-seekers in the exurban community in which the call center would be located.

In setting grade levels for this work, however, and in its advertising, recruiting, and interviewing processes, the location manager and personnel staff of National Services decided that it wanted a mixed work force—men and women, black and white, and older as well as younger workers. Its experience told it that morale is higher and employee satisfaction greater in such a diverse working group, and this firm has an anticipative approach to equal employment opportunity (EEO) and affirmative action considerations. The location–staffing objective was aided by two other factors: the weak job market when they opened this facility and the strong national reputation of this firm as a good employer. These factors provided them with a large applicant pool of men as well as women, and people of varied backgrounds. In addition, the company was able to offer transfers to this location for a varied group of its own employees who were being affected by a major reorganization this firm had also undergone. The result was about as evenly balanced a customer-service work force at the VDTs as any political party convention manager or EEO visionary could imagine, by sex, race, and age.

Since the pay levels at National Services are above average for customer-service work in the area, since there is a generous benefits policy, and since the firm has a history of providing strong job security, it was not surprising that individual VDT operators we interviewed considered working at this site an "outstanding job." They particularly liked the mixture of people they worked with. "I used to operate a VDT at an all-women's job," one young woman in her twenties commented, "and it was a sorority house all day. Here, there are men of various ages, and things are just more interesting."

Of 10 women we specifically asked about their career plans at this company, 6 were working to go into supervision or programming and felt they had good prospects of succeeding in these ambitions. One was entering a sales training course offered by the company. The other three said they expected to keep on working at their customer-service jobs for the near future. This firm has an annual career-planning exercise at which each employee and manager discuss the employee's skills, performance, and aspirations and develop a blueprint for advancement for those employees seeking it.

Two Companies, Two Pathways

These two companies illustrate two different pathways to office technology implementation. At Great Northern, because of its reorganization and consolidation, VDT customer-service work will probably remain almost all female, unsatisfying for the career concerns of many of these women employees, and likely to make Great Northern's employees less accepting of management progress on other VDT issues (ergonomics, work quotas, stress effects, etc.). The attitude of top management and especially its information system experts has been highly deterministic; they feel that using the technology "requires" that certain work force patterns be adopted to achieve maximum efficiency. They assume that "people problems" created by a need to rush in their new VDT system will disappear as employees "get used to the work." As of 1984, the concerns of some personnel staff at Great Northern had not led to any basic change in top management's blueprint or its attention to women's issues.

At National Services, top management, its technical specialists, and its personnel staffs have a philosophy that office systems technology should be used in ways that further the firm's basic employee relations and "people policy," rather than undercut these. Management set out to create a certain kind of VDT work force at its new center, and they achieved it. They report that productivity, the employee climate, and overall facility effectiveness have been excellent; and our interviews confirmed high employee satisfaction, especially among women. National Services follows the same policies as to equality and opportunity for all its employees: clericals, professionals, and managers. It has uniform policies in all its installations, in central cities as well as suburbs and rural areas, and it has facilities in all types of communities. Its approach is also carried through in bad as well as good economic times, rather than being an approach that is tailored to exploit economic pressures.

RESEARCH IMPLICATIONS

The larger study on which this paper is based draws on data generated in an exploratory field study. We identified issues relating to office technology and women clerical workers which should be fully explored and studied through structured and representative social research. However, there are many conceptual and methodological difficulties associated with trying to measure "technology impact," especially on the interests of women workers.

First, the treatment of women at the workplace and their opportunities to achieve good jobs, equal pay, and fair participation with men is shaped by very large social forces and not just office technology applications. These forces include the following: overall economic conditions, national and local labor markets, changing requirements for particular occupations or skills, and industry employment and staffing trends. They also reflect patterns of sex discrimination in American society and institutions that have been built up over long periods of time and that are not easily dismantled. Although some of these discriminatory attitudes and practices at the workplace are in the process of being changed in our time by new social values, women's rights pressures, and EEO law enforcement, they remain significant factors affecting most working women, especially in long-time sex-segregated areas such as clerical and secretarial jobs.

Second, quality of work life and equality issues for women clericals are powerfully affected by the general levels of employment available in our society. This will be shaped significantly by the overall strength of the U.S. economy and competitiveness of American companies in a global economy marked by high-tech tools and low-wage work forces; by the levels of government employment available in the next decade (and the fiscal strengths of the economy that undergirds this); by social policies in education and retraining of workers, job sharing, and work week length; and by the distribution of the rewards of achievement among various claimants in the social system.

Finally, in terms of social impact, the introduction of new office technology can have one of several alternative effects on the equality and quality of work-life interests of women clerical workers:

- OA could produce important positive changes in the objective condition of women clerical workers, along dimensions such as pay, job quality, working conditions, career opportunities, etc.
- OA could have no appreciable effects one way or the other on the equality and equity interests of women, proving to be a weak

or even negligible factor when measured against larger economic, social, or legal forces unfolding in contemporary offices.

- OA could reinforce existing negative aspects of the status quo, perpetuating patterns of differential treatment of women clerical workers in aspects such as pay, promotion, and participation. OA would therefore operate to retard or weaken social efforts to close the equality gaps between women and men office workers.

- Finally, OA could actively increase discriminatory treatment of women clerical workers, by enlarging the differential treatment of women in office work under what were perceived by managements as imperatives for effective technological utilization and economic efficiency.

Researchers therefore need to frame studies that set baselines of pre-OA conditions; measure changes in objective conditions and perceived worker satisfaction in OA settings and compared to non-OA work; factor in the presence of changing economic conditions, social values, and legal standards; and produce as solid an empirical description as can be assembled for all scenarios.

THE FUTURE OF GOOD USER POLICIES

Events are moving rapidly in the evolution of user policies toward the "people" and "quality of work life aspects" of installing and expanding office system technology. Both the positive and negative incentives we noted earlier are increasing the motivation of managements to address these VDT issues. In addition, models for management have been suggested by negotiated provisions on VDT work in collective bargaining contracts, such as those at Boston University, Equitable Life Assurance, and others. Following the pattern in other areas of technology–society relations, such as privacy and databank issues in the 1964–1980 period, a set of value judgments, organizational policy frameworks, operating standards, and implementation procedures have begun to emerge as "organizational software" for dealing with VDT applications; and the successful experiences of pioneering organizations are beginning to be made available for adoption by mainstream managements. There has been a surge of "how to do it" educational materials and seminars for user managements, developed by industry and government user associations, vendor organizations, university and consulting groups, and many others.

If we were to rank the breadth of adoption of good user policies involving VDTs among the 110 organizations we studied, our estimate as of mid-1986 would run something like this:

- The most widely developing management responses are directed at ergonomics—better terminals, more user-friendly software, adjustable workstations, and proper work environments. This is the "nuts and bolts" aspect of better VDT policies, and while it involves significant costs, it is essentially noncontroversial. Ergonomics can be "sold" within organizations on a combination of productivity gain, health claim avoidance, and decent treatment of employees arguments.

- Better employee communication on health and safety issues is next in rank. Because the great weight of scientific evidence supports the position that VDTs cannot be shown to cause disease, managements are increasingly communicating with employees on this issue, preparing briefing booklets and stories in employee newspapers that report scientific findings and explain their conclusions. The "don't make waves" concept of not talking to employees about VDT health issues has given way in most organizations we visited to direct communications, including practical guides for exercises to relieve musculo-skeletal tensions, resting the eyes from intensive VDT work, dealing with job stress, and so on. Reducing potential worker compensation claims, absences, and high turnover provide important employer incentives here.

- Next in order of emerging policies would be matters of job design and performance evaluation. Providing variety in tasks, allowing employees some discretion in work pacing, setting fair work standards, giving employees access to work records, and similar matters are being considered, as more powerful office system applications are applied to claims processing, customer-service work, and secretarial–administrative functions. The key here is usually whether the personnel or human resources function is brought into the application planning, as opposed to having this done exclusively by a DP or OA function. Increasingly, personnel departments were being brought into VDT planning in the organizations we visited.

- Employee involvement seems to be the next most widespread policy we saw being adopted. Clerical work has not been as frequent an occupational sector for "quality circle" or other employee participation programs as factory work has been in the past 6 to 8 years. This was changing at the sites we visited. In 1984–1986, use of employee involvement mechanisms for clerical groups was clearly growing and almost half of the organizations we visited were making some use of formal employee involvement programs in office automation.

• As far as unique women's issues in clerical VDT operations are concerned—such as pay equity, internal career opportunities, and sex-segregated work grouping—innovative management policies in this area were not developing as fast in 1984–1986 as the other aspects of VDT-based work. Only 25 percent of the sites we visited were addressing women's issues directly. This is probably due to a combination of factors: the deeply institutionalized nature of organizational policies in these areas; the absence of clear or relatively cheap "fixes" for these problems; the absence of regulatory pressures on these issues from the Reagan administration, federal or state EEO agencies, or the courts; and labor-market conditions that currently provide employers with ample supplies of willing women clerical workers.

As of 1986, then, new policies addressing the quality of work life aspects of VDT use were developing widely among the organizations we studied, following the most common to least common patterns we have just estimated. Our observation of user publications and educational efforts suggests that this trend is also taking place among most substantial users of VDTs, especially in the clerical sectors which have generated the greatest publicity and controversy. These data are reported in Westin (1987).

However, it is not clearly established whether these employer initiatives are coming primarily from users' own learning as to sound employee-relations policies for using office systems technology effectively, or whether employers are acting primarily to head off threats of regulatory action and to defuse attacks by unions and activist groups. Our own judgment is that the office automation controversy has not caused the development of good policies among leading-edge organizations, such as the company we called "National Services." However, the controversy has accelerated the process of mainstream-user consideration of quality of work life aspects of office automation and has also strengthened the position inside mainstream organizations of those staff and management groups that believe such policies should be pursued.

Since policy initiatives are under way in the user community, regulatory action may not be necessary. However, at this time, attitudes toward the need for regulation depend more on the analyst's philosophy about the scope and timing of social regulation than on any objective or empirical measures of VDT usage conditions. The key questions in deciding about regulatory proposals will be (1) whether the need for regulation can be preempted by widespread usage of effective, substantive measures in the user community and (2) whether regulatory advocates can produce evidence of harm to employee health or well-being that convinces policy makers that the substantial costs employers would have to bear would be worthwhile.

We have shown that there are good policies present among some user organizations we studied, addressing both the quality of work life and women's equality issues of concern to millions of women clericals in business, government, and nonprofit organizations. These policies work well, are not prohibitively expensive, contribute to strong employee job satisfaction and women's equality interests, and support the productivity goals of organizations in a time of challenge and competition. How widely and well these approaches will be adopted in the next few years is therefore an issue of enormous importance, not only to women clericals but to all employees and employers in the United States and to American society as a whole.

REFERENCES

Asher, R.
1983   Unpublished transcripts of interviews for the Project on Connecticut Workers and Technological Change. Storrs: University of Connecticut.

Westin, A.F.
1987   *VDT Update Report: User Policies and Practices in Applying Office System Technology.* New York: The Educational Fund for Individual Rights.

Westin, A.F., H. Schweder, M. Baker, and S. Lehman
1985   *The Changing Workplace: A Guide to Managing the People, Organizational, and Regulatory Aspects of Office Technology.* Westchester, N.Y.: Knowledge Industries.

New Office and Business Technologies: The Structure of Education and (Re)Training Opportunities

BRYNA SHORE FRASER

THE IMPORTANCE OF TRAINING FOR WOMEN

Will the introduction of new technologies into a wide range of business and commercial settings enhance the skill and job opportunities of those affected? Are existing education and training strategies adequate to help women workers take advantage of new opportunities, or will they only serve to maintain the existing opportunity structure? The introduction of new office and commercial technologies is of particular concern to working women, who, in 1983, accounted for 99 percent of all secretaries, 97 percent of typists, 92 percent of bookkeepers and bank tellers, 87 percent of cashiers, and 70 percent of retail clerks (Serrin, 1984:A3). This paper seeks to determine how these types of jobs are being affected by new computer technologies, how workers are being trained or retrained in their use, and, wherever possible, how women's experiences differ from those of men in the use of the new technologies and in their access to training.

Studies to date on the differing effects of technological change on men and women are not encouraging. Data from the first national study of technological change show that proportionately

343

more women than men operate machines, are more exposed to machines that have alienating effects, and suffer more from the negative effects of technological change. Relatively more men operate machines that require skill and encourage work autonomy. Moreover, the changes for men enhance their job skills and improve their opportunities for advancement. Not so for women (Form and McMillan, 1983). Gutek and Bikson (1984), in a study of 55 offices in 26 different private sector organizations, reported similar findings. Women used computers more than men and used them more routinely, while men's computer use was more flexible and autonomous. The authors concluded that "nothing in our data suggests that these 55 offices will use technological innovation as an occasion for improving the situation of working women" (p. 16).

A recent survey of 300 senior human resource executives in Fortune 1500 firms found that 44 percent of the companies are most likely to hire new employees with required skills rather than retrain workers whose skills have become obsolete. Two other frequently used options, cited by 40 percent of the companies, are (1) switching employees into new positions that require no additional skills and (2) reducing the number of employees. On a more hopeful note, the report states that a shrinking work force may make it more difficult for companies to rely on new workers and may make worker retraining a more attractive long-term solution (ITT Educational Services, 1984). Some companies do retrain their employees. IBM, for example, supports a policy of full employment, meaning that employees should not lose their jobs due to advancing technologies, among other circumstances. The company maintains no records on the amount of retraining given each year "because it is business as usual to move people from one job to a totally different job" (IBM Corporation, 1985:13).

The most sophisticated—as well as the simplest—equipment will not increase productivity unless those using it have the knowledge and motivation to make it work. Recent studies show that the prospect of working with new technology is welcomed by most people when it is first suggested. One recent survey of more than 500 secretaries and administrative assistants found that "office automation has been accepted with open arms" (Gallant, 1984:24). On a scale of emotional responses ranging from love to hate, 83 percent of the respondents said they loved the word-processing equipment, while none expressed any hatred of the equipment.

Eighty-seven percent said they felt that their word-processing skills would lead to new career opportunities, while 88 percent expressed the belief that these skills would result in salary increases.

But the same survey revealed some troubling disparities between respondents' beliefs and the reality of their situations. Only 30 percent had actually received pay raises as a result of acquiring word-processing skills, and while 75 percent said that the equipment freed them from typing chores and allowed them more time for work involving decision making, when asked what new responsibilities the electronic equipment had allowed them to undertake, almost all cited traditional secretarial tasks such as drafting letters and researching reports.

The survey pointed to the importance of *age* as a factor. Forty-eight percent of the respondents under age 25 reported pay raises resulting from word-processing skills, compared with much lower figures among older secretaries. The younger secretaries said their knowledge of word processing was more important than such customary skills as shorthand, while the older secretaries placed more value on traditional abilities. In addition, almost a third of the respondents under age 25 had already had training in either COBOL or BASIC programming, compared with a very small percentage of the older respondents. In another survey of more than 1,200 secretaries and 900 managers in 443 information-intensive businesses, younger secretaries were also found to view automated equipment more favorably than their older counterparts. In this survey secretaries in particular cited training as the single most important change needed when introducing automation into the workplace. The most frequent suggestion made for improving productivity in businesses where automation already existed was more and better training (Keefe, 1984:23).

As new technology is introduced into more and more work environments, changes will be needed in work skills and patterns. Changed tasks, roles, and machine pacing must be learned. For example, a secretary who moves from a typewriter to a word processor has to learn to increase concentration on work (due to the machine's sensitivity); hand-eye coordination (due to the speed of the information flow); and ability to respond to signs rather than complete symbols (due to the shorthand language of the computer). All of this learning depends, in turn, on mental flexibility. Even under the best working conditions, it is difficult for workers to learn so many new skills well, and all at once. Adults often cite a variety of reasons, however, for not participating in (re)training and education programs that would help them learn new skills. These barriers can be categorized as follows (Charner, 1980; Charner and Fraser, 1984).

Situational factors arise out of an individual's position in a family, workplace, or social group at a given time. Within this category, costs, lack of time, age, and level of education head the list.

Social/psychological factors are related to an individual's attitudes and self-perceptions or to the influence of significant others (family, friends, etc.) on the actions of an individual. Included are lack of confidence in ability, feeling of being too old, lack of interest, and lack of support from family or friends. Only small proportions of adults report such factors as barriers to their participation in education or training activities. Women more frequently than men report that they feel they are too old to begin. Men, on the other hand, cite lack of confidence in ability more than women.

Structural factors are policies and practices of organizations that overtly or subtly exclude or discourage adults from participating in (re)training and education activities and include scheduling problems (course and work); location and transportation problems; lack of courses or relevancy of courses; procedural problems (red tape, credit, admission, required full-time attendance); and information/counseling problems. These factors fall between situational and social/psychological barriers in the proportion of adults reporting such factors as deterring their participation. Location, scheduling, and lack of courses are most often mentioned as barriers, with few differences among subgroups of adults.

Given the general barriers confronting adults participating in any (re)training/education program, how does a clerical worker, secretary, telephone operator, or any of the millions of workers in service and retail occupations go about getting trained in up-to-date technological skills for office and commercial settings?

The next three sections briefly describe a variety of programs currently provided by employers, educational institutions, and government agencies that can be used by women workers. A final section outlines education and training policies that, if adopted, would contribute to a smooth transition for women workers from the old work environment to the new. One of the most important policy areas discussed is the need for more information. Indeed, the following description of available programs suffers from a lack of published information. Not only do we not know how many programs are available to which workers, we also know little about their effectiveness. Careful review of the latest journals, newsletters, and publications dealing with the retail trades, office automation, computer technology, management, and training and development yielded little in the way of gender-specific examples of training in new office and business technology for this population. Furthermore, most companies are reluctant to provide detailed descriptions of company-specific training courses, and while almost all organizations with 500 employees or more have at least one full-time person responsible for training activities, many office and commercial enterprises employ less than 100 employees and have no one in-house with even part-time training responsibilities. Therefore, much of the program-specific information related below has been based on the limited published material available or on anecdotal information provided by researchers or program sponsors.

EMPLOYER-PROVIDED EDUCATION AND (RE)TRAINING PROGRAMS

Employer-provided training includes a wide variety of programs that are either provided or sponsored by an employer. Although private and public employers provide the lion's share of training in the United States, spending $30 billion annually according to the American Society for Training and Development (more than three times the amount spent by federal, state, and local governments combined), most of these programs are concentrated in only 200–300 of the largest companies. Furthermore, businesses are spending more and more money on remedial math and reading instruction rather than on focused skill training (Business–Higher Education Forum, 1984:30).

A substantial portion of corporate training is generally geared to respond to changes in a company's technology, organization, or products. In the case of technological innovation, for example, manufacturers of office computer equipment usually provide training for employees of companies buying their equipment. There are no statistics on the volume of this training, but prevailing wisdom suggests that this is a major mode of training, if not the most important one.

Subjects in which training is provided include the operation of computers of various sizes with already-prepared programs, programming, maintenance and repair, systems management, other management problems associated with computers, communications systems, and operation and programming of computer-assisted design or manufacturing equipment.

The courses are typically brief, lasting from 1 to 5 days, although some courses go on for several weeks. They tend to be quite specific, focusing on a single model of equipment, use of a single program, teaching a single programming language, and so on. Thus, an employee wishing to advance beyond this level may need to take additional courses to round out the skills acquired. Moreover, since the technology is changing rapidly, the employee may need retraining in order to learn new equipment.

Self-study is used extensively. Textbooks, programmed learning books, and computer-based training programs are available for many of the subjects. A growing proportion of this material is being produced in the form of video cassettes, computerized instruction, satellite-transmitted teleconferences, and other ways of allowing the necessary training to take place in many locations and at flexible times. At the same time there continues to be much use of traditional printed manuals. Only rarely, however, is this material geared to the needs of a particular group.

Employer-provided/sponsored training generally falls into one of four categories: (1) in-house programs, (2) contracts with a postsecondary educational institution, (3) tuition assistance programs, and (4) union-negotiated (re)training programs. Various anecdotal examples of each type of program are presented below.

IN-HOUSE PROGRAMS

In-house training programs are usually delivered by company staff, frequently by a part- or full-time trainer. Employers either develop their own training curricula or buy/lease prepackaged training programs. A third option is to bring in outside consultants to design and/or deliver training courses at the worksite.

A good example of an employer-designed and delivered program is provided by the Intel Corporation, a manufacturer of integrated circuits, which recently installed 65 personal computers in its microprocessor division over a 6-month period (Johnson, 1985).

Implementation activities focused on three efforts: the Continuous Learning Center (CLC), the Office Systems Center (OSC), and twice-monthly meetings for all the microprocessor division secretaries. The CLC was designed as a place where people would both learn how to use the PC and bring their new applications for others to learn. The OSC provided "hot line" help for anyone who needed immediate assistance with either the hardware or the software. Currently, the OSC's primary activities are training and software applications and evaluation.

To evaluate the success of the implementation process, Intel used as a control group secretaries who had been given the same PCs but who had received a more conventional 8 hours of training from in-house word-processing instructors. Based on the self-reports of 20 microprocessor division secretaries and 9 control group secretaries, 52 percent of the former reported an increase in productivity compared with 15 percent of the controls; 80 percent of the first group reported new procedures developed compared with 10 percent of the control group; and 70 percent of the microprocessor division secretaries reported new uses in place compared with 20 percent of the control group secretaries. In addition, the secretaries in the first group had freed up 2 hours a day they had previously spent in typing revisions. They were using this time to (1) support more people; (2) provide better support for their managers (e.g., drafting routine reports previously done by their managers); (3) eliminate the need for temporaries; and (4) develop more PC skills—they now have time to spend in the CLC, as they are completing their other work in half the time it used to take. These secretaries have become a creative source of new applications and have been rewarded by their managers for their creativity. They have also gained new respect within the company for their use of PCs as information tools. Further follow-up of these different training approaches by Intel could assess the longer-range career impacts of each approach to PC training for secretaries.

United Virginia Bank, which purchased a computer-based training program designed to increase the effectiveness of its teller training efforts, provides an example of employer delivery of a purchased program. The bank determined that a generic computer training program could be purchased from a local vendor at much less cost than developing an interactive videotape system in-house.

The purchased program consisted of 22 lessons, supporting texts, and other materials.

Each year, more than 100 tellers in the Richmond region, the vast majority of whom are women, attend the bank's 4-week teller course. The trainees in each class spend the first 4 days of their training on the terminals. The program presents lessons and asks the students relevant questions. It also tells them whether they have answered correctly. Students move at their own pace. The instructor is free to help students who require one-on-one assistance; meanwhile, the rest of the class members stay busy at their terminals. Trainees say they enjoy learning from a computer and they now score higher on final tests—90 percent or more—and are being taught 15 percent more than with traditional methods. The program also shaves 1 day from classroom work. Overall, United Virginia Bank views its experience with computer-based training very positively, and the bank intends to continue to experiment with the concept and expand the program (Coleman, 1983).

With the help of outside consultants, Metropolitan Life Insurance Company developed a program to train 20,000 employees at 1,250 sites to use the company's recently acquired minicomputer-based network. Metropolitan is spending more than $30 million for the network hardware and approximately $3 million for the training program. Applications of the system include data entry and editing, a client data base specific to each sales office, word processing, electronic mail, and policy and contract illustrations. Almost all Metropolitan employees will be users of the system.

Metropolitan's training plan was developed with the help of an outside consulting firm. Called a "top-down" training program, it resembles an inverted pyramid in structure. Senior executives in the personal insurance field were trained first, senior sales staff were trained second, and key people in eight regional head offices were trained next. Each regional office became home to a nucleus of six to eight trainers. Next in line were the "critical users"— sales managers and office managers in 1,100 U.S. sales outlets. These users traveled to the company's eight regional head offices for training. When the sales and office managers were trained, they became responsible for training sales office staff. The training emphasized hands-on experience, with 20 percent of the time spent in lectures and the rest of the time spent actively using the system (Desmond, 1984).

Outside consultants can also be used to deliver complete training programs. ITT Educational Services, Inc., Business Division, offers employers complete training programs (including provision of facilities) in such areas as automation, bank teller, computer programming, data processing, electronic office-machine technology, keypunch operator, retail technical sales, secretarial, telecommunications, and word processing. In addition to generic or custom-designed training programs, ITT offers to take care of all arrangements, including site selection, employee recruitment, student enrollment, assessment, basic/remedial education, English as a second language, skill training, career counseling, and support service coordination. ITT also offers more advanced training beyond the initial level for supervisory personnel, as well as courses that provide part of the training at the trainee's workstation on the job.

CONTRACTS WITH POSTSECONDARY EDUCATIONAL INSTITUTIONS

Many employers, particularly those smaller businesses that do not have an in-house training capability of their own, are contracting with postsecondary educational institutions for both custom-designed and generic training programs. A growing number of colleges—mainly 2-year community colleges—have established offices or centers to offer the colleges' educational services, resources, and facilities to local business and industry, although, overall, institutions of higher education provide only a small amount of employer-sponsored education and training. The majority of contracted programs involve a small number of employees and are of short duration, ranging from a 1-hour seminar to a full-semester course. These programs may be standard courses identified in the college catalog that are presented at times and locations convenient to the firm and in time blocks appropriate to circumstances; they may be customized versions of standard college offerings; or they may be totally new programs, structured to meet the specific demands of the company. They may be taught by college faculty or by instructors hired specifically for the course.

The Vermont State Colleges Office of External Programs (OEP), for example, assists employers, particularly in small businesses, to identify their education and training needs. Through its

Educational Brokering Service, OEP communicates these employers' needs and specifications to more than 30 educational institutions in the state. Interested schools then bid on providing the training services, with the employers making the final selection of the desired program provider.

TUITION ASSISTANCE PROGRAMS

A very high proportion of companies, particularly the larger ones, have some form of tuition aid or tuition assistance programs under which employees receive partial or full reimbursement of the costs incurred for courses taken on their own. Generally, these programs have a very low participation rate, particularly among lower-level, nonmanagement employees.

Unlike most programs, the Polaroid Corporation's Tuition Assistance Plan has a very high rate of participation, even among hourly employees. Polaroid has developed a systematic and comprehensive series of courses and programs for its employees which includes internal education and skills training programs; technology-based programs and seminars for technical and nontechnical personnel; and career counseling workshops to help employees determine career goals and methods for achieving them.

The Tuition Assistance Plan prepays 100 percent of the costs of approved educational programs successfully completed by employees—both hourly and salaried, with all those working 20 or more hours per week eligible to participate in the plan on a pro-rated basis (30 hours equals 75 percent payment). Acceptable courses and programs include

- Any basic course in reading, writing, or arithmetic
- Courses or programs that will improve the employee's skill on his or her present job
- Courses or programs that relate to the next job in the employee's job family
- Courses or programs required or relevant to a trade or craft licensing or certification program appropriate to the individual's career and specific to Polaroid's need for the trade- or craft-specific degree programs (associate, bachelor's, and graduate degrees). All engineering, science, mathematics, accounting, finance, and secretarial programs. All general business management, marketing, transportation, economics, journalism, nursing, and criminal justice programs, if currently job related.

According to company figures, about 6,000 (50 percent) of its domestic employees participated in an average of 1.5 internal or external education and training programs in a recent year. Ten percent of the eligible domestic work force participated in the Tuition Assistance Plan, and of these, 40 percent were from the hourly ranks (Knox, 1979).

UNION-NEGOTIATED (RE)TRAINING PROGRAMS

Unions are very active in the support of training and retraining for their members. A number of union-negotiated agreements call for advance notification of expected technological changes and the retraining of those workers who would be displaced. A recent example is the Communications Workers of America (CWA) National Training Fund, under the retraining provisions negotiated with the seven regional Bell System holding companies. A provision in the agreement stipulates that retraining will be provided for any worker who needs or desires it. Local committees have been established in each of the seven regions and are responsible for the development of appropriate programs in response to local membership needs.

CWA Local 8519 has developed, through its Arizona Training Fund (ATF), a 600-hour, 15-course curriculum leading to a Level I certification in telecommunications. Interested CWA members can enroll in courses ranging from Basic Circuit Reading to Digital Electronics as well as an elective computer literacy course. All courses are fully accredited, and tuition costs are reimbursed by Mountain Bell and AT&T. Of the 316 CWA members who have taken one or more ATF courses, about 55 percent are female. Thus far, no one has failed, but 26 persons have dropped out with an additional 9 incompletes, resulting in an overall retention rate of nearly 90 percent. The ATF training program is aimed at developing "broad, generic skills that will be useful to CWA members inside or outside the Bell system" (Hilton, 1984:4). As a result of their participation in the program, many CWA members have been promoted, while others, threatened with job loss, have found new jobs outside the Bell companies.

Only a very small number of workers in offices and businesses belong to a union. The majority of employees in these work settings are dependent on employer-provided (re)training or must look to other sources of education and training for programs.

SUMMARY

Corporate training that is mandated, provided, and/or paid for by the worker's employer can eliminate a significant number of the barriers facing employed adults noted above. Some of these barriers and the means used for overcoming them include

- Financial constraints—employer finances the total costs of the training.
- Time and location constraints—programs are offered at the workplace or a nearby training facility during regular working hours.
- Problems due to prior educational attainment—remedial courses are offered; programs are held in familiar or nonthreatening settings (e.g., the workplace); active, hands-on participation by the learner is encouraged.
- Scheduling problems—programs are generally short term, at or near the workplace, with flexible curricula.

In addition, training is provided on state-of-the-art equipment and frequently gives the trainee important, transferable skills useful for job and career transitions.

Unfortunately, not all workers have the opportunity to receive technology training from their employers. And, of course, there are thousands more unemployed adults who desire such training. They must rely on other providers.

EDUCATIONAL INSTITUTIONS

The range of education and training opportunity currently available, in addition to that provided or sponsored by employers, is considerable and is offered by a wide variety of institutional providers and organizations. While it is likely that, for the foreseeable future, employers will continue to provide the majority of training in a variety of new technologies, educational institutions are increasingly offering training in a variety of new technologies as part of their educational programs.

NONCOLLEGIATE POSTSECONDARY SCHOOLS

A growing number of people are turning to noncollegiate postsecondary schools (often called proprietary or trade and technical schools) for courses in electronics, communications, computers, health care, and secretarial fields. In the past 2 years, enrollments in these schools have increased by 25 percent. More than 1.5 million people are enrolled annually in these public and private training institutions. Women, once a minority in these schools, currently constitute 52 percent of their enrollments.

Many proprietary schools are small and independently owned and specialize in training students for a single vocation. But many others are part of chains of three, four, or more schools. Large national corporations are active in the field, too. ITT Educational Services, Inc., is the leading example, operating a nationwide network of 28 proprietary schools offering technical and business programs and 19 career training centers. ITT trains more than 15,000 people annually in 39 business and technical skill areas. Offering primarily vocational and technical courses on a part-time and full-time basis, noncollegiate postsecondary schools do not grant degrees. Programs last from 2 weeks to 2 years. Tuition for a typical 10-month course held 5 days a week, 5 hours a day averages $2,000, a price that clearly puts it out of reach of the average low-skilled, low-paid worker or unemployed would-be worker. There is no guarantee of a job upon completion of a course, although the schools frequently emphasize the high starting salaries offered in sought-after fields and the schools' close links to community employers.

Noncollegiate postsecondary schools maintain a high degree of flexibility in admissions requirements and in courses offered and are generally responsive to local employment needs. In regard to the effectiveness of these schools in training students for actual jobs, however, evidence to date is mixed at best. Several studies have found that relatively few graduates of professional or technical-level training courses actually find jobs in that area. This is particularly true for graduates of computer courses. Clearly, the need for obtaining information on quality of the program, completion rates, entry requirements, costs, financial aid, job placement rates and assistance, and refund policies is crucial for any individual seeking (re)training in hopes of obtaining a new or better job (Kaercher, 1983).

TWO-YEAR COLLEGES

The nation's 1,296 2-year community and junior colleges offer a variety of courses in technology training and updating, for those currently employed as well as those seeking to enter or reenter the labor market. Because the majority of the 2-year schools are publicly supported, tuition and fees are generally low and affordable. Also, because of their liberal admissions policies, 2-year colleges may be particularly attractive to those would-be adult learners who have not fared well within the traditional formal education system.

Recent data reveal that the community and junior college population is a *working* population (in 1985, more than 70 percent of full-time students at 2-year colleges were employed), with particular interest in the occupational pay-off of the programs in which they are enrolled. The data also show that the 2-year colleges are serving an extremely varied clientele consisting of adults (the average age of community college students is 27), women (who comprise 55 percent of enrollment), minorities, and the "disadvantaged," as well as substantial numbers of conventional postsecondary students (Charner and Fraser, 1984).

These schools have been very responsive to the learning and training needs of adult workers in their communities, particularly blue-collar workers. A recent study indicated that 41 percent of community colleges had developed programs in response to union requests. Twenty-five percent were offering classes off-site in workplaces, union halls, and community centers. Programs included skill-upgrading in such areas as electronics, welding, and secretarial work. The main unions involved were the electrical workers, machinists, carpenters, plumbers, and sheet-metal workers (Goldstein, 1984). It is likely that this responsiveness on the part of community colleges accounts for the finding that a higher percentage of blue-collar and service workers enrolled in adult education were in 2-year colleges than in any other type of institution (National Center for Education Statistics, 1979).

Community and junior colleges also work effectively with local business and industry. These partnerships take a variety of forms, most frequently including plant-specific training provided by the college under contract with a local employer or employers, equipment use or donation, industry assistance in developing programs, faculty assignments in industry, industry personnel as part of the instructional staff, sharing of facilities, and on-the-job training.

One cooperative program is the Associate Degree Program for Motorola Technicians operated by the Rio Salado (Arizona) Community College. Its goal is to train entry-level workers to develop knowledge and skills sufficient to earn an Associate in Applied Science degree in Electronic Technology and to allow them to return to the workplace at a higher-level job. Traditionally technicians in this industry have been men while women have tended to fill the ranks of the assembly-line. The program's objective is to move more women into higher-skilled, better-paying technician positions.

Normally a 2-year degree program, the 64-credit program has been compressed into 1 year. The curriculum leads to an Associate of Science degree for either an electrical technician or semiconductor technician and was developed jointly by the college and the industry. Courses are concentrated in a short time period of 5 weeks with classes meeting for 3.5 to 4 hours, 5 days per week. Among the courses included are Introduction to Algebra, Economics, General Psychology, Electronics I, Speech, Stress Management, Digital and Logic Circuits, and Solid State Devices. Finally, all participants take part in on-the-job training cooperative work experience when they actually work at technician jobs in the plant. In addition to instruction, the college provides counseling and other student services.

Motorola provides the students for the program from the ranks of its assembly-line employees. The company pays the employee's salary for the entire year of the program, in addition to all applicable tuition and book costs. The company also has provided a Technical Training Center at the work site consisting of 2 classrooms (for instruction) and 18 lab stations (for instruction and practice). A full-time director, lab technician, and secretary are also provided by the company. The cost for the program runs about $18,000 per student. This includes student salaries but not facility and staff costs.

Participants in the program included 130 individuals, almost all women, over 2 years. Although placement in technician positions was not guaranteed, 98 percent of participants completed the program, and 95 percent of the participants were promoted, on a competitive basis, to either electronic technician or process technician positions in the company. The average salary increase after program completion was approximately $2.00 per hour, from $8.25 per hour as an assembly line-worker to $10.00 per hour as a starting technician.

Four-Year Colleges and Universities

Colleges and universities have long been involved in the further education of adults through their continuing education and extension departments. Approximately 1,230 4-year institutions of higher education operate such programs or variations thereof. In general, the range of courses is broad and varied, although usually not for degree credit. The participants in these continuing education programs are usually well educated and fairly well-off, and the programs are generally supported almost entirely from student fees.

Recent trends in overall college enrollment indicate that more women and adults are entering the regular departments of colleges and universities. Overall the proportion of college students who were women rose from 43.1 percent in 1972 to 51.5 percent in 1982. Students 25 years old and over accounted for 28 percent of enrollment in 1972 and for 35.6 percent in 1982. Part-time students increased from 34.1 percent of the entire student body to 41.9 percent in the same time span (National Center for Education Statistics, 1983:98). Given the decline in the traditional youthful population and the increase in adult students, higher education institutions may be forced to move away from what some critics have called prejudice against the adult worker toward a "new understanding of adult learning" (Barton, 1982:143).

Colleges and universities are providing more learning opportunities for adults through two separate approaches: adapting the delivery of traditional programs to accommodate a nontraditional student population and offering nontraditional programs to both traditional and nontraditional students. Among the modifications being made are scheduling classes at night and on weekends; offering classes at diverse locations, such as libraries, employment sites, and union halls; using the media to transmit courses, lectures, and reading materials; easing admission requirements and formal entry qualifications for certain courses of study, including the granting of credit for life experience; and encouraging greater use of independent study.

An unusual example of a nontraditional program in technical training is the Grass Roots Computer Literacy for Rural Adults Project operated by the University of Idaho Cooperative Extension (with funding from the U.S. Department of Education's Fund for the Improvement of Postsecondary Education). This project, started in the fall of 1983, has two goals. The first is to design, test, and evaluate a curriculum to teach computer literacy to rural adults, particularly women. By computer literacy, the project means the ability to understand simple computers and to be able to use mini- and microcomputers in work or home settings. The second goal is to develop a delivery system that is appropriate for teaching in rural communities. In developing the curriculum, the designers recognized the necessity of incorporating rural values and experiences.

This curriculum eliminates a number of the known barriers to adult participation in the project. There are no costs to the participants in the program, because they are covered through the project's federal grant. Courses last for 4 weeks (2 evenings per week) and are located at local high schools. The curriculum includes a math-readiness component that covers math concepts, problem solving, and manipulation skills. A language-readiness component focuses on logical thinking and the communication skills involved in information processing. Participants are encouraged to share feelings and successes by teaching each other and by encouraging and facilitating ideas to be exchanged. Classes are small (12 per class) to allow for group interaction and discussion.

Community people, small business persons, farmers, and homemakers participate in the delivery of the program as supervised peer teachers. These peer teachers are selected by local advisory committees and trained by project staff to recruit students and teach the course.

All of the program participants have become computer literate. To date over 600 students have enrolled in the program.

Both colleges and universities seem to be moving toward greater flexibility in accommodating diverse new populations of would-be learners. Practices vary significantly, however, as does the level of institutional responsiveness to the special needs of workers in search of specialized technology training. Innovative approaches such as those cited above represent, in most instances, isolated departures from traditional delivery systems geared toward traditional student populations.

PROFESSIONAL ASSOCIATIONS

Professional associations are composed of member practitioners within a particular occupational group and are aimed at advancing the interests of the occupation as a whole as well as enhancing the occupational competence of its individual members. These associations are organized on a national, regional, state, or local basis and consist of such diverse memberships as engineers, real estate brokers, doctors, secretaries, and sociologists. They serve their members through meetings and conferences, professional publications, workshops, courses, and other educational activities. These activities are almost always part time and are usually paid for by the participants or their employers.

The American Management Association (AMA) is a major provider of education, with its 7,500 lecturers and discussion leaders and the provision of almost 100,000 courses for business personnel in a recent year (Anderson, Kasl, and Associates, 1982). Most of the courses last 1 to 4 days and include subjects such as Production Planning and Control, Utilizing Computer-Aided Engineering for Better Design, Pre-retirement Planning, Career Workshop for Executive Secretaries, and Improving Interviewing Skills. Recently the AMA began offering courses on integrated office systems to assist in making the changeover to the automated office. For those unable to leave their places of business, the AMA provides in-house courses for groups or supplies multimedia packages and a trainer for companies to use.

GOVERNMENT AGENCIES

Government agencies provide a wide range of programs offering technology training at low cost or no cost to the participant. Very few programs, however, are aimed at the adult female worker who has been, or expects to be, affected by the introduction of technology into the office or business.

PUBLIC SCHOOL SYSTEMS

Local school systems, though mainly focused on educating youth, have long offered adult education courses. With projected stabilization and, in some cases, decline in enrollments, it is likely that the trend of offering programs for adults will increase, particularly at the secondary level. Many schools, especially vocational schools, are upgrading their equipment through donations from and partnerships with employers, and schools throughout the country are benefiting from contributions from computer companies in particular. It is very likely, therefore, that computer training courses in a variety of fields will be increasingly available to community members through adult education programs.

One example of such a program is the "Computers for the Medical Assistant" course offered by the Fairfax County (Virginia) Public Schools Office of Adult and Community Education. The class, which meets weekly at a local high school for 5 weeks, explores the use of automation in the doctor's office. Another course covers the coding system being implemented in hospitals, insurance companies, and doctors' offices. Classes are held at night, and costs are very low.

LOCAL COMMUNITY PROGRAMS

Increasing numbers of community agencies and organizations are offering courses in technology use, particularly the operation of microcomputers and computer literacy. One example is a free computer education program started in 1983 by the Tacoma (Washington) Public Library. Local library officials developed the pilot program, named Compulit, after learning that while computer education courses were available in area schools, no such programs were available for adults. Compulit consists of three computer literacy classes, a microcomputer laboratory, and a computer checkout service in which class enrollees are allowed to take home a microcomputer. The computer laboratory is equipped with a variety of microcomputers and many popular home and business software programs. The students have been about equally divided between men and women, and slightly more than half have been between 36 and 64 years old (Computerworld, 1984:34).

FEDERAL EMPLOYMENT AND TRAINING PROGRAMS

The federal government, through an array of employment and training programs, provides significant education and (re)training opportunities, focusing on entry-level training for the disadvantaged would-be worker, with some attention paid to the retraining of the dislocated worker. Most recently, federal programs for unemployed and disadvantaged workers have included the Comprehensive Employment and Training Act of 1973 (CETA) and its successor, the Job Training Partnership Act (JTPA); the Work Incentive (WIN) program; and the Trade Act of 1974. The types of training provided through these programs include machine tool, welding, secretarial, electronics, clerical, and nursing (LPN). The CETA program, which focused mainly on disadvantaged workers, relied increasingly during its life span on public sector employment as its chief mechanism, with training accounting for only one-quarter of program expenditures by the end of the 1970s. Despite the negative image often associated with CETA, it was found that the program helped raise earnings substantially for women and male workers with little or no recent work experience (U.S. Congress, Office of Technology Assessment, 1986:170).

The current Job Training Partnership Act (JTPA) is expected to produce 800,000 to 1,000,000 trainees in fiscal year 1984 at a cost of $3.5 billion. The bulk of this money was to support the training of disadvantaged youth in marketable skills. In FY 1983, about $215 million was allocated under Title III for the retraining of adult workers who lost their jobs in heavy industry because of automation or the 1981–1982 recession. The program emphasizes training in fields where job openings are increasing, i.e., the service industries: health care, food services, clerical work, and computer sciences. According to the Office of Technology Assessment (OTA), only 4 percent of eligible displaced workers are estimated to have participated in Title III programs in 1983, the majority of whom were white males (U.S. Congress, Office of Technology Assessment, 1986:174). In addition, OTA expresses concern over whether displaced workers in these programs are getting enough chances at training for new skills and occupations. Some critics, moreover, believe that trainees, particularly women, are being shortchanged because the program emphasizes short-term training for low-level jobs that could be obtained without the training (Johnson, 1984:9).

For eligible workers (those losing jobs due to foreign competition), the Trade Act of 1974 provides some important benefits not available under Title III of JTPA: support payments for workers in training and generous relocation assistance. The numbers served, however, are very small and are decreasing; in 1984, only 6,538 workers entered training under the program, compared with

20,386 in 1981 (U.S. Congress, Office of Technology Assessment, 1986:197).

The Work Incentive (WIN) program provides training and employment services for Aid to Families With Dependent Children (AFDC) participants, 90 percent of whom are women. In FY 1985, approximately 350,000 WIN participants found employment, generally entry-level positions in maintenance/clerical fields, park service, and human services. In keeping with the aims of the WIN program (to help participants lessen their dependence on welfare), the bulk of the training provided focuses on remedial education, job search techniques, and basic occupational skills, with little emphasis on higher-skilled technology training (*Employment and Training Reporter*, 1986:647).

Since 1980, and particularly under JTPA, local partnership programs have been preferred as both the locus of responsibility and service deliverer for federally funded training programs. These partnerships take a variety of forms but, in almost every case, always include the involvement of one or more major employer(s) in the community. The presence of the employer is designed to assure that training programs are up-to-date and provide training in skills needed for current or projected jobs in local industry and businesses. The programs described below are typical of the collaborative efforts focusing on the provision of technology training at the state and local levels.

Word Processing Training Centers are currently operating in 32 cities across the country. These centers are run by local community-based organizations in partnership with the IBM Corporation, with additional funding from the Job Training Partnership Act. Training in word processing, computer operation, and computer programming is provided to some 3,000 individuals annually, most of whom are women in their late twenties and thirties, although ages range from 18 to 55. The training is done on up-to-date equipment provided and updated periodically by IBM, which also provides loaned staff to the centers for the first 3 years of operation, at which time centers are expected to be self-sufficient, although IBM continues to donate and upgrade equipment.

One specific example, the Washington, D.C., Word Processing Center, is operated by the Washington Urban League and serves three main categories of workers: women returning to the work force, workers whose jobs have been terminated, and public assistance recipients. Ninety-eight percent of the program participants are female. The training course, which is promoted heavily through local advertising, lasts for 26 weeks and consists of 6 hours a day, 5 days a week. While no stipend is offered to trainees, they do receive $35 a week to cover transportation, and other support services, including counseling, are provided. The center trained 153 word processors in 1983, over 85 percent of whom were placed in jobs with an average starting salary of $13,400. In a follow-up of trainees placed during the center's first 3 years of operation, 75 percent had been retained by their employers, and several of the trainees had moved up to become administrative assistants or managers. Its operators are convinced that the program offers participants not just entry-level skills but also the skills needed to gain upward mobility within the employing organization. Twenty-three new centers were added to the national program in the summer of 1985.

A state-funded cooperative effort, the Bay State Skills Corporation (BSSC) was created by the Massachusetts state legislature in 1981 to act as a catalyst in forming partnerships between businesses and educational institutions to train workers in skills needed by growing industries in the state. BSSC provides grants to public or nonprofit education and training institutions, which link up with one or more growing companies to train workers for specific jobs. Participating companies are required to match the grant with contributions of equipment, materials, staff time, or cash.

The training can take place at community colleges, vocational schools, 4-year colleges, universities, and community-based employment and training organizations throughout the state. The training is not restricted to unemployed or poor individuals. Because employers' major criteria are the need for skilled workers, BSSC's primary focus is on training people for jobs, regardless of their economic status. The programs cover a variety of training levels, including entry-level training, employee upgrading, retraining, and advanced (college- and university-level) programs and run from 20 weeks to 20 months. Training is provided in a wide variety of new and emerging occupations, such as nuclear medicine technology, computer-aided design/computer-aided manufacturing, plastics technology, and advanced automation and robotics, in addition to the more traditional occupations of the machine trades, licensed practical nursing, and junior accounting.

To date, BSSC has served approximately 1,500 adults in its training programs. Women tend to predominate in the technician-level training courses and are currently underrepresented in the higher-skilled programs, such as robotics and manufacturing engineering. Several mid-level programs have been targeted for women and minorities and have been successful in moving them into jobs as technical writers and computerized materials managers (at annual salaries averaging between $15,000 and $25,000). In addition, BSSC has contracted with the Women's Technical Institute of Boston to provide training for women in higher-level electronics jobs and with Northeastern University to provide programs for women in engineering and in information systems.

IN SEARCH OF TECHNOLOGICAL TRAINING EQUITY

Probably the most typical technology training for women workers today is several hours of instruction in word processing, provided by the employer to meet its immediate needs. A few of the innovative technology training programs described in the preceding sections offer some hope that attention is beginning to be paid to the broader needs of women for training and retraining in new office and business technologies. A wide variety of educational and training programs is available, but very few focus on training for higher-skilled, higher-level positions in emerging occupations. Nor is training being designed to meet the differing needs of women at varying stages over the life span. Very few programs appear to differentiate between the training needs of women and men. Counseling and career development are included in only a few programs.

It is possible, perhaps, that this review does not reflect the bulk of what is currently happening in individual programs, but it is unlikely that a significant number of programs are operating in relative obscurity. The limited information available and the growing concern over women's role in the "Office of the Future" lead us to a discussion of appropriate research and actions to better meet the technological training and educational needs of women.

INFORMATION GAPS

There is an imperative need for better and more comprehensive information on education and training for occupations and jobs affected by the new office and business technologies. Studies such as the National Commission for Employment Policy's project, "Technological Change and Employment: The Effects of Computer-Based Equipment," are beginning to fill some of the information gaps, but currently there does not exist a single data base that examines the complete system of training opportunity in the United States. Within this larger category, specific data are needed on the structure of (re)training opportunities for women and men in terms of the providers of (re)training services; the need for (re)training in terms of changing occupational skill requirements due to technology; and the demand for technology (re)training by individuals and employers.

Specifically, an inventory of technology training programs needs to be developed, particularly for service and information occupations. Such an inventory should provide a history of programs (goals, objectives, population served, and outcomes) as well as descriptions of training and services offered and instructional approaches. Complementing the inventory, additional information could be obtained through a longitudinal data collection component that would emphasize patterns of occupational mobility, attitudinal and behavioral changes, and patterns of technology education and training for women and men at different stages of their life spans. Analysis of such longitudinal data could track patterns of participation; assess the short-term and long-term nature of barriers to participation for population subgroups; measure the impacts of different education and training experiences on job mobility, attitudes, and behaviors; and assess the impacts of institutional initiatives aimed at increasing the technology training opportunities for women. This information could be collected on a regular basis by the federal government, perhaps as part of the National Center for Education Statistics' survey of participation in adult education.

A parallel information collection effort would focus on a series of case studies of a selected number of technology training programs in service and information occupations designed to train women for middle-level and higher skilled positions in these industries. These case studies could help identify specific components that best serve the needs of or eliminate the barriers for different groups of women in obtaining the skills required for the higher tier of jobs within those occupations affected by new technology.

One approach to conducting these case studies might be to build on the groundwork laid by the authors of *In Search of Excellence* (Peters and Waterman, 1984). The majority of companies identified as "excellent" were in the service, information, and high-technology sectors and were judged to be far above the norm in the amount of time they spent on training activities. Although systematic data on training were not collected and no mention was made of these companies' policies with regard to women specifically, several of the companies have reputations for being particularly responsive to the education and training needs of their office workers. It would be worthwhile to examine more closely some of these companies' policies and programs relating to the introduction of new technology into the workplace.

Case studies should also be conducted of programs offered by educational institutions and by other public and private training providers, particularly those developed by groups with a long-term interest in the technological preparation of women for occupations, such as those operated by unions and community service organizations.

Dissemination of the information resulting from the case studies as well as from the inventory and the longitudinal study should not be limited to researchers and government policy makers. A central clearinghouse with direct access to employers and educators is essential to the implementation of any recommendations arising from the information collection efforts. One possible site for such a clearinghouse might be the recently established Center for Education and Employment, operated by Teachers College, Columbia University, whose mission is to explore education and training alternatives that contribute to lifelong learning and retraining for both personal development and effective instruction.

EDUCATION POLICY

Beyond the collection of more and better-quality information on training for new technologies, special attention must be paid to what is (and is not) currently happening at the various levels of education today, with particular concern focused on long-range occupational and career impacts relating to women and technology.

Early emphasis at the elementary and secondary school levels must be placed on access to math and science skills for girls, so that more options will be open to women on completion of secondary schooling for training in higher-level scientific and technical occupational skills. This is true for all students, not simply those traditionally college-bound. Such education is increasingly a prerequisite for those wishing to enter 2-year technology training programs without first having to participate in remedial courses. Currently, too many options for advanced technology training appear to be closed to women due to the lack of an adequate background in science and related fields.

Vocational education is often criticized for perpetuating sexual segregation in training offered to students at the secondary level. Girls are still being tracked, for the most part, into clerical and secretarial courses, while boys are encouraged to enter the more technical training programs. Frequently, critics charge, even the technical courses lag behind economic realities, teaching skills that are no longer in demand on equipment that is already obsolete for jobs that are being eliminated. Clearly, the role of vocational education in preparing women and men for emerging technological occupations needs to be reassessed and perhaps restructured.

As far as postsecondary education is concerned, reference was made earlier to higher education's "prejudice" against the adult learner. In an age when there is an expanding need for the retraining of adults and a dwindling number of traditional young students, colleges and universities must start rethinking their policies regarding the education and training required for an increasingly knowledge-intensive, service-oriented economy. This rethinking process has already begun at some institutions, as evidenced by several of the innovative programs referenced earlier in this paper. It should be noted, however, that most of these programs operate on the fringes of the sponsoring educational institutions and are generally not held in the same regard as the more traditional mainstream offerings.

Community and junior colleges have historically been responsive to local economic conditions and the training needs of area employers. In 1978, 2-year colleges became the course providers most frequently cited by adult education participants. Reflecting their concern for the learning and training needs of adult workers in their communities, these schools offer a wide variety of occupational programs. Information is lacking, however, on the level of technological skills offered in many of these programs and on how course completers fare in the job market and in their career development. Concern has been expressed by some that the focus on narrow job-specific training may limit the general employability of program participants and may ultimately reduce the adaptability of the work force. The inventory of technology training programs recommended earlier would contribute much-needed information on these issues.

Educational institutions at all levels would do well to rethink their missions in terms of changing demographic, economic, and technological factors. Training and retraining will become ever more important as new skills are needed by workers over their life span. Educators should begin thinking in proactive terms, anticipating changing educational demands, rather than simply reacting to crisis situations related to the immediate needs of the moment.

EMPLOYER RESPONSIBILITIES

Perhaps, as Lewis Perelman suggests in his recent book, it is time for employers, managers, and workers to "rethink the social contract surrounding the human capital they employ" (Perelman, 1984:58). In 1982, for example, companies invested an average of $3,600 per worker in new facilities and equipment, much of which was probably linked to the introduction of new technologies. Yet these same companies invested an average of just $300 per worker for training. Research from *In Search of Excellence* indicates that all of the "excellent" companies treat their people (they are not thought of simply as workers) as the primary source of productivity gains—not capital spending or automation. The most pervasive theme in these companies is "respect for the individual." The common practice among most companies of letting employees leave rather than retrain them for new technology reflects little of such respect.

Unfortunately, existing federal policies tend to favor physical capital over human capital development (witness many of the tax provisions), and the current climate is unlikely to favor additional drains on the treasury. Therefore, traditional recommendations, such as offering federal tax incentives to encourage employers to establish or enhance in-house technical training, are highly unlikely to be implemented at this time. How then might employers be encouraged to allocate more resources to (re)training office workers to allow them to benefit from opportunities generated by new technologies?

Perhaps changing demographic and economic factors will force employers to reverse their underinvestment in training for this population. As the supply of entry-level workers declines, women and minority workers, in whom human capital investments have been least, will comprise a greater share of available workers. This reality may require that employers invest more heavily in training to provide themselves with the skilled employees that they need. Particular attention will have to be paid to the retraining needs of employed workers whose skills no longer match the needs of their employers, as well as the basic skill needs of workers entering the labor market.

A CONTINUING EDUCATIONAL SYSTEM

If such demographic and economic conditions do not bring employers to invest more resources in industry-provided training, then, once again, the responsibility will revert to the educational system. As Noyelle, Perelman, and others have suggested recently, we may be moving toward a "truly continuing educational system—one that is more equitable, more flexible, better adapted to shorter term passages, more ubiquitous, and perhaps less specialized in orientation than it has traditionally been" (Noyelle, 1984:39).

For the educational system to be responsive to the needs of adults, particularly women, preparing for new office and business technologies, it must look beyond its traditional role of education of youth toward its emerging role in training adults. The educational system must be responsive to the diverse needs of a diverse society, but education and training providers cannot work alone; they must work collaboratively with business, labor, government, and other educational organizations.

Such collaborative efforts are important because few technologies have expanded as rapidly as the computer or penetrated so many sectors of the economy so quickly. Twelve to 15 million workers (one out of every eight employed Americans) currently use computers in their jobs. More than 2 million business computers were sold in 1984 alone, added to the 7.5 million already in the workplace. This has resulted in a formidable training task, involving workers currently on the job as well as young and older would-be workers. It is critical that this process ensure the equitable availability of training in new technologies for all current and future members of the work force.

REFERENCES

Anderson, R.E., E.S. Kasl, & Associates
1982 *The Cost and Financing of Adult Education and Training.* Lexington, Mass.: Lexington Books.
Barton, P., and the National Institute for Work and Learning
1982 *Worklife Transitions.* New York: McGraw-Hill.
Business–Higher Education Forum
1984 *The New Manufacturing: America's Race to Automate.* Washington, D.C.: Business–Higher Education Forum.
Charner, I.
1980 *Patterns of Adult Participation in Learning Activities.* Washington, D.C.: National Institute for Work and Learning.
Charner, I., and B.S. Fraser
1984 *Different Strokes for Different Folks: Access and Barriers to Adult Education and Training.* Washington, D.C.: National Institute for Work and Learning.
Coleman, J.S.
1983 Virginia bank says micro teller training works. *ABA Banking Journal* (June):58.
Computerworld
1984 Library's computer course swamped with registrants. *Computerworld* (March 26):34.
Desmond, J.
1984 Insurer's network training program works from top down. *Computerworld* (August 6):8.
Employment and Training Reporter
1986 Education and Labor Committee calls for fewer program cuts than Reagan budget. *Employment and Training Reporter* (February 26):646–647.
Form, W., and D. McMillan
1983 Women, men, and machines. *Work and Occupations* 10(2):147–178.
Gallant, J.
1984 Survey reveals OA accepted with open arms. *Computerworld* (March 5):24.
Goldstein, H.
1984 Institutional Sources of Education and Training in the Adult Years. Unpublished paper.
Gutek, B., and T. Bikson
1984 Differential Experiences of Men and Women in Computerized Offices. Unpublished paper.

Hilton, M.
  1984   CWA Training: Local Success Stories. Unpublished paper. Communications Workers of America, Washington, D.C.
IBM Corporation
  1985   IBM Education: Notes for the Presentation. Unpublished paper. Armonk, New York.
ITT Educational Services
  1984   *America at Work: The Management Perspective on Training for Business.* Washington, D.C.: ITT Educational Services.
Johnson, B.
  1985   Organizational Design of Word Processing from Typewriter to Integrated Office Systems. Paper presented at American Federation of Information Processing Societies, Office Automation Conference, Atlanta, Ga.
Johnson, S.
  1984   Retraining's come a long way, baby. *The New York Times* (October 14), Section 12:9.
Kaercher, D.
  1983   Trade school: ticket to a better job? *Better Homes and Gardens* (November):57-62.
Keefe, P.
  1984   Three unresolved issues identified for OA users. *Computerworld* (March 26):23.
Knox, K.
  1979   *Polaroid Corporation's Tuition Assistance Plan: A Case Study.* Washington, D.C.: National Manpower Institute.
National Center for Education Statistics, U.S. Department of Education
  1979   *Survey of Participation in Adult Education, 1978.* Washington, D.C.: U.S. Government Printing Office.
  1983   *Digest of Education Statistics 1983-84.* Washington, D.C.: U.S. Government Printing Office.
Noyelle, T.
  1984   *Work in a World of High Technology: Problems and Prospects for Economically Disadvantaged Workers.* Knoxville: University of Tennessee.
Perelman, L.
  1984   *The Learning Enterprise: Adult Learning, Human Capital, and Economic Development.* Washington, D.C.: Council of State Planning Agencies.
Peters, T.J., and R.H. Waterman, Jr.
  1984   *In Search of Excellence: Lessons From America's Best-Run Companies.* New York: Warner Books.
Serrin, W.
  1984   Experts say job bias against women persists. *The New York Times* (November 25):A1, A3.
U.S. Congress, Office of Technology Assessment
  1986   *Technology and Structural Unemployment: Reemploying Displaced Adults.* Washington, D.C.: U.S. Government Printing Office.

The New Technology and the New Economy: Some Implications for Equal Employment Opportunity

Are sex and race still major determinants of employment discrimination? Is the new computer technology changing the demand for labor to such an extent as to reshape the terms under which women and minorities encounter discrimination? As I argue in this paper, using evidence from empirical studies of the retail, insurance, and financial sectors, both questions deserve qualified answers (Noyelle, 1986; 1987).

While major advances have been made in alleviating sex and race discrimination in the workplace, discriminatory barriers based on sex and race remain. Still, other bases for discrimination, which in the past played a lesser role, loom larger today. For example, there may be an increasing tendency to use age to differentiate youth and some groups of older workers from others in the labor market today. During the 1950s or 1960s, the age factor seemed relatively unimportant. More significantly, the role played by socioeconomic status may be growing in importance because of its implications for access to formal schooling and higher education. While our economy places increasing value on formal education as a criterion for hiring, our society continues to lag behind in providing equal access to quality education.

The new technology is changing the nature of many jobs and skills and, as a result, is redefining the demand for labor. In the process, it is loosening the hold of particular groups of workers on specific occupations. But its displacement effects are not restricted to women and minority workers. At the same time, the new technology cannot be viewed in isolation. Deep economic and social changes and dramatic industry shifts have acted to alter the overall occupational structure and to increase the importance of formal schooling and higher education for employment opportunity. The new wave of technological change simply reinforces these trends.

The overall thesis of this paper is straightforward. I argue that the current labor market transformation is altering fundamentally employment and mobility opportunities by changing, in particular, the need for training and the way training is provided. Further, I argue that this transformation has disturbed an earlier balance among sources of discrimination.

A principal conclusion of the paper is that while direct equal employment opportunity (EEO) enforcement in the workplace must continue, the reach of EEO enforcement must be widened from an almost exclusive focus on the workplace to one that links the workplace to the educational arena. At the federal level, this may require a redefinition of the scope of activities of the Equal Employment Opportunity Commission (EEOC) through new legislation, since, under Title VII of the Civil Rights Act of 1964, the scope of the Commission is largely restricted to the workplace. Currently, equal opportunity in federally financed educational programs is mandated by other portions of the 1964 Civil Rights Act, as amended, and other legislation, and is the responsibility of other federal agencies. Enhancing equality of opportunity in the transformed labor market may well require a consolidation of enforcement power and an awareness of the increasingly important link between the two.

The paper is divided into three main parts. The first part traces trends in aggregate employment data and shows which groups of workers have tended to gain in their employment opportunities and which have tended to lose. The second part emphasizes key changes that have occurred in the structure of the U.S. economy and the concomitant changes in the demand for labor. The third discusses the changing nature of discrimination with examples from back-office and retail employment and with special reference to various groups of women and minorities. Policy implications are discussed in the conclusion of the paper.

TECHNOLOGY AND DISCRIMINATION: EVIDENCE FROM AGGREGATE DATA FOR 1970–1980

What can be discerned about the critical linkages between technology and discrimination from employment aggregates? To seek some answers, I developed two sets of measures—one based on decennial census data, the other on EEOC data.

Table 1, based on 1970 and 1980 census data, presents an industry shift-share analysis for six major groups of workers: youth (ages 16–19), black females, Hispanic females, white females, black males, and Hispanic males. For each group, employment growth (or decline) in an industry has been broken down among three components: first, growth (or decline) associated with the relative growth (or decline) of the industry; second, growth (or decline) associated with an increase (or decrease) in the group's participation in the employed labor force; and third, growth (or decline) associated with the pure "shift" of the group in or out of the industry. In other words, the "shift" measure indicates the gains or losses in a given group's penetration in a particular industry, everything else being held constant. For each group, the "shift" measure is shown as a "turnover" ratio indicating the number of workers "shifted" during the 10-year period shown as a percentage of the group's 1980 employment. In addition, the positive and negative shifts are distributed in percentage terms among industries. The overall impact of the shift is shown by means of normalized shares for 1970 and 1980. The share of employment of a group in an industry is divided by its share in the total labor force. This ratio shows the group's standing in an industry relative to the economy as a whole. A ratio below 1 means that the group penetration in the industry is lagging; a ratio above 1 means that the group is overrepresented.

For example, Table 1 shows an aggregate turnover measure of 2.6 percent for white women, indicating that 2.6 percent of the 34,806,839 white women found themselves in 1980 in an industry different from that in which they would have been employed had there been no change in the penetration of white women in various

TABLE 1 Industry Shifts of Major Groups of Workers and Distribution of Positive and Negative Shifts Among Industries

Industry	Employment Distribution: All Sexes, Races, Ages (percent)		Youth (16-19 Years Old) Normalized Share		Shift (percent)	Black Female Normalized Share		Shift (percent)	Hispanic Female Normalized Share		Shift (percent)
	1980	1970	1980	1970		1980	1970		1980	1970	
1. Health	7.4	5.5	0.68	0.93	-21.3	2.35	2.35	+0.3	1.42	1.81	-23.6
2. FIRE[a]	6.0	5.0	0.67	0.85	-13.2	1.03	0.70	+15.1	1.23	1.17	+3.4
3. Social	1.8	1.6	0.87	0.70	+3.1	2.13	1.32	+10.5	1.48	1.18	+10.7
4. Business services[b]	6.6	5.7	0.72	0.90	-14.7	0.60	0.85	-10.6	0.73	0.83	-6.6
5. Education	8.6	8.0	0.62	0.75	-13.5	1.59	1.49	+9.4	1.14	1.11	+12.4
6. TCU[c]	7.3	6.8	0.33	0.59	-23.2	0.71	0.44	+14.8	0.52	0.49	+6.8
7. Wholesale	4.3	4.1	0.71	0.68	+0.8	0.34	0.32	+0.8	0.71	0.81	-7.3
8. Construction	5.9	6.0	0.71	0.52	+12.9	0.10	0.06	+1.4	0.14	0.11	+0.8
9. Public adm.	5.3	5.5	0.40	0.37	+1.9	1.51	1.07	+18.2	0.90	0.73	+16.8
10. Consumer services[d]	20.3	21.4	2.46	2.11	+80.6	1.06	1.70	-86.1	1.23	1.39	-62.5
11. Other goods[e]	4.0	4.5	1.06	1.02	+0.7	0.20	0.33	-3.4	0.59	0.56	+0.2
12. Manufacturing	22.4	25.9	0.60	0.64	-14.1	0.78	0.60	+29.4	1.14	0.96	+52.3
1980 Employment			6,973,441			4,659,177			2,168,649		
Turnover[f]			8.3			13.9			5.7		

NOTE: The 12 industries are ranked by rate of growth between 1970 and 1980 from the fastest growing (health) to the slowest growing (manufacturing). The industry breakdown used is based on classification of service industries found in Stanback et al. (1981). The first two columns show the distribution of all employed among the 12 industries in 1970 and 1980. The positive and negative "shift" is distributed for each group on a percentage basis. The normalized shares of major groups of workers shown for 1970 and 1980 are computed by dividing the share of employment held by each group in each industry by that same group's share of employment in all industries combined. An index below 1.00 indicates underrepresentation; above 1.00, overrepresentation. For definition of "shift," see text.

[a] Finance, insurance, and real estate.
[b] Legal, accounting, advertising, and the like.
[c] Transportation, communications, and utilities.
[d] Retailing and personal services.
[e] Agriculture, mining.
[f] Total shift for given group measured as percentage of 1980 employment. See text.

SOURCE: Bureau of the Census, 1974, 1984.

TABLE 1 (continued)

Industry	Black Male Normalized Share 1980	Black Male Normalized Share 1970	Shift (percent)	Hispanic Male Normalized Share 1980	Hispanic Male Normalized Share 1970	Shift (percent)	White Female Normalized Share 1980	White Female Normalized Share 1970	Shift (Percent)
1. Health	0.65	0.58	+7.7	0.42	0.46	-3.4	1.74	1.93	-28.4
2. FIRE[a]	0.58	0.53	+4.5	0.54	0.61	-8.3	1.43	1.41	+14.7
3. Social	0.84	0.86	-2.1	0.48	0.61	-7.4	1.45	1.32	+8.1
4. Business services[b]	0.82	0.84	-4.9	0.98	0.96	+7.2	0.92	0.90	+11.5
5. Education	0.68	0.54	+16.4	0.42	0.45	-6.9	1.53	1.70	-37.9
6. TCU[c]	1.72	1.45	+38.5	1.12	1.17	-11.3	0.56	0.59	-1.5
7. Wholesale	0.96	1.00	-7.2	1.18	1.25	-11.3	0.67	0.65	+4.7
8. Construction	1.37	1.56	-29.5	1.70	1.47	+34.4	0.21	0.17	+10.8
9. Public adm.	1.33	1.32	-1.7	0.87	1.12	-44.0	0.88	0.77	+25.8
10. Consumer services[d]	0.72	0.74	-16.7	0.90	0.90	-2.9	1.30	1.28	+3.4
11. Other goods[e]	0.88	1.30	-37.8	2.04	1.97	-4.5	0.40	0.27	+20.9
12. Manufacturing	1.29	1.21	+32.9	1.26	1.10	+58.4	0.72	0.77	-32.1
1980 Employment	4,674,871			3,288,208			34,806,839		
Turnover[f]	4.3			3.3			2.6		

sectors of the economy between 1970 and 1980. In addition, the table shows that this shift was primarily due to increased penetration in public administration (explaining 25.8 percent of the positive shift); other goods (+20.9 percent); finance, insurance, and real estate (FIRE) (+14.7 percent); and business services (+11.5 percent), matched by decreased penetration in education (explaining 37.9 percent of the negative shift), manufacturing (−32.1 percent), and health (−28.4 percent).

On the whole, Table 1 points to the following: industry shifts were extensive among black females (turnover of 13.9 percent for the entire group) and youth (8.3 percent turnover) and rather limited among white females (2.6 percent turnover), Hispanic males (3.3 percent), and black males (4.3 percent).

The largest exit move for black females was out of the personal services industries where large numbers used to be employed as domestic servants. Their greatest gains were in manufacturing (+29.4 percent); public administration (+18.2 percent); and FIRE and transportation, communications, and utilities (TCU) (+29.1 percent combined) where they made substantial gains in clerical work; and the educational sector (+9.4 percent). Youth's greatest losses were in TCU, FIRE, and business services (51.1 percent of their losses combined), while their greatest gains were in retailing (a staggering 80.6 percent).

The patterns of gains and losses among Hispanic females tended, with some discrepancies, to resemble those of black females. Among black males and Hispanic males, there were limited positive shifts, overwhelmingly concentrated in some of the least-dynamic and slowest-growing sectors of the economy: manufacturing and TCU for black males (+71.4 percent), and manufacturing and construction for Hispanic males (+92.8 percent). Lastly, the key finding for white women remains that industry shifts over the decade were very limited, with an overall turnover of only 2.6 percent.

The second set of data, presented in Table 2, shows changes in the normalized shares of five demographic groups of workers in major occupations between 1966, 1978, and 1981. These data are for large private-sector firms only (100 or more employees) and are based on EEO-1 reports, which large employers must file every year. They show the progress made by various groups of workers in what has been traditionally the most progressive sector of the economy in terms of EEO enforcement—that of large employers.

Some major changes are worth highlighting. The data show white women advancing out of clerical positions and making large gains in professional ranks; black women and Hispanic women, respectively, moving out of service worker and laborer positions while, in both cases, gaining in clerical positions; and black men and Hispanic men shifting out of laborer positions and into operative and craft positions. Despite some scattered gains, minority males in general continue to trail considerably in the fast-growing white-collar occupations. Of all groups, Hispanic males appear to be the least mobile.

Together these two data sets suggest the following: (1) a relative narrowing of job opportunities for youth as their concentration in retailing increased; (2) a relative improvement in the position of women as shown by the gains of minority women into clerical positions and the advances of white women into professional positions; and (3) a general lack of progress by minority men in entering the relatively fast-growing service industries and white-collar occupations.

Findings regarding age-based discrimination are incomplete. Aside from the patterns observed among youth, the statistical analysis developed for this paper appeared too crude to yield significant evidence of age-based discrimination among other groups, although it is thought to exist.

THE TRANSFORMATION OF THE AMERICAN ECONOMY AND CHANGES IN THE DEMAND FOR LABOR

THE RISE OF THE NEW SERVICE ECONOMY AND ITS IMPACT ON THE INDUSTRY-OCCUPATION STRUCTURE

For some time now, the U.S. economy has been in the midst of a major transformation, involving the shift of capital and labor out of the smokestack industries and into high-tech and service industries. While this transformation had been in the making through much of the early postwar period, the acceleration in the internationalization of the economy after the first oil crisis of 1973 contributed to speeding the redeployment of resources, as many older industries were put through the wrenching test of worldwide competition (Noyelle, 1984; Stanback and Noyelle, 1982; Stanback et al., 1981; Ginzberg and Vojta, 1981).

TABLE 2 Employment by Sex, Race, and Occupation in EEO Reporting Firms: All Industries, 1981, 1978, 1966

Occupation	EEO Firm Employees Distributed by Occupation			Normalized Shares White Male			White Female			Black Male			Black Female			Hispanic Male			Hispanic Female		
	1981	1978	1966	1981	1978	1966	1981	1978	1966	1981	1978	1966	1981	1978	1966	1981	1978	1966	1981	1978	1966
Managers and administrators	11.7	10.8	8.2	1.54	1.56	1.47	0.55	0.48	0.32	0.47	0.41	0.12	0.27	0.21	0.08	0.50	0.48	0.31	0.27	0.21	0.10
Professionals	9.7	8.6	6.6	1.17	1.21	1.38	1.01	0.96	0.46	0.32	0.30	0.13	0.44	0.40	0.24	0.35	0.39	0.37	0.32	0.32	0.16
Technicians	5.7	5.0	4.5	1.10	1.10	1.09	0.98	0.98	0.99	0.63	0.57	0.26	0.89	0.92	1.03	0.68	0.68	0.53	0.59	0.63	0.56
Sales workers	9.0	8.8	7.1	0.86	0.88	0.98	1.40	1.39	1.30	0.48	0.43	0.17	0.80	0.77	0.56	0.56	0.52	0.41	1.00	0.89	0.92
Clerical workers	16.3	15.6	16.7	0.27	0.30	0.43	2.07	2.16	2.43	0.35	0.30	0.16	1.73	1.65	1.05	0.29	0.29	0.31	1.73	1.68	1.39
Craft workers	12.1	12.6	14.2	1.63	1.58	1.46	0.21	0.21	0.20	1.20	1.10	0.55	0.22	0.21	0.17	1.38	1.32	1.01	0.27	0.32	0.33
Operatives	19.1	21.1	25.4	1.06	1.04	1.00	0.72	0.75	0.85	1.68	1.67	1.46	1.09	1.12	0.98	1.41	1.39	1.30	1.18	1.16	1.15
Laborers	7.5	8.5	9.7	0.92	0.89	0.86	0.70	0.74	0.66	2.08	2.06	3.07	1.16	1.21	1.45	2.47	2.48	2.79	1.73	1.84	1.74
Service workers	9.1	9.0	7.7	0.61	0.60	0.66	1.15	1.21	1.13	1.65	1.60	2.32	2.20	2.35	3.93	1.47	1.35	1.62	1.59	1.58	1.57
Total	100.0	100.0	100.0																		
Percent employed in EEO reporting firms				48.0	50.2	60.6	33.0	31.7	28.0	6.0	6.3	5.7	5.5	5.2	2.5	3.4	3.1	1.7	2.2	1.9	0.8

NOTE: The first three columns of the table show the distribution of all EEO firm employees (all sex and race combined) by occupation for 1966, 1978, and 1981, respectively. These three columns give an indication of the changing relative importance of the major occupations in EEO reporting firms in 1966, 1978, and 1981. The normalized shares of major groups of workers shown for 1966, 1978, and 1981 in the remainder of the table are computed by dividing the share of employment held by each group in each occupation by that group's share of all employment in EEO reporting firms (shown on the last line of the table). An index below 1.00 indicates underrepresentation; an index above 1.00, overrepresentation.

SOURCE: U.S. Equal Employment Opportunity Commission, 1966, 1978, and 1981.

Between 1970 and the last quarter of 1984, 27.2 million net new jobs (*Employment and Earnings*, household survey data) were added to the economy, of which nearly 95 percent were in the service industries. Looking at the Reagan years only, the shift to services was even sharper since, by November 1984, employment in the goods-producing industries—agriculture, mining, construction, and manufacturing—had not even caught up with their January 1981 level (*Employment and Earnings*, establishment survey data). In *net* terms, this means that employment growth, since early 1981, had been 100 percent in the services.

In occupational terms, the labor market transformation of the 1970s has led to more than 7 out of every 10 workers being employed in either white-collar or service-worker occupations. Simultaneously, a very sharp drop in the share of blue-collar workers—from 39.2 percent to 29.3 percent of the nonagricultural labor force—occurred between 1965 and 1983 (*Employment and Earnings*, household survey data). In short, growth has shifted to service industries dominated by white-collar or service-worker occupations, technological change in manufacturing accelerated the shift to managerial, engineering, technical, sales, and clerical occupations, away from blue-collar jobs.

As Tables 1 and 2 indicate, these shifts have been tilted toward women and minority workers. During the 1970–1984 period, nearly two-thirds of the new jobs were filled by members of these groups. By late 1984, white males, for the first time, no longer constituted the majority of the labor force: their share of the employed had dropped from nearly 55 percent in 1970 to 49.5 percent by late 1984.

THE EARLY YEARS OF EEO: OPENING INTERNAL LABOR MARKETS TO WOMEN AND MINORITY WORKERS

The aforementioned statistics mean little until one analyzes who gets hired, for which jobs, and through which mechanisms. Looking back at the record of the postwar period, it is surprising to see the extent to which employers used to rely on internal labor market structures to train workers and staff the ranks of their organization, and how rapidly this practice began changing in the early 1970s (Edwards, 1979; Osterman, 1982a, 1982b; Noyelle, 1986). It is important to stress that this earlier reliance on "internal labor markets" was extensive not only among the manufacturing giants that typified the era—the IBMs and the GMs—but also among many medium-sized firms, including those in the service sectors (Appelbaum, 1984; Noyelle, 1986). Thus, the recent loosening of the reliance on internal labor markets cannot solely be ascribed to the overall industry shift to the services, but must be seen as part of a total labor market transformation affecting *both* manufacturing *and* service industries.

In the insurance industry, for example, most workers entered firms straight out of high school, at the very bottom of the organization as messengers or file clerks. Through on-the-job training and seniority, they would move up the ranks. For example, the most successful would move gradually from an entry-level clerical into a professional position, from, say, messenger to statistical clerk, claims examiner, or policy rater and later to assistant underwriter or underwriter (Appelbaum, 1984; Noyelle, 1986). In the department store industry, workers would enter as stockroom clerks and would move into sales positions (possibly to a commissioned sales position in a high-ticket department such as furniture, household, appliances, etc.), or even to department manager, assistant buyer, and buyer positions (Noyelle, 1986).

There were important differences among industries and firms, however. In the construction sector, for example, mobility ladders were industry and craft based rather than firm based, with trade unions often playing a central role in operating the mobility system (Gallo, 1983). In addition, most small firms lacked both the resources and the range of employment opportunities necessary to operate internal labor markets and relied extensively on the open labor market. More important, perhaps, sex and race stereotyping was often used to create sex- or race-labeled occupations. In turn, these were used to restrict mobility opportunities available through internal labor markets to white males, by channeling women and minority workers into dead-end jobs. A good deal of the mid-1970s literature on internal labor markets sought to account for many of these differences and the way they contributed to discrimination among different groups of workers.

Consistent with the dynamics of labor markets prevailing at the time, a principal focus of EEO policy, when first formulated, was to open internal labor markets through both hiring quotas and internal quotas to those who, for reasons of race or sex, had been left out or left behind. Much attention was focused on industries that were then the pillars of the economy: manufacturing and the public sector. The efforts of the federal government to accelerate the promotion of minorities and women within its own agencies, as well as within the private sector, through major consent decrees such as those secured in 1973 between AT&T and the Equal Employment Opportunity Commission (Northrup and Larson, 1979), and in 1974 between the Commission and the steel industry (Ichnowski, 1983), typified that period of EEO enforcement.

Although these decrees led to substantial gains during the 1970s, in retrospect, we can see that these efforts were focused on industries and work settings that were declining in economic importance. We are left with only limited clues as to how to approach and solve labor market discrimination in today's economy. Over the past decade, the role of internal labor markets has weakened dramatically across a broad range of industries. The reasons for this declining role are numerous and diverse, but it is evident that firms are increasingly externalizing the cost and responsibility for the training process, are relying more and more on external labor markets for new workers, and are putting in place new arrangements affecting whom they hire and promote (Noyelle, 1986). Two primary forces are responsible for this new dynamic: the postwar expansion of schooling and higher education and the new wave of technological change.

THE POSTWAR EXPANSION OF SCHOOLING AND HIGHER EDUCATION AND ITS IMPACT ON HIRING REQUIREMENTS AND MOBILITY LADDERS

The first factor behind the transformation in hiring and mobility opportunities—the postwar expansion of schooling and higher education—albeit slow in the making, is nevertheless irreversible. The transformation has been largely a case of supply changes leading to demand changes. By changing the makeup of the labor supply, the expansion of the educational system put pressure on all firms to adjust their hiring procedures to the new availabilities of a labor supply increasingly differentiated by grades and types of education. For example, whereas only slightly more than 10 percent of those between age 25 and 29 had received 4 or more years of college education in 1960, by 1980 their share had risen to nearly 25 percent.

The expansion of formal education led to a major shift to outside hiring, first felt most strongly at the level of professional and managerial personnel—the so-called "exempt workers." This trend significantly weakened some traditional internal ladders, especially those designed to move the ablest workers from nonexempt positions into supervisory and middle managerial positions. No longer could a sales clerk expect to become a buyer for a major retail organization, or a messenger expect to become an insurance executive by simply moving through the ranks. Rather, most companies began recruiting exempt workers directly from college (Noyelle, 1986). In that respect, the 1970s represent a turning point as the cumulative effect of several decades of expansion of the educational systems and the coming of age of the baby boom were felt massively on the supply side of the labor market.

The Impact of the New Technology on Skill Requirements and the Acceleration of Changes in Hiring and Mobility Opportunities

Whereas earlier changes in hiring and mobility opportunities had been mostly supply driven, recent changes have been largely demand driven. They are the result of the introduction of the new computer-communications technology and its impact on skills. Broadly speaking, the new technology has acted to reinforce the tendency toward a weakening of internal ladders. Two preliminary observations are warranted to support this point.

First, vast areas of work are being transformed and reorganized around the processing of information through interaction with computerized systems. Until recently, the areas most directly affected had tended to be primarily in the middle range of occupations, from relatively low-level clerical positions or even blue-collar operative positions, all the way up to low- or middle-level professional workers (Hirschhorn, 1984; Bertrand and Noyelle, 1984; Appelbaum, 1984). Today, however, higher-level technical, professional, and/or managerial work are also being unaffected. Only in the case of the lowest-level occupations—primarily laborers, service workers, and low-level sales and clerical classifications—has the new technology, thus far, had little or no direct impact on work and skills. It may be relevant to note here that these low-skilled occupations, including sales clerks, building janitors, guards, orderlies, cooks, and others have been among the fastest-growing areas of employment and that mobility ladders are conspicuously absent in these occupations (Bureau of Labor Statistics, 1984).

Second, the new technology does not, as many initially believed, lead ineluctably to downskilling but rather to varying degrees of upskilling. This generalization does not preclude occasional downskilling or occasional lags between current and potential uses of technology by firms. Upskilling comes about for three principal reasons: first, because the most efficient use of the new technology often seems to lead to a reintegration of tasks previously parcelled out among different workers; second, because, as intelligent systems take over "processing functions," workers are left with "diagnosis" and "problem-solving" functions; and third, because the shift to "problem-solving" functions at lower levels of the organization calls for a simultaneous decentralization in decision-making power (Adler, 1984; Hirschhorn, 1984; Rajan, 1984; and others reviewed in Bertrand and Noyelle, 1984).

As the new technology changes skill requirements for many jobs, it also leads to the homogenization of skills across a wide range of industries, encouraging the externalization of training for many middle-level workers. This means that the jobs of bank clerks processing letters of credit or fund transfers on a computerized system, of insurance examiners processing claims, of airline agents processing reservations and ticketing, or even of telephone switchmen routing and managing traffic flows through switches are becoming not only more demanding in terms of skills, but also increasingly similar in terms of skills required (Appelbaum, 1984; Noyelle, 1984). Not surprisingly, a major focus of the current "training debate" about the need for more sophisticated training institutions concerns this middle range of occupations, because these are occupations, that, in their older configurations, had rarely been brought within the purview of formalized training processes. These were jobs for which skill training was traditionally acquired on the job through internal labor market mechanisms. Hirschhorn (1984) refers to this transformation as the process of "para-professionalization." Thus, the institutions most directly concerned with the new demand for training are clearly not simply high schools but, increasingly, vocational-educational institutions, community colleges and even 4-year colleges.

Technological Change and Increasing Institutional and Geographical Mobility

Since formal education and training have become increasingly important in determining a worker's position in the labor market, there is a presumption that better-prepared workers should have an edge particularly in terms of improving their earnings. Thus far, this has not necessarily been the case. The tendency toward universalization/homogenization of skills has also weakened the degree to which workers are sheltered from competition as they once were when skills were more specific to the output of the industry or firm. Further, this has been aggravated by a context of weakening unionization.

In addition, the new technology makes it increasingly feasible and cost efficient to separate geographically so-called back-office functions (dominated by clerical and service worker occupations) from "front-office" functions (dominated by technical, sales, professional, or managerial occupations). Two consequences follow. First, the separation contributes to breaking the institutional job linkages that used to exist when entire departments, from the bottom up, were located in the same physical location. Second, the increasing mobility of back-office establishments puts workers on the defensive because the rise in two-wage-earner households is hindering geographic mobility for many.

THE SHIFTING NATURE OF DISCRIMINATION

The broad changes that have taken place on the demand side of the labor market and the gains made by certain groups of workers in selected occupations and industries as a result of early EEO efforts have both acted to shift the nature of discrimination.

Two examples will serve to illustrate some aspects of the shift: (1) back-office clerical employment and (2) sales employment in the retailing sector. In the first example, technology is brought in to reform, reorganize, and rationalize work involving large concentrations of workers. As suggested above, the introduction of technology has led to some degree of upskilling and associated changes in the demand for labor. In the second case, the direct impact of technology on sales and related occupations is relatively modest. Technology figures in mostly indirectly in that it permits great improvements in the control and coordination of the organization itself (in buying, inventory control, and accounting). To the extent that changes in labor demand can be observed, these are unlikely to be associated directly with technology.

These two examples are instructive because they cover work situations in which large numbers of women and minority workers have traditionally found and continue to find employment.

THE REORGANIZATION OF BACK-OFFICE EMPLOYMENT

This example relates to the reorganization of clerical work typical of the back offices of banks, insurance companies, telephone and other utilities, and other organizations with large processing facilities. In the 1960s and early 1970s, these firms hired large numbers of youth as messengers and file clerks directly out of high school to staff entry-level clerical positions. Later, many of these young workers would be trained in-house and would move up the ladder as they matured.

As Appelbaum (1984) has noted, the long-standing tendency in back offices was to discriminate between white men and women and minority workers by operating a two-track system. One track, reserved mostly for white men, lead those workers into professional or managerial employment; the other, used primarily for women and minority workers, would channel most of them into dead-end positions. By forcing companies to do away with these practices, EEO, for a time at least, opened new avenues of opportunities to women and minority workers. Yet, no sooner had these avenues been opened than their access was considerably curtailed as the result of the tendency toward the weakening of internal labor markets, and in particular the delinking of nonexempt from exempt jobs. This did not completely shut out access for women and minorities to many managerial and professional positions; but, typically, it forced them to enter through another route, that of higher education. At the same time, changes were also occurring at the traditional entry level, with impacts on both adult workers and youth.

For many years companies with large back-office employment were known for their close links to the local high schools. During the 1970s, however, this situation changed dramatically as a result of the new technology. As one executive of a large New York insurance firm reported in a recent interview: "Up until the early 1970s, we hired nearly 2,000 kids every summer. Today, we hire at most 100 kids. Nowadays, most entry takes place at a higher level— typically community college or equivalent—straight into claim examiner positions. Most of the filing and messenger functions have been eliminated through computerization."

In a recent study of the youth labor market in New York City, Bailey and Waldinger (1984) found that of the nearly 40,000 jobs lost by youth in New York City during the last decade (1970–1980), nearly half could be attributed to the sheer contraction of the city's economy. The other half—that is nearly 20,000 jobs—could be attributed to the elimination of filing clerks, messengers, and similar positions in local public utilities (telephone, gas, and electric), banks, and insurance firms. The industry shift data for youth presented above corroborate this finding for the nation as a whole. Beyond the magnitude of the numbers involved, these losses implied that by the late 1970s a major group of workers—youth with high school or equivalent diplomas—no longer had available to them entry opportunities with built-in promotion ladders. They had largely been relegated to entering retail and consumer services, with far more limited opportunities for upward mobility.

The trend just discussed, which was set in motion in the early 1970s when large back-office organizations began investing in centralized EDP, is being followed by yet another trend growing out of the deployment of distributed data processing in the late 1970s and early 1980s. The new generation of computer-communications technology permits geographic separation of back offices from front offices of the firm and permits the parent organization to seek new locations away from the central districts of very large cities such as New York, Los Angeles, Chicago, Philadelphia, and other places where back-office jobs have traditionally been located. The greatest impact of this new trend appears to fall on minority women, who had made great gains in entering clerical ranks during the 1970s but who may now be left behind in the inner cities where they reside, while back-office jobs are being moved elsewhere (Noyelle, 1986, especially Ch. 5).

While some groups are losing, others are clearly gaining from this restructuring/relocation of back-office work. In general, employers relocate their facilities not only in areas where operating costs (rent, utilities) and labor costs are lower, but also often in areas where they can find an infrastructure of community colleges (or equivalent) that will help them prepare and train employees.

Typically, such moves bring firms to the suburbs where they seek large pools of middle-aged, married, usually white women. In some cases, they bring employers to communities with large military installations where they hire both married wives of enlisted men and retired military clerks willing to put in a few more years of work. The advantage of hiring from these groups is that these are workers who typically demand little by way of mobility opportunities, something that most employers can no longer offer because of delinking between back-office clerical positions and higher-level jobs.

THE TRANSFORMATION OF RETAIL EMPLOYMENT

Retail is one sector where employment transformations appear to be less directly linked to recent or past technological changes. This does not mean, however, that the new technology has not found its way into this sector, but that its impact has been more diffuse and indirect.

The postwar period witnessed the rapid growth and diffusion of large chain organizations. Up until the 1940s, organizations such as Sears or A&P were exceptions. The postwar period saw a rapid growth of multiunit organizations in foods, dry goods, hardware, gasoline, and many other areas, penetrating markets traditionally dominated by "mom-and-pop" businesses. The resulting shift in the scale of operations made possible substantial rationalization, with accompanying major productivity gains in buying, inventory control, and accounting, facilitating the further growth of large sales organizations with relatively thin administrative staffs. These changes also made it easier for large retail organizations to follow their customers into the suburbs, where they were able to tap into underutilized pools of suburban married women often eager to work.

Simultaneously, the cumulative effect of changes in work habits and spending patterns (e.g., two-worker families) led retail organizations to stay open for more hours during the week and to make more use of part-time employees. In place of the basic 9-to-5, 40-hour work week, many retail organizations, today, are open 65 hours a week (10 hours on weekdays; 7.5 hours on Saturday and Sunday). In some of the largest metropolitan areas, supermarkets compete on a 24-hour, 7 days-a-week basis. The impact of these changes on employment patterns has been dramatic: the reliance on part-time employees has skyrocketed. In department stores, the breakdown between full-time and part-time employment shifted from 65 percent full time/35 percent part time in the mid-1960s to the reverse ratio nowadays as stores added half-time and short-hour shifts (Noyelle, 1986).

Much of the employment expansion in retail was first based on the hiring of women—first white women, later minority women. Clearly, the expansion of part-time jobs was aimed in part at facilitating the employment of married women, many of whom preferred not to put in a full work week. While large retail organizations were leaders in uncovering those underutilized pools of women, the discovery did not go unnoticed for long in other industries. As noted previously, large clerical organizations are now actively seeking such employable women by relocating back-office facilities in the suburban rings of large cities. In the process, these organizations are creating new pressures on the adult women labor market. As a result, many retail organizations are now seeking to recruit more actively from among high school youth, many of whom are now available, because, short of educational credentials higher than a high school diploma, they are blocked from competing for more desirable jobs.

POLICY IMPLICATIONS

For more than 20 years now, this nation has had a policy of equal employment opportunity enacted into law, administered by a specialized federal agency, and enforced through the courts.

Because EEO was shaped under specific historical circumstances, namely, as an outgrowth of the civil rights and, later, women's movements, and because it was shaped in response to the reality of the labor markets of the 1960s and early 1970s, the principal emphasis of early EEO policy was to stress the elimination of sex-based or race-based discrimination in the workplace. Workplace discrimination, at the time, was primarily rooted in blatant sex or race job stereotyping, perpetuated not simply through cultural biases but quite concretely by excluding women and minority workers from entering white men's jobs and from accessing opportunity ladders available to white men. In a period when the large majority of workers was rarely educated beyond high school, formal education beyond the acquisition of basic skills was seen as playing a relatively minor role in determining what happened to workers once they entered the labor market. Still, considerable effort was also placed on desegregating schools to increase the likelihood that minority youth would acquire basic skills and be able to enter the labor market on the same terms as white youths.

To assert that sex or race discrimination in the workplace has been eliminated and no longer needs the nation's attention would be ridiculous and wrong. But it would be equally wrong to write off the past 20 years of EEO enforcement and assert that nothing has changed.

This paper suggests that we need (1) a stronger assessment of the changes that have occurred in the labor market as a result of earlier EEO efforts, the increasing importance of education, technological change, and the structural shift from manufacturing to services; (2) a stronger assessment of the impact of these changes and their role in bringing to the fore factors of discrimination other than sex or race, especially age and socioeconomic status; and (3) a stronger assessment of the way in which these new factors of discrimination may be used either independently or in connection with sexual or racial characteristics to bring about different patterns of discrimination.

Formal education is clearly becoming a major determinant of a worker's long-term position in the labor market. This is not simply a case of growing credentialism for the sake of erecting new barriers, although the tendency may also be at work. While professions have traditionally used formal accreditation or licensing based on educational degrees as a way to keep entry restricted, the rising importance of education is also a reflection of a growing reliance on externalization of training. This tendency has been in the making for several decades, especially among the upper echelons of the occupational structure. Still, the new technology is intensifying the trend, by accelerating the formalization of training and education for workers employed in a broad range of middle-level occupations.

The increasing importance of education appears to be creating both new opportunities and potential problems for groups of workers that have traditionally been the target of discrimination. On the one hand, the process of externalization of training may make it increasingly difficult for employers to close off access to skill acquisition as a way to discriminate against women and minority workers. The substantial progress of women over the past two decades in professional occupations attests to this. On the other hand, the externalization of training is unlikely to be problem-free. For example, the current structure of our higher educational system—characterized by considerable disjunction among various levels (2-year colleges, 4-year colleges, graduate schools) and often lacking flexibility—makes it difficult to find workable continuing-education solutions that are increasingly necessary in order to progress upward in the labor market during one's work life. In addition, to the extent that employers may partly control access to higher education, for example, by financing retraining programs at the community college level or tuition reimbursement programs at 4-year colleges, there may be room for discrimination to creep back in.

In general, these developments point to the increasing importance of the issue of who gets access to preferred education and why. In a society that is still far from having an equitable educational system in place, one's family socioeconomic status may largely determine one's future position in the labor market. It has been primarily middle-class women, mostly although not exclusively white, who, over the past two decades, have been most successful in advancing to professional positions through the higher educational route. Short of major changes, this trend may accelerate.

In concluding, three points must be emphasized. First, I believe that EEO's traditional emphasis on eliminating cultural biases and institutional arrangements that perpetuate discrimination in the workplace must be maintained. But I also believe that EEO policy must begin to reach outside the employing institution to the educational process in order, ultimately, to strengthen enforcement in the workplace. As noted at the outset, this may require new legislation to bring about a more coordinated enforcement effort in the two areas.

Second, the linkage between work achievement, education, and socioeconomic background may have major implications for women and minority groups that have traditionally used "sex" or "race" as a lever in the workplace. Increasingly, sex or racial groups may become differentiated along socioeconomic class lines, so that recourse to "sex" or "race" as rallying points in the workplace may lose some strength.

Finally, as the aggregate data indicate, we may need to put in place special efforts to assist minority men who appear to be failing in entering many of the white-collar occupations in the service sector where much of the future lies. The unrelenting high unemployment among young minority workers must be a matter of special concern. We must find ways to intervene and turn this trend around.

REFERENCES

Adler, P.
  1984 Rethinking the Skill Requirements of New Technologies. Working Paper HBS 84-27, Harvard Business School, Division of Research, Cambridge, Mass.
Appelbaum, E.
  1984 The Impact of Technology on Skill Requirements and Occupational Structure in the Insurance Industry, 1960–1990. Working Paper. Temple University, Department of Economics, Philadelphia. April.
Bailey, T., and R. Waldinger
  1984 A skill mismatch in New York labor market? *New York Affairs* (Fall):3–18.
Bertrand, O., and T.J. Noyelle
  1984 Development and Utilization of Human Resources in the Context of Technological Change and Industrial Restructuring: The Case of White Collar Workers. Expert Report, Organization for Economic Cooperation and Development, Center for Educational Research and Innovation, Paris, OECD/CERI/CD(85/8).
Bureau of the Census
  1974 *Census of Population: 1970. Detailed Characteristics.* Report PD(1)D. Washington, D.C.: U.S. Department of Commerce.
  1984 *Census of Population: 1980. Detailed Characteristics.* Report PC80-1-D. Washington, D.C.: U.S. Department of Commerce.
Bureau of Labor Statistics
  Var. years *Employment and Earnings.* Washington, D.C.: U.S. Department of Labor.
  1984 *1995 Industry-Occupational Employment Outlook.* Washington, D.C.: U.S. Department of Labor.
Edwards, R.
  1979 *Contested Terrain.* New York: Basic Books.
Gallo, C.
  1983 The Construction Industry in New York City: Immigrants and Black Entrepreneurs. Working Paper. Conservation of Human Resources, Columbia University, New York.
Ginzberg, E., and G. Vojta
  1981 The service sector of the U.S. economy. *Scientific American* 244 (March):48–55.
  1985 *The Large Corporation at Risk.* New York: Basic Books.
Hirschhorn, L.
  1984 Information Technology and the Office Worker: A Developmental View. Working Paper. Management and Behavioral Center, University of Pennsylvania, Wharton School, Philadelphia.

Ichnowski, C.
  1983   Have angels done more? The steel industry consent decree. *Industrial and Labor Relations Review* 36(2):181–198.
Northrup, H.R., and J.A. Larson
  1979   *The Impact of the AT&T-EEO Consent Decree*, Vol. #20. Labor Relations and Public Policy Series, University of Pennsylvania, Wharton School, Industrial Research Unit, Philadelphia.
Noyelle, T.J.
  1984   Work in a World of High Technology: Employment Problems and Mobility Prospects for Disadvantaged Workers. Paper prepared for the Educational Resources Information Center, U.S. Department of Education and the University of Tennessee, Office for Research in High Technology Education, Knoxville.
  1986   *Beyond Industrial Dualism: Market and Job Segmentation in the New Economy.* Boulder, Colo.: Westview Press.
  1987   *Technological Change and Employment in the Financial Service Industries.* Conservation of Human Resources, Columbia University, New York.
Osterman, P.
  1982a   Internal Labor Markets in White Collar Firms. Working Papers #90. Boston University, Department of Economics.
  1982b   Employment structures within firms. *British Journal of Industrial Relations* 20(3):349–361.
Rajan, A.
  1984   *New Technology and Employment in Insurance, Banking and Building Societies: Recent Experience and Future Impact.* Gower and Aldershot, U.K.: Institute of Manpower.
Stanback, T.M., Jr., and T.J. Noyelle
  1982   *Cities in Transition.* Totowa, N.J.: Rowman and Allanheld.
Stanback, T.M., Jr., P.J. Bearse, T.J. Noyelle, and R. Karasek
  1981   *Services/The New Economy.* Totowa, N.J.: Rowman and Allanheld.
U.S. Equal Employment Opportunity Commission
  1966   *EEO-1 Report on Minorities and Women in Private Industry.* Washing-
  1978   ton, D.C.: U.S. Equal Employment Opportunity Commission.
  1981

Managing Technological Change: Responses of Government, Employers, and Trade Unions in Western Europe and Canada

FELICITY HENWOOD AND SALLY WYATT

NEW TECHNOLOGY IN THE
CURRENT ECONOMIC CLIMATE

Technological change has always been a major factor in the uneven development of industries and occupations. It is often suggested that the development of radical new technologies has provided the impetus for major changes in the pattern of economic development both within and between countries. The restructuring of industry that accompanies such technological innovation then leads to significant changes in the level and structure of employment and in the nature and organization of work. The ways in which these changes are managed differ between countries according to the part played by governments, employers, and workers' organizations. Furthermore, the role of each of these groups changes over time and is closely related to the overall economic climate—in particular, the level of unemployment.

In the 30 years after World War II, many Western industrialized countries experienced faster technological change than during any period since the Industrial Revolution, and yet these changes were largely managed within a cooperative environment, by mutual agreement between unions and managers. The relative lack of worker resistance to technological change during this period is, of course, directly related to the fact that this was also a period of economic growth and prosperity in most western European countries. By the mid-1970s, however, economic recession and rising unemployment had led to the reemergence of debates about the relationship between technological change and unemployment. It has been during this last decade or so that there has been, in most of these countries, a serious challenge to the established framework for managing technological change.

Clearly, on one level, employers can be seen as having the prerogative in many of the decisions surrounding technological change. It is they who make investment decisions and they who have the final right to hire and fire their employees. The relationship between labor and capital in market-oriented economics has been described as a "compulsory symbiosis in which the employers are in a fundamentally favorable position" (Markmann, 1985:141). There are many examples, however, of government intervention and worker participation in technological decision making that have resulted in more favorable outcomes for employees. Through government initiative in establishing more progressive frameworks for labor-management negotiations around technological change, many countries are now realizing the benefits of involving workers in such negotiations. In the next section, we discuss and compare the parameters of government, employer, and trade union intervention in technological decision making in several western European countries and Canada. This discussion forms the backdrop for the discussion in the following sections, which examines, in some detail, the part played by each of these groups in resolving conflicts over specific issues related to the introduction of new technologies, such as job design, changing locations and hours of work, and education and training.

The overall aim of this paper is to examine these issues with specific references to women and women's employment. We shall pay particular attention to the different experiences of women and men. It is important to examine women and men as distinct groups when analyzing the relationship between new technology and paid work and, therefore, when developing policies aimed at alleviating the problems that are encountered when new technology is introduced into the workplace. Reasons include the following: First, the labor markets in the countries under consideration are characterized by a high degree of occupational segregation in which women are concentrated primarily at the lower levels in a few occupations. Not only does this help to explain women's lower earnings on average and their relative powerlessness, it also makes women more (or less) vulnerable to changes in technology. Second, women's participation and experience in paid work will continue to be different from men's as long as women continue to bear major responsibility for household work and child care. (Table 1 presents indicators of women's position in the labor market for selected industrialized countries.) Government legislation against sex discrimination and in favor of equal pay exists in most Western industrialized countries; it is generally recognized, however, that these measures have not yet achieved equal opportunity in the workplace nor have they begun to address women's and men's unequal family roles.

THE MANAGEMENT OF TECHNOLOGICAL CHANGE

The management of technological change takes different forms in different countries according to the political organization, industrial relations, and cultural environments of the different countries (Evans, 1983:154). However, it is possible to point to three main methods of management which, to a greater or lesser extent, can be found in most western European countries. Jostein Fjalestad of the Norwegian Computer Centre has described these methods as (1) regulation—based on legislation, standards, and rules; (2) negotiations—resulting in technology agreements; and (3) local developments—which ensure that agreements are relevant to particular workplaces (Fjalestad, 1981). Table 2 summarizes the variety of procedures adopted in different European countries.

Evans (1983:156) has argued that regulation, negotiation, and local developments should be seen as complementary approaches to the effective management of technological change:

> Laws and standards define minimum requirements. National, sectoral and corporate technology agreements establish the procedures and broad actions to be followed and the mechanisms to resolve conflicts. They set out the framework to be used in negotiating acceptable arrangements at local levels. Without genuine local agreement, however, the other methods will fail to achieve their aims.

We shall discuss briefly the relative importance of each of these methods for the management of technological change in several

TABLE 1 Selected Indicators of Women's Position in the Labor Market for Selected Countries, 1982

Indicator	Belgium	Denmark	Federal Republic of Germany	France	Sweden	United Kingdom	Canada	United States
Women as percent of economically active population	30.7[a]	45.7[b]	33.9	33.5	46.3	35.9	41.2	40.3
Percent of women who are economically active	48.7[b]	72.0[b]	50.1[b]	52.5[b]	70.0[c]	57.3[b]	52.8[b]	
Women as percent of total employees in employment	36.9	44.8[b]	38.6	38.8	46.1	41.1	41.2	43.5
Unemployment rate								
Total	13.8	9.8	7.5	8.5	3.1	12.1	11.0	9.7
Women	20.0	10.4	8.6	10.8	3.4	7.8	10.8	9.4
Women's wages in non-agricultural activities as percent of men's	73.6	83.9	72.7	88.6		69.1	72.0[a]	

Percent of women in employment who work part time (less than 30 hours per week)	29.0[a]	42.0[a]	24.0[a]	20.0[a]	51.5[c]	46.0[a]	24.0[b]
Usual contractually agreed hours of work of industrial workers (weekly)	37.5-40	40.0	40.0	39.0		37.5-40.0	
Union members as percent of all workers	72.5	75.5	42.0	25.0		52.5	

[a] Data for 1980.
[b] Data for 1981.
[c] Data for 1983.

SOURCES: Compiled by the authors from data in ILO (1983), Berner (1984), Equal Opportunities Commission (1984), David-McNeil (1984), Department of Employment (UK) (1984), Boulet (1984), Liisa Rantalaiho (personal communication, 1985), Johannesson and Persson-Tanimura (1984), and Peitchinis (1984).

TABLE 2 Examples of Procedures for Regulation of Technological Change in Several European Countries (to 1983)

| Country | Laws and Regulations | Collective Agreements | | Company or Plant Level |
		National Agreements	Sectoral Level	
West Germany	Works Constitution Act 1972 Works Safety Act 1973 plus VDT regulations 1981	None	Job protection agreements in metal working, textiles, footwear, leather, paper processing, printing	Over 100 agreements concluded
U.K.	Health and Safety at Work Act 1985	None	Parts of public sector	Over 200 agreements concluded
Norway	Working Environment Act 1977, plus VDT Regulations, 1982	1975 Employer/Union Agreement on computer-based systems	Banking	Most of industry and services covered by local agreements

Sweden	Working Environment Act of 1978, plus VDT Regulations 1981 Codetermination Act 1977	1976 Employer/Union Work Environment Agreement	Technology agreement in printing. Co-determination agreements in public government and private industry	Use of legislative rights
Various	Health and Safety Laws (France, Italy, and elsewhere) Codetermination laws (e.g., in Austria) Statute of Workers Rights 1970 (Italy)	1981 agreement for private sector in Denmark	Printing sector in Netherlands, Belgium, Austria, and Greece; metal working in Italy	In USA, 1979 Ford agreement on procedures for introducing technology. General Motors quality of working life programme.
				In Japan, company unions consensus in return for job security and income sector.

SOURCE: Evans (1983:155). Reprinted with permission from Francis Pinter Publishers.

European countries, in some cases comparing European experiences with those of the United States and Canada.

THE ROLE OF GOVERNMENTS

Most western European governments take the view that employment will be generated only if and when the "new technology" industries are established. Thus, a major part of government activity in the new technology area is concerned with the promotion of research and development (R&D) in the fields of microelectronics, telecommunications, and computers and in the strengthening of links between government, research establishments, and industry. There are important differences between countries regarding the extent and nature of government intervention in such programs. For example, the French government, unlike the United Kingdom and West German governments, believes that it is legitimate and necessary for politicians to control industry overtly, not only to strengthen it in a general way. Over the last few years, several broad, new programs were launched: for example, the 3-year program for the promotion of "productique" in France, the Technological Development Program in Denmark, and the Alvey program in the United Kingdom (Commission of the European Communities, 1984b). In early 1984, a European Economic Community (EEC) initiative—the European Strategic Program for Research on Information Technologies (ESPRIT)—was given the go-ahead. Like the national programs, the main purpose of the EEC program is to promote cooperation among enterprises, research centers, and universities through public subsidies, with a view to creating or consolidating European industrial potential in new technology fields such as advanced microelectronics, software technologies, advanced information processing, office automation, and computer-integrated manufacture.

The above examples of government initiatives to promote new technologies illustrate the separation that is so often made by governments between the growth of new technology industries and the employment problems that such growth may cause. In many cases, the priority for governments is the development of the new technologies. The "effects" of the new technology, such as job displacement and changing skill requirements, are generally dealt with "after the fact" by separate employment and/or training policies, usually administered by various government departments.

Governments in some countries, however, are beginning to take a more interventionist role in attempting to prevent, rather than simply alleviate, the most adverse effects of new technologies.

Of course, the relationship between technology and the demand for workers is complex. The industries based on the new technologies, once established, may or may not generate many jobs. And job displacement and changing skill requirements can occur for reasons unrelated to technological change. Uneven economic growth, international competition, and shifts in demand generate employment change as well. Moreover, changes in work organization, such as subdividing or integrating jobs, occur more or less continuously, often without the facilitating influence of specific innovations. Nevertheless, current technological developments are widely recognized as having enormous potential for both productivity improvement and work reorganization, with substantial, if not totally known, effects on workers. And, as noted above, these rapid technical developments have also occurred during a period of economic difficulty. Interventions by government aimed at shaping technological change, though important, necessarily do not address all factors affecting employment.

Legislation to set minimum standards in technological decision making is used in several countries in two key areas: health and safety and "co-determination." The 1977 Norwegian Work Environment Act is a good example of government intervention to ensure that the health and safety of employees is maintained with the introduction of new technologies. Among its provisions (quoted in Deutsch, 1986:37) are the following: "Technology, organization of the work, working hours and way systems shall be set up so that the employees are not exposed to undesirable physical or mental strain and so that their possibilities of displaying caution and observing safety measures are not impaired." The Act also extends to encouraging workers' personal and professional development, avoiding undiversified and repetitive work, and involving employees and their elected representatives in planning work and work changes. Another example of legislation being used to set minimum standards is the 1976 Swedish Act of Co-determination. Employers are required by it to inform trade unions about plans for future developments and to initiate discussions and negotiations on new technology before any changes take place or any final decisions are made on the nature of the system (Evans, 1983:157). West Germany also has a form of co-determination legislation.

Under this law, any plant or company of more than five employees must have a works council composed solely of representatives of employees. Works councils have found it difficult, however, to use information disclosed to them because they are outside the mainstream of collective bargaining, which takes place between employers' associations and union confederations (Evans, 1983:164).

THE ROLE OF EMPLOYERS AND TRADE UNIONS

The role of government in influencing the pattern of introduction of new technology in any particular workplace is limited. The most important negotiations about technological change at this level take place between the employers or management and the workers, often, although not always, via the local trade union branch. During the 1970s, a fairly coherent and comprehensive approach toward negotiating about technology began to emerge in several western European countries. The "new technology agreements" or "technology agreements" had the effect of placing on the agenda of collective bargaining "a range of topics which affect all aspects of technological and organizational change" (Evans, 1983:158). This development has been an important one that has marked a shift, on the part of organized labor, from what might be seen as a reactive strategy toward new technology, to a more proactive one.

The 1975 agreement between national management organizations and unions in Norway can be seen as the archetypal technology agreement that influenced discussions and actions around the world. Evans (1983:158) has described the principle stated in that agreement as one where "the social effects of new technology should be regarded with equal importance to economic and technical considerations." Both procedural and substantive elements are found in technology agreements. The former is concerned with the methods of introducing the new technology and the latter with the operational conditions once the technology is implemented. A summary of the main clauses to be found in most technology agreements can be found in Table 3.

In spite of a great deal of discussion among organized workers concerned with broad issues such as the future of work and the ways in which different groups of workers are affected by the introduction of new technology, technology agreements on the whole

TABLE 3 Summary of Main Clauses Found in Technology Agreements

---

Procedural provisions in technology agreements

    A commitment by all parties to encourage the introduction of new technology and the successful management of change.

    The provision by management of full and timely information, in clear and jargon-free language, about plans for technological change. To be useful, the information must be provided at an early stage, before decisions are implemented. The agreement should be explicit about the likely effects of change and the options available.

    The establishment of joint management/union bodies to discuss, monitor, and negotiate change at corporate and local levels.

    The opportunity for the election and training of "technology representatives" or "data stewards" with responsibility for monitoring the introduction of new technology on behalf of staff, and who keep in close touch with grassroots experience and opinion.

    The arrangements by which unions can have access to outside expertise, just as management hires external consultants.

    The establishment of a procedure for monitoring and regulating the collection and use of personal data on individuals working in the organization.

    A status quo clause which gives the unions a right to veto changes unless they have been consulted and an agreement reached.

Substantive issues on technology agreements

    Job security following the introduction of new technology. This could aim to maintain the same number of job posts (total volume of employment) or, if some reduction in employment is unavoidable, to offer guarantees of no compulsory redundancy.

    The provision of adequate retraining opportunities to staff whose jobs are changed or eliminated by new technology and the establishment of guidelines on the maintenance of status and pay in the new job.

    Methods for sharing the benefits of new technology with employees through, for example, improved pay, shorter working hours, and a better working environment.

    For older staff, the offer of adequate schemes for voluntary early retirement.

    Monitoring of the impact of new technology on the workplace in terms of issues such as stress, alienation, reduced social contact, or increased central control and supervision.

    Health and safety regulations on aspects of working with computers, based on independent guidelines encompassing physical, software, and psychological ergonomics factors.

    Protection of the confidentiality of personal information collected about employees and guaranteeing that such information will be limited to activities of direct relevance to work at the organization. Many countries have Data Protection Legislation to provide the basic guidelines.

SOURCE: Evans (1983:162).

have been primarily concerned with protection of existing jobs and conditions of work for existing employees. This narrow focus has led to the making of agreements that have implicitly discriminated against women. "No redundancy" (layoff) clauses, for example, have protected existing employees but have done nothing to protect jobs for which there is a high turnover, as is the case for many women's jobs. In many instances, employers have relied on these high turnover groups to provide "natural wastage" (attrition). Clearly, unions are working under enormous constraints when negotiating around new technology, with technology agreements being seen by some employers as "interfering with the manager's right to manage." However, unions have an obligation to represent the interests of all their members fairly; recognition of existing differences and a commitment to overcoming existing inequalities are necessary first steps.

Insofar as trade unions are an important vehicle through which workers can influence the shape of technological change, women's participation in the unions is important. Again, there are significant differences between countries in this respect (see Table 1). In relation to negotiations around new technology, women can be seen as both disadvantaged and well placed to negotiate in these areas. In the following discussions of specific issues that arise in negotiating around technological change, we discuss how, while women may be disadvantaged in terms of their position in the labor market and their low levels of unionization relative to men, they have, by virtue of their particular experiences of work, both paid and unpaid, some very important contributions to add to these negotiations. We argue that this is particularly the case in relation to quality of work issues: job design, changing location and changing hours of work, and education and training.

POLICY ISSUES

JOB DESIGN

— Many studies of women's work and new technology have focused on changes in office work, where women workers predominate, and it is with this area of work that we shall be most concerned in the following sections. Although research has highlighted a host of changes associated with the introduction of new office technologies, such as changes in job content, skills required, increasing specialization, and/or routinization of jobs for secretaries and clerical workers, most successful negotiation has tended to focus on the narrower, although perhaps more tangible, question of ergonomics. Successful negotiation about the ergonomic aspects of video display terminals (VDTs) and about the length of time people can be required to work on them without a break has occurred in most European countries. As many commentators have pointed out, however, increased stress and other psychological problems associated with the use of VDTs are not entirely due either to the physical arrangement of the workstation or to the time spent on the machines.

A comprehensive German study which examined the effects of working with VDTs points out that the "stress" associated with the use of VDTs is related to the nature of the job itself (Cakir et al., 1978). The study found significant differences in levels of stress experienced by workers depending on whether they were using the VDTs as a tool in their job or whether their job was to operate a VDT. Thus, VDT operators were found to have much higher stress levels than programmers and publishing editors. Clearly, it is not possible to be absolutely certain as to the reasons for the higher levels of stress found among VDT operators, but the study's finding of a high correlation between the time spent working at the screen and the feeling that all the details of the work were too rigidly defined suggests that broader aspects of the job than time spent on VDTs must be taken into consideration.

Some interesting work done at the Norwegian Computing Centre on visual display terminals and the working environment makes a similar point (Thoresen, 1983:85). This research illustrates that tackling ergonomics alone will not necessarily improve the job overall because so many additional factors affect the quality of work. Thoresen describes how, in attempting to overcome the physical and psychological problems associated with the use of VDTs, attention has generally been focused on the physical arrangement of the workstation—the desk, chair, lighting, display unit, and keyboard. She points out, however, that "one soon discovers that such measures only have limited effects" (Thoresen, 1983:85) and that other aspects of work, not associated with the physical arrangement of the workplace, must be considered. Following the concept of work adopted in the Norwegian Work Environment Act of 1977, Thoresen stresses the opportunities for professional and personal learning and development that a job can provide.

Bjorn-Anderson (1983), in his study of the changing roles of secretaries and clerks following the introduction of new technology, identified four main factors central to the design of jobs. These are job content, work autonomy and control, ergonomics, and psychological aspects. In his research he found that new technology, as currently used, tends to lead to overspecialization, which in turn leads, especially at the lower levels of the office hierarchy, to the creation of boring jobs with limited scope for learning and initiative, and that overcontrol by the computer has led to loss of autonomy for individual workers. However, he found that this need not be the case. He argues that, provided the computer system has been designed with enough flexibility, most job functions in the office can be enlarged to encompass a variety of activities and skills.

As noted above, employers in most European countries are moving toward the recognition of the importance of worker participation. In many cases, employer support for such participation has been won by persuading them that dissatisfaction among workers will, in the end, result in less-efficient workplaces. Bjorn-Anderson (1983) addresses employers when he argues that the most effective and acceptable way of overcoming any staff resistance to new technology is to allow staff to take an active part in designing their own work environment. Obviously, the extent to which employees are able to exert influence depends on numerous factors, including access to the relevant information at the right time, the level of organization among those affected, and the support they receive from other workers, especially those seen by management as essential workers. In many cases, where women's jobs at the lower end of the job hierarchy are particularly affected, this may mean relying on the support of the more secure, often male, workers. Conflicts of interest between workers at different levels of the occupational hierarchy will have to be faced and to some extent overcome if workers are to be effective in influencing decision making.

Numerous examples of successful negotiations around job design have resulted in maintenance or even improvement of the quality of work after the introduction of new technologies. The most successful have been those that have been concerned with more than ergonomic issues and have looked at job design in the broader sense discussed here. Some good examples include (1) the Copenhagen Business School in Denmark where some secretaries took on responsibilities for new tasks following the introduction of new technology, which reduced their previous work load and removed some of the decision making from their jobs (see Bjorn-Anderson, 1983:123); (2) the introduction of a new computer-based system into the Norwegian savings banks: as a result of union involvement and negotiation with the systems designers at the banking industry's research and development center, the workers were able to retain certain decision-making aspects of their jobs which most certainly would have been removed had they not been involved in the discussions (Howard and Schneider, 1985:30); and (3) the case of the postal workers in Norway where the workers managed to retain some elements of their jobs which they believed contributed to their sense of job satisfaction: customer contact was retained despite attempts by the postal authorities to introduce a system which would have prevented direct contact between an individual worker and a customer (Bermann, 1985).

In considering the gender dimension of these debates and negotiations, we found that some of the most important and progressive approaches to questions of job design and quality of work have been informed by the experience of women's work. Indeed, Bermann (1985) suggests that women's involvement in people-oriented service work means that they are in a far better position than men to assess how the qualitative aspects of jobs may change with new technology. As she also notes, women's influence is not always directed through the trade unions. In discussing the importance of informal worker influence, Bermann (1985:235) describes "self-selected groups of women organizing word-processing units and gaining considerable competence in programming and repairing machines and in organizing work, [and] groups of women working to rule after computer systems had been 'dumped' on them." She goes on to point out that, whereas the women's supervisors saw their work only in terms of "narrow, formalized, 'functions'—the reproduction of signs—these women made their broader knowledge relevant" (Bermann, 1985:235). As a result of the women's efforts, several regional and sector-specific union chapters started to provide for the exchange of such experiences in the form of courses or seminars that then provide the basis for mobilization. This example illustrates both how women have valued aspects of their work that their superiors would have overlooked and how they were, therefore, in the best position to represent their own interests.

The importance of discussion and negotiation about job design is the recognition that the organization of jobs and the use of machinery and equipment in those jobs are the result of political struggle and political decision making. As we have noted, there are often significant differences of interest and certainly differential access to the decision-making structures both between employers and employees and between groups of workers, not least between women and men. There are also institutional differences between countries concerning the extent to which different groups are able to effect change. In Denmark and Norway, for example, there is a much stronger tradition of worker participation than in either the United States or the United Kingdom.

When we examine the debates around the changing locations of work and the changing hours of work facilitated by the new technology, we find, as with job design, that women's experiences of work have often led them to make demands different from those of men. For example, in the debates around homeworking, women's and men's different experiences of work have led them to focus on different concerns (Huws, 1984; Monod, 1984). In particular, groups of office workers have been concerned about the possible increase in the use of homeworkers in data-entry and data-processing type jobs because these workers are not likely to escape the disadvantages that traditional homeworkers have faced, such as low pay, little job security, and inadequate working conditions. While women in the more professional groups of new homeworkers, such as software designers and programmers, may be better placed than clerical workers to cope with the problems associated with homework, insofar as they still have the major responsibility for housework and child care, they, too, will remain disadvantaged relative to the majority of men.

In the discussions around changing working hours, women and men have again had different priorities, largely attributable to women's greater domestic responsibilities and their particular experience of paid work. The Organization for Economic Cooperation and Development (OECD) conducted an informal survey of the institutions of its member countries and found a wide variety of attitudes and policies related to working time adjustments (OECD Sectretariat, 1985:188–189):

1. In many countries, notably Scandinavia, the reduction of working time is discussed in terms of the improvement of social welfare.

2. Some other countries, France for example, regard policies for reducing working time as fundamental in the fight against unemployment.

3. Employers are generally against the reduction of working time. They are worried about its effects on production costs and, thus, on their competitive position.

4. In nearly every case, unions are in favor of reduced working time, though they are concerned with the timing of any measures.

5. There exists considerable uncertainty as to the actual impact on employment and unemployment. Estimates vary in the basic assumptions adopted and do not always take account of secondary effects.

The Commission of the European Communities is concerned primarily with how to reduce working time in order to reduce the high levels of unemployment that exist in its member countries. The Commission issued some (legally binding) directives earlier this decade which were intended to ensure that part-time and temporary workers had the same rights and obligations as full-time workers. One obvious goal of the directives was to provide legal safeguards for forms of work that deviate from the current norm, but it is interesting to note that such directives were issued at a time when unemployment was at an unacceptably high level. By making part-time work relatively more attractive to workers, the Commission may have hoped to reduce the demand for full-time jobs. The Commission of the European Communities (1984a:21) is also concerned with changing the norm through supporting measures aimed at redistributing work; rather than issue a binding policy directive, however, they issued a set of guidelines and objectives concerned with the reduction and/or redistribution of working time, which includes the following:

1. The competitiveness of enterprises should not be affected; i.e., unit production costs must not rise.

2. The reorganization of working time should result in more flexible utilization of capital equipment; i.e., actual production time should be lengthened.

3. Special measures should be taken, where necessary, to avoid shortages of particular types of workers.

4. The characteristics of particular sectors and specific types of enterprises, particularly small firms, must be taken into account.

Policies attempting to reduce or reorganize working time fall into one of the following categories: part-time work and job sharing, reductions in the length of people's working lives, longer leisure blocks and redistribution of working time, and reductions in working time for everyone. Such policies may not be primarily motivated by the current wave of technological change, just as the current unemployment may have no direct relation to technical advances, but enacting such policies may be facilitated by the new innovations. And many believe that the productivity-enhancing characteristics of the new innovations may make such policies increasingly necessary in the future.

Part-Time Work and Job Sharing

Most part-time workers are women, and many women who work, work part-time (see Table 1). Part-time work almost inevitably means low pay, low status, and little job security. The decision to work part-time is not often one of positive choice by women but rather one of necessity, particularly when there is minimal public provision for the care of children or the elderly.

Job sharing has become an acceptable alternative form of part-time work; it refers to the sharing of a full-time, usually professional, position with commensurate rights and responsibilities. Job sharing is on the increase in the United Kingdom, especially in the public sector. Employers benefit because staff are more likely to return after maternity leave, the job is covered when one person is ill or on holiday, and, as one personnel manager says, "Two heads are often better than one and because staff are content and committed, they often put in more than a week's work" (Meade-King, 1985:9). Job sharing also gives the employee the option of meeting domestic responsibilities or of pursuing other interests while maintaining some career continuity. So far, however, job sharing has not been widespread among low-paid women or men. Among its disadvantages as a policy are that it is an individual solution, rather than a direct attack on a broader problem, and it leaves unchallenged the notion that the full-time week is the norm.

One OECD commentator expressed his concern that the increased availability of part-time work or job sharing will not actually lead to a reduction in the level of unemployment because the only effect will be to induce more women to enter the labor market (Barou, 1985:221). This is a good illustration of the fact that when many people talk about a return to full employment what they mean is full-time male employment, rather than everyone's right to paid work.

The United Kingdom government has found a way of not challenging the classic definition of full employment while, at the same time, promoting part-time work. The Job Splitting Scheme provides cash incentives for employers who split a job in order to offer part-time work to unemployed people seeking full-time employment. This scheme explicitly excludes married women who, since 1983, are not recognized as unemployed if they are living with a man who has a paid job (Meade-King, 1985:9).

Reductions in the Length of People's Working Lives

Together with a move to longer schooling—compulsory education or youth training schemes (see below for further discussion of training and education)—a feature of recent years has been to lower the retirement age and promote early retirement schemes. One example is the early retirement law, which came into effect in Germany in May 1984. The retirement age, for women and men, was lowered from 59 to 58. When firms, on the basis of collective agreements or individual agreements between workers and employers, agree to early retirement schemes they receive a subsidy from the government if they replace the retiree with an unemployed person or with someone under age 26 (Commission of the European Communities, 1984a:101).

Many firms were able to lower the average age of their staff, adjust their skill mix, and reduce their total wage bill as a result of the departure of long-serving workers on high rates of pay. The effect on unemployment was significant. While such measures do relieve labor market congestion in the short term, there are costs involved such as the subsidies to employers (though this must be offset against the costs of paying unemployment benefits or welfare to those young people who might otherwise have remained unemployed), and the economy is deprived of the accumulated experience of older workers (Barou, 1985:215–216).

Longer Leisure Blocks and Redistribution of Working Time

The phenomenon of long periods of free time is still relatively new, and the 8-hour day, 5-day week is still the norm. Interest in the redistribution of working time is growing: workers can gain longer periods of free time and employers can use their capital equipment for longer periods, if not continuously, through flexible shifts. In Italy and the United Kingdom, experiments have been conducted with five crew members shiftworking in either 8- or 12-hour shifts (Commission of the European Communities, 1984a:64). Such plans could have the effect of further excluding women from certain areas of the labor market because, in many countries, women are prohibited from working night shifts in selected manufacturing industries.

Women's and men's different responsibilities have affected their views on redistributing working time. In Scandinavia, in broad-based discussions regarding the overall reduction of working time, women have tended to favor the option of a shorter working day, whereas men favor a shorter working week (DELFA, 1984:3). One suggestion (to our knowledge, as yet untried) has been for a 30-hour week to become the norm, because it provides for many different possibilities of work organization, such as a 4-day week for workers, but the firm itself would operate for 5 or 6 days; a 6-hour day, 5-day week, in which case the firm could operate for 12 hours a day, with relatively acceptable working hours for its workers; variable working hours related to seasonal activities, i.e., 6 months with a 20-hour week and 6 months with a 40-hour week (Barou, 1985:221).

For any of these arrangements, it is important to see whether they complement the worker's other responsibilities. Cooperation of the work force is necessary because all of these arrangements have the potential to profoundly affect people's daily and weekly routines. Care must also be taken to ensure that new work policies do not reinforce existing gender inequalities; indeed, such arrangements could contribute to redistributing unpaid work more equally between men and women, notably caring for children, older people, and sick or disabled people.

Reductions in Working Time for Everyone

Overall reductions in working time are most often the result of collective bargaining. Many different agreements have been reached in Europe. In some cases the government has not been involved, in others, such as the Netherlands, the government has made recommendations, and in some, notably France, the government has played a much more active role.

One obvious way to reduce working time is to introduce longer periods of paid holiday. In Germany, a sixth week of annual leave is fast becoming the norm. The first agreement was reached in the metal-working sector in 1978. Since then the proportion of workers entitled to 6 weeks leave has risen from 4 percent in 1980 to 25 percent in 1981 to 38 percent in 1982. Other workers whose terms of employment are governed by collective agreements (90 percent of all wage earners) are entitled to at least 5 weeks. Employers consider this method to be the least disruptive of production; however, this may not be the case in countries such as France where whole firms usually close in the August holiday period. For that reason when a fifth week of holiday was introduced in France it was explicitly stated that it could not be taken consecutively with the other 4 weeks (Barou, 1985:216).

For countries where weekly working time is statutory, another method of reducing working time is simply to change the law. This was done in France at the beginning of 1982. Five weeks holiday and a statutory 39-hour week were introduced, with maximum working hours reduced to 48 in a given week and to a weekly average of 46 over a 12-week period; detailed arrangements at the enterprise or sectoral level were settled subsequently. Studies done by the French authorities to assess the impact of these measures estimate that 70,000 nonagricultural jobs were saved or created by these reductions in working time (Barou, 1985:216–218).

In addition to the statutory measures introduced in France, some collective agreements were reached at the enterprise level. In one "solidarity contract" the aim was to achieve a 35-hour week with a planned 5 percent increase in the number of jobs and a 10 percent increase in productivity. The package was worked out between workers' representatives and management, with the government providing the legal framework and some financial aid. This scheme aims to achieve an expansion of business, together with a reduction in unemployment. The advantage of this scheme is that the objectives of the workers regarding employment opportunities are in line with the management's objective of maintaining or improving their competitive position through reducing unit production costs. In this case, it was possible for management and workers to share productivity gains.

There are many ways of reducing working time that are of benefit to both workers and employers. The most effective are those that are more flexible and innovative than traditional shift work and that are agreed to on a collective basis at the enterprise level, though governments have a role to play in facilitating discussion and providing financial assistance in order to have a positive impact on employment levels. These new initiatives can be at least partly funded through gains in productivity, achieved either through the use of new capital equipment or through the extended use of equipment currently owned. Collective bargaining should allow for differences between workers; individuals should have the option of choosing between working patterns, which might be dependent on their life-cycle stage. In addition to providing greater choice for individual workers, such schemes should also aim to redistribute the unpaid work in society, at present, largely performed by women. The widespread use of part-time work is not a substitute for a collective policy on reducing working time. The introduction of new technologies and the possibilities it offers for a reorganization of working time create potential for radical social change that could benefit both men and women.

TRAINING AND EDUCATION

There is little agreement among the "experts" regarding precisely what skills will be needed in the future (Townson, 1983; Women's Bureau, Labour Canada, 1982; Leontief and Duchin, 1986). It is not clear what new jobs there will be nor how existing jobs will be changed. It is agreed, however, that at the very least people will require some generic scientific and technical training to prepare them for the rapid changes in technology that are characteristic of today's industrialized economies.

Training is often seen as the key factor in enabling people to take advantage of the opportunities provided by new technology. Without training or retraining, workers are more likely to become unemployed or stuck in routine, unskilled jobs. Over the last few years, many training programs and courses offering new technology-related skills have been initiated, some aimed specifically at women.

Training and educational initiatives need to be taken at many different levels in order to widen the opportunities provided by new technology to as many people as possible. In this section, we shall discuss public awareness, training, educational initiatives taking place within schools (and, to a much lesser extent, universities), and vocational training. In all cases we shall pay particular attention to the specific needs of women. At the outset, we outline some of the major differences between the countries under consideration in terms of what types of training and education are provided and who is responsible for administering them.

Government, Employer, and Union Responsibilities for Training and Education

In each member country of the European Community the education and training systems have evolved over a period of 100 years or more; therefore, the very terms "training," "education," and "school" are not always strictly comparable across countries. In many ways the education systems in Great Britain and Ireland differ significantly from those on the continent. However, most variation occurs in the provision of facilities for continuing education and training (for further details, see CEDEFOP [1984a,b]).

Employers contribute to the cost of vocational training in all EEC countries, though the extent to which they do so varies from one country to another. Even in France, where most training is provided by schools or other state institutions, employers play an important part in continuing vocational training, although not in the initial training of young people. This is similar to the situation in the United Kingdom. In both France and the United Kingdom, a major role is played by intermediary training centers and organizing bodies; para-governmental organizations and facilities run by joint training boards are particularly important. Many of the latter are funded by a wide variety of bodies, including government, industry, foundations, chambers of trade and industry, donations, and professional associations (CEDEFOP, 1984b:51).

In contrast to France and the United Kingdom, firms in the Federal Republic of Germany are very active not only in continuing training but also in the initial training of young people. As a result, employers contribute a larger share of the total cost of training than the government (CEDEFOP, 1984b:22). In Italy and Luxembourg, continuing education and training are largely financed through government subsidies; and in Belgium, the financial burden is carried jointly by the government, employers, trade unions, and professional institutions (CEDEFOP, 1984a:43).

Training centers run on a purely commercial basis are extremely rare. In all member countries, young people do not have to pay any fees for initial training; they receive grants that vary in amount, however. A legal right to educational leave exists in Belgium, France, Italy, Luxembourg, and some of the individual states of Germany (CEDEFOP, 1984a).

Methods adopted by different EEC members for financing and organizing training vary enormously. It is not possible to identify an ideal solution. Both Germany's system of considerable industry involvement and the Netherlands' system of state-funded, school-based vocational training appear to be stable and efficient within the context in which they operate. Italy's new system of a regionally devolved approach to vocational training might be better able to meet labor market problems, given the very different structural problems of its individual regions. Presumably decentralized solutions will be more flexible and appropriate in such countries.

Public Awareness

Many commentators express the need for increasing public awareness of the broader social implications of information technology (Menzies, 1981; Berner, 1984; Sjørup and Thomsen, 1984; Thomsen, 1984). People need to be alerted about the need to undertake training at various times throughout their working lives, and women need to be alerted to changing conditions in clerical jobs. Understanding the broader implications of information technology would also help to equip workers to act more effectively in negotiations with employers.

The Women's Bureau of Labour Canada (1982) identifies components necessary to a local awareness campaign run by a city or local government (see Table 4). In the United Kingdom, the Equal Opportunities Commission, the Manpower Services Commission, and the Engineering Industry Training Board declared the year 1984 to be Women Into Science and Engineering (WISE) Year. While some courses were developed for target groups such as 14- to 16-year-old girls, women returning to paid work, and unemployed women, its major function was to increase public awareness

TABLE 4　Components of a Local Awareness Campaign Run by a Local Council

---

Press and the electronic-mail paid advertising
Public service announcements
Interviews with press and television media
Related film clips and fillers to be provided to local television
　stations
Films and audiovisual programs about women and microtechnology for use
　in schools, community groups, etc.
Establishment of a speaker's bureau
Sponsoring of speakers on the subject
Organization of workshops to inform the public about the high-tech
　industry and its human resource requirements
Preparation and circulation of a manual containing details of local
　training programs

SOURCE: Women's Bureau, Labour Canada (1982:50-51).

regarding engineering as a career choice for women. This initiative arose out of British industry's often-expressed need for more engineers and technicians—women were a hitherto unexploited source of such labor. Activities during the year appear to have broadened discussion about women entering engineering and technical jobs.

Many informal efforts to increase public awareness have also been made. The women's movement in Copenhagen has started a course to teach women about specific technical skills and about the social impacts of information technology. A group of women researchers, technicians, and users in Denmark have formed "Forum," whose role is to provide public education (Thomsen, 1984). The Brighton Women and Technology Group has twice organized a 10-week course, through the local adult education authority, concerned with the impact of technology on various aspects of women's lives. There are now many other similar courses across Europe.

Schools

Many European countries are beginning to adapt their educational systems to meet the changing technological environment. Policies adopted have been quite similar, especially where the introduction of microcomputers into schools is concerned. In Denmark, children are obliged to participate in courses dealing with microcomputers and information processing in both primary and secondary school (Thomsen, 1984). By June 1983, nearly half of the primary schools in the United Kingdom had ordered or received a microcomputer under a grant scheme organized by the Department of Trade and Industry. By the same date, 7,000 microcomputers had been installed in 800 secondary schools in France. The plan is to have 100,000 installed by 1988. Also, four centers have opened for teacher training in information technology. A major concern in many countries is the lack of qualified teachers at all levels (Dirrheimer, 1983; Commission of the European Communities, 1984a:110). In the Netherlands, government initiatives are being supplemented by private enterprises. The Dutch Savings Bank, in cooperation with Philips, is planning to supply microcomputers for courses taking place during the last 2 years of primary school. There is a similar initiative in Belgium. In Italy, some national firms involved in robotics have agreed to produce 200 robots for demonstration purposes in technical schools (Commission of the European Communities, 1984a:110).

While such programs will enable children to become familiar with the capabilities of microcomputers, they are not entirely unproblematic. The Canadian Union of Public Employees (CUPE) objects to the widespread introduction of microcomputers into schools. They maintain that children should not be subjected to the possible negative health effects, particularly since growing children may be more susceptible to physical problems and may not be able to effectively express any problems they do experience (CUPE Research Department, 1982:8).

Another problem, specifically facing girls, is that they might have difficulty in gaining access to the machines without interference from boys (Harding, 1983; Thomsen, 1984). Berner (1984) points to the need for affirmative action programs in this area that should act on three levels: counteracting stereotypes, providing options, and strengthening self-confidence. In Sweden, technical subjects are compulsory at all levels; the possibilities of opting out of mathematics or science courses before the age of 16 are limited. Also, additional points are given to girls who choose traditionally masculine subjects and to boys who choose traditionally feminine subjects. She also cites many cases where girl-only workshops are provided in order to give the girls the support they require (Berner, 1984:233).

The United Kingdom's Engineering Industry Training Board (EITB), as part of WISE Year, organized a pilot program to encourage more girls to consider becoming technicians or engineers. Thirty girls, aged 14 to 16, participated in a 4-day residential course during which they visited firms and engineering departments in polytechnics, and met with women technicians and engineers (Engineering Industry Training Board, 1984). The pilot was thought to be successful. Similar programs are now being organized on a regional basis. The EITB is also considering whether to run 1-day courses for 12 to 14 year olds, in order to provide them with more information before they make their "O level" choices.[1] Such programs are valuable and necessary as long as girls continue to be socialized away from scientific and technical subjects in their early school careers; ideally, if girls were encouraged and expected to develop their scientific and technical capabilities from an early age, such programs would not be necessary.

In the meantime, for girls who have gone through the education system without receiving adequate scientific and technical training some remedial action is necessary. The Chelmer Institute of Higher Education in England was awarded a grant by the European Social Fund of the EEC to retrain women in surveying, microprocessing and computer technology, accountancy, and management. The first part of the course includes basic study skills and mathematics. To date, some of the women who have completed the course have found jobs, many others have used it as a bridge into higher level courses, and about 30 percent have, through necessity or choice, opted out of the labor market (Commission of the European Communities, 1983a:75–77).

Vocational Training

One of the most frequent themes in the literature on vocational training involves, though not always explicitly, the relative merits of on-the-job training and formal training (Women's Bureau, Labour Canada, 1982; Dirrheimer, 1983; CEDEFOP, 1984a; EOSYS Ltd., 1984; Gensior, 1984; Goldstein, 1984; Johansen, 1984; Thomsen, 1984). One advantage of on-the-job training is

---

[1] "O level" examinations are taken at the age of 16. They are important because they determine what "A levels" a student can take (at 18) and thus what subject at university.

that it is more likely to provide a work force with the skills relevant to the employer's needs. Also, the difficulties associated with fulfilling domestic and child care responsibilities outside of working hours are not so acute if training is provided on the job, within regular working hours.

The disadvantages of on-the-job training are that the skills learned are not always formally recognized and that the unemployed and those outside the labor force are excluded (see below). The fact that skills learned on the job are not always formally recognized means that worker mobility is reduced. Both women and men will be less able to move outside the firm. And women may also experience difficulty moving within the firm, particularly where management discriminates against women, either because they think a secretary only types even if she actually possesses quite advanced information-technology-related skills, or simply because they think women should not have professional or high-paying jobs.

The major advantage of formal training is that skills learned are recognized. The skills needed in office work include knowledge of routines; knowledge of the firm and branch; ability to interpret questions, combine information, and solve nonroutine cases; and social skills. Often, only the first of these skills is visible to management (Lie and Rasmussen, 1984:6). Not only does formal training improve worker mobility, it also overcomes some of the problems typical when workers are insufficiently trained. Clerical workers who are not aware of all of the capabilities of a piece of equipment are often dissatisfied. The Danish Union of Commercial and Clerical Employees, together with some schools of commerce, has initiated courses in word processing for its members (Thomsen, 1984). The disadvantages of formal training are related to (lack of) time and money.

Ways to combine the advantages of both types of vocational training include having formal training paid for by industry or the state and scheduling it within working hours, or introducing some means of assessing skills gained on the job. The usual objection raised by employers to paying for formal training is precisely that it will increase worker mobility: why pay for someone else's work force? In the long run, however, training for a skilled and flexible work force will benefit everyone.

As noted above, on-the-job training does nothing to meet the needs of the unemployed. Unemployment, particularly youth unemployment, is becoming an increasingly serious problem in most of the countries under consideration. The tremendous increases in unemployment are partly a result of new technology and partly a result of the more general economic climate. In most countries, training for people who are not in paid employment is seen as the primary responsibility of the government. As Goldstein (1984) argues, some government schemes have negative elements. In her view, the New Training Initiative (NTI) of the current British government is an attack on the conditions of paid work, disguised as training to meet changing market and technological conditions.

The publicly funded Youth Opportunities Program (YOP) provided young people with jobs for 6 months during which they were paid a weekly allowance. Employers received free labor. YOP workers were heavily concentrated in distributive, retailing, and administrative jobs; opportunities for learning new skills were few. In 1981–1982, more school leavers were in YOP than in regular jobs. Employers have admitted that 30 percent of these represented abuses of the goals of YOP; they substituted YOP workers for regular workers (Goldstein, 1984:100). The chief disadvantage of YOP, Goldstein (1984) argues, is that they have given credibility to the notion that putting people in the workplace to serve employers' short-term needs represents training.[2] Training need no longer lead to gaining skills or access to long-term paid employment. This type of program also undercuts organized labor and diverts resources away from other types of training. The problems associated with shortages of skilled labor remain.

Similar programs have been adopted in other countries. In Belgium, both private and public enterprises with more than 50 employees are required to recruit between 1 and 2 percent of their

---

[2] The Community Programme scheme designed to help the long-term unemployed does not even pretend to provide anything but the most broadly based "introduction to work"-type training. It is mentioned here because it illustrates the government's attitude to women's right to paid work. The scheme authorizes local authorities to hire the long-term unemployed to work on projects for 4 days a week for the benefit of the community. Those eligible include people over the age of 25 who have been unemployed for more than 1 year (Goldstein, 1984:86). The wage may not exceed an average of £63 (1985 figure) per week. Since 1983, women who are living as married with a man in paid work are not eligible for these schemes, since they are not officially recognized as unemployed.

work force from people under 30 years of age with no previous work experience for a maximum period of 1 year. Not only are employers required to pay only 90 percent of the agreed wage rate, they also receive a grant from the government for each trainee, above the minimum 1 percent (Commission of the European Communities, 1984a:90).

Some more positive training schemes aimed at unemployed women have been developed. The Ministry of Education in Denmark, together with the equality of opportunity consultants, has initiated the formation of a number of "data centers" for women who would not otherwise receive any training (Thomsen, 1984). Other schemes have begun in various cities in the United Kingdom. They involve women teaching other women nontraditional skills, often programming and electronic engineering but also carpentry and plumbing. The schemes are supported by the local councils and the European Social Fund. They all include the following: a creche, or child care allowances; a training allowance; a schedule to coincide with school hours; and assertiveness training. Women over 25 with no formal qualifications are given priority. Links with local employers are more established in some schemes than in others (informal discussion with E. Cousins, Women's Technology Scheme, Liverpool).

These schemes are a good example of how women's needs can be taken into account. Courses offered in the evenings are often inaccessible for women with children, and company training is sometimes only provided to full-time workers, while women are more likely to work part time. Training "open to all" is insufficient if it is not recognized that women face restrictions on their ability to participate.

A study done for the Women's Bureau of Labour Canada (1982) surveyed different groups of women regarding their attitudes to technology and training. They found that women who were not in the labor force were the group most afraid of technology and that they would prefer full-time training during the day. Women in the labor force, but not in technology-related jobs, preferred some form of apprenticeship. Lack of confidence, time and money, fatigue, and stress were the difficulties cited in relation to out-of-hours training. They felt it was the employers' responsibility to train them. Women using word processors had usually been trained either by their employer or by the equipment supplier. The latter is usually a marketing exercise; women receiving such training thought it was not always adequate. Women working in electronic assembly received informal, on-the-job training. Their employers sometimes offered to pay for night-school courses, but the women felt night school would be too much, in addition to their existing work and domestic responsibilities. Women in both arts and science subjects in postsecondary education were aware that they would probably work with technology in some form; however, science students were more confident about their job prospects (Women's Bureau, Labour Canada, 1982:27–33).

Many training initiatives aim to develop specific industrial skills. Given the rapid change that characterizes industrial economies, it may be more appropriate for training and retraining to be aimed at developing broader skills, such as basic scientific understanding, computer literacy, logical thinking, and communications skills. Training focused in this direction would enhance worker mobility, whereas training in specific skills increases the danger of creating the job ghettos of the future (Canadian Advisory Council on the Status of Women, 1982; Dirrheimer, 1983).

Training and educational initiatives need to be taken at many different levels in order to widen the opportunities provided by new technology to as many people as possible. The aim of any training or educational initiative must be to increase workers' mobility and their ability to participate in technological decision making. Governments and employers have a responsibility to at least contribute to the cost of training, especially because they benefit from having access to a skilled work force. Also, it is important to remember that not all workers are starting from the same point in terms of training and education; therefore, for women and other disadvantaged groups, some positive action is necessary.

SUMMARY AND CONCLUSION

Today, the industrialized countries of the world and many of the newly industrializing countries are experiencing major changes in employment and work patterns as the rapid diffusion of the current "new technologies," based on microelectronics, is transforming the industrial structure of their economies. Both government intervention and negotiations between employers and trade unions concerning the introduction of new technologies are becoming increasingly widespread. Employers attempting to maintain profit levels in increasingly competitive market situations can do so in various ways; technological change is only one of the options available, but productivity-enhancing, labor-saving technologies are an obvious tool to employ.

We have noted that the unequal distribution of power between social groups means that some groups have more influence over technological decision making than others. The roles played by governments, employers, and trade unions in this process differ from country to country. We have noted that women and men often have different priorities and choose different strategies.

In the European countries, governments have a crucial, if limited, role, mainly through the provisions of legislation, which sets minimum standards to which employers must adhere. Most negotiations about the introduction of specific technologies take place between employers and trade unions, as negotiations around job design illustrate.

To negotiate around job design is, we argued, to reject the notion of technological determinism. It accepts that technology, as such, does not determine how jobs are defined, how the work should be done, and how the person doing the job relates (or does not relate) to other people in the workplace. The importance of discussions of job design is the recognition that the organization of jobs and the use of machinery and equipment in those jobs is the result of political struggle and decision making, involving groups of people with different amounts of power to influence those decisions. Such discussions also move the focus away from the important, yet narrow, question of ergonomics, to the broader, more fundamental questions of quality of work.

Important differences between countries concern the extent to which employees are able to effect change; these differences depend, in large part, on the different traditions of worker participation and on the relationship between employers and workers. In Denmark and Norway, for example, there is a much stronger tradition of worker participation than in either the United States or the United Kingdom. There is also a much higher rate of unionization in these countries (see Table 1). It is not surprising, therefore, that some of the most progressive examples of workers securing a degree of control over decisions surrounding new technology are found in these countries.

Women's position in the labor market and in the occupational hierarchy gives them less access to decision-making structures (via the trade unions) than men. But their position has both positive and negative aspects. In particular, we have argued that women's relationship to work, both paid and unpaid, has led them in many cases to have different priorities from many male trade unionists. Many of women's priorities have proved particularly relevant in discussions of the quality of work and have since been taken up more widely by the trade unions.

Our discussion of changing locations and changing hours of work showed that there currently exists the potential for radical social change. The pervasiveness of the new technologies has opened a debate about the role of work in advanced industrial societies. Gender relations could both affect and be affected by changes in the role of work. The various proposals should be evaluated in terms of their benefit to individual workers, and not merely their effect on reducing unemployment levels; furthermore, discussions of, and choices about, the relative merits of the different schemes must take into account the existing differences between women and men in their relation to work, especially unpaid work. By recognizing women's and men's different starting points, strategies and policies could, if the political will existed, set out to redress existing imbalances, resulting in a genuine redistribution of all forms of work (paid and unpaid) that would enable both women and men to achieve greater work fulfillment.

In our discussion of the role of governments, employers, and trade unions in providing education and training, we argued that education and training should aim to increase the availability to individual workers of opportunities for satisfying work and should not merely aim to reduce unemployment in the short term. Further, it is not enough to provide training for all; efforts must be made to identify factors that prevent certain groups from taking advantage of such opportunities. The difficulties women face in taking part in education and training programs are well documented. In addition to providing the necessary support services (such as child care) that will enable more women to participate in training schemes, trainers and educators must take into account the very different relationships girls and boys, women and men have to technology, and structure their training programs in such a way as to best overcome past discrimination and socialization in this area.

The formulation of strategies and policies aimed at dealing with the issues raised in this paper should start by identifying existing differences and inequalities between groups of workers. We have been concerned here with gender inequality but there are many others—age, race, and skill all divide workers and sometimes lead to conflicts of interest. Until these differences are recognized and a commitment is made to overcome resulting inequalities, it will be impossible for employees to make the best of opportunities that now exist for their participation in decision making regarding technological change. This commitment must be demonstrated at all levels, by governments, employers, and trade unions.

ACKNOWLEDGMENTS

We would like to thank the following people who sent us material: Isa Bakker, Paula Bennett, Patricia Blackstaffe, Fernande Faulkner, Iris Fitzpatrick-Martin, Michael Gurstein, Michael Mc-Bane, Kathryn McMullen, Marylee Stephenson, and Jane Stinson from Canada; Jannet Grønfeldt, Janni Nielsen, and Karen Sjørup from Denmark; Andreas Drinkuth, Sabine Gensior, Camilla Grebsbach-Gnath, Werner Kleges, Heinz Murer, Barbel Schöler, and Suzanne Seeland from the Federal Republic of Germany; Liisa Rantalaiho from Finland; Marie-Thérse Letablier, Yvette Lucas, Elsbeth Monod, Martina Ni Cheallaigh, and Claire Terlon from France; Bente Rasmussen and Kari Thoresen from Norway; and Boel Berner, Lars Ingelstram, Karin Ohrt, Lesley Palmer, Inga Persson-Tanimura, and Ulla Weigelt from Sweden. We are also grateful to Heidi Hartmann and members of the Panel on Technology and Women's Employment for their comments on an earlier draft. Their help greatly facilitated our task. Responsibility for errors of interpretation or of fact remain, of course, our own.

REFERENCES

Barou, Y.
    1985   Reduction of working time: collective bargaining and government action. Pp. 211–226 in *Employment Growth and Structural Change*. Paris: OECD.
Bermann, T.
    1985   Not only windmills: female service workers and new technologies. Pp. 231–248 in A. Olerup, L. Schneider, and E. Monod, eds., *Women, Work and Computerisation*. Amsterdam: North-Holland.
Berner, B.
    1984   New technology and women's education in Sweden. Pp. 227–239 in S. Acker, ed., *World Yearbook of Education 1984, Women and Education*. New York: Kogan Paige, Nichols Publishing Co.

Bjorn-Anderson, N.
  1983   The changing roles of secretaries and clerks. Pp. 120–137 in H.J.
          Otway and M. Peltu, eds., *New Office Technology: Human and
          Organisational Aspects.* London: Francis Pinter.
Boulet, J.-A.
  1984   La diversification professionnelle des femmes en milieu de travail.
          Paper presented at a Colloquium on the Economic Status of
          Women in the Labor Market, Montreal, Canada.
Cakir, A., H.J. Reuter, L. von Schmude, and A. Armbruster
  1978   Anpassung von Bildschmirmarbeitsplatzen an die physiche und
          psychishe Funktionsweise des Menschen. Bonn, Germany: Bun-
          desminister für Arbeit und Sozialordnung.
Canadian Advisory Council on the Status of Women
  1982   *Microelectronics and Employment: Issues of Concern to Women.* A
          Brief to the Task Force on Microelectronics and Employment.
          July. Ottawa, Ontario.
CEDEFOP
  1984a   *Vocational Training Systems in the Member States of the European Com-
          munity, Comparative Study.* Luxembourg: Office for Official Publi-
          cations of the European Communities.
  1984b   *Vocational Training Bulletin Number 15.* Luxembourg: Office for
          Official Publications of the European Communities.
Commission of the European Communities
  1983a   *Social Europe Special Issue.* Directorate-General for Employment, So-
          cial Affairs and Education. Brussels: Commission of the European
          Communities.
  1983b   *Social Europe,* 0(September) Directorate-General for Employment,
          Social Affairs and Education. Brussels: Commission of the Euro-
          pean Communities. September.
  1984a   *Social Europe,* 3(December) Directorate-General for Employment,
          Social Affairs and Education. Brussels: Commission of the Euro-
          pean Communities.
  1984b   *European National Actions on Information Technology.* Information
          Technology Task Force, Intelligence Unit. Brussels: Commission
          of the European Communities, June.
  1984c   *European Women in Paid Employment 1984.* Brussels: Commission
          of the European Communities.
CUPE Research Department
  1982   *CUPE's Response to the Report of the Labour Canada Task Force on
          Microelectronics and Employment—In the Chips: Opportunities, People,
          Partnerships.* Ottawa: CUPE.
David-McNeil, J.
  1984   *The Female Labour Force: A New Place in the Canadian Economy.*
          Ottawa: Economic Council of Canada.
Department of Employment, United Kingdom
  1984   *Employment Gazette* 92(12). London: Her Majesty's Stationery
          Office.
DELFA, The Committee for the Study of Working Hours
  1984   *Preferred Working Hours.* DELFA Debate Report No. 3. Stockholm:
          Ministry of Labour.

Deutsch, Steven
  1986   International experiences with technological change. *Monthly Labor Review* (March):35–40.
Dirrheimer, A.
  1983   *Information Technology and the Training of Skilled Workers in the Service Sector.* Report of the Evaluation of the Literature and of Interviews with Experts. Luxembourg: CEDEFOP.
Engineering Industry Training Board
  1984   *Girls and Technical Engineering.* London: EITB.
EOSYS Ltd.
  1984   *Case Studies in Information Technology and Career Opportunities for Women.* A Study by EOSYS Limited for the Manpower Services Commission. Sheffield, England: Manpower Services Commission, Training Division.
Equal Opportunities Commission
  1984   *The Fact About Women Is . . .* Manchester, U.K.: EOC.
Evans, J.
  1983   Negotiating technological change. Pp. 152–168 in H.J. Otway and M. Pletu, eds., *New Office Technology: Human and Organisational Aspects.* London: Francis Pinter.
Fjalestad, Jostein
  1981   *Information Technology and Participation: Problems and Experiences.* Oslo, Norway: Norwegian Computer Centre.
Gensior, S.
  1984   New Technologies—Possibilities for a New Valuation of Women's Work. Berlin: The Berlin Institute for Social Research and Sociological Practice. Mimeograph.
Goldstein, N.
  1984   The new training initiative: a great leap backward. *Capital and Class* 23(Summer).
Harding, J.
  1983   *Switched Off: The Science Education of Girls.* York, England: Longman for Schools Council.
Howard, R., and L. Schneider
  1985   Worker Participation in Technological Change; Interests, Influence, and Scope. Paper prepared for the Panel on Technology and Women's Employment, Committee on Women's Employment and Related Social Issues. Washington, D.C.: National Research Council (February).
Huws, U.
  1984   *The New Homeworkers—New Technology and the Changing Location of White-Collar Work.* Low Pay Pamphlet No. 28. London: Low Pay Unit.
ILO
  1983   *Yearbook of Labour Statistics 1983.* Geneva: ILO.
Johannesson, J., and I. Persson-Tanimura
  1984   *Labour Market Policy Under Reconstruction—Studies of the Swedish Labour Market and the Effects of Labour Market Policy.* An English summary of the report *Arbetsmarknadspolitik under omprovning, sou 1984:31* from the Delegation for Labour Market Policy Research (EFA). Stockholm: Swedish Ministry of Labour.

Johansen, D.
1984　Eroding jobs by bits and bytes. *Our Times,* May.
Leontief, W., and F. Duchin
1986　*The Future Impact of Automation on Workers.* New York: Oxford University Press.
Lie, M., and B. Rasmussen
1984　Office Work and Skills. Paper presented at the IFIP "Women, Work and Computerization" conference, Italy.
Markmann, H.
1985　The role of trade unions in coping with the labour implications of technological change. Pp. 141–147 in *Employment Growth and Structural Change.* Paris: OECD.
Meade-King, M.
1985　Two into one will go. *Guardian,* June 27.
Menzies, H.
1981　*Women and the Chip: Case Studies of the Effects of Informatics on Employment in Canada.* Montreal, Canada: Institute for Research on Public Policy.
Ministère de l'éducation nationale
1984　Note d'information. Vanves, France: Ministère de l'éducation nationale.
Monod, E.
1984　Telecommuting—A New Work, but Is It Still Just the Same Old Story? Paper presented at the IFIP "Women, Work and Computerization" conference, Italy.
OECD Secretariat
1985　The current debate on working-time adjustments. Pp. 188–196 in *Employment Growth and Structural Change.* Paris: OECD.
Peitchinis, S.
1984　Microelectronic Technology and Female Employment. Paper presented at the Colloquium on the Economic Status of Women in the Labour Market, Montreal, Canada.
Sjørup, K., and F. Thomsen
1984　The Future: Do Women Play a Part? Roskilde, Denmark: Roskilde University Centre. Mimeograph.
Thomsen, T.
1984　Country Report: Denmark. Roskilde, Denmark: Roskilde University Centre. Mimeograph.
Thoresen, K.
1983　Working with visual display units. Pp. 85–104 in E. Fossum, ed., *Computerisation of Working Life.* Chichester, England: Ellis Horwood.
Townson, M.
1983　The Impact of Technological Change on Women. Paper presented at the Canada Tomorrow Conference, Ottawa.
Women's Bureau, Labour Canada
1982　Towards the Integration of Women into the High Technology Labour Force in the National Capital Region. Discussion Paper No. 1 in Series B *Changing World of Work,* prepared by Communicado Associates, Ottawa: Labour Canada.

Biographical Sketches of Contributors

EILEEN APPELBAUM is associate professor of economics at Temple University. She is on the editorial boards of the *Journal of Post Keynesian Economics* and *Computers and the Social Sciences* and serves as a consultant to the Office of Technology Assessment and the Mayor's Commission for Women in Philadelphia. Her research and writing encompass both theoretical and applied work in labor economics, with emphasis on implications for women workers. She is the author of *Back to Work* (Auburn House, 1981), an econometric analysis of the experiences of mature women returning to the labor force. Appelbaum is also the author of several articles on employment and technology issues as well as on part-time and temporary work. She has a B.A. in mathematics from Temple University and a Ph.D. in economics from the University of Pennsylvania.

CAROLYN L. ARNOLD is a Ph.D. candidate in the sociology of education at Stanford University. Previously she was a community college instructor in women's studies, social sciences, and statistics; a project associate at Far West Laboratory for Educational Research and Development; and a counselor and funding coordinator in a community women's health clinic. She has conducted research on women's education, gender segregation in the labor market (with Myra Strober), and women's participation in high technology. She is currently researching the development of stratification by gender in technical occupations. Arnold has a B.A. from Smith College, an M.A. in women's studies from San Francisco State University, and an M.S. in statistics from Stanford University.

BARBARA BARAN is a postgraduate research fellow at the Berkeley Roundtable on Internal Economy (BRIE) currently working on a study to examine work reorganization and skill change in manufacturing and service industries for the Carnegie Forum on Education and the Economy. Her research has focused on the technological transformation of white-collar work, with particular emphasis on changes occurring in the structure of women's employment, and included a study of technological change in the insurance industry. Prior to returning to school, she served as a chairperson of the San Francisco Women's Union and was editor of a community newspaper in San Francisco. She has a B.A. in history from the University of Wisconsin, Madison, and an M.A. and a Ph.D. in city and regional planning from the University of California, Berkeley.

BRYNA SHORE FRASER is a senior program officer at the National Institute for Work and Learning in Washington, D.C. She is the editor of the Postsecondary Education for a Changing Economy series and the director of the National Study of Employment in the Fast Food Industry. She has done extensive research on employment-related education and training for youth and adults. Her most recent publications have focused on the impact of computers and new technologies on training and the workplace. Fraser has a B.A. from Brandeis University and an M.A. in Slavic languages from Indiana University.

ELI GINZBERG is A. Barton Hepburn professor emeritus of economics and director of Conservation of Human Resources, Columbia University. From 1941 to 1981 he served as a consultant to various departments of the federal government, including State, Defense, Labor, Health and Human Services, and the General Accounting Office. He is the author of 100 books, primarily on human resources and health policy, the most recent of which is *Understanding Human Resources* (Abt, 1985). Ginzberg has an

A.B. in social sciences and an A.M. and a Ph.D. in economics, from Columbia University.

CLAUDIA GOLDIN is professor of economics at the University of Pennsylvania, research associate at the National Bureau of Economic Research, and editor of the *Journal of Economic History*. She has previously held positions at Princeton University and the University of Wisconsin. Her research interests are in American economic history, and her research subject matter has included urban slavery in the American South, early industrialization, the impact of the Civil War, the postbellum southern economy, and, most recently, the evolution of the female labor force from 1790 to the present. She is currently writing *Understanding the Gender Gap* (to be published by Oxford University Press). Goldin holds a B.A. from Cornell University and an M.A. and a Ph.D. from the University of Chicago.

HEIDI I. HARTMANN is study director (on leave) of the Committee on Women's Employment and Related Social Issues, the Panel on Technology and Women's Employment, and the Panel on Pay Equity Research at the National Research Council (NRC). She has edited or coedited a number of NRC reports on comparable worth and other women's employment issues. Previously she taught economics on the Graduate Faculty at the New School for Social Research. Her research has concentrated on employment issues related to women and minorities, particularly discrimination and internal labor markets, women's economic independence, and political economy and feminist theory. In the 1986–1987 academic year she is an American Statistical Association fellow doing research on women in poverty at the Bureau of the Census. Hartmann has a B.A. from Swarthmore College and an M.Ph. and a Ph.D. from Yale University, all in economics.

FELICITY HENWOOD is a social scientist studying gender and technology issues. While working on her contribution to this volume, she was a research fellow at the Science Policy Research Unit. She has published mainly in the area of new technology and women's employment and works in adult education, teaching courses on women and science/technology. Henwood is currently studying for a Ph.D. in the Arts Graduate School of the University of Sussex.

H. ALLAN HUNT is manager of research at the W.E. Upjohn Institute for Employment Research in Kalamazoo, Michigan. He has been at the Institute since 1978 and in his current position since

1982. His professional experience has involved him in the areas of workers' disability compensation, employment and training policy, and the employment impacts of technological change. Hunt has taught at Lehigh University; California State University, Hayward; and the University of Connecticut. He studied at the University of Wisconsin; Lehigh University; and the University of California, Berkeley, where he received a Ph.D. in economics.

TIMOTHY L. HUNT has been a senior research economist at the W.E. Upjohn Institute for Employment Research since 1981. In 1983, he co-authored an Institute monograph entitled *Human Resource Implications of Robotics,* which examines the employment impacts of robots in the United States by 1990. With the support of the National Research Council and the National Commission for Employment Policy, Hunt has recently completed several other studies exploring various aspects of the employment implications of technological change. He has published numerous papers and given presentations to government agencies and various other groups at the state, national, and international levels. He holds a B.A. in history from Otterbein College, an M.S. in economics from South Dakota State University, and a Ph.D. in economics from Kansas State University.

MARY C. MURPHREE is New York regional administrator for the Women's Bureau of the U.S. Department of Labor. She formerly served the Women's Bureau as an expert consultant, directing the bureau's study of the impact of computer-based technology on women clerical workers. She is the author of the recent Women's Bureau publication *Women and Office Automation: Issues for the Decade Ahead.* Murphree has taught college-level courses, served as a consultant to government and private industry, and written and spoken widely on the subject of women and technology. She received a B.A. from Hollins College and an M.A. and a Ph.D. in sociology from Columbia University.

THIERRY J. NOYELLE is senior research scholar at Conservation of Human Resources, Columbia University. His areas of expertise include labor market segmentation; technology, change, and employment; the service industries, especially financial and business services; and the internationalization of services. He has a B.A. in economics from the University of Lyons (France), an M.S. in engineering from the École Centrale of Lyons (France), and an M.A. in regional science and a Ph.D. in city and regional planning, both from the University of Pennsylvania.

MYRA H. STROBER is an associate professor of education at Stanford University. She has been on the faculty at the University of Maryland; the University of California, Berkeley; and the Stanford Business School. Her research focuses on women's employment, particularly the relationship between work and family among educated women. Strober's most recent work is on occupational segregation. She was one of the founders of the Center for Research on Women at Stanford and served as its director for 7 years and was also the first chair of the board of the National Council for Research on Women. Currently, she is the director of the Stanford Education Policy Institute. Strober has a B.S. in industrial and labor relations from Cornell University and a Ph.D. in economics from the Massachusetts Institute of Technology.

SHARON HARTMAN STROM is a 1986–1987 fellow at the Bunting Institute of Radcliffe College, on leave from the University of Rhode Island, where she is professor of history and a former coordinator of the women's studies program. She recently served as a consultant on several projects related to women's work and technology for the Office of Technology Assessment. She has published work on the history of women's clerical work unions and is currently completing a monograph on the history of the American office between 1910 and 1950. Strom has a B.A. from Whittier College and an M.A. and a Ph.D. from Cornell University, where she studied social and intellectual history.

ALAN F. WESTIN is professor of public law and government at Columbia University, where he has taught since 1959. A specialist in constitutional law, civil liberties, and civil rights, he has for 30 years studied the effects of new information technologies on organizations, individuals, and society and the impacts of the public policy choices that such developments raise in democratic nations. Among his works are *Privacy and Freedom* (Atheneum, 1967); *Databanks in a Free Society* (Quadrangle, 1972); and *The Changing Workplace: A Guide to Managing the People, Organizational, and Regulatory Aspects of Office Technology* (Knowledge and Industry Publications, 1985). He is president of the Educational Fund for Individual Rights, a nonprofit research foundation that studies employee rights issues at the workplace. Westin has a B.A. from the University of Florida and an L.L.B. and a Ph.D. in political science from Harvard University.

SALLY WYATT is a research associate for The Program on Information and Communication Technology at the Economic and Social Research Council, London, England. Previously she was an economist at the Science Policy Research Unit of the University of Sussex, where she worked on various science and technology policy issues. She is currently conducting research on the transfer of technology from the western oil companies to China's offshore oil industry. She received a B.A. from McGill University and an M.A. from the University of Sussex, England, both in economics.